**FROM ~~CY YOUNG~~ TO**
**KE~~~~**
**FRO~~~~**
**TO BA~~~~**
**IT'S T~~~~**
**BOOK OF BASEBALL FEATS,**
**FACTS & FIRSTS!**

- Do you know that Barry Bonds became the only
  National League player to receive three
  consecutive MVP awards when the honor came
  to him again in 2003?

- Do you know that in the nine years of play since
  the 1994 strike more players have hit 50 or
  more single-season home runs than ever before?

- Do you know that only three players since the
  1930s have cracked the top ten list for most total
  bases scored in a season, and that two of the
  three managed the feat in 2001? Do you
  know who those two players were?

Test your memory and knowledge of America's favorite pastime with the most comprehensive sourcebook
of unusual, intriguing, and amazing baseball achievement—plus special sections featuring the evolution of
season and career hitting, fielding, and pitching records—that everyone, from fan to fanatic, will devour.

**DAVID NEMEC** is a novelist and baseball historian.
He has written *The Beer and Whisky League*, *The
Great Encyclopedia of 19th-Century Major League
Baseball*, and the historical sections of *The Ultimate
Baseball Book*.

# GREAT BASEBALL FEATS, FACTS & FIRSTS (2004)

## DAVID NEMEC

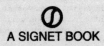

A SIGNET BOOK

SIGNET
Published by New American Library, a division of
Penguin Group (USA) Inc., 375 Hudson Street,
New York, New York 10014, U.S.A.
Penguin Books Ltd, 80 Strand,
London WC2R 0RL, England
Penguin Books Australia Ltd, 250 Camberwell Road,
Camberwell, Victoria 3124, Australia
Penguin Books Canada Ltd, 10 Alcorn Avenue,
Toronto, Ontario, Canada M4V 3B2
Penguin Books (N.Z.) Ltd, Cnr Rosedale and Airborne Roads,
Albany, Auckland 1310, New Zealand

Penguin Books Ltd, Registered Offices:
80 Strand, London WC2R 0RL, England

Published by Signet, an imprint of New American Library,
a division of Penguin Group (USA) Inc. Previously published in a Plume edition.

First Signet Printing, April 1989
First Printing (2004 Edition), April 2004
10  9  8  7  6  5  4  3  2  1

To my father, Joseph Sylvester Nemec,
who was ahead of his time
but balanced matters by having a son
who is an anachronism in his.

# Contents

# SECTION 3

# SECTION 4

# SECTION 5

# SECTION 6

# SECTION 7

# Acknowledgments

A book like this one is often the product of a single, highly skewed imagination, but usually there have been many minds along the way that have triggered, fostered and helped refine it.

Among those I especially wish to cite are: first and foremost, Scott Flatow for his knowledgeable and painstaking assistance in updating the book each season; Phillip Von Borries, baseball historian, whose favorite province is the old American Association and in particular Pete Browning; Bill Weiss, Pacific Coast League statistician, for providing me with copious material on the minor leagues; Dino Restelli for introducing me to many old players and fans in the San Francisco Bay area; Tony Salin for his suggested refinements; Bob Tiemann for sharing his many nineteenth-century discoveries; Jill Grossman and Larry Zuckerman for their supportive and helpful editing; and Fran Collin for her representation of my interests in the publishing industry.

Finally, I want to thank the many readers who have written to apprise me of errors they've found in earlier editions. With their help this book is now as accurate as I know how to make it, although I suspect there still may be some glitches. Baseball research, in many areas, is still in its infancy and much new information has been unearthed since I began this project. In any case, I hope readers will continue to let me know where I'm still short of the mark, which is always absolute perfection.

# Foreword

It probably won't come as a surprise to those of you familiar with my other baseball history and memorabilia books to learn that I'm in a shrinking minority. I don't believe there is any way at the moment to compare George Brett's accomplishments to those, say, of Home Run Baker. Nor do I think anyone ever will devise a satisfactory method to do it. We are doomed to debate forever whether Babe Ruth would have out-homered Mark McGwire if he too had been in his prime in 1998, or whether Cy Young would have won 500 games or just 400, or not even 300, if he had pitched under the same conditions and against the same batters that Greg Maddux faces. Give me an argument if you like—I'm still open to being convinced that one or the other of our sabermetricians now on the case will discover a system to measure Reggie Jackson against Chuck Klein—but, meanwhile, it doesn't make me overly despondent not to know who was the greatest hitter or pitcher or shortstop of all time. Life—and baseball—are full of uncertainties. Differences of opinion are a large part of what makes them fun.

In the next breath, I'm going to haul off and say that I do have some suggestions that I think will help you make order out of the chaos that exists whenever baseball analysts gather to thrash out and attempt to settle once and for all the metaphysical issues of their profession. First off, many of them like to dismiss all records set before 1893 because the geometry of the playing field hadn't yet been properly established. This is a convenient way to dispose of a lot of unwieldly 50-win and 400-strikeout seasons, but ultimately it's an evasion of the problem. A record achieved in 1886 isn't any less meaningful because it happened when the pitcher's line was only 50 feet from home plate. That it was accomplished by a pitcher who played left field between starting assignments or had a 6.90 ERA after the mound was moved to its present location is also beside the point. A record is a record regardless of when or under what circumstances it occurred. If five pitchers win 200 games in the course of a decade, but only one wins 250, then we all agree that one pitcher has the best mark for that particular 10-year-period. But if no pitchers win 200 games in the following decade, and only two win as many as 150, we'll all agree again that it doesn't necessarily mean those two pitchers aren't at least the equal of the five who won 200 a decade earlier and perhaps even as good as the 250-game winner. What it comes down to is that for us to grapple successfully with the many enormous disparities that exist between batting averages in the twenties and batting averages in the sixties, pitching strikeouts in 1906 and pitching strikeouts in 1996, shortstops' fielding averages in 1882 and shortstops' fielding averages in 1982, we can't simply call some of the figures unrepresentative and drop them from consideration. Instead, we have to set up a few ground rules. One that I've found helpful in winding my path through the record books is to divide the game into eight periods:

1. 1876, the year the National League began, through 1892
2. 1893, the first year the pitcher's mound was 60 feet six inches from the plate, through 1900
3. 1901, the American League's inaugural year as a major circuit, through 1919
4. 1920, the unofficial beginning of the lively ball era, through 1941
5. 1942, the first year World War II altered the game appreciably, through 1960
6. 1961, the first wave of expansion, through 1976
7. 1977, the third wave of expansion, through 1993
8. 1994, the beginning of three divisions in both leagues and the addition of a wild-card qualifier creating three rounds of postseason play, through the present

To some extent these points of demarcation are arbitrary. Many, for example, feel that the seventh phase really began when the strike zone was redefined after the 1968 season and a second wave of expansion took place, or else when the American League adopted the designated hitter rule in 1973. If you want to side with either of those contentions, I have no quarrel. Neither will I be unhappy if you happen to think the National Association was a major league and the first phase should therefore begin with the 1871 season. Almost every generalization that is made about baseball invites speculation, if not outright argument. Everybody is in accord that the game entered a new phase when the pitcher's mound was moved 10 feet farther away from the plate, because it altered the balance between batters and pitchers radically in favor of the former and immediately led to more hitting and scoring. But I have yet to unearth a good explanation for why batting averages and run production jumped in 1893, really took off for the stratosphere in 1894 and then returned for the next few years to about the level reached in 1893. What happened during the 1894 season? Why was it that hitters really feasted the second year—rather than the first year—after the mound was moved? I don't know the answer. I can't even make a reasonable guess why somebody like Hugh Duffy hit .440 in 1894, 78 points higher than he did in any other season. The record books are full of feats, facts and firsts that defy logic and leave us hungering for explanations. And the books themselves aren't always logical or consistent. For my purposes, I usually go with *Total Baseball* when there is a conflict—but I haven't found *Total Baseball* so trustworthy that I'd be willing to stake my reputation on its data. What I've done when a serious dispute exists is attach an alert signal, letting you know that before you hold forth on Paul Hines, for one, at your favorite watering hole or the next SABR convention, you ought to be prepared for somebody to jump in and say, "Now wait a minute ace. According to the *Sporting News,* the first Triple Crown winner was . . ."

In any event, I think you'll have a good time looking through this book and seeing who holds a certain record and who held it before him. You'll also note how and why several dozen pitchers who were active before 1920 had career ERAs under 2.50 while only two pitchers who were active between 1920 and 1960 had career ERAs under 3.00. Maybe you already know who those two pitchers are. If so, you can still expect to find a fair amount you don't know, or haven't quite thought of in the same way I have, and will appreciate having it in a compact form. Enjoy yourself.

—David Nemec
San Francisco, California

# The System for Evaluating Feats

In college, I had a coach who used to start out each season by telling us that baseball was essentially a simple game. Three strikes, three outs; nine players, nine innings. There was an inherent order to it, and when it was played right it worked like a mathematical equation. Listening to our coach, I always got a bad feeling in my stomach. He wasn't explaining baseball to us but reducing it. Seeing the game merely in terms of numbers and logic was deeply disturbing to me. It was so much more.

Yet, once I began to write about baseball, I realized that he had a point. It really is a game with a magic number, and that number beyond all doubt is three. Along with three strikes and three outs and a structure that is built on multiples of three, in the scheme of things 300 wins and 3000 hits have become the twin pinnacles that, when attained by a pitcher or a batter, assure him of eventual selection to the Hall of Fame. On a seasonal basis, a .300 or higher batting average for a hitter is almost exactly as likely to occur as a 3.00 or lower ERA for a pitcher, and in the utopian year there would be about 10 or 12 of each. To my knowledge that utopia has never been achieved in a season. Probably it never will be. One faction or the other will inevitably hold an edge, and in the ebb and flow of rule changes and developments in equipment and playing surfaces that edge will constantly swing back and forth like a pendulum. Arguably, the balance between hitters and pitchers is more even now than it's ever been. In recent years there have been about the same number of .350 hitters and pitchers who have allowed fewer than two earned runs a game, and that, historically, has not always been the case. Indeed there have been times when virtually no pitchers could hold the opposition below three runs a game—forget two—and a .350 batting average just barely got its owner into the top 10 hitters. The 1930 season was like that. The 1968 season, however, in the American League especially, was the exact opposite. Was it because most of the great hitters were born around 1905 and somewhere in the early thirties something in the genes changed around and resulted in a lot of super pitching arms being hatched? Maybe, but there are several much more likely explanations. Wherever the truth lies, though, those two seasons and others like them created scads of records for batting zeniths and pitching nadirs or vice versa—records that in some instances are so skewed as to be all but unbreakable. Nobody in the past 60 years has come anywhere near to collecting 191 RBIs in a season or posting a 7.71 ERA in over 150 innings or rapping 36 triples. What that means, to me, is that a straight fact and record book, while interesting, leaves something to be desired, namely a perspective that allows for other notable feats to receive their due. I've tried to provide that perspective, first by noting the all-time record and, where it's possible to do it without disrupting the continuity of the book, featuring it in the period in which it occurred, and then by tracing the evolution of the record and noting some of the significant high points and low points since it was set. In other words, touching on not only the major record but the records for each period as well.

It's not an altogether new approach, but what is unique, I think, is the manner in which it's been organized and served up to you. The main course is full of the staples that you rightfully want in a book of feats, facts and firsts, but it's spiced with flavors that ought to do some exciting things to your taste buds.

# Introduction

The first section of this book, covering the years from 1846 through 1900, differs somewhat in design from the other sections. Though I'm not writing a history of baseball, I do feel both the obligation and the desire to offer up a backdrop—a setting of the stage, if you will.

In Section 1, along with the great feats and firsts that occurred in the last century, I'll introduce all of the various elements that are present in a typical day or night at a baseball game with the exception of the managers and the stadiums, which we'll meet in Section 2 when both subjects really began to come into their own. Tucked in amid the introductions are chapters on first basemen's records, some of the most interesting teams of the era and a few of the more intriguing bit players who flitted across the stage for only a moment or two but sometimes stole the show before disappearing into the wings. Some comments with regard to chapters on team and individual record holders: Although each for the most part is located in the section focusing on the era when the all-time record was set—i.e., Home Run Feats is found in Section 5, the period when Roger Maris and Hank Aaron set single-season and career home run marks—all include the bulk of significant records established since 1901. Secondly, the seasons of 1918 and 1919, which were abbreviated due to World War I, and the strike-shortened 1981, 1994 and 1995 seasons have been omitted from consideration except in cases when the number of games played had no bearing on the record figure. And finally, the names in capital letters designate the all-time record holders for the specified era or position, as distinguished from the names in regular case, which designate either league record holders or runners up to an all-time record.

# SECTION 1

# Famous Firsts: 1846–1900

The precise origins of many things about baseball that we take for granted are heavily shrouded by the almost impenetrable veils of the past. It would be wonderful to know who first thought of putting webbing in his glove or what pitcher was the first to pick a runner off base, but it is impossible even to pinpoint with any degree of certainty the moment of transition between ancient games like rounders and stoolball and to say this is how and where baseball began. There are still many people, some current major-league players among them, who believe that Abner Doubleday invented the game as we know it. The more tenable opinion for the past half-century has been that Alexander Cartwright was the inventor and that the first game under the Cartwright rules was played on June 19, 1846, at Elysian Fields in Hoboken, New Jersey, between the New York Nine and Cartwright's club, the Knickerbockers. There is no longer any serious dispute that this game took place; a complete record of it exists. We know that the final score was 23–1, and the game ended when the New York Nine scored their 21st run, then called an ace, in the fourth inning, added two more for safe measure, and then held the Knickerbockers scoreless in their last turn at bat. We even know that Cartwright, umpiring the game, levied a six-cent fine for swearing against a New York Nine player named Davis.

But was it really the first game? If so, how did the Knickerbockers, purportedly the first club ever to organize mainly for the purpose of playing baseball, manage to lose so egregiously? Who were the New York Nine? When and where did they assemble and start mastering the intricacies of the new sport? How sure are we that they didn't secretly play a slew of games to prepare for Cartwright's bunch and that those games weren't the first ones? Well, the unhappy truth is that we're not at all sure; nor, probably, will we ever be. Therefore be warned that some of the firsts you will encounter at the beginning of each section of this book may in fact have been seconds or thirds or, in some instances, no more than myths fashioned by the ageless pairing of a writer with space to fill and a player with an eye to posterity. But in any event, they are well worth sharing.

**1849**—The Knickerbockers adopt the first official club uniform, which consists of blue woolen pantaloons, a white flannel shirt and a straw hat; in 1855, a broad patent leather belt is added and the straw hat gives way to a mohair cap.

**1857**—The first league is formed and calls itself the National Association of Baseball Clubs. All games are played at the Fashion Race Course in Jamaica, New York, and spectators are assessed a 50¢ admission fee. The season runs from July to October because some clubs contend the weather is too hot before July.

**1857**—After the formation of the National Association, a nine-inning format replaces the first-team-to-score-21-runs-wins rule, with five innings constituting a legal contest.

**1859**—The Brooklyn Excelsiors become the first team to go on tour.

**1859**—The National Association of Baseball Players is formed, taking control of the game away from the Knickerbockers Club and giving it a national flavor to induce western clubs to participate. The Association also swiftly has the corollary effect of demolishing baseball's image as strictly a gentleman's game.

**1862**—Jim Creighton of the Brooklyn Excelsiors, highly paid pitcher and the first famous pro player, suffers a ruptured spleen while batting in a game and dies at his home. A large granite monument is erected over his grave in Brooklyn's Greenwood Cemetery. Carved on the granite and encircled by a wreath is a design featuring a pair of crossed bats, a scorebook, a base and a baseball cap. Above the granite design is the single scrolled word *Excelsior,* and balanced on the summit of the granite column rests a stone baseball.

**1864**—Second baseman Al Reach, later a sporting goods manufacturer and founder of the *Reach Baseball Guide,* becomes the first "revolver" when he jumps the Eckfords club to sign with the Philadelphia Athletics.

**186?**—Pitcher Candy Cummings discovers how to make a baseball curve . . . maybe. Cummings himself claims not to be the discover, but he nevertheless makes the Hall of Fame for it. In the years to come other pitchers will be credited with discovering various new types of deliveries, but it's open to speculation which of them did and which of them didn't. Elmer Stricklett is credited with discovering the spitball; or maybe it was Bill Hart, who claimed he first used it in 1896 after being taught how to throw it by Baltimore catcher Frank Bowerman; or maybe it was Frank Corridon. Nat Hudson is credited with the sinker; Dave Danforth, the shineball; Russ Ford, the emeryball, and maybe the knuckler too, or at least one of the first good ones; Christy Mathewson, the screwball, the first great one anyway, called a fadeaway; and Eddie Plank, the first great palmball.

**187?**—Nat Hicks of the Mutuals becomes the first catcher to play directly behind the bat; others claim it is Deacon White, who is almost definitely seen doing it in 1875, at any rate with runners on base.

**1871**—The National Association forms into an organized professional league and plays its first game on May 4, with Cleveland (Forest City) pitted against Fort Wayne (Kekionga). Bobby Mathews of Kekionga pitches a 2–0 shutout over Forest City's Uncle Al Pratt. Deacon White, catcher for Cleveland and the most famous player in the game, goes 3-for-4.

**1871**—Rynie Wolters, the first Dutch player, debuts with the New York Mutuals.

**1871**—Boston and Cleveland keep batting averages for all players, and the other National Association clubs soon do likewise. Previously only runs have been recorded.

**1872**—Oscar Bielaski, the first Polish player, debuts with the Washington Nationals.

**1874**—The Boston Red Caps and Philadelphia Athletics embark on the first overseas tour to promote baseball, traveling to England in July. While there, the two clubs play a series of exhibition baseball games as well as several cricket matches. The tour is neither a financial nor an artistic success as the British seem singularly uninterested in the new game.

**1875**—Fred Thayer of Harvard invents the first catcher's mask and shows it to classmate Jim Tyng, who tests it in a college game. Later Thayer is also credited by some with developing the first inflated chest protector.

**1875**—Joe Borden of the Philadelphias, aka Joe Josephs,

pitches the first recorded no-hitter on July 28 against the Chicago White Stockings.

**1875**—The Boston Red Caps turn a profit for the season of $2261.07, which is not lost on other National Association club owners and spurs them to begin thinking of forming a more tightly run league and getting rid of weak clubs, corrupt players and lackadaisical team officials.

**1876**—William Hulbert, taking the bit in his teeth, forms a new circuit and calls it the National League after getting Boston's four star players, Deacon White, Ross Barnes, Al Spalding and Cal McVey, to desert the Red Caps and sign with his Chicago club. Cynics contend Hulbert's motive in forming the National League isn't to provide a better-run operation but because he fears the National Association will expel the four players and his Chicago team in the bargain.

**1876**—The first National League game is played on April 22 at Philadelphia, with Joe Borden, now with Boston, beating Lon Knight of the Athletics 6–5. Boston's Jim O'Rourke gets the first National League hit, a single in the top of the first inning. Third baseman Ezra Sutton of the A's has the distinction of having also played in the first National Association game, five years earlier, with Cleveland.

**1876**—Al Spalding appears on the field wearing a black kid glove with layers of padding to reduce the sting of a thrown or hit ball. (If you prefer another player of the time, feel free to substitute his name for Spalding's. Literally dozens are credited with having been the first to use a glove.)

**1876**—Philadelphia and New York are booted out of the new circuit for failing to complete their last western road trips. Not until 1883 will the two largest cities in the country again be permitted to have franchises in the National League.

**1877**—The first uniform playing schedule is adopted so that fans in all cities will know in advance which dates their club will be playing at home and can plan accordingly.

**1877**—The National League starts its second season with a new rule, which states that for a batted ball to be fair it must stay within the foul lines until it passes a base or else is fielded. The rule is put in to curb Ross Barnes, Davy Force and other batsmen who are adept at slicing hits that land in fair territory and then carom foul, forcing infielders to play outside the boundaries when they come to bat. Other players who will force rules to be changed in the years ahead are George Wright and Dickey Pearce, specialists at trapping pop flies before the infield fly rule is created; Will White and Jack Schappert, deft at hitting and intimidating batters without penalty until it occurs to somebody that maybe these wounded batsmen should be awarded first base; King Kelly, who is credited, perhaps falsely, with instigating a rule that prevents him from hopping off the bench when a foul fly heads his way and announcing himself into the game as a substitute in order to catch it; Roy Thomas, so skilled at fouling off pitches that the National League finally, in 1901, decides to start counting foul balls as strikes; and Germany Schaefer, whose crowd-catching device of setting out from second base to steal first causes a rule to be written that the bases can no longer be run backward.

**1878**—For the first time a commercial league, the National, plays all its scheduled games. Always before at least one team has failed to finish the season.

**1879**—Boston owner Arthur Soden devises the reserve clause. At first it protects only five players on each team, but with time it's expanded to include the whole roster.

**1879**—The Providence Grays build the first wire screen behind home plate and across the grandstand in their park to protect spectators from foul tips in a seating area that has become known as the "Slaughter Pens." That same year or maybe a year earlier the Grays are also, some say, the first team to install a turnstile in their park.

**1880**—Rules are put in to declare a runner out if hit by a batted ball and to award a base on balls on eight balls instead of nine.

**1880**—The *Chicago Tribune* begins reporting RBIs, but RBI records are not consistently kept until 1907 and then are not officially recognized until 1920.

**1881**—The pitcher's box is moved to 50 feet from home plate instead of 45 feet.

**1882**—"Hustling" Horace Phillips and Cincinnati sportswriter Opie Caylor create the American Association as a competitor to the National League. The AA puts teams in cities dropped by the NL, charges 25¢ admission instead of 50¢, says it's okay to play games on Sunday where the blue laws allow and to sell liquor at them, and outfits its players in gorgeous silk uniforms. Best of all, as far as the players are concerned, it chooses not to honor the NL's blacklist and to go after all players not bound to the NL by the reserve clause. The NL reacts to the threat by trying to ignore it.

**1882**—The number of balls needed to get a walk is knocked down to seven.

**1882**—Providence centerfielder Paul Hines trots out to his position wearing sunglasses. Fred Clarke is later credited with being the first player to wear pull-down sunglasses attached to his cap.

**1882**—Pete Browning of the Louisville Eclipse club wins the American Association batting title with a .378 average, 36 points higher than the runner-up, as only four players in the new league break the .300 mark. Two years later Browning will have the first modern baseball bat made for him by J. A. "Bud" Hillerich, an accidental occurrence that leads to the formation of Hillerich and Bradsby, the world's most famous batmaker. (A century later players credited with inventing curveballs and shin guards will be immortalized on bronze plaques in the Baseball Hall of Fame. Browning, the owner of a .341 career batting average, the first player to have his bats custom made and one of the most colorful and controversial characters in a league replete with them, will not.)

**1883**—The term *fan* is coined by St. Louis Browns manager Ted Sullivan when team owner Chris Von Der Ahe calls the club's followers fanatics. Heretofore the popular word for a baseball fan has been *krank,* and kranks have already been analyzed in depth by Thomas Lawson in his book *The Krank: His Language and What It Means,* which contains a lexicon that includes many phrases that will still be in vogue 100 years later—to wit, the umpire as a 10th man or a robber, a bat as a willow or an ash, outstanding fielding plays as circus catches. The first great krank emerges around the time Sullivan thinks up a shorter word for him. His name is Arthur Dixwell, and he lives in Boston. Independently wealthy, he lavishes rewards on Beaneater players who do something unexpectedly fine and boosts the minor leagues in the New England area with his award of the coveted Dixwell trophy. When excited, Dixwell is heard to scream, "Hi! Hi!" and hence becomes known as Hi! Hi! Dixwell.

**1884**—Pitchers are allowed to employ shoulder-high deliveries instead of being restricted to those in which their hands must pass below their hips. As a sop to hitters, who now must face overhand fastballs from only 50 feet away, the number of balls needed for a walk is cut to six. In 1886, when observers feel that games are cluttered with too many walks, the figure is again hiked to seven.

**1884**—Henry Lucas, a young real estate scion who had been operating a minor league called the Union Association, grows convinced that baseball players are little more than chattels and vows to build his minor league into a powerful new major league that will not have the reserve clause. Lucas pilfers many good players from the American Association and National League, but his circuit fails when he stacks his own team, the St. Louis Maroons, with most of the good players and places competing UA teams in such thriving metropolises as Wilmington and Altoona.

**188?**—Harry Stevens, the "Scorecard Man," aka "Hustling Harry," comes out of the woodwork. By 1900 Harry has nailed down the scorecard and food concessions at most major-league parks, a distinction that his heirs still carry on in 2004. His sales prompt fans to beg owners to put numbers on players' uniforms so that better use can be made of the scorecards; some owners actually oblige their fans for a week or two, but the players resist, not liking the idea of wearing a number. Meanwhile, Stevens is so flush from his commissions that by 1910 he has sent his son to Yale Law School.

**1886**—The New York Giants set a record when 20,709 attend a Memorial Day game at the Polo Grounds. Later in the season the Giants get nearly 30,000 to a game.

**1886**—Cincinnati owner Aaron Stern observes that women swarm to the Reds ball park on days that handsome Tony Mullane is scheduled to pitch. Shrewdly, Stern begins designating games that Mullane will work against weak teams that normally draw poorly as special "Ladies Day" events. Mullane becomes known as "The Apollo of the Box" and receives credit from many historians for starting Ladies Days, but further research turns up Ladies Day games as far back as 1876. Whatever the truth of the matter is, Ladies Day games mushroom in the 1880s, and clubs like Brooklyn begin making every day except holidays Ladies Day in the belief that women add a certain tone to the crowd and curtail rowdyism and drunkenness. Brooklyn owner Charles Byrne also points out to his fellow moguls that it's a lot cheaper than hiring special police.

**1887**—Batters are no longer permitted to call for high or low pitches, and the strike zone is now defined as the area between the tops of the shoulders and the bottoms of the knees rather than above or below the waist. Also in 1887, the NL belatedly goes along with the Association and gives a batter first base if hit by a pitch. To further complicate things for umpires, a base on balls is reduced to five balls, and a strikeout requires four strikes instead of three. Major-league rulers, still not content, next decide to count walks as base hits. After all this, Tip O'Neill and Pete Browning post astronomical batting averages in the Association, which are discounted because they were compiled by men who got four strikes and received many walks. (Years later, after statisticians have removed the walks from their hit totals, their averages remain well over .400 and are still viewed as flukes.)

**1887**—Before the season, Chicago peddles King Kelly to Boston for $10,000, a record transaction. Two years earlier the Detroit Wolverines had shelled out only $7000 to obtain four players nearly as good as Kelly from Buffalo.

**1887**—Cap Anson takes his champion Chicago White Stockings to Hot Springs, Arkansas, to prepare for a preseason series with the defending AA champion St. Louis Browns and is credited with originating the concept of spring training.

**1887**—Several St. Louis Browns tout Merrell's Penetrating Oil as a cure for bruises and muscle pulls, the first player endorsement of a product, some say, although players have already begun appearing on cigarette and chewing tobacco cards.

**1887**—Henry Chadwick decides it's time to revise won-lost records for pitchers. Previously a pitcher who worked the most innings in a game was credited with the decision regardless of the score when he departed. Chadwick, called "the father of the game," was born in England in 1824 and became a sportswriter in 1848. By 1887 he has long since invented the box score, begun editing *Spalding's Official Baseball Guide,* authored the first rule book and originated the scoring system still in use today.

**188?**—Third baseman Arlie Latham of the St. Louis Browns takes it upon himself to start coaching his teammates when they're on base. A torrential heckler and ace sign stealer, Latham soon becomes so popular with fans that it's feared efforts to control his antics may cut attendance. In 1907, John McGraw pays Latham to do nothing more than act as a base coach for the Giants, making him the first contracted coach.

**1888**—Detroit begins issuing rainchecks, which state, "In case rain interrupts the game before three innings are played this check will admit the bearer to grounds for the next league game only." Other clubs also adopt the practice, and the next-league-game rule will remain the custom for a long while.

**1888**—Pitcher Tim Keefe of the New York Giants designs and sells to his team their tight-fitting all-black uniforms with white raised letters that spell NEW YORK across the chest. Called "Funeral" uniforms at first, their color will soon catch on. The 1889 Baltimore Orioles, for one, play in black pants with white side stripes, white shirts and maroon stockings, and black-and-white-striped caps.

**1888**—Officials finally have it all figured out: Batters should get only three strikes, and that's it. The following year four balls, for the first time, constitute a walk.

**188?**—Philadephia manager Harry Wright introduces pre-game batting practice and also starts fungoing fly balls to his outfielders before games.

**1889**—For the first time in major-league history a pennant race is decided on the last day of the season. On October 5, New York beats Cleveland while lowly Pittsburgh is downing Boston's ace pitcher John Clarkson. Had the Beaneaters won, and New York lost, Boston, and not the Giants, would have claimed the NL flag.

**1889**—Indianapolis owner John T. "Tooth" Brush waits until Monte Ward, organizer of the first major league players union, goes on a world tour and then sneaks through a classification rule wherein players are graded from A to E, with A players limited to salaries of $2500 and E players able to earn no more than $1500—Ward explodes when he comes home and learns that salaries have been capped.

**1890**—Ward, Ned Hanlon and several other angry players get Cleveland street railway magnate Albert Johnson to influence other capitalists to loan money to players so that they can build parks in eight cities and start a new league. By the spring of 1890, the Players League has corraled most of the top players in the AA and NL and is a reality. Six months later the Players League concludes its first and only season of play, and Ward and its other leaders are unaware that the AA and NL are near collapse. In their ignorance, the players agree to return to the fold, after getting a few concessions from the owners that are quickly reneged on when the AA ceases operation in the fall of 1891 and the NL absorbs its four strongest franchises, leaving the players with only one major league to which to sell their talents and no recourse but retirement or the minors if they don't like what they're offered.

**1890**—Harry Decker perfects the "Decker Safety Catching Mitt"—a forerunner of modern mitts. Previously, catchers used heavily padded mittens. Buck Ewing, the first to use Decker's mitt, enthusiastically endorses it.

**1891**—The substitution rule is liberalized, allowing a player to enter a game at any time and at any position, the only restriction being that the player for which he is substituted cannot reenter the game.

**1891**—Pittsburgh fines outfielder Pete Browning for not wearing spikes on his shoes. Spikes have been in general use for several years and by now are mandatory equipment.

**1892**—The new 12-team National League for the first time plays a 154-game schedule, clubs meeting each of their rivals 14 times. (The longer schedule is tried again later in the decade, then reduced to 140 games, where it remains until 1904.)

**1892**—On June 2, Benjamin Harrison becomes the first president to attend a game while in office, when he watches Cincinnati beat Washington 7–4 in 11 innings.

**1893**—The pitcher's mound is moved from 50 feet to 60 feet 6 inches from home plate, and a rule is added that bats must be completely round, eliminating all the bats that are flat on one side or sawed off at the end. It puzzles officials at first why those extra six inches were tacked onto the new mound distance, until they learn that a surveyor misread the blueprint, which correctly read 60 feet 0 inches.

**1893**—Clifford Spencer proposes that, in conjunction with increasing the mound distance, the field should be made pentagonal with four bases for better balance, fewer foul balls, more stealing and higher status for second basemen. Many are intrigued by the idea, but it's shelved for the moment because the lengthened mound distance immediately leads to more scoring and revitalizes fan interest.

**1894**—To curb pesky hitters like Willie Keeler who stick out their bats and deliberately poke pitches foul until they get one to their liking, a batter for the first time is charged with a strike for hitting a foul bunt.

**1894**—Players on the Baltimore Orioles conspire with groundskeeper Tom Murphy to landscape the baselines in their home park in order to prevent their bunts from rolling foul while at the same time leaving the outfield grass high to hide illegal balls that can be put into play at propitious moments. Murphy also loosens the dirt in front of the pitcher's mound to stymie rival hurlers like Cy Young and Amos Rusie and reduce them to a par with Baltimore's moundsmen, who are among the worst in the league.

**1895**—The infield fly rule is adopted, and a strike is now assessed a batter on a foul tip—but not as yet on a foul ball. Umpires are left to judge between a tipped ball and a fouled one.

**1896**—A Princeton professor named Hinton invents the first mechanical pitching machine, a smoothbored breechloading cannon mounted on two wheels and fitted with curved prongs attached to the sides of the muzzle in order to curve a ball.

**1897**—Eddie Abbaticchio, the first Italian player of note, debuts with Philadelphia.

**1897**—Oliver Perry Caylor dies. Although never himself a major league player, Caylor helped to found the American Association, managed the Cincinnati Reds and the New York Metropolitans for two seasons and part of a third, subsequently edited *Reach's Official Baseball Guide* and then became baseball editor of the *New York Herald* and official scorer for the Giants. His witty, cutting style and iconoclastic viewpoint are sorely missed in the next decade.

**1898**—The first modern balk rule is put in the book; also the modern rule for recognizing stolen bases, making it forever impossible to compare Ty Cobb, Lou Brock and Rickey Henderson to Harry Stovey, Billy Hamilton and other early base thieves.

**1899**—The Cleveland Spiders are the first major league team to become a traveling road show when they play all but a handful of their games in rival cities after the 4th of July owing to poor home attendance; an entirely predictable result after the team's best players are shifted en masse to St. Louis prior to the season, leaving a crew of dregs in the Forest City that lose an ML record 134 games and win a mere 20.

**1900**—A pentagon-shaped home plate is unveiled, replacing the old diamond-shaped one.

**1900**—At the conclusion of the season, the infield fly rule is modified so that it's in effect with none out as well as with one out. The National League also decides to start calling foul balls strikes in 1901, unable to care less that the upstart Western League, which has changed its name to the American League and began billing itself as a major circuit, doesn't want to go along with the foul-strike rule and will not conform until 1903.

# Season Record Holders Prior to 1901

It would take an entire book to chronicle the rules that were used to determine batting and pitching records in the 19th century, the exceptions that were made to them, the numerous seasons in which incomplete statistics were kept and the many disputes that are still raging over whether a certain batter hit .492 one year or only .435 and whether a certain pitcher struck out 513 batters another year or only 505. Suffice it to say these are the consensus records of an era that was not as yet consumed by the mystique of records and the devotion to minutiae needed to keep them accurately.

The record holders prior to 1893 played when the pitcher's mound was either 45 feet or 50 feet from home plate. The record holders between 1893 and 1900 played under present rules for the most part but in a period when there was only one 12-team league, no meaningful postseason play, and a batter was still allowed to hit an unlimited number of foul balls without a strike being charged against him.

## 1876 THROUGH 1892

### Batting

| Department | National League | American Association |
|---|---|---|
| Batting Average | .429, Ross Barnes, Chicago, 1876 | .435, TIP O'NEILL, St. Louis, 1887 |
| Slugging Average | .590, Ross Barnes, Chicago, 1876 | .691, TIP O'NEILL, St. Louis, 1887 |
| Home Runs | 27, NED WILLIAMSON Chicago, 1884 | 19, Harry Stovey, Philadelphia, 1889 |
| | | 19, Bug Holliday, Cincinnati, 1889 |

| Department | National League | American Association |
|---|---|---|
| RBIs | 166, SAM THOMPSON, Detroit, 1887 | 123, Tip O'Neill, St. Louis, 1887 |
| Runs | 153, Dan Brouthers, Detroit, 1887 | 177, TOM BROWN, Boston, 1891 |
| Hits | 205, Jack Glasscock, Indianapolis, 1889 | 225, TIP O'NEILL, St. Louis, 1887 |
| Doubles | 49, Ned Williamson, Chicago, 1883 | 52, TIP O'NEILL, St. Louis, 1887 |
| Triples | 26, John Reilly, Cincinnati, 1890 | 31, DAVE ORR, New York, 1886 |
| Total Bases | 311, Sam Thompson, Detroit, 1887 | 357, TIP O'NEILL, St. Louis, 1887 |
| Bases on Balls | 136, JOHN CROOKS, St. Louis, 1892 | 119, Dummy Hoy, St. Louis, 1891 |
| Stolen Bases | 111, Billy Hamilton, Philadelphia, 1891 111, Monte Ward, New York, 1887 | 138, HUGH NICOL, Cincinnati, 1887 |

*Note:* This book disagrees with *Total Baseball*'s recent decisions to count walks as times at bat in 1876 and as hits in 1887.

## Pitching

| Department | National League | American Association |
|---|---|---|
| Wins | 60, HOSS RADBOURN, Providence, 1884 | 52, Guy Hecker, Louisville, 1884 |
| Losses | 48, JOHN COLEMAN, Philadelphia, 1883 | 41, Larry McKeon, Indianapolis, 1884 |
| Innings Pitched | 680, WILL WHITE, Cincinnati, 1879 | 671, Guy Hecker, Louisville, 1884 |
| Strikeouts | 441, Hoss Radbourn, Providence, 1884 | 513, MATT KILROY, Baltimore 1886 |
| Complete Games | 75, WILL WHITE, Cincinnati, 1879 | 72, Guy Hecker, Louisville, 1884 |
| Shutouts | 16, GEORGE BRADLEY, St. Louis, 1876 | 12, Ed Morris, Pittsburgh, 1886 |

| Department | National League | American Association |
|---|---|---|
| ERA | 1.23, George Bradley, St. Louis, 1876 | 1.21, DENNY DRISCOLL, Pittsburgh, 1882 |

# 1893 THROUGH 1900

## Batting

| Department | Record Holder | Runner-up |
|---|---|---|
| Batting Average | .440, HUGH DUFFY, Boston, 1894 | .424, Willie Keeler, Baltimore, 1897 |
| Slugging Average | .696, SAM THOMPSON, Philadelphia, 1894 | .694, Hugh Duffy, Boston, 1894 |
| Home Runs | 25, BUCK FREEMAN, Washington, 1899 | 19, Ed Delahanty, Philadelphia, 1893 |
| RBIs | 165, SAM THOMPSON, Philadelphia, 1896 | 147, Sam Thompson, Philadelphia, 1894 |
| Runs | 198, JESSE BURKETT, Cleveland, 1896 | 166, Billy Hamilton, Philadelphia, 1895 |
| Hits | 240, JESSE BURKETT, Cleveland, 1896 | 238, Ed Delahanty, Philadelphia, 1899 |
| Doubles | 55, ED DELAHANTY, Philadelphia, 1899 | 51, Hugh Duffy, Boston, 1894 |
| Triples | 31, HEINIE REITZ, Baltimore, 1894 | 29, Perry Werden, St. Louis, 1893 |
| Total Bases | 374, HUGH DUFFY, Boston, 1894 | 352, Sam Thompson, Philadelphia, 1895 |
| Bases on Balls | 128, BILLY HAMILTON, Philadelphia, 1894 | 124, John McGraw, Baltimore, 1899 |
| Stolen Bases | 100, BILLY HAMILTON, Philadelphia, 1894 | 87, Billy Hamilton, Philadelphia, 1895 |

Note: Some sources still credit Werden with 33 triples in 1893.

## Pitching

| Department | Record Holder | Runner-up |
|---|---|---|
| Wins | 36, AMOS RUSIE, New York, 1894 | 35, Cy Young, Cleveland, 1895 |

| Department | Record Holder | Runner-up |
|---|---|---|
| Losses | 35, RED DONAHUE, St. Louis, 1897 | 30, Jim Hughey, Cleveland, 1899 |
| Innings Pitched | 482, AMOS RUSIE New York, 1893 | 447⅓, Ted Breitenstein, St. Louis, 1894 |
| Strikeouts | 239, CY SEYMOUR, New York, 1898 | 208, Amos Rusie, New York, 1893 |
| Complete Games | 50, AMOS RUSIE, New York, 1893 | 46, Ted Breitenstein, St. Louis, 1894, 1895 |
| Shutouts | 6, WILEY PIATT, Philadelphia, 1898 6, JACK POWELL, Cleveland, 1898 | 5, done by six different pitchers |
| ERA | 1.88, CLARK GRIFFITH, Chicago, 1898 | 2.10, Al Maul, Baltimore, 1898 |

## TEAM SEASON RECORD HOLDERS

### 1876 through 1892

| Highest | National League | American Association |
|---|---|---|
| Batting Average | .337, CHICAGO, 1876 | .307, St. Louis, 1887 |
| Slugging Average | .446, CHICAGO, 1884 | .413, St. Louis, 1887 |
| Winning Pct. | .788, CHICAGO, 1880 (67–17) | .705, St. Louis, 1885 (79–33) |
| *Lowest* | | |
| Batting Average | .208, Washington, 1888 | .204, BALTIMORE, 1886 |
| Slugging Average | .261, New York, 1876 | .258, BALTIMORE, 1882 |
| Winning Pct. | .138, CINCINNATI 1876 (9–56) | .196, Louisville, 1889 (27–111) |

# 1893 through 1900

|  | Highest | Lowest |
|---|---|---|
| Batting Average | .350, Philadelphia, 1894 | .247, St. Louis, 1898 |
| Slugging Average | .484, Boston, 1894 | .305, St. Louis, 1898<br>.305, Cleveland, 1899 |
| Winning Pct. | .705, Boston, 1897 (93–39) | .130, Cleveland, 1899 (20–134) |

# The Four Most
# Interesting Teams Before 1901

## 1884 PROVIDENCE GRAYS
## W-84 L-28
## Manager: Frank Bancroft

**Regular Lineup**—1B, Joe Start; 2B, Jack Farrell; SS, Arthur Irwin; 3B, Jerry Denny; RF, Paul Radford; CF, Paul Hines; LF, Cliff Carroll; C, Barney Gilligan: P, Hoss Radbourn; P, Charlie Sweeney.

Fifth in the National League in batting and fifth in runs scored, the Grays nonetheless won the pennant by 10½ games. Their lineup had just one .300 hitter, Hines, and Radford hit only .197, one of the poorest averages ever for a regular outfielder. The Grays had finished third in 1883 and seemed destined to drop out of contention altogether when Sweeney jumped the club midway in the 1884 season and signed with St. Louis in the Union Association. Sweeney reportedly had the best fastball in the game at the time and was, moreover, an excellent hitter—good enough to play the outfield on the days Radbourn pitched. After Sweeney's defection, manager Bancroft tried to find a replacement for him, but there were three major leagues in 1884, and experienced pitchers were scarce. Finally Bancroft in desperation struck a bargain with Radbourn, who had been under suspension for drunkenness when Sweeney left. Radbourn offered to pitch every game for the rest of the season if in return Providence released him from his contract. Then he proceeded to fulfill his part of the deal by posting an all-time record 60 wins. Radbourn didn't literally pitch every game down the stretch— other Providence players, Radford among them, took a turn on the mound now and then to spell him—but he did work far more often than necessary considering the Grays' runaway win, and it took its toll on his arm. After 1884 he was only an average pitcher and was out of baseball entirely eight years later.

Upon leaving the game, Radbourn opened a billiard parlor and spent his days there, drinking and schmoozing with patrons until he suffered an injury that left his face partially paralyzed. Self-conscious, he retired to a back room, where he sat most of the time in dim light, which concealed his disfigurement. He died of paresis in 1897.

His team fared no better. The smallest city in the National League, Providence, despite winning the pennant, could not draw enough fans to meet its payroll and withdrew from the majors after the 1885 season, never to return.

## 1882 CINCINNATI REDS
## W-55 L-25
## Manager: Pop Snyder

**Regular Lineup**—1B, Dan Stearns; 2B, Bid McPhee; SS, Chick Fulmer; 3B, Hick Carpenter; RF, Harry Wheeler; CF, Jimmy Macullar; LF, Joe Sommer; C, Pop Snyder; P, Will White.

Expelled from the National League after the 1880 season for playing games on Sunday and selling beer in its park, the Cincinnati franchise was quick to regroup when the American Association formed in time to begin the 1882 season. The Reds signed White, Sommer, Carpenter and Wheeler, all members of the 1880 team who were either released or left unprotected by National League clubs, and then snatched catcher Snyder away from the Boston Red Stockings to serve as player-manager. These five players became the nucleus of the only Cincinnati club to win a pennant before 1919. Joining with them were 22-year-old second baseman McPhee, getting his first opportunity to play in the majors, and shortstop Fulmer, who had been blacklisted by the National League early in the 1880 season. In the Association's inaugural year, the Reds were easily the class of the league, romping home 11½ games ahead of Philadelphia. Whether they were as good as Chicago, the NL champ in 1882, was never settled—a post-season series between the two teams ended in controversy after each had won a game—but they were undoubtedly the best Cincinnati nine since the legendary Red Stockings. The club remained strong for several more years but was never again able to mount a serious pennant bid as the St. Louis Browns emerged as the league's powerhouse team.

## 1894 PHILADELPHIA PHILLIES
### W-71 L-57
### Manager: Arthur Irwin

**Regular Lineup**—1B, Jack Boyle; 2B, Bill Hallman; SS, Joe Sullivan; 3B, Lave Cross; RF, Sam Thompson; CF, Billy Hamilton: LF, Ed Delahanty; C, Jack Clements; P, Jack Taylor; P, Kid Carsey; P, Gus Weyhing; util., Tuck Turner.

The Phillies had an all-time record team batting average of .350, averaged over nine runs a game and featured three .400 hitters. But the club could do no better than finish a distant fourth, 10 games behind third-place Boston. At a glance, the reason would seem to be inadequate pitching—the Phillies mound staff had an aggregate 5.63 ERA in 1894—but every team except the New York Giants had the same problem that year. With the mound now 60 feet 6 inches from the plate, hitters in 1894 were so far ahead of pitchers that the league batting average was .310, and five teams scored over 1000 runs.

The better explanation for the Phillies' failure to challenge for the pennant probably lay in manager Irwin. Boston, New York and Baltimore, the three clubs that finished ahead of Philadelphia, were piloted by Frank Selee, Monte Ward and Ned Hanlon, three of the best minds in the game, and I have a hunch that Irwin found himself on the wrong end of a lot of 10–9 and 10–8 scores when he came up against them.

## 1899 CLEVELAND SPIDERS
### W-20 L-134
### Managers: Lave Cross and Joe Quinn

**Regular Lineup**—1B, Tommy Tucker; 2B, Joe Quinn; SS, Harry Lockhead; 3B, Suter Sullivan; RF, Sport McAllister;

CF, Tommy Dowd; LF, Dick Harley; C, Joe Sugden; P, Jim Hughey; P, Charlie Knepper; P, Frank Bates; P, Crazy Schmit.

One of the National League's best clubs earlier in the decade, the Spiders were disemboweled by their owners, the Robison brothers, after they bought the St. Louis franchise and gauged that its fans would be more supportive of a good team. Syndicate ownership was outlawed shortly thereafter—but too late to save the Spiders. The Robisons shipped every single regular from the 1898 club to St. Louis, leaving manager Cross with only three quality players—himself, Quinn and Dowd—plus aging Tommy Tucker, talked out of retirement to play one more season. After the club lost 30 of its first 38 games, Cross was mercifully transferred to St. Louis, which needed a third baseman, and the reins were handed to Quinn. Under Quinn, the Spiders had a 12–104 record and were so inept that they no longer dared to show their wares in front of a Cleveland crowd. After June, with the exception of a few games in late August, the club played out the season on the road, where it lost 102 of 113 games and became known as the Wanderers. The leading pitcher, Knepper, had a .154 win percentage, and no hurler won more than four games. Amid all this, Tommy Dowd hit a respectable .278 in 147 games. Dowd, in his 10-year career, had the unpleasant distinction of playing on just about every rotten team in the period. Ironically, he began with the pennant-winning 1891 Boston AA team but played only four games with them before being swapped to Washington, which finished in the cellar. There is a theory that Lave Cross, whose career stats are better than many contemporary players who made the Hall of Fame, never got in because he played for and managed—albeit for only a few weeks—the 1899 Spiders, the worst team in history.

# Wild Men
# On the Mound

Bases-on-balls statistics prior to 1893 require that anyone interested in interpreting them read a rule book for each season. As an illustration, in 1883 Pud Galvin of Buffalo walked only 50 batters in 656 innings; seven years later he walked 62 in 247 innings. What happened to Galvin's control? Nothing—the fact is it probably got better. But in 1883 a batter had to receive seven balls before he drew a walk. By 1889 the number of balls needed for a walk had dropped to four, and the following year Amos Rusie of the Giants set an all-time record when he granted 289 free passes. In 1893 the mound was moved 10 feet 6 inches farther from the plate, but by that time most pitchers, Rusie included, had adapted, at least partially, to the less liberal margin for errant tosses, and pitchers on the whole issued fewer walks at the longer distance.

## MOST BASES ON BALLS, SEASON

|  |  | Team | League | Year |  |
|---|---|---|---|---|---|
| 1893–1900 | Amos Rusie (R) | New York | National | 1893 | 218[1] |
|  | Cy Seymour (L) | New York | National | 1898 | 213 |
| 1901–19 | Bob Harmon (R) | St. Louis | National | 1911 | 181 |
|  | Nap Rucker (L) | Brooklyn | National | 1908 | 125 |
| 1920–41 | Bob Feller (R) | Cleveland | American | 1938 | 208[2] |
|  | Ken Chase (L) | Washington | American | 1941 | 143 |
| 1942–60 | Sam Jones (R) | Chicago | National | 1955 | 185[3] |

|  |  |  |  |  |
|---|---|---|---|---|
| Tommy Byrne (L) | New York | American | 1949 | 179[4] |
| 162-Game | Nolan Ryan (R) | California | American | 1977 | 204[5] |
| Schedule | Sam McDowell (L) | Cleveland | American | 1971 | 153 |

[1]Probably the wildest pitcher in history, Rusie got better as his career went along. By 1897 his control had improved so much that he gave up only 87 walks in 322 innings.

[2]Both the 20th-century record and the American League record.

[3]The 20th-century National League record.

[4]The 20th-century record for a left-hander.

[5]Walked 202 in 1974 and is the only pitcher in the 20th century to issue 200 or more walks in a season twice.

## Most Seasons League Leader in Bases on Balls

AL—6—Nolan Ryan, last in 1978; Ryan also led the NL in 1980 and 1982.

NL—5—Amos Rusie, 1890–94 consecutive

NL since 1901—4—Jimmy Ring, 1922–25 consecutive;
Bob Veale, last in 1968

## Most Intentional Walks, Season

23—Mike Garman, 1975, St. Louis, NL
Dale Murray, 1978, Cincinnati, NL
Kent Tekulve, 1982, Pittsburgh, NL

## Most Hit Batsmen, Season, Since 1893

NL—41—Joe McGinnity, 1900, Brooklyn

AL—31—Chick Fraser, 1901, Philadelphia

## Fewest Bases on Balls, Season, by League Leader in Bases on Balls (Strike Seasons Excepted)

NL—82—David Cone, New York, 1992

AL—89—Tanyon Sturtze, Tampa Bay, 2002

## Most Bases on Balls, Game, Nine Innings

NL—16—Bill George, New York Giants, May 30, 1887, versus the Chicago White Stockings. George, a 22-year-old rookie left-hander, set the record in a season when five balls were still needed for a walk. Some sources contend that in 1887 White Stockings rookie George Van Haltren also gave up 16 walks in a game.

NL since 1893—14—Henry Mathewson, New York, October 5, 1906, versus Boston. Christy's younger brother, Mathewson set the modern NL record while making his only major league start.

AL—16—Bruno Haas, Philadelphia, June 23, 1915, versus New York. In 1915 A's pitchers issued an all-time record 827 walks—only 28 of them by Haas, who was released soon after his record-shattering performance. Six years later, however, he resurfaced as a halfback in the newly formed National Football League.

## Most Consecutive Bases on Balls, Game

7—Dolly Gray, Washington, AL, August 28, 1909. Gray walked eight batters altogether in the course of the inning, also a record. But it must have been only a momentary lapse, for he walked just 77 batters in 218 innings that season.

## Co-Winners of the "Why Let a Few Walks Bother You" Award

Yankees Hall of Famer Lefty Gomez pitched a shutout on August 1, 1941, despite giving up 11 walks. On May 21, 1970, Mel Stottlemyre of the Yankees was relieved with one out in the ninth inning after surrendering 11 walks in a game that also ended as a shutout.

## MOST BASES ON BALLS, CAREER, TOP 10

|   | | Years Active | BB |
|---|---|---|---|
| 1. | Nolan Ryan | 1966–93 | 2795 |
| 2. | Steve Carlton | 1965–88 | 1833[1] |
| 3. | Phil Niekro | 1964–87 | 1809 |
| 4. | Early Wynn | 1939–63 | 1775 |
| 5. | Bob Feller | 1936–56 | 1764 |
| 6. | Bobo Newsom | 1929–53 | 1732 |
| 7. | Amos Rusie | 1889–1901 | 1707 |
| 8. | Charlie Hough | 1970–94 | 1665[2] |
| 9. | Gus Weyhing | 1887–1901 | 1570[3] |
| 10. | Red Ruffing | 1924–47 | 1541 |

[1]The lefty career record.

[2]When Hough garnered his 200th career win in 1992, it meant, for what it's worth, that all ten hurlers on the most walks list have notched at least 200 victories, led by Carlton with 329.

[3]Like Rusie, his control began to improve dramatically after the mound distance was increased.

**Most Hit Batsmen, Career, since 1901**

206—Walter Johnson, 1907–27. He also once held the AL record for wild pitches with 21, but the mark now belongs to Juan Guzman with 26 in 1993. The NL record since 1901 is held by Red Ames of the Giants, who let 30 pitches get away from him in 1905.

**The Amos Rusie Award for the Most Consistent Lack of Control**

Left-hander—Tommy Byrne, 1943–57. Byrne spent most of his career with the Yankees, but in 1951, while pitching for the St. Louis Browns, he walked 16 Washington Senators in a 13-inning game. Over his career, he gave up 1037 bases on balls in only 1362 innings.

Right-hander—Dick Weik, active between 1948 and 1954 with the Senators, Indians and Tigers. Weik made only 26 starts but four times walked 10 or more batters in a game. In 1949 he issued 103 walks in only 95 innings, and if his control improved after that his stats didn't show it. Lifetime, he had a 6–22 won-lost record and 237 walks in 214 innings. Despite it all the Indians liked him enough to trade Mickey Vernon for him in 1950. Three years later Vernon won his second AL batting crown while Weik had a 13.97 ERA in 12 games.

Weik's control problems were equally manifest in the minors. In his very first pro game, with Charlotte in the Tri-State League in 1946, he walked 15 men. Two years later he led the Southern Association in bases on balls, issuing 173 in just 132 innings.

# Owners

George Steinbrenner, Marge Schott, Ted Turner and Claude Brochu are poles apart in their philosophies on operating a major league baseball franchise, and each may seem like one of a kind. But the truth is that each of them has had numerous prototypes throughout the game's history. Here are fourteen of my favorite owners; by no means the most famous fourteen, nor the most influential, nor the wackiest—just a representative selection from the legion of fascinating men and women who have had a hand in shaping events.

## The First Steinbrenner

Aaron Champion became president of the Cincinnati Red Stockings baseball club in 1867 and immediately embarked on a no-holds-barred commercial expansion program. He pushed through an $11,000 stock issue so that the Red Stockings could refurbish their home grounds, Union Field, and then set out with manager Harry Wright to obtain the best players available regardless of the price. The Red Stockings were not, as some historians have written, the first professional team. Rather, they were the first nationally successful one by dint of being the first all-salaried team, a device to hold players to full-season contracts and prevent them from "revolving," or jumping to rival teams. For more about the Red Stockings see "Team Records," but let's look for a moment at the salaries of the 1869 Red Stockings as a point of comparison to, say, what Yankee regulars got in 2003.

| | |
|---|---|
| Harry Wright, CF | $1800 |
| George Wright, SS | $1800 |
| Asa Brainard, P | $800 |
| Charlie Gould, 1B | $800 |
| Fred Waterman, 3B | $800 |

| Charlie Sweasy, 2B | $700 |
| Doug Allison, C | $700 |
| Andy Leonard, LF | $700 |
| Cal McVey, RF | $700 |
| Dick Hurley, Sub | $600 |
| Total salaries: | $9400 |

## The First Wayne Huizenga

Arthur Soden was principal owner and team president of the Boston Beaneaters from 1877 through 1906. To stop revolving, Soden instituted the reserve clause and later was a leader in the movement to limit players' salaries. Tight-fisted, intransigent, Soden was nevertheless highly successful—Boston was the National League's strongest team as late as 1898—until the American League arrived on the scene. Refusing to match the huge sums of money dangled in front of his stars by AL clubs, Soden had lost virtually every player of merit by the time the two leagues reached a peace settlement in 1903. Boston deservedly finished deep in the cellar in 1906—his last season as its owner.

## The First August Busch/Charlie Finley/Ted Turner

Chris Von Der Ahe was owner and sometimes manager of the St. Louis Browns in the American Association. Von Der Ahe was just one of several brewery magnates who helped start the Association in 1882, but by the middle of the decade he stood alone. Outfitting his players in elegant multicolored silk uniforms, bickering with umpires and rival owners, getting more press than all the other club officials combined, Von Der Ahe at the same time gave Browns fans high-quality baseball. Sadly, the game swiftly passed him by when the Association folded after the 1891 season, and he died nearly broke.

## The Biggest Reason the American Association Failed

The Metropolitan Exhibition Company owned both the American Association New York Metropolitans and the National League New York Giants in the mid-1880s. Convinced that the NL would survive the civil war between the two circuits, company officials stocked the Giants with many of the Mets' best players after the club won the 1884 Association pennant and even included in the package the Mets manager,

Jim Mutrie. When the Pittsburgh Alleghenies switched to the National League after the 1886 season, the Association was left without any strong owners except Von Der Ahe. The Metropolitan Exhibition Company's machinations were a forerunner of the syndicate ownership practices of the Robison brothers and the von der Horsts, which nearly ruined the National League too in the late 1890s.

## Big City Versus Little City I

When Fredrick Stearns bought the Detroit National League franchise in the mid-1880s, the automobile was still only a fantasy, and Detroit was one of the smallest cities to have a major-league team. The Buffalo franchise, likewise serving a small city, was on the verge of collapsing, and Stearns, thinking he saw a quick way to enliven his franchise, purchased Buffalo's four best players—Deacon White, Dan Brouthers, Jack Rowe and Hardy Richardson—at the close of the 1885 season. With the addition of the "Buffalo Four," Detroit became an instant contender in 1886 and won the NL pennant the following year, but Stearns was thwarted from reaping the benefits he had anticipated. His plan, since Detroit had too small a population to draw many fans regardless of the quality of the team, was to make the Wolverines the top road attraction in the game and earn the bulk of his money on visits to Chicago, Boston, Philadelphia and New York. But team owners in these cities abruptly changed the rules governing the sharing of gate receipts when they fathomed Stearn's strategy, and by 1889 Detroit had folded and would be without major-league baseball again until 1901.

## Big City Versus Little City II

Andrew Freedman, the New York Giants owner in the late 1890s, believed that having possession of the team in the largest population center in the country entitled him to run it any way he pleased, and for eight years he did. Even more penurious than Arthur Soden and far and away the most loathed baseball mogul in his day, Freedman aborted the career of his star pitcher Amos Rusie by forcing Rusie to hold out one entire season. By the end of the decade the Giants had sunk to last place and seemed destined to stay there unless Freedman was removed. After a bitter struggle, he sold out to a group headed by John Brush, and within a few months Brush had induced John McGraw to desert the American League for the Giants managerial post, and the franchise was on its way to becoming once again the most financially successful in the game.

## Big City Versus Little City III

Horace Fogel was part of the new regime that Brush brought with him when he took over the Giants—Fogel even managed the club for a while in 1902—but by 1912 he had switched allegiance to Philadelphia and bought a chunk of the moribund Phillies. He was forced to divest himself of his stock and barred from the game when he allegedly charged that St. Louis manager Roger Bresnahan had allowed the Giants to beat the Cardinals in a crucial series near the end of the 1912 season so that Bresnahan's crony John McGraw would be assured of winning the pennant. The accusation had really emanated not from Fogel and the Phillies camp but from Cubs owner Charles Murphy, who headed the one NL franchise that was on a par at the time with New York's and was thus too powerful to oust. Interestingly, the only other owner ever banned was another Phillies mogul, Billy Cox, who was given the gate by Commissioner Judge Landis early in World War II for betting on his own team. Cox departed meekly and sold the club to the Carpenters, who installed their youngest son, Bob, as team president.

## The First Marge Schott

Helen Britton assumed control of the St. Louis Cardinals in 1911 after her uncle, Stanley Robison, died, and she ran them through 1916 when her marriage came apart and she sold the team. After Britton and her husband separated, she took over his post as club president for the 1916 season, making her the first woman ever to act in that capacity on a major league level.

## The Federal League Legacy I

In 1915 Harry Sinclair bought a controlling interest in the Newark Federal League franchise and quickly found a way to recoup his losses—and then some—after the Feds closed up shop. As part of the peace settlement with organized baseball, Sinclair was allowed to take over the contracts of many Federal League players and sell them to major-league clubs, earning himself a sizable piece of change and in the process becoming a broker of players and the greatest trader in human merchandise since the abolition of slavery. If the name seems to ring a bell, you're right—it's the same Harry Sinclair who was later implicated in the Teapot Dome Scandal.

## The Federal League Legacy II
Another stipulation of the peace settlement with the Federal League granted Fed moguls Phil Ball and Charles Weeghman the privilege of purchasing the St. Louis Browns and the Chicago Cubs respectively. Ball did little to improve the Browns plight, but Weeghman provided a sharp contrast to former Cubs owner Charles Murphy and indeed to most major-league magnates of his time. In 1916 Weeghman began the groundwork that would soon make Wrigley Field a national treasure. Among his many innovations was to build concession booths in back of the stands so that fans weren't continually being disturbed by hawkers peddling scorecards and refreshments.

## The Braves Have That History
Atlanta owner Ted Turner decided in 1977 that he could manage his team better than anyone else and handled the Braves for one game before Commissioner Bowie Kuhn, probably fearing that George Steinbrenner, Ray Kroc and Charlie Finley would soon get the same brainstorm, ordered Turner to cut out the nonsense. Back in 1929, however, Commissioner Landis sat quietly by while Braves owner Judge Fuchs ran the club. Manager Fuchs, the last mogul foolish enough to station himself in his team's dugout for a full season, finished a dreary last, thanks largely to the assistance he'd received from owner Fuchs, who sent Rogers Hornsby to the Cubs prior to the season for a packet of cash, a pocketful of minor leaguers and second baseman Freddie Maguire, whom Hornsby outhit in 1929 by a mere 128 points.

## The Greatest Innovator Prior to World War II
Many would vote for Branch Rickey, who brought Jackie Robinson to the majors and was the first major-league mogul to operate a minor-league "farm" system to develop young players, but equally high marks should go to Larry MacPhail. As owner of the Cincinnati Reds in 1935, MacPhail introduced night baseball to the majors and later brought it to Brooklyn and the Yankees when he took over those clubs. Furthermore, he orchestrated the first televised World Series

in 1947 and the first official old-timers' game, also in 1947, to commemorate Babe Ruth, ill with throat cancer, Ruth's Foundation for Boys receiving the entire proceeds. But perhaps his most significant act of all was to bring Red Barber with him when he moved from Cincinnati to Brooklyn. Try, if you can, to summon back a vision of Ebbets Field in the forties and fifties without hearing Barber's voice as a counterpoint to it.

## The Greatest Innovator Since World War II

Bill Veeck—and there's no one else even close. Over and above the countless zany and delightful spectacles he gave his fans, Veeck owned the last Cleveland team to win a World Championship, the last Chicago team to win a pennant and the last team, in 1953, to play under a name that will always be among the most tradition-laden in history—the St. Louis Browns.

## The Greatest Innovator Since Veeck

Charlie Finley has been with us too recently to get into perspective. We laughed when he adorned his Kansas City A's in green, white and gold uniforms in the fifties, and we groaned when he scheduled weekday World Series games exclusively at night, but history, I think we're going to find, will be very generous to him.

# Famous Brother Acts

After the Cincinnati Red Stockings broke up, Harry Wright and his brother George signed with the Boston Red Caps in the newly formed National Association. In 1876 they were joined on the Boston club, now in the National League, by a third brother, Sam, for a short time. Hence the Wrights were not only the first brothers to play in the major leagues, they were also the first trio of brothers. In 1877 a second set of brothers arrived on the scene in Boston when Deacon White was joined on the Red Caps by his younger brother Will. The following season both White brothers jumped to the Cincinnati club and formed the first sibling battery in the National League, with Deacon catching and Will pitching. They stayed together through the 1880 season; when the Cincinnati franchise folded, Deacon caught on with Buffalo while Will was cast adrift until the American Association was organized two years later.

### First Brother Battery in the American League
Homer and Tommy Thompson with the 1912 Yankees. You might have missed seeing them since Tommy pitched only 33 innings and Homer didn't even catch one entire game.

### Second Brother Battery in the American League
Milt and Alex Gaston with the 1929 Red Sox. Both played several seasons in the AL but were together only in 1929.

### First Brother Battery in the National League after 1900
Jack and Mike O'Neill with the 1902–03 Cardinals. Mike, the pitching half, also served as the Cardinals' main pinch hitter—on June 30, 1902, he hit the first pinch grand slam in history, off Togie Pittinger of the Braves. A few years later, two younger brothers, Steve and Jim, arrived in the majors.

Steve, who managed the 1945 Tigers to a World Championship, is the lone O'Neill remembered today, but all four brothers made a dent.

## Most Successful Brother Battery

AL—Rick and Wes Ferrell played together from 1934 through 1938 with the Red Sox and Senators. Rick is in the Hall of Fame, and Wes not only won nearly 200 games but was perhaps the best hitting pitcher ever. In 1948, seven years after leaving the majors, he led the Western Carolina League with a .425 average while serving as a player-manager for Marion.

NL—Mort and Walker Cooper helped power the Cardinals to three pennants in the early forties. Mort won 20 games three years in a row, and Walker was voted to several All-Star squads.

## Oldest Player to Act as His Brother's Batterymate

Johnny Riddle, nearly 43 years old, caught his brother Elmer for the 1948 Pirates.

## First Brothers to Oppose Each Other as Starting Pitchers

Jesse and Virgil Barnes on June 26, 1924; pitching for the Giants, Virgil helped beat Jesse and the Braves 8–1. Earlier in the decade the two had both been with the Giants and formed the first brother starter-reliever combo, Virgil acting the part of savior.

## Second Brothers to Oppose Each Other as Starting Pitchers

Joe Niekro, then with the Cubs, faced his brother Phil on July 4, 1967, the first of what would be many duels between them, Phil and the Braves winning 8–3.

## Only Pitcher to Start Against His Brother in His First Major-League Game

By special arrangement, Pat Underwood of the Tigers faced his brother Tom of the Blue Jays in his major-league debut on May 31, 1979.

## First Brothers Each to Win 20 Games in a Season

Harry and Stan Coveleski. Harry first collected 20 wins with the 1914 Tigers, Stan with the 1918 Indians. The Coveleskis played for rival teams in the AL for several years but made a pact not to pitch against each other and never did.

## Only Brothers to Win a Combined 40 Games in a Season as Teammates

Dizzy Dean won 30 games and brother Paul won 19 for the 1934 Cardinals.

## Only Brothers to Pitch a Combined Shutout

Rick and Paul Reuschel of the Cubs on August 21, 1975, 7–0 over the Dodgers.

## Brothers with the Best Combined Career Winning Percentage, Each Winning at Least One Game

The famous Hovlik brothers. Ed was 2–1 with the 1918–19 Senators, and Joe was 2–0 with the 1911 White Sox, giving them a family winning percentage of .800.

Among brothers with more than 250 career decisions combined, the Deans rank first with a .631 winning percentage. The three Clarksons, thanks chiefly to John, posted a combined winning percentage of .623 to top all brothers who figured in more than 500 career decisions.

## First Twins to Play in the Major Leagues

John and Phil Reccius with the 1882–83 Louisville club in the American Association. Recently discovered information casts doubt, though, on whether the Recciuses were really twins.

## Only Twins in the 20th Century to Play Beside Each Other

Johnny and Eddie O'Brien formed a keystone combination for the 1953 Pirates; later they both also pitched for the Pirates.

## First Brothers to Play Beside Each Other in the Outfield

Jim and John O'Rourke of the 1880 Boston Red Stockings.

## First Brothers to Play Beside Each Other in the Infield

Bill and Jack Gleason of the 1882 St. Louis Browns, Bill at shortstop and Jack at third base.

## First Brothers to Oppose Each Other in a World Series

Doc and Jimmy Johnston in 1920, Doc with Cleveland and Jimmy with Brooklyn. The second pair of brothers to face each other in the Series were the Meusels in 1921, Bob with the Yankees and Emil with the Giants. In 1908 the Clarke brothers, Fred and Josh, narrowly missed becoming the first brothers to play against each other in a Series when Fred's

Pirates lost the NL pennant on the last day of the season and Josh's Naps finished ½ game behind the victorious Tigers.

## First Black Siblings to Play in the Major Leagues
Fleet and Welday Walker, in 1884, with Toledo in the American Association.

## First Black Siblings to Play in the Major Leagues in the 20th Century
Sammy and Solly Drake, Solly with the 1956 Cubs and Sammy four years later, also with the Cubs.

## Only Brothers to Have 100 or More RBIs, Season, in the Same League
Bob and Roy Johnson, Bob with the Philadelphia A's and Roy with the Red Sox. Two other sets of brothers—the Meusels and Joe and Vince DiMaggio—also had 100 RBI seasons but in different leagues.

## Most Home Runs, Season, by Brothers Who Were Teammates
54—Tony Conigliaro (36) and Billy Conigliaro (18), 1970 Red Sox.

## Brothers With the Highest Combined Career Batting Average
The Sherlocks. Monk hit .324 for the 1930 Phillies, and Vince hit .462 for the 1935 Dodgers; their combined career average is .335.

## Brothers With the Highest Combined Season Batting Average
The Waners. Playing side by side in the outfield for the 1927 Pirates, they hit a combined .367, Paul leading the NL with a .380 average and Lloyd hitting .355—between them they also had a brother-record 460 hits.

## Only Brothers Who Celebrated Their Major-League Debuts More Than 25 Years Apart
Jesse and Art Fowler. Born in 1898, Jesse broke in with the 1924 Cardinals. Art, 24 years younger, first appeared with the 1954 Reds.

## First Brothers to Share the Same Position for the Same Team
Patsy and George Tebeau. When Patsy, the Cleveland Spiders' manager–first baseman, was injured in 1895, brother George, pre-

viously a spare outfielder, replaced him at the initial sack. A third Tebeau, Pussy, also played two games for the 1895 Spiders.

## Player With the Most Brothers Who Preceded Him in the Major Leagues

Joe Delahanty. By the time he broke in with the 1907 Cardinals, four of his brothers—Ed, Tom, Jim and Frank—had paved the way for him. Hall of Famer Ed, who drowned in 1903 after falling from a railroad trestle over Niagara Falls, was the best of the Delahantys.

## Last Trio of Brothers to Play in Same League, Same Season

NL—Technically, the Cruzes—Jose, Hector and Cirilio—but Cirilio played only a few innings. Felipe, Matty and Jesus Alou were the last trio of brothers in the NL who were all quality players.

AL—The Alous in 1973. Jesus was with Oakland and Felipe and Matty played with the Yankees.

## TOP 10 BROTHERS, CAREER HITS*

| | | |
|---|---|---|
| 1. | Paul and Lloyd Waner | 5611 |
| 2. | Felipe, Matty and Jesus Alou | 5094 |
| 3. | Joe, Dom and Vince DiMaggio | 4853 |
| 4. | Ed, Jim, Frank, Joe and Tom Delahanty | 4217 |
| 5. | Hank and Tommy Aaron | 3987 |
| 6. | Cal and Billy Ripken | 3857 |
| 7. | Joe and Luke Sewell | 3619 |
| 8. | Ken, Clete and Cloyd Boyer | 3559 |
| 9. | Honus and Butts Wagner | 3474 |
| 10. | Bob and Roy Johnson | 3343 |

## BROTHERS WITH 1,750 OR MORE CAREER RBIS

| | | |
|---|---|---|
| 1. | Joe, Dom and Vince DiMaggio | 2739 |
| 2. | Hank and Tommy Aaron | 2391 |
| 3. | Ed, Jim, Frank, Joe and Tom Delahanty | 2153 |
| 4. | Eddie and Rich Murray | 1924 |

*Including only brothers who contributed to the family's total figure. For example, Cloyd Boyer had 20 hits but no home runs; Tommy Sewell was hitless in one at bat; and the Mathewsons and Whites were omitted from the pitchers' list because in each case one brother failed to win a game.

5. Cal and Billy Ripken                          1920
   6. Paul and Lloyd Waner                          1907
   7. Bob and Emil Meusel                           1886
   8. Bob and Roy Johnson                           1839
   9. Ken, Clete and Cloyd Boyer                    1803
  10. Lee and Carlos May                            1780

## BROTHERS WITH 350 CAREER HOME RUNS

   1. Hank and Tommie Aaron                          768
   2. Joe, Vince and Dom DiMaggio                    573
   3. Eddie and Rich Murray                          505
   4. Jose and Ozzie Canseco                         462
   5. Cal and Billy Ripken                           451
   6. Lee and Carlos May                             444
      Ken, Clete and Cloyd Boyer                     444
   8. Graig and Jim Nettles                          406
   9. Dick, Hank and Ron Allen                       358

## BROTHERS WITH 1,800 OR MORE CAREER RUNS

   1. Joe, Dom and Vince DiMaggio                   2927
   2. Paul and Lloyd Waner                          2828
   3. Ed, Jim, Frank, Joe and Tom Delahanty         2309
   4. Hank and Tommie Aaron                         2276
   5. Felipe, Matty and Jesus Alou                  2213
   6. Bob and Roy Johnson                           1956
   7. Cal and Billy Ripken                          1934

## BROTHERS WITH 200 OR MORE CAREER WINS

   1. Phil and Joe Niekro                            539
   2. Gaylord and Jim Perry                          529
   3. John, Dad and Walter Clarkson                  383
   4. Greg and Mike Maddux                           346
   5. Ramon and Pedro Martinez                       301
   6. Stan and Harry Coveleski                       297
   7. Bob and Ken Forsch                             282
   8. Gus and John Weyhing                           260
   9. Jesse and Virgil Barnes                        214
  10. Al and Mark Leiter                             210
  11. Dizzy and Paul Dean                            200

# Invisible Men: Umpires

Don Denkinger achieved a unique distinction in 1985—he became the first umpire ever to be the most memorable performer in a World Series. Years from now, long after it has grown misty whose pinch single finally won Game Six, his controversial safe call on Jorge Orta's seeming ground-out will still seem vivid. But whether Denkinger himself will become a major figure in the umpires' pantheon remains to be determined. If he does, he'll have a lot of company.

## The First Famous Umpire

In the early days umpires were required to be consummate gentlemen, and the man appointed to umpire a game was generally deemed to be both the most honorable and the most knowledgeable club member. But when baseball became a business and players were no longer necessarily of the gentleman class, a new breed of umpire appeared. The first such man was probably Bill McLean, an ex-prizefighter. Officiating in the National Association in the early 1870s, McLean earned the nickname "King of Umpires" because of the vigorous manner in which he took charge of games. McLean later umpired in the National League through the 1884 season. Living in Providence, he customarily walked from his home to work an afternoon game in Boston, rising at 4:00 A.M.

## First to Make Umpiring a Full-Time Profession

Nobody knows for sure, but a good guess would be "Honest" John Gaffney, who joined the National League in 1884 and introduced the style of working behind the catcher with no runners on base. By 1888 Gaffney was paid $2500 plus expenses for a season's work, more than most players received. Only a few years earlier umpires had earned just $5 a game, paid by the visiting team while the home team absorbed all other expenses.

## First League to Put Its Umpires on a Regular Salary

In 1883 the American Association paid its umpires $140 a month and $3 per diem for travel expenses. Accordingly, the AA had a better overall caliber of umpiring than the National League in the early eighties. The AA's most highly esteemed umpire was probably Ben Young, who pioneered in forming a code of ethics for umpires before he was killed in a railway accident en route to an assigned game. Before his death, Young was also instrumental in getting the AA to provide training for its umpires, issue them blue coats and caps, and experiment with a double umpire system. The NL regarded two umpires as a needless extravagance and preferred to put each game in charge of just one man like Gaffney or Bob Ferguson, a former NL player and manager, whose philosophy after becoming an umpire was "Never change a decision, never stop to talk to a player—make 'em play ball and keep their mouths shut and never fear but the people will be on your side and you'll be called the king of umpires." As late as 1908, in fact, both the National and the American League had a staff of only six umpires, one of whom served as an alternate, meaning that three umpires each day worked a game entirely alone.

## Most Difficult Call for an Umpire Prior to 1884

Whether or not a pitch was legally delivered. Until 1884 pitchers were restricted to below-the-waist deliveries, much like fast-pitch softball pitchers. Umpires in the early days often consulted with players and sometimes even with fans before rendering a decision on a play or a pitch.

## Only Umpire Banned for Rigging Games

Dick Higham, a former National League player and a good one. Higham was suspected of throwing games while playing, which makes you wonder what the NL expected when he was hired in 1882 to umpire. His downfall came midway in the season while he was umpiring a string of games that involved Detroit and kept making questionable calls against the Wolverines. Detroit officials were finally led to inspect his mail, much of which was in code and not a particularly sophisticated one. From it, they were easily able to deduce that Higham was in collusion with gamblers who were making a nifty sum, thanks to his help, by betting against Detroit.

## First Former Player to Have a Lengthy Career as an Umpire

Bob Emslie joined the National League umpiring staff in 1891 after pitching for three seasons with Baltimore in the American Association and remained an umpire until 1924. Emslie was working the bases in the famous "Merkle Game" between the Giants and the Cubs in 1908, and it was actually his responsibility to decide whether Giants rookie Fred Merkle touched second base after Al Bridwell singled home the apparent winning run. But when Emslie claimed not to have seen the play, the onus fell on home plate umpire Hank O'Day, himself a former National League pitcher. O'Day ruled that Merkle was out, and pandemonium reigned at the Polo Grounds, making it impossible for O'Day and Emslie to clear the field and resume the game. Instead it had to be replayed at the end of the season when the Giants and Cubs wound up in a dead heat. The Cubs won the makeup game and the pennant and then went on to win their second and— to date—last World Championship in the Series that fall against the Tigers. Hence Emslie and O'Day are well remembered by both Giants and Cubs fans for their role in the Merkle game, and the game itself was pivotal for major league baseball as a whole in that it, along with several other controversial games in that same period, eventually forced officials to realize that more umpires were needed.

## First World Series Game to Have More Than Two Umpires

The fourth game of the 1909 Series between the Pirates and the Tigers found Bill Klem behind the plate, Billy Evans working the bases and Silk O'Loughlin and Jimmy Johnstone on the foul lines after a bitter dispute in Game Three over whether a batted ball had been fair or foul.

## Umpire with Most Seasons of Service

NL—Bill Klem. In 1909 Klem was in the fifth season of what would be a record 37-year career. He also officiated in a record 18 World Series, the last in 1940.

AL—Tommy Connolly served 31 years, from 1901 through 1931, and umpired in eight World Series. He, Klem, Hank O'Day, Cy Rigler, Billy Evans, Bill McGowan and Bill Summers are the only umpires to work more than seven Series.

**Active Umpire with Most Seasons of Service**

Bruce Froemming with 33 seasons.

**Umpire Who Started the Custom of Raising His Right Arm to Signal a Strike**

Cy Rigler. He reputedly initiated it so that Dummy Hoy, a deaf-mute, could keep track of the count while on base or playing in the outfield. The problem with this story is that Rigler first raised his arm to call a strike around 1905, by which time Hoy had already been out of the game for several years.

**First Hall of Fame Player Later to Umpire**

Tim Keefe. But many outstanding players became umpires after their playing careers ended. Among them were the aforementioned O'Day and Emslie, plus George Moriarty, Babe Pinelli, Lon Warneke, George Pipgras, Al Orth, Sherry Magee, Charlie Berry, Bob Caruthers, Firpo Marberry, Ed Rommel, Mal Eason, Butch Henline, Bill Dinneen, Lip Pike, Chief Zimmer and Ed Swartwood.

**Men Who Both Played and Umpired in a World Series**

Dinneen, Warneke, Moriarty, Rommel, Pipgras and Frank Secory, a substitute with the 1945 Cubs. Former umpires Ken Burkhart and Bill Kunkel were also members of World Series teams, but neither got into a game.

**The "Right Man for the Job" Award**

The home plate umpire for the famous double no-hit game on May 2, 1917, between Fred Toney of the Reds and Hippo Vaughn of the Cubs was former pitcher Al Orth. In 1908 Orth and Vaughn had been teammates on the Yankees for a brief while.

**The "Lou Gehrig in Blue" Award**

Bill McGowan, who worked in the American League from 1925 through 1954, umpired a record 2541 consecutive games over a 16½ year period. Born in 1896, McGowan began his umpiring career in the Tri-State League in 1913 at age 17.

**The "Going Out with a Bang" Award**

Babe Pinelli served as a home plate umpire for the final time in his long career on October 8, 1956. His last official action that day was to signal a called third strike on Dodgers pinch hitter Dale Mitchell and thus ring down the curtain on Don Larsen's perfect World Series game.

### The "Umpires' Best Friend" Award

Tom Lynch, former National League umpire, became the NL president after Harry Pulliam committed suicide in 1909. Lynch was the first official to back umpires to the hilt in their war to reduce player rowdyism. He was so successful that he became despised by owners and players alike and was soon fired.

### First Umpire to Wear Glasses on the Field

Ed Rommel on April 18, 1956, at Washington in a game between the Senators and Yankees. Larry Goetz was the first National League umpire to do it.

### The "Longest Day" Award

On October 2, 1920, the Pirates and Reds played the last major-league tripleheader. Peter Harrison worked behind the plate in all three games—until darkness began to descend over Forbes Field in the sixth inning of the finale, with the Pirates ahead 6–0, and he was at last able to call a halt to the marathon without argument.

# First Basemen's Records

Prior to 1900 most of the dominant hitters in the major leagues were first basemen. Then as now size and batting prowess were the key qualities sought by managers when testing players at the position. Four first sackers of the game's first phase—Dan Brouthers, Roger Connor, Cap Anson and Dave Orr—hold most of the pre-1900 career batting records. Others, like Harry Stovey, Long John Reilly, Tommy Tucker, and Jake Beckley, also ranked consistently among the leading hitters and sluggers. Connor, Anson, Beckley, and Brouthers are in the Hall of Fame, and several more of their contemporary gateway guardians probably should be. Achieved during a time when the season schedule called for far fewer games than are played today, the bulk of their season and career marks have long since been eclipsed. So too have the fielding standards that were set by men, like Joe Start and Charlie Comiskey, who used rudimentary gloves and in some cases none at all. In fact, only one first baseman's season record that was established before 1900 is still on the book—for most triples.

## SEASON BATTING RECORDS

| Department | National League | American League |
|---|---|---|
| Batting Average | .401, Bill Terry, New York, 1930 | .420, GEORGE SISLER, St. Louis, 1922 |
| Slugging Average | .752, Mark McGwire, St. Louis, 1998 | .765, LOU GEHRIG, New York, 1927 |
| Home Runs | 70, MARK MCGWIRE, St. Louis, 1998 | 58, Hank Greenberg, Detroit, 1938 |
| RBIs | 150, Andres Galarraga, Colorado, 1996 | 184, LOU GEHRIG, New York, 1931 |

| Department | National League | American League |
|---|---|---|
| Runs | 152, Jeff Bagwell, Houston, 2000 | 167, LOU GEHRIG, New York, 1936 |
| Hits | 254, Bill Terry, New York, 1930 | 257, GEORGE SISLER, St. Louis, 1920 |
| Doubles | 59, Todd Helton, Colorado, 2000 | 64, GEORGE BURNS, Cleveland, 1926 |
| Triples | 29, PERRY WERDEN, St. Louis, 1893 <br> 22, Jake Daubert, Cincinnati, 1922* | 20, Lou Gehrig, New York, 1926 |
| Total Bases | 405, Todd Helton, Colorado, 2000 | 447, LOU GEHRIG, New York, 1927 |
| Stolen Bases | 67, FRANK CHANCE, Chicago, 1903 | 52, Frank Isbell, Chicago, 1901 |
| Bases on Balls | 162, MARK MCGWIRE, St. Louis, 1998 | 137, Roy Cullenbine, Detroit, 1947 |
| Strikeouts | 182, Jim Thome, Philadelphia, 2003 | 185, JIM THOME, Cleveland, 2000 |
| Fewest Strikeouts Minimum 500 ABs) | 6, Stuffy McInnis, Boston, 1924 | 5, STUFFY MCINNIS, Cleveland, 1922 |

*Record since 1901. Records are otherwise since 1893 for NL players and 1901 for AL players with the all-time holder's name in caps.

Note: Some sources still credit Werden with 33 triples in 1893, but most reference works have now uniformly credited him with 29. In 1932 Jimmie Foxx hit 58 homers for the Philadelphia A's but played 13 games at third base; similarly, Stan Musial of the Cardinals had 50 doubles in 1946 but played 42 games in the outfield. Hence both Foxx and Musial are not recognized as record holders here because a significant portion of their accomplishments occurred while they were playing other positions.

## Most Games, Career, at First Base
2413—Eddie Murray, 1977–97

## Most Consecutive Games at First Base
885—Lou Gehrig, New York Yankees, June 6, 1925, through September 27, 1930

# EVOLUTION OF SEASON RECORD FOR BEST FIELDING AVERAGE

|  | Team | League | Year | Average |
|---|---|---|---|---|
| Joe Start | New York | National | 1876 | .964[1] |
| Joe Start | Hartford | National | 1877 | .964 |
| Chub Sullivan | Cincinnati | National | 1878 | .975 |
| Cap Anson | Chicago | National | 1879 | .975 |
| Cap Anson | Chicago | National | 1880 | .978 |
| Joe Start | Providence | National | 1884 | .980 |
| Dave Orr | New York | Amer. Assoc. | 1886 | .981 |
| Roger Connor | New York | National | 1887 | .993 |
| Patsy Tebeau | Cleveland | National | 1897 | .994 |
| Dan McGann | New York | National | 1906 | .995 |
| Ed Konetchy | St. Louis | National | 1913 | .995[2] |
| Ed Konetchy | Pittsburgh | National | 1914 | .995 |
| Stuffy McInnis | Philadelphia | American | 1914 | .995 |
| Fritz Mollwitz | Cincinnati | National | 1915 | .996 |
| Chick Gandil | Chicago | American | 1919 | .997[3] |
| Stuffy McInnis | Boston | American | 1921 | .999[4] |
| Frank McCormick | Philadelphia | National | 1946 | .999 |
| Wes Parker | Lost Angeles | National | 1968 | .999 |
| Jim Spencer | Calif.–Texas | American | 1973 | .999 |
| Steve Garvey | Los Angeles | National | 1981 | .999 |
| Eddie Murray | Baltimore | American | 1981 | .999 |
| Steve Garvey | San Diego | National | 1984 | 1.000 |

[1] Several sources credit him with being the first first sacker to play off the bag with the bases empty.

[2] Among the better first basemen in his time, but hidden away on bad teams until late in his career.

[3] He and Hal Chase were two of the *enfants terribles* in the teens. Chase got all the raves for his glove, but Gandil got the stats—he led the AL in fielding four consecutive years, 1916–19, whereas Chase, ironically, was never a fielding leader.

[4] For a player who was never considered among the greats, even in his time, McInnis holds an awful lot of records. His .999 average was better than any of the .999 FAs that followed in that he handled more chances.

## Best Career Fielding Average, Minimum 1,000 Games
.996—Don Mattingly, 1982–95

## Most Seasons League Leader in Fielding Average
NL—9—Charlie Grimm, last in 1933
AL—6—Joe Judge, last in 1930

## Most Consecutive Errorless Games
193—Steve Garvey, San Diego Padres, June 26, 1983, through April 14, 1985

## Most Consecutive Errorless Chances
1700—Stuffy McInnis, Boston Red Sox and Cleveland Indians, May 31, 1921, through June 2, 1922

## Most Chances Accepted, Career
25,505—Jake Beckley, 1888–1907

## Most Chances Accepted, Season
1986—Jiggs Donahue, Chicago White Sox, 1907

## Most Chances Accepted, Game, Nine Innings
NL—22—Ernie Banks, Chicago, May 9, 1963 (22 putouts)
AL—22—Done several times; last by Alvin Davis,
    Seattle, May 28, 1988 (22 putouts)

## Most Assists, Season
184—Bill Buckner, Boston Red Sox, 1985: breaking his old record of 161, set in 1983 with the Cubs, which in turn had broken his 1982 mark of 159. The current NL mark is 180, set in 1990 by Sid Bream of Pittsburgh.

## Most Seasons League Leader in Assists
NL—8—Fred Tenney, last in 1907
AL—6—George Sisler, last in 1927
   Vic Power, last in 1962

## Most Double Plays, Season
194—Ferris Fain, Philadelphia A's, 1949. That year the A's turned 217 double plays, an all-time team record, and then topped 200 again in 1950 and 1951.

## Best Glove Man Ever at First Base
Hal Chase had the rep, Vic Power was compared to him, and Keith Hernandez has the most Gold Gloves—11—but don't overlook Paul Campbell. In 1941, playing with Montreal

in the International League, Campbell set an all-time record for first baseman by starting 26 double plays; the major-league record is 18. Furthermore, Campbell tied a major-league single-game mark on May 14, 1949, when he performed two unassisted double plays for the Tigers.

# Under the Lights

If you thought night baseball was a comparatively recent innovation, you might be surprised to learn that the first night game was played on September 2, 1880, between Jordan Marsh & Company and R. H. White & Company, two Boston department stores. The two company nines battled to a 16–16 tie at Nantasket Bay near Hull, Massachusetts, as part of a series of lighting displays put on by the Northern Electric Company of Boston to prove the far-reaching value of the incandescent lamp, invented by Thomas Edison only the year before.

There were other night games during the latter part of the 19th century, but few had the foresight to envision that night baseball would ever be anything more than a novelty. One who did was sportswriter O. P. Caylor. In 1893 Caylor wrote:

> Should the time ever come when by some system of illumination base ball could be played as well at night as in the daytime the possibilities of the game's earnings could hardly be estimated. . . . But the chances are that the time will never come when base ball at night will be possible. . . . However, it is a subject which will be worth consideration. If any one ever does discover a system of out-of-door lighting sufficiently good for base ball playing in the open air at night he will at once take ranks with the millionaires of the land.

Caylor's remarks are quite prescient in all, but his last statement makes me wince each time I read it. George Cahill, the man who first discovered a way of economically staging night games, never made anything close to a million from his invention and indeed is largely forgotten today.

By 1910 Cahill had devised a portable lighting system good

enough to get the grudging permission of Charlie Comiskey to stage a game under artificial glare at the new White Sox park. Some 20,000 fans watched two local amateur teams play a full nine innings under the gleam of twenty 137,000-candlepower arc lights and from all accounts thoroughly enjoyed the proceedings. But Comiskey and other major-league owners saw no future in night baseball, and it would be another 25 years before Cahill realized his dream.

The first major-league night game did not take place until 1935. On May 24, at Crosley Field, Paul Derringer of the Reds beat the Phillies 2–1 after President Franklin Roosevelt turned on the lights by pushing a button in the White House. The first to bat under artificial light in a major-league game was Phillies outfielder Lou Chiozza. Among the 20,422 in attendance, though no great ceremony was made of it, was the man who had the largest hand in making it all possible, George Cahill.

Although the first major-league team to install lights, the Reds were far from being the first team in organized baseball to do so. On April 28, 1930, Independence, Kansas, of the Class C Western Association staged the first official pro night game, losing 13–3 to Muskogee, and by 1935 many other minor-league clubs had already begun playing under the lights.

### Second Major-League Team to Install Lights

The Dodgers, and they could not have had a better sense of timing. Their guests on June 15, 1938, for the inaugural night game at Ebbets Field, were the Reds. Four days earlier the Reds scheduled starting pitcher, left-hander Johnny Vander Meer, had pitched a no-hitter against the Braves, and in case you don't know what he did to the Dodgers in front of the first crowd in the New York area to witness a major-league game under the lights, see "No-hitters and Perfect Games."

### First American League Team to Install Lights

The Indians, but the Athletics were the first team actually to play at home under the lights. A complete list follows of the opening night games for the 16 franchises that were around when it all started.

| Stadium | Date | Result |
|---------|------|--------|
| At Crosley Field | May 24, 1935 | Reds 2, Phillies 1 |
| At Ebbets Field | June 15, 1938 | Reds 6, Dodgers 0 |
| At Shibe Park | May 16, 1939 | Indians 8, A's 3, 10 innings |
| At Shibe Park (Phillies) | June 1, 1939 | Pirates 5, Phillies 2 |
| At Cleveland Stadium | June 27, 1939 | Indians 5, Tigers 0 |
| At Comiskey Park | August 14, 1939 | White Sox 5, Browns 2 |
| At Polo Grounds | May 24, 1940 | Giants 8, Braves 1 |
| At Sportsman's Park | May 24, 1940 | Indians 3, Browns 2 |
| At Sportsman's Park (Cards) | June 4, 1940 | Dodgers 10, Cardinals 1 |
| At Forbes Field | June 4, 1940 | Pirates 14, Braves 2 |
| At Griffith Stadium | May 28, 1941 | Yankees 6, Senators 5 |
| At Braves Field | May 11, 1946 | Giants 5, Braves 1 |
| At Yankee Stadium | May 28, 1946 | Senators 2, Yankees 1 |
| At Fenway Park | June 13, 1947 | Red Sox 5, White Sox 3 |
| At Briggs Stadium | June 15, 1948 | Tigers 4, A's 1 |
| At Wrigley Field | August 9, 1988 | Cubs 6, Mets 4 |

## First Night All-Star Game

July 13, 1943, at Shibe Park, won by the American League 5–3. However, the last part of the 1942 game, at the Polo Grounds, was played under the lights when darkness began to set in after a lengthy rain delay.

## First Night World Series Game

October 13, 1971, at Three Rivers Stadium, when the Pirates beat the Orioles 4–3 to even the Series at two games apiece.

# World Series Play: 1876–1900

## FRANCHISE SUMMARY

| Team | League | WS Record | Years in Series |
|------|--------|-----------|-----------------|
| New York Giants | National | 2–0–0 | 1888, 1889 |
| Providence Grays | National | 1–0–0 | 1884 |
| Detroit Wolverines | National | 1–0–0 | 1887 |
| Louisville Eclipse | Association | 0–0–1 | 1890 |
| Cincinnati Red Stockings | Association | 0–0–1 | 1882 |
| St. Louis Browns | Association | 1–2–1 | 1885, 1886, 1887 1888 |
| Chicago White Stockings | National | 0–1–2 | 1882, 1885, 1886 |
| Brooklyn Bridegrooms | Both | 0–1–1 | 1889, 1890 |
| New York Metropolitans | Association | 0–1–0 | 1884 |

**Yearly Highlights**

1882—Cincinnati (AA) and Chicago (NL) tied 1 game to 1

At the conclusion of the American Association's first season as a major league, the pennant winners in the AA and the National League played a "World Series" to settle which circuit was superior. But the Series ended abortively after two games when AA president Denny McKnight wired the Red Stockings that they would be expelled if they continued play. Cincinnati was prepared to defy McKnight, but Chicago manager Cap Anson withdrew his White Stockings from the Series in what he believed was the best interest of both teams.

1884—Providence (NL) defeated New York (AA) 3 games to 0

Responding to a challenge from New York manager Jim Mutrie, Providence manager Frank Bancroft brought his Grays to the Mets' home park, the original Polo Grounds, for a three-game World Series. The first contest was played on October 23, 1884, before a crowd of 2500 in blustery conditions and under Association rules, which called for hit batsmen to be given first base. As a result, both Providence leadoff batter Paul Hines and second batter Cliff Carroll reached base after being hit by the Mets' Tim Keefe. Hines scored the first run on a wild pitch and a passed ball, and the Grays won 6–0 behind their 60-game winner Hoss Radbourn. The following day Radbourn won 3–1 on a three-run homer by Jerry Denny and then closed out the Series with 12–2 win in even rawer conditions, which caused the third game to be terminated after six innings. The Grays played all three games without using a single substitute.

1885—St. Louis (AA) and Chicago (NL) tied 3 games to 3

The Browns and White Stockings played seven games and wound up deadlocked at three-all, with one contest a tie, in what was now called "The World Championship Series," so named by Alfred Spink, the creator of the *Sporting News*. Players did not take the games seriously because the owners, in their greed, were more concerned with attracting spectators than making for good baseball, and the crowds at times overran the field. Neither team's players received a penny for participating in this Series, which was sloppily played and ineptly umpired.

1886—St. Louis (AA) defeated Chicago (NL) 4 games to 1

The first best-four-of-seven Series played to a conclusion. After splitting the first two games in Chicago, the teams moved to St. Louis, where the Browns won three straight, the finale in the 10th inning when Curt Welch scored from third base on a wild pitch that sailed over the head of Chicago catcher King Kelly. Welch was the first Series hero to be immortalized for a feat that was largely fiction. His "$15,000 Slide," which was made to seem the tail end of a brazen dash for the plate, wasn't even necessary—he could have jogged home and scored standing up.

## 1887—Detroit (NL) defeated St. Louis (AA) 8 games to 3

Frederick Stearns, eager to take full advantage of his slugging Wolverines, challenged Browns owner Chris Von Der Ahe to a 15-game Series, with the two teams traveling in a special train of parlor cars and playing in all major cities as well as St. Louis and Detroit. Von Der Ahe further agreed to hiking admission prices to one dollar and to Stearns's suggestion that two umpires be used, "Honest John" Kelly and "Honest John" Gaffney. In search of a way to plug her acting career, Helen Dauvray, wife of New York Giants shortstop Monte Ward, hit upon the notion of awarding a cup in her name to the winning team. Detroit won the first Dauvray Cup, which has disappeared over the years, by taking 8 of the first 11 games, but the teams played the last four anyway.

## 1888—New York (NL) defeated St. Louis (AA) 6 games to 2

Jim Mutrie, having switched his loyalty to the NL in 1885, became the first man to manage Series teams in two leagues. His war cry to herald his Giants was "We are the people!" Nobody quite knew what it meant, least of all Mutrie, but it sounded good and a song went with it. A 10-game Series was arranged and played out even though the Giants won six of the first eight games. Von Der Ahe, supported by his players and in particular Arlie Latham, a notorious rabble-rouser, blamed the umpires for his club's defeat, even accusing umpires Kelly and Gaffney of betting on the Giants. This Series also had the first goat, Browns shortstop Bill White, who had replaced the popular Bill Gleason after Gleason was traded to Philadelphia. White was unfairly chastised—his fielding cost St. Louis one game at most—and never again played in the majors. The Dauvray Cup came to Helen's husband and his Giants, to be kept by them pending the results of the following year's Series.

**1889—New York (NL) defeated Brooklyn (AA) 6 games to 3**

The Giants played the Bridegrooms in what would have been the first subway Series if there had been subways in 1889—at the time New York and Brooklyn were still separate cities. The Giants won in nine games, making the 10th game unnecessary, and now had two legs up on the three Series wins required to take permanent possession of the Dauvray Cup.

**1890—Louisville (AA) tied Brooklyn (NL) 3 games to 3**

It was the last Dauvray Cup World Series, as the war between the two leagues in 1891 made postseason play between their pennant winners out of the question. The Bridegrooms, after switching to the NL intact with no key players lost to Players League raids, beat Louisville three of the first four games. But Louisville won the next two, in Brooklyn no less, evening the Series. The weather was so dreadful for the deciding seventh game that only 300 fans showed up and the contest was called off, the Series ending, as it had begun eight years earlier, in a tie.

**Postscript**

In 1892 the National League, now inflated to 12 teams after absorbing 4 clubs from the defunct Association, played a split schedule for the first and only time in major-league history, the Cleveland Spiders winning the first half season and the Boston Beaneaters the second. After the first game of the post-season series ended in a tie, Boston swept five in a row and terminated proceedings. No championship was played in 1893, but William Temple, president of the Pittsburgh Pirates, which unexpectedly finished second to Boston that year, felt cheated of a crack at the Beaneaters and proposed a plan whereby the second-place team at the end of each season would challenge the first-place team to a best four-of-seven series and win by default if the first place team refused the challenge. He then ordered a cup in his name for $800 from New York jeweler A. E. Thrall and stipulated that, like the Dauvray Cup, permanent possession of the Temple Cup would go to the first team to win it three times. To Temple's chagrin, the Baltimore Orioles won easily in 1894, and the Giants finished second while his Pirates plummeted to seventh place. To the chagrin of all club owners in the league, the

Orioles merely went through the motions in their series with the Giants and dropped four straight games. When the same lack of player enthusiasm persisted the next three years, the Temple Cup series was scrapped, owners citing low motivation and secret agreements between teams to split the take fifty-fifty regardless of the result. The irony was that the Orioles, after dismal performances in the 1894 and 1895 series, had revved up their act and taken the next two series in a row, putting them on the brink of seizing permanent ownership of the Temple Cup, which now resides, instead, in the Hall of Fame.

# SECTION 2

# Famous Firsts:
# 1901–19

**1901**—The American League opens its first season as a major league on April 24 but runs into bad luck—three of the four scheduled lid-lifters are rained out. Hence the honor of playing the first AL game falls exclusively to Chicago and Cleveland, which meet at the Chicago Cricket Club in front of 14,000 or so. Chicago, behind rookie right-hander Roy Patterson, wins 8–2. Bill Hoffer, himself a record-shattering rookie 31-game winner in the National League only six years earlier, goes all the way for Cleveland in defeat but is released a few weeks later with a 3–8 record. Cleveland outfielder Ollie Pickering earns the distinction of being the first player to bat in an AL game while his teammate, second baseman Erv Beck, goes 2-for-2 and gets the game's only extra-base hit, a double. The following day Beck hits the first AL home run.

**1902**—Tom Rice of the *Brooklyn Eagle* begins campaigning for scoreboards and other fan conveniences like having teams announce lineup changes; his efforts lead, among other things, to announcers with megaphones strolling about the grounds and calling out starting lineups and substitutions.

**1903**—The first moving picture of a baseball game is made, featuring Nap Lajoie and Harry Bay of Cleveland during a post-season series with Cincinnati. In 1910 the National Commission receives $500 for World Series movie rights; the figure climbs to the gigantic sum of $3500 in 1911. Four years later Harry Aitken of the Mutual Film Corporation talks John McGraw of the Giants into becoming the first manager to film his players during spring training for instructional purposes.

**1905**—Roger Bresnahan experiments with a batting helmet—called a "pneumatic head protector"—after being beaned. In 1907 Bresnahan catches the opening game of the season for the Giants wearing shin guards. The game winds up being forfeited to the Phillies when the Polo Grounds crowd gets unruly, but Bresnahan nonetheless makes the Hall of Fame, in part for his experimentation with headgear and shin guards. Nig Clarke, a rookie catcher for Cleveland who regularly wore soccer guards under his socks in 1905, becomes a footnote in the shin guard story.

**1907**—Albert Spalding creates a commission to unearth the origins of baseball and names A. G. Mills to head it. Mills, a former National League president, after some months of digging attributes the game's invention to his old friend Gen. Abner Doubleday, who purportedly concocted it one afternoon in 1839 in Cooperstown, New York, while still a West Point cadet. Mills's report is nine-tenths fiction and one-tenth the vague testimony of Abner Graves, a boyhood friend of Doubleday's who claimed to have seen the first game. On the basis of Mills's findings, the Hall of Fame and National Baseball Museum are placed in Cooperstown, and a centennial celebration of the game's birth is planned for 1939. Long before 1939 all the historical material accumulated by Mills is reportedly destroyed in a fire, making verification of it impossible. But the hoopla attending the centennial celebration is so vast that it reaches all the way to Hawaii, where Bruce Cartwright, grandson of a man named Alexander Cartwright, writes a letter in 1938 and encloses supporting evidence that touches off an investigation that seems to prove beyond all doubt that the Mills Commission's findings were phony and Alexander Cartwright was the true inventor of baseball. Hall of Fame committee members, upon deliberation, buy grandson Bruce's evidence, and Doubleday, the man responsible for the shrine's placement in Cooperstown, is himself never enshrined.

**1908**—George Baird of Chicago invents an electric scoreboard that instantly records balls, strikes, runs, etc.

**1908**—In July the Giants stun the baseball world by paying $11,000 for Rube Marquard, an unproven minor-league pitcher.

**1908**—On August 4 the Cardinals and Dodgers play a full game at Brooklyn's Washington Park using only one ball. There is nothing to attest that this was the last time it was done, only that it was still something that happened as late as 1908.

**1909**—On July 18 Cleveland shortstop Neal Ball, in a game against the Red Sox, performs the first for-sure unassisted triple play. The previous year, while playing for the Yankees, Ball led the majors with 80 errors and fielded .898.

**1910**—President Taft throws out the first ball at the Senators' opener on April 14, then watches Walter Johnson pitch a one-hit 3–0 shutout over the Athletics. Taft likes the experience so much that he decides to make it an annual event.

**1911**—It becomes mandatory for home teams to wear white uniforms and visiting teams dark uniforms. The Giants and the Phillies are the first to start doing this as a way for both fans and players to distinguish one team from the other.

**1911**—A cork-and-rubber-center ball replaces the dead-as-duck-feathers rubber-core ball; Ty Cobb hits .420, Wildfire Schulte of the Cubs cracks 21 homers, and batting averages as a whole in the American League skyrocket 30 points.

**1912**—Ty Cobb is suspended by AL president Ban Johnson for going into the Hilltop Park stands on May 15 and fighting with Yankees fan Claude Lueker. The Tigers react to Cobb's suspension by going on strike before their game on May 18 against the Athletics, forcing Detroit manager Hugh Jennings to use Philadelphia seminary student Aloysius Travers, later a priest, on the mound, local amateurs at other positions, and 48-year-old coach Deacon McGuire behind the bat. Travers pitches a complete-game 26-hitter, losing 24–2, while McGuire singles and scores a run, and 30-year-old third baseman Ed Irvin, playing his only major-league game, raps two triples in three at bats, giving him a record 2.000 career slugging average. Late in the game, Jennings inserts himself as a pinch hitter and avoids getting hit by a pitch, thereupon failing in his last big-league at bat to increase his all-time career record for being hit 287 times by pitches.

**1914**—The Federal League opens its first of two seasons as a major circuit after luring many major-league players into its camp. The first to jump ship is St. Louis Browns first baseman George Stovall. Joe Tinker is the first star to join the Feds. Walter Johnson signs a Fed contract, then recants when Washington owner Clark Griffith gives him a raise, plus a healthy bonus, which is subsidized by other American League owners to keep him out of the Feds' clutches.

**1915**—The Tigers, the last team to wear collars on their uniforms, finally abandon them. The Yankees, meanwhile, wear pinstriped uniforms for the first time.

**1915**—The National League makes it a rule that all clubs must have canvases to cover their fields in the event of rain so that play can resume when it stops without resorting to the ancient method of burning wood and spreading oil and sawdust.

**1915**—The American League starts the policy of giving each player two passes, good for any park in the league.

**1915**—Cardinals officials, convinced that St. Louis can't support two major-league teams and the Browns are the stronger franchise, attempt to move the team to Baltimore when Federal League owners of the Baltimore club express an interest in buying the Cardinals and transferring them, but other National League owners block the move. Thirty-nine years later the Browns move to Baltimore.

**1916**—Cubs owner Charles Weegham comes up with the revolutionary idea of allowing fans to keep balls hit into the stands, seemingly bringing to an end the warfare between park policemen and fans trying to obtain souvenir balls. But as late as 1923 a Philadelphia boy is arrested and housed overnight in the slammer for keeping a ball hit into the Baker Bowl bleachers, and in 1937 a Yankees fan is vigorously pummeled by ushers when he attempts to retrieve a ball lodged in the home plate screen. His suit against the Yankees, in which he wins $7,500, results in a sort of truce between club officials and fans on the issue.

**1917**—The Cardinals establish the first "Knothole Gang" for kids. The brainchild of St. Louis insurance man W. E. Bilheimer to combat juvenile delinquency, it is so successful that in 1920 the Cardinals admit an estimated 64,000 boys to their games for free.

**1917**—On June 27 Braves catcher Hank Gowdy becomes the first major leaguer to enter the military service in World War I. In October of the following year, former Phillies third baseman Eddie Grant becomes the first major-league player ever to be killed in combat.

**1919**—The Cardinals pay $10,000 to Kansas City for pitcher Jesse Haines. Haines is the last minor leaguer to be purchased by the Cardinals until World War II, as their farm system, for the next quarter of a century, supplies them with all the talent they need.

# A Short History
# of Team Names

Unlike the Kansas City Royals and several other expansion teams whose names were chosen logically and systematically by their fans, most of the 16 teams that constituted the major leagues from 1901 through 1960 had a number of names before settling on the one now in vogue. To eliminate confusion, all references to teams for the remainder of the book will use their current names.

## American League

Anaheim Angels (1961)—Originally the Los Angeles Angels, they became the California Angels when the franchise moved to its new stadium in Anaheim and in 1997 began calling themselves the Anaheim Angels.

Baltimore Orioles (1901)—During the 1901 season the franchise was located in Milwaukee. Moving to St. Louis in 1902, the team became known as the Browns because of the brown trim on its uniforms, a carryover from the old St. Louis Browns in the American Association. When the franchise shifted to Baltimore in 1954, team officials and fans were eager to rid the club of all association with the losing Browns and revive the old Orioles tradition. All Baltimore major league teams since 1885, with the exception of the Federal League Terrapins, had been called the Orioles, as had the International League franchise, the city's lone link to organized baseball from 1916 through 1953.

Boston Red Sox (1901)—Called the Pilgrims or the Puritans in the early years of the American League, and also for a time the Somersets—after owner Charles Somers—they became the Red Sox when new owner John Taylor decided the club needed a zippier name. For a time the club was labeled the Red Stockings, the name of the original Boston National

League team, but sportswriters soon shortened it to Red Sox, and in later years, to BoSox.

Chicago White Sox (1901)—Called the Invaders at first when the American League "invaded" Chicago before the opening of the 1900 season, the club then assumed the name White Stockings, which had been discarded by its National League counterpart in the late 1880s, but the sobriquet was immediately abbreviated to fit into sports page headlines. Within a few years it began being shortened, still more, to ChiSox. Also called the Pale Hose, as opposed to the Red Sox, who are known as the Crimson Hose.

Cleveland Indians (1901)—Known as the Broncos in 1901, then the Blues because of their uniforms, and then the Naps when Nap Lajoie became the team's player-manager, the Indians didn't settle finally on a name until 1915. From 1912 through 1914 they were called the Molly McGuires since many of their players were Irish, but when they finished last in 1914, it seemed time for a completely fresh start. Some believe the name Indians was chosen to commemorate Louis Sockalexis, the ill-fated Penobscot Indian who played with the Cleveland Spiders in the 1890s. Also called the Tribe.

Detroit Tigers (1901)—The team began as the Wolverines, after the Detroit National League entry which had adopted the name of the state animal, but sportswriter Phil Reid of the *Detroit Free Press* noticed that the blue-and-orange-striped stockings worn by the 1901 club resembled Princeton's colors and started calling them the Tigers. Also known as the Bengals.

Kansas City Royals (1969)—The name was chosen by the team's fans.

Minnesota Twins (1901)—Named for the twin cities of Minneapolis and St. Paul. From 1901 through 1960, the team was known as both the Senators and the Nationals, sometimes abbreviated to Nats, because its home was the nation's capital.

New York Yankees (1901)—Began in 1901 as the Baltimore Orioles. Shifted to New York in 1903, the team was called the Highlanders because its home ground, Hilltop Park, was so high and also because its first president was Joseph Gordon, whose name suggested the Gordon Highlanders, at the time a crack regiment in the British army. Around 1914 Jim Price of the *New York Press* coined the current name. Also called the Bronx Bombers.

Oakland Athletics (1901)—Began in 1901 as the Philadelphia Athletics; moved to Kansas City in 1955 and then to Oakland in 1968. The name has a long and rich history that both Kansas City and Oakland officials fortunately chose to preserve. In 1871 the Philadelphia Athletics won the first National Association pennant. Also called the A's.

Seattle Mariners (1977)—The name was adopted to honor the nautical tradition of the Pacific Northwest. The first major-league team in Seattle survived only one season—1969—before moving to Milwaukee, and was called the Pilots. There was some sentiment to name the team the Rainiers, after the Seattle club in the Pacific Coast League, but Mariners was a more popular choice.

Tampa Bay Devil Rays (1998)—Name chosen by fans.

Texas Rangers (1961)—Upon leaving Washington after the 1971 season, the franchise assumed the name of the state's traditional lawmen and took the example of the Minnesota team by coupling it with Texas so as not to slight either Dallas or Forth Worth.

Toronto Blue Jays (1977)—Name chosen in a fan contest.

## National League

Arizona Diamondbacks (1998)—Name chosen by fans.

Atlanta Braves (1876)—The team moved from Boston to Milwaukee in 1953—the first franchise since 1903—then abandoned Milwaukee for Atlanta after the 1965 season. While in the National Association the team was dubbed the Red Caps. The red hosiery they sported led to their being called the Red Stockings after they joined the National League, but by the 1890s they were more commonly known as the Beaneaters. The name Braves came into existence in 1912 because owner Jim Gaffney was a Tammany Hall chieftain. Prior to that they had also been known as the Doves, while the team president was George Dovey, and the Pilgrims after the Red Sox dropped that name. A horrible season in 1935 spurred team officials and fans to call the club the Bees from 1936 to 1940, but the name never really caught on.

Chicago Cubs (1876)—Originally the White Stockings, the team became known as the Colts after player-manager Cap Anson appeared on stage in a play called *Runaway Colt* in the late 1880s. When Anson left the club after being denied the share of the franchise he'd been promised, people began calling them the Orphans. For several years they were also known as the Cowboys and the Broncos, but in 1901 Chicago sportswriters George Rice and Fred Hayner began referring to them as the Cubs because their roster was stocked with so many young players after American League raids had depleted it. Also known as the Bruins.

Cincinnati Reds (1890)—Short for Red Stockings, the name of the great Cincinnati team in the late 1860s. Briefly called the Red Legs in the 1940s when *reds* was an evil word in America.

Colorado Rockies (1993)—Team based in Denver, where several teams have carried the nickname.

Florida Marlins (1993)—Named after the Miami Marlins, former Triple A team.

Houston Astros (1962)—First called the Colt 45s. Became the Astros when the Astrodome was opened in 1965.

Los Angeles Dodgers (1890)—Based in Brooklyn until 1958, the club shrewdly kept the Dodgers name after moving to the West Coast, thereby retaining the loyalty of its East Coast fans and also appealing to the many transplanted New Yorkers in the L.A. area. In 1889, while the franchise was still in the American Association, the team acquired the name Bridegrooms after three players got married in the off-season. When Ned Hanlon became manager in 1899, the team was called the Superbas because there was a popular vaudeville troupe at the time known as "Hanlon's Superbas." The club was also called the Atlantics—after the old Brooklyn National Association team—and later the Robins when Wilbert Robinson became manager, but by World War I the Dodgers name had taken hold. It had its roots in "Trolley Dodgers," the pejorative sobriquet given turn-of-the-century Brooklynites by New Yorkers.

Milwaukee Brewers (1970)—The name of the first National League team representing Milwaukee in 1878; also the name of the first American League team in 1901 and the minor-league American Association team.

Montreal Expos (1969)—Named after Expo '67, the World's Fair exposition.

New York Mets (1962)—Short for Metropolitans, a revival of the name borne by the New York American Association franchise in the 1880s.

Philadelphia Phillies (1883)—The original name of the Philadelphia team in the National League, it was spelled Fillies at first, as in female horses. Also briefly called the Quakers and later the Bluejays when the Carpenters bought the team during World War II and tried to create a new image, but neither name stuck.

Pittsburgh Pirates (1887)—The team was called the Alleghenies while it was in the American Association and then, facetiously, the Innocents after the franchise traitorously deserted the AA and switched to the National League. Became the Pirates in 1891 when the club "pirated" Lou Bierbauer, star second baseman the Philadelphia American Association team neglected to protect after he jumped to the Players League. Also called the Bucs or the Corsairs.

St. Louis Cardinals (1892)—Originally the St. Louis Browns American Association franchise, accepted into the National League when the AA folded after the 1891 season. Also known in the late 1890s as the Maroons and the Perfectos. In 1899 the Robison brothers, who owned both the Cleveland and the St. Louis franchises, not only stocked St. Louis with all of Cleveland's best players but also brought along the Spiders' uniforms. St. Louis sportswriter Willie McHale, observing the red trim, coined the name Cardinals.

San Diego Padres (1969)—Assumed the nickname of the old Pacific Coast League team whose place they took in town.

San Francisco Giants (1883)—Like the Dodgers, the Giants retained their name when they moved from New York to the West Coast in 1958. But though the Dodgers also successfully kept their identity, the Giants failed. It is doubtful that very many San Francisco fans know much about the franchise's history, let alone that the team name was originated in 1885 by manager Jim Mutrie, who called his charges "My boys, my Giants!" Before Mutrie came along the club was known as the Green Stockings or the Gothams.

# Where the Games
# Are Played

During the period between 1909 and 1915 more than half the teams then in the major leagues either built new stadiums or made massive renovations in the parks they were using. There were several reasons for the feverish construction, not the least of which were the ever-present threat of fire in the old wood parks and the many lawsuits the Phillies faced when a section of the rickety Baker Bowl grandstand collapsed in 1903, killing several spectators.

The first ballpark on record was built in 1862 when William Cammeyer, the owner of the Union Club's grounds in Brooklyn, conceived the notion of enclosing his field and charging admission to games. Cammeyer's park did not survive long, nor did the majority of other parks that were built in the last century—the lifespan for most was only a few years—but Sulphur Dell, built in 1866, was the home of the Southern Association Nashville Volunteers until 1963 and set an all-time park longevity record of 97 years. Prior to 1991 the oldest major-league park was Comiskey, home of the White Sox, which opened in 1910. To keep you abreast of who is playing where at the moment, and how long they have been there, here is a list—which includes mention of some historic parks formerly used by the 30 current major league teams.

## AMERICAN LEAGUE
### Edison Field, Anaheim Angels

First game—April 19, 1966; Chicago 3, California 1.
Seating capacity—64,593. Natural surface.

Clean, efficient, yet spacious and without a single major flaw. The Angels first played in tiny Wrigley Field, which they inherited from the Los Angeles franchise in the Pacific Coast League, and then, for several years, shared Chavez Ravine with the Dodgers while waiting for their own new park to be completed.

**Oriole Park at Camden Yards, Baltimore Orioles**
First game—April 6, 1992; Baltimore 2, Cleveland 0.
Seating capacity—48,262. Natural surface.

The Yard is a new stadium deliberately built to look like an old one. In 1992, their first year of occupancy, the Orioles drew 3,567,819 fans. The Yard marked the third new AL park to open since 1989. Two years later Cleveland and Texas made it five new parks in just six seasons.

**Fenway Park, Boston Red Sox**
First game—April 20, 1912; Boston 7, New York 6, 11 innings.
Seating capacity—33,871. Natural surface.

Considered the ultimate in parks when it was built, but within a year the Red Sox already had a sneaking suspicion it was too small and that its left-field wall would always be both a boon and a burden.

**U.S. Cellular Field, Chicago White Sox**
First game—April 18, 1991; Detroit 16, Chicago 0.
Seating capacity—44,321. Natural surface.

With the closing of Comiskey Park I at the finish of the 1990 season, Tiger Stadium and Fenway Park became the oldest facilities in the majors. Ironically, the White Sox also lost their lid-lifter in Comiskey I, 2–0 to the St. Louis Browns on July 1, 1910.

**Jacobs Field, Cleveland Indians**
First game—April 4, 1994; Cleveland 4, Seattle 3, 11 innings.
Seating capacity—42,865. Natural surface.

Has its share of flaws, but one of them is not a lack of charisma. Jacobs Field is the first park in decades to be named after a team's owner, which may not be a wise investment in view of the Indians' tumultuous ownership history in recent years. Cleveland Stadium, the Indians' former park, was used by the NFL Cleveland Browns until they moved.

**Comerica Park, Detroit Tigers**
First game—April 11, 2000; Detroit 5, Seattle, 2.
Seating capacity—40,000. Natural surface.

A raw 40-degree day held attendance at Comerica's debut to less than capacity (39,168) and forced more than half the crowd to flee after just an inning or two. Conditions were so bitter that Seattle shortstop Alex Rodriguez wore a ski mask on the field to keep warm. Comerica replaced Tiger Stadium, which in turn replace Bennett Park in 1912. The Tigers' original home was named for Charlie Bennett, a catcher who lost both legs in a railway accident. Bennett Park seated only 8500 and was the smallest facility in the majors when it closed.

### Kauffman Stadium, Kansas City Royals
First game—April 10, 1973; Kansas City 12, Texas 1.
Seating capacity—40,625. Natural surface.

Features a 322-foot-wide water spectacular with a fountain and a 10-foot waterfall from the upper cascade plus two lower pools that empty into five more 10-foot falls. The Royals played in Municipal Stadium, with a seating capacity of 30,611, until their new park was finished.

### The Metrodome, Minnesota Twins
First game—April 6, 1982; Seattle 11, Minnesota 7.
Seating capacity—44,457. Artificial surface and sky.

The Twins' home from 1961 until 1982 was Metropolitan Stadium.

### Yankee Stadium
First game—April 18, 1923; New York 4, Boston 1.
Seating capacity—57,545. Natural surface.

Closed for two years in the middle seventies, the Yankees sharing Shea Stadium with the Mets during the hiatus. Before it was built the Yankees shared Polo Grounds with the Giants from 1912 through 1922 after forsaking Hilltop Park, their original home field. Yankee Stadium took 284 days to build—the renovation took more than twice that long and reduced the capacity by some 13,000 seats.

### Network Associates Coliseum, Oakland Athletics
First game—April 17, 1968; Baltimore 4, Oakland 1.
Seating capacity—43,662. Natural surface.

The park was there waiting for the A's when they moved from Kansas City, where they used Municipal Stadium. While the franchise was based in Philadelphia, the A's played in Columbia Park, located at Twenty-ninth and Columbia Avenue, until 1909 when Shibe Park was completed. Shibe was the first all concrete-and-steel stadium in the majors.

### Safeco Field, Seattle Mariners
First game—July 15, 1999; San Diego 3, Seattle 2.
Seating capacity—47,000. Natural surface.

Nicknamed "The Safe," Seattle's new park cost a record $517.6 million and replaced the dreary Kingdome, the Mariners' home for their first 22½ seasons. Complete with a retractable roof, Safeco was the first major-league park in history to host an interleague game on its inaugural day.

**Tropicana Field, Tampa Bay Devil Rays**
First game—March 31, 1998; Detroit 11, Tampa Bay 6.
Seating capacity—45,200. Artificial surface and sky.

**The Ballpark at Arlington, Texas Rangers**
First game—April 11, 1994; Milwaukee 4, Texas 3.
Seating capacity—49,178. Natural surface.

The Rangers' old park was Arlington Stadium, a former minor-league stadium upgraded to major-league capacity.

**SkyDome, Toronto Blue Jays**
First game—June 5, 1989; Milwaukee 5, Toronto 3.
Seating capacity—50,516. Artificial surface.

A triumph of modern architecture and technology, the Blue Jays' space-age facility helped them to set a new American League attendance record in its first year of operation.

## NATIONAL LEAGUE

**Bank One Ballpark, Arizona Diamondbacks**
First game—March 31, 1998; Colorado 9, Arizona 2.
Seating capacity—48,569. Natural surface.

**Turner Field, Atlanta Braves**
First game—April 4, 1997; Atlanta 5, Chicago 4.
Seating capacity—49,200. Natural surface.

Previously the Braves used Fulton County Stadium after moving from Milwaukee to Atlanta. Before transferring to Milwaukee from Boston, the team played in Braves Field, which opened in 1915, replacing South End Grounds, the oldest park in the majors, home to Boston in the National Association as far back as 1873.

**Wrigley Field, Chicago Cubs**
First game—April 23, 1914; Chicago Whales 9, Kansas City Packers 1.
First NL game—April 20, 1916; Chicago 7, Cincinnati 6, 11 innings.
Seating capacity—38,765. Natural surface, natural everything.

Called North Side Park originally, it was taken over by the Cubs from the Whales when the Federal League folded. The Cubs had previously played in West Side Park at Polk and Lincoln.

**Great American Ball Park, Cincinnati Reds**
First game—March 31, 2003; Pittsburgh 10, Cincinnati 1.
Seating capacity—42,036. Natural surface.

Until 1970 the Reds played in Crosley Field which held fewer than 30,000, making it the smallest park in the majors.

Called Redland Field when it opened in 1912, it also had the distinction of having the first "artificial" surface—in 1937, when the Reds dyed the sun-burned outfield grass green.

**Coors Field, Colorado Rockies**

First game—April 26, 1995; Colorado 11, New York 9, 14 innings.

Seating capacity—50,200. Natural surface.

The Rockies' thrilling win in their opener at Coors was the longest debut game for a new ballpark in the 20th century, both in length and time (4:47).

**Pro Player Stadium, Florida Marlins**

First game—April 5, 1993; Florida 6, Los Angeles 3.

Seating capacity—41,855. Natural surface.

The summer heat in Florida makes night baseball a must at Pro Player. In 1993, their inaugural season, the Marlins played just 35 day games, the fewest in the majors.

**Minute Maid Park, Houston Astros**

First game—April 7, 2000; Philadelphia 4, Houston 1.

Seating capacity—41,583. Natural surface.

The short porch in left field led to Minute Maid being labeled a "bandbox" park the day it opened its doors. In contrast, Minute Maid's predecessor, the Astrodome, was a notorious pitchers' park. Prior to 1965, when the $31,600,000 Astrodome debuted, the Astros played in Colts Stadium, built in 1962 for the new Houston National League entry.

**Dodger Stadium, Los Angeles Dodgers**

First game—April 10, 1962; Cincinnati 6, Los Angeles 3.

Seating capacity—56,000. Natural surface.

Their first four seasons in L.A., the Dodgers played in Memorial Coliseum where they set an all-time attendance record on May 7, 1959, when they drew 93,103 for an exhibition game honoring Roy Campanella. They also set an Opening Day attendance record of 78,672 in their first game in the Coliseum on April 18, 1958, against the Giants. In Dodger Stadium, also known as Chavez Ravine, they set a single-season attendance record in 1982. Before transferring to L.A. from Brooklyn, the team played at Ebbets Field, which held only 32,111; nevertheless the Dodgers attracted 1,807,526 fans in 1947, at the time an NL record.

**Miller Park, Milwaukee Brewers**

First game—April 6, 2001; Milwaukee 6, Cincinnati 4

Seating capacity—42,400; Natural surface

The Brewers' new park has a retractable dome. Unfortunately, in 2001, the Brewers performed so poorly that it sometimes seemed home fans came out to watch the closing of the dome after games rather than their team. Milwaukee formerly played in County Stadium, opened in 1953 to house the city's first major-league franchise since 1901.

### Olympic Stadium, Montreal Expos

First game—April 15, 1977; Philadelphia 7, Montreal 2.
Seating capacity—46,500. Artificial surface.

The Expos originally played in Jarry Park, home of the minor-league Montreal Royals. The last games in Jarry Park were on September 26, 1976, when the Phillies won a division-clinching doubleheader from the Expos, their first title of any sort in 26 years.

### Shea Stadium, New York Mets

First game—April 17, 1964; Pittsburgh 4, New York 3.
Seating capacity—55,777. Natural surface.

Windy, too close to the airport, a tough place to spend an evening in the fall or early spring—unless you're a pitcher. While waiting for Shea to be built, the Mets played their first two seasons in the Polo Grounds.

### Veterans Stadium, Philadelphia Phillies

First game—April 10, 1971; Philadelphia 4, Montreal 1.
Seating capacity—62,238. Artificial surface.

Features a monstrous TV screen and probably the fastest turf in the majors. The Phillies played in Shibe Park from July 4, 1938, through 1970. Prior to switching to Shibe and sharing it with the A's, the club had called Baker Bowl home for over half a century. Refurbished a number of times, especially after the 1903 disaster, the Baker Bowl seated just 18,000 and hosted its first game on April 30, 1887, the Phils beating the Giants 15–9.

### PNC Park, Pittsburgh Pirates

First game—April 9, 2001; Cincinnati 8, Pittsburgh 2
Seating capacity—38,127; Natural surface

The Reds also bested the home team in the Pirates's opening game at their former domicile, Three Rivers Stadium. In 1970, Three Rivers replaced Forbes Field, at the time the oldest major-league park in existence. The first fully modern park in the majors when it opened in 1909, Forbes had triple-decker stands, elevators, electric lights, telephones, inclined ramps instead of stairs and maids in the ladies' restrooms. Moreover, it shared with Shibe Park the distinction of having the first visitors' dressing room, ending the custom of visiting teams dressing at their hotels and then riding to the park in open horse-drawn buses.

**Busch Stadium, St. Louis Cardinals**
First game—May 16, 1966; St. Louis 4, Atlanta 3, 12 innings.
Seating capacity—57,078. Natural surface.

Before 1966 the Cardinals played in Sportsman's Park, a relic that dated back to 1876 when it was used by the first St. Louis team in the National League. The park was later taken over by Chris Von Der Ahe's American Association Browns and then renovated by the St. Louis Browns American League team and used by them until they moved to Baltimore. Until 1920 the Cardinals played in Robison Field, built by the St. Louis Maroons for their 1884 season in the Union Association. The final game played at Robison Field, the last wood park in the majors, was on July 6, 1920.

**Qual Comm Park, San Diego Padres**
First game—April 8, 1969; San Diego 2, Houston 1.
Seating capacity—56,133. Natural surface.

Underrated, in some ways the best all-around facility in the majors. The last major-league park to be built without a carpet prior to the new White Sox stadium.

**Pac Bell Park, San Francisco Giants**
First game—April 11, 2000; Los Angeles 6, San Francisco 5.
Seating capacity—40,800. Natural surface.

In Pac Bell's lid-lifter, Dodger shortstop Kevin Elster, after sitting out the entire 1999 season, slammed three home runs and the Giants also "went yard" three times. The breathtaking panoramic view of the San Francisco Bay area from the upper deck along with the park's funky contours immediately charmed fans and the media alike. The Giants' sensational season in 2000 also helped to disguise the fact that Pac Bell, even more so than Comerica and Enron, has major problems. The seats are cramped and getting to and from them, particularly in the upper deck, is an adventure that most spectators could do without. Pac Bell's predecessor was Candlestick (aka 3Com) Park. While waiting for Candlestick's completion in 1960, the Giants played in Seals Stadium, one of the finest ballparks ever constructed. Before moving to the Bay Area in 1958, the Giants called the Polo Grounds home. Polo Grounds was famed for 250-foot home runs and 450-foot outs. Candlestick (3Com) was famed for being the only major-league park where a pitcher—Stu Miller in the 1961 All Star Game—committed a balk when a sudden blast of wind blew him off the mound.

# Managers' Records

Connie Mack took over the Pittsburgh manager's job late in the 1894 season, lasted through 1896 and then was replaced by Patsy Donovan. He had to wait until 1901 to get a second opportunity to manage in the majors. John McGraw had a similar experience, guiding the Baltimore Orioles to an unexpectedly high fourth-place finish in 1899 and then having to endure a one-year hiatus in St. Louis as a player only before Baltimore was granted an American League franchise and he was given the reins in 1901. By the time Mack and McGraw were done managing, they held almost every dugout longevity record.

**Most Years as Manager, League**

AL—50—Connie Mack, Philadelphia, 1901 through 1950

NL—32—John McGraw, Baltimore, 1899; New York Giants, 1902 through 1932.

**Most Games Won as Manager, League**

AL—3582—Connie Mack, Philadelphia. Mack also holds the AL record for most losses, 3814.

NL—2690—John McGraw, Baltimore and New York Giants. McGraw also suffered the most losses in the NL, 1863.

**Most Pennants Won as Manager, League**

AL—10—Casey Stengel, New York, last in 1960

NL—10—John McGraw, New York, last in 1924

**Most World Series Won as Manager, League**

AL—7—Joe McCarthy, New York, last in 1943; Casey Stengel, New York, last in 1958

NL—4—Walter Alston, Brooklyn-Los Angeles, last in 1965

## Most Consecutive Pennants Won as Manager, League
AL—5—Casey Stengel, New York, 1949–53
NL—4—John McGraw, New York, 1921–24
AA—4—Charlie Comiskey, St. Louis, 1885–88

## Most Clubs Managed
7—Frank Bancroft, Worcester, NL; Detroit, NL; Cleveland, NL; Providence, NL; Philadelphia, AA; Indianapolis NL; Cincinnati, NL. Bancroft managed less than nine full seasons and had just one pennant winner, the 1884 Providence Grays, but he spread his work over a 22-year period and was the only man to manage in the NL before the American Association came into existence and after the American League replaced the Association as the NL's rival. One of the game's first great promoters and missionaries, Bancroft took a team to Cuba in 1879, the first such expedition in history, and later staged a wedding at home plate. He spent the last 30 years of his life as the Cincinnati Reds business manager and traveling secretary.

## Most Clubs Managed, since 1901
6—Jimmy Dykes, Chicago, AL; Philadelphia, AL; Baltimore, AL; Cincinnati, NL; Detroit, AL; Cleveland, AL.
John McNamara, Oakland, AL; San Diego, NL; Cincinnati, NL; California, AL; Boston, AL; Cleveland, AL.
Dick Williams, Boston, AL; Oakland, AL; California, AL; Montreal, NL; San Diego, NL; Seattle, AL.

## Most Clubs Managed to Pennants
3—Bill McKechnie, Pittsburgh, NL; St. Louis, NL; Cincinnati, NL
Dick Williams, Boston, AL; Oakland, AL; San Diego, NL

## Most Clubs Managed to Division Titles
4—Billy Martin, Minnesota, AL; Detroit, AL; New York, AL; Oakland, AL

## Only Manager to Lead Same Club to Consecutive Pennants in Two Different Leagues
Bill McGunnigle steered Brooklyn to the American Association flag in 1889, then repeated in 1890 after the Bridegrooms transferred to the National League.

**First Manager to Pilot Two Clubs to Pennants, Same League, since 1901**
  NL—Pat Moran, Philadelphia, 1915; Cincinnati, 1919
  AL—Joe Cronin, Washington, 1933; Boston, 1946

**First Manager to Pilot Pennant Winners in Two Leagues, since 1901**
  Joe McCarthy, Chicago, NL, 1929; New York, AL, 1932

**Most Years Managed Without Winning a Pennant**
  26—Gene Mauch, Philadelphia, NL, 1960 into 1968; Montreal, NL, 1969 through 1975; Minnesota, AL, 1976 into 1980; California, AL, 1981 through 1982, 1985 through 1987

**Only Man to Win a Pennant in His Lone Season as a Manager**
  George Wright, Providence, NL, 1879

**First Man to Win a World Championship in His First Full Season as Manager**
  AL—Tris Speaker, Cleveland, 1920
  NL—Rogers Hornsby, St. Louis, 1926

**First Manager to Pilot Club in World Series without Managing It for Full Season**
  NL—Charlie Grimm, Chicago, 1932
  AL—Bob Lemon, New York, 1978. Lemon piloted the Yankees in two Series—1978 and 1981—without ever managing the club a full season.

**Only Managers to Win Four Pennants since 1901 and Not Make the Hall of Fame**
  Billy Southworth, St. Louis, NL, 1942, 1943, 1944; Boston, NL, 1948; Dick Williams, Boston, AL, 1967; Oakland, AL, 1972, 1973; San Diego, NL, 1984

**Only Player-Manager to Win Back-to-Back World Championships and Not Make the Hall of Fame**
  Bill Carrigan, Boston, AL, 1915 and 1916. Carrigan retired after the 1916 triumph but in the late twenties was coaxed into returning to manage a string of awful Red Sox teams.

## Last Manager to Win Four Consecutive Pennants

Joe Torre, New York Yankees, AL, 1998–2001. The last NL manager to win as many as three flags in a row was Billy Southworth with the 1942–44 Cardinals.

## Highest Career Winning Percentage as Manager

.615—Joe McCarthy, 24 seasons, 2125 wins and 1333 losses

## Lowest Career Winning Percentage as Manager, Minimum 1000 Games

.401—Jimmie Wilson, nine seasons, 493 wins and 735 losses. Wilson's best team was the 1943 Cubs, who finished fifth.

## Lowest Career Winning Percentage as Manager, Minimum 500 Games

.313—John McCloskey, five seasons, 190 wins and 417 losses. McCloskey, who helped found the Texas League, skippered the 1908 Cardinals, probably the National League's most dismal team in the deadball era.

## First Great Manager Who Was Never a Major-League Player

Frank Selee. After managing the Boston Beaneaters to five pennants in the 1890s, Selee moved to the lackluster Chicago Cubs in 1902. Within a year he had the Cubs in contention and was just putting the finishing touches on a club that would win three consecutive pennants (1906–8) when failing health forced him to step down in 1905 and turn the reins over to Frank Chance, his personal choice as his replacement.

## First Manager to Win 1000 Games

Cap Anson of the Chicago White Stockings and Harry Wright, then in his last season as the Philadelphia Phils skipper, both went over the 1000 mark in 1893.

## Youngest Manager to Win 1000 Games

Fred Clarke, who became player-manager of the Louisville Colonels in 1897 when he was only 24 years old, collected his 1000th win at age 35 in 1908 while at the helm of the Pittsburgh Pirates. Only 42 when he stepped down at the end of the 1915 season, Clarke departed with 1602 wins, the most by any manager in history to that point.

## Oldest Rookie Manager

Tom Sheehan was 66 years old when he took over the San Francisco Giants in June 1960 and steered them to a 46–50 record for the remainder of the season before giving way to Al Dark.

## Youngest Rookie Manager, since 1901

Roger Peckinpaugh was only 23 years old when he served as the Yankees player-manager for the last 17 games of the 1914 season.

## Youngest Player-Manager to Lead Club for Full Season, since 1901

Lou Boudreau bid for and was given the Cleveland manager's post at age 24 in 1942. Six years later he became the last player-manager to steer his club to a pennant.

## Last Player-Manager to Win a National League Pennant

Technically, Leo Durocher, who played a few games for his Brooklyn Dodgers in 1941. The last to do it while still a full-time player was Gabby Hartnett with the 1938 Chicago Cubs.

## Last Year Both Teams in World Series Were Led by Player-Managers

1934—Frankie Frisch, St. Louis Cardinals, and Mickey Cochrane, Detroit Tigers. The Tigers repeated in 1935 under Cochrane and played the Cubs, led by Charlie Grimm, who'd played two games during the regular season but didn't appear at all in the Series.

## First year Both Teams in World Series Were Led by Player-Managers

1903—Jimmy Collins, Boston Red Sox, and Fred Clarke, Pittsburgh Pirates. Player-managers were so common then that the 1905 World Series, when McGraw's Giants played Mack's A's, was the only one until 1911 in which neither team was led by a manager who was also a full-time player.

## Only Pitchers to Win a Pennant as Player-Managers

NL—Al Spalding, Chicago, 1876
AL—Clark Griffith, Chicago, 1901

**Only American League Manager to Win Two Pennants between 1936 and 1968 for Teams Other Than the Yankees**

Al Lopez, Cleveland, 1954; Chicago, 1959

## Winners of the "Might Have Been Another Casey Stengel" Award

Burt Shotton. Fired by the Phillies in 1933 after managing a string of rotten teams, he lucked into the Dodgers' managerial post in 1947 when Leo Durocher was suspended for the season, won a pennant and then won again in 1949 as Durocher's replacement after Durocher was axed. In 1950 Shotton lost the NL pennant to the Phillies in the last game of the season when he failed to replace slow-footed Cal Abrams with a pinch runner and saw Abrams thrown out at the plate trying to bring home the run that would have tied the Dodgers with the Phillies and forced a pennant playoff. That lapse as much as anything else caused the Dodgers to can him. Over the next six seasons Brooklyn won four pennants under Chuck Dressen and Walter Alston with basically the same team that Shotton had in 1950. If Shotton had stayed with the club, we can only wonder now what might have happened—but it's a fairly strong possibility that fans in the 1950s would have had the treat of watching two eccentric senior citizens trying to outmaneuver one another each fall.

# The Three Most Interesting
# Teams Between 1901 and 1919

### 1908 PITTSBURGH PIRATES
### W-98 L-56
### Manager Fred Clarke

**Regular Lineup**—1B, None; 2B, Eddie Abbatichio; 3B, Tommy Leach; SS, Honus Wagner. RF, Owen Wilson; CF, Roy Thomas; LF, Fred Clarke; C, George Gibson; P, Vic Willis; P, Nick Maddox; P, Howie Camnitz; P, Lefty Leifield; P, Sam Leever.

Led by Wagner and player-manager Clarke, this team finished only one game shy of the pennant and in so doing immortalized Fred Merkle and the Cubs infield of Tinker, Evers and Chance. Merkle's "boner" probably would have been overlooked amid the welter of strange occurrences in 1908 if the Pirates had won their final game of the season, against the Cubs, clinching the pennant and making it unnecessary for the Cubs and Giants to replay the game in which Merkle neglected to touch second base. As it is, the Pirates' own boner that year has been largely overlooked. The club played all season without a decent first baseman after cutting Jim Nealon, who had an off year in 1907 after leading the National League in RBIs as a rookie in 1906. In preference to Nealon, the Pirates alternated Harry Swacina, Jim Kane and Al Storke, none of whom could do the job. The following year the Pirates picked up Bill Abstein, won the pennant and then released him after he had a poor World Series. Without Abstein, the club once again had a gaping hole at first base that would go unplugged until 1920, when Charlie Grimm emerged.

# 1913 WASHINGTON SENATORS
## W-90 L-64
## Manager: Clark Griffith

**Regular Lineup**—1B, Chick Gandil; 2B, Ray Morgan; 3B, Eddie Foster; SS, George McBride; RF, Danny Moeller; CF, Clyde Milan; LF, Howard Shanks; C, John Henry and Eddie Ainsmith; P, Walter Johnson; P, Joe Boehling; P, Bob Groom.

After finishing second to the Red Sox in 1912, the Senators seemed ready to provide Washington fans with their first major-league pennant, especially when rookie left-hander Boehling looked sharp in spring training. Boehling continued to shine when the season started—he finished with a 17–7 record, combining with Johnson to post 53 wins and only 14 losses. But the rest of the mound staff had a dismal 37–50 record, and the Senators again could do no better than second place. Griffith, in his search for supporting moundsmen, tried 23 pitchers all told in 1913, ranging from his own 43-year-old arm to that of 18-year-old Jack Bentley. It was a shame none of them worked out because Johnson had an incredible season. In 1913 he won 36 games, lost only 7 and had a 1.14 ERA and an .837 win percentage. All of his stats towered over those of the second-best pitcher in the league, Cleveland's Cy Falkenberg, who had a 23–10 record. The following year Boehling slumped to only 13 wins, and the Senators slipped to third place and did not seriously contend again until a decade later.

# 1916 PHILADELPHIA ATHLETICS
## W-36 L-117
## Manager: Connie Mack

**Regular Lineup**—1B, Stuffy McInnis; 2B, Nap Lajoie; 3B, Charlie Pick; SS, Whitey Witt; RF, Jimmy Walsh; CF, Amos Strunk; LF, Rube Oldring; C, Wally Schang; P, Elmer Myers; P, Joe Bush; P, Jack Nabors; P, Tom Sheehan.

The A's had the worst team in this century only two years after they won their fourth pennant in five seasons. Mack blamed Federal League defections and his having to sell stars like Home Run Baker, who wanted more money than he could pay, but his explanation didn't quite wash then, and history has made it look even lamer. After the Federal League folded, there were a number of good players floating loose whom Mack could have gotten cheaply, but they weren't his kind of people, and he played out the season instead with the few members of the 1914 crew who'd remained loyal to him, plus 41-year-old Lajoie and a pack of rejects from other clubs. Myers and Bush, two quality pitchers, had a combined 29–47 record, but the rest of the staff lost 70 games and won only 7. A truly embarrassing operation, from 1915 through 1921 the A's finished in the cellar a record seven straight years.

# ERA Records

The National League didn't officially begin keeping earned run averages until 1912, and the American League didn't follow suit until the following year. As a result, many of the ERA records that were set before 1912 have been unearthed only after today's standards were applied to what, in some cases, were previously uncalculated statistics.

**Lowest ERA, Season, 1901 through 1919**
 AL—0.96—Dutch Leonard, Boston, 1914; the all-time season record
 NL—1.04—Three Finger Brown, Chicago, 1906; the all-time National League record

**Lowest ERA, Season, 1920 through 1941**
 NL—1.66—Carl Hubbell, New York Giants, 1933
 AL—2.06—Lefty Grove, Philadelphia, 1931

**Lowest ERA, Season, 1942 through 1960**
 AL—1.64—Spud Chandler, New York, 1943
 NL—1.75—Howie Pollet, St. Louis, 1943

**Lowest ERA, Season, 1961 through 1976**
 NL—1.12—Bob Gibson, St. Louis, 1968
 AL—1.65—Dean Chance, Los Angeles, 1964

**Lowest ERA, Season, 1977 through 1993**
 NL—1.53—Dwight Gooden, New York, 1985
 AL—1.74—Ron Guidry, New York, 1978

**Lowest ERA, Season, since 1994**
 NL—1.56—Greg Maddux, Atlanta, 1994
 AL—1.74—Pedro Martinez, Boston, 2000

## Most Seasons League Leader in ERA

AL—9—Lefty Grove, last in 1939

NL—5—Pete Alexander, last in 1920; Sandy Koufax, 1962–66 consecutive

## Lowest ERA, Season, Team, since 1901

NL—1.73—Chicago, 1907

AL—1.78—Philadelphia, 1910

## Last Team with an ERA below 2.25, Season

NL—Chicago, 1919 (2.21); Cincinnati, 1919 (2.23)

AL—Washington, 1918 (2.14)

## Last Team with an ERA below 2.50, Season

NL—St. Louis, 1968 (2.49)

AL—Chicago, 1967 (2.45); the best ERA by any team since 1919

## Lowest Team ERA, Season, since 1968

AL—Baltimore, 1972 (2.54)

NL—Houston, 1981 (2.66)

## TOP 10 IN ERA, CAREER, SINCE 1893

### (Minimum 1500 innings)

| | | Years Active | ERA |
|---|---|---|---|
| 1. | Ed Walsh | 1904–17 | 1.82 |
| 2. | Addie Joss | 1902–10 | 1.89 |
| 3. | Three Finger Brown | 1903–16 | 2.06 |
| 4. | Christy Mathewson | 1900–16 | 2.13 |
| 5. | Rube Waddell | 1897–1910 | 2.16[1] |
| 6. | Walter Johnson | 1907–27 | 2.17[2] |
| 7. | Orval Overall | 1905–13 | 2.23 |
| 8. | Ed Reulbach | 1905–17 | 2.28 |
| 9. | Jim Scott | 1907–17 | 2.32 |
| 10. | Eddie Plank | 1901–17 | 2.35 |

[1] Lefty record holder.

[2] Only member of the career top 10 who pitched in the lively ball era.

## Lowest Career ERA, Pitcher Active Exclusively after 1910

2.43—Jeff Tesreau, 1912–18

**Lowest Career ERA, Pitcher Active Exclusively between 1920 and 1945**

2.98—Carl Hubbell, 1928–43. Hubbell is the only pitcher in that period who had an ERA under 3.00 in over 1500 innings.

**Lowest Career ERA, Pitcher Active Exclusively between 1940 and 1960 at Least Ten Full Seasons**

2.92—Harry Brecheen, 1940–53. Brecheen and Hubbell are the only two pitchers active between 1920 and 1960 who had career ERAs under 3.00.

## TOP 10 IN ERA, CAREER, SINCE 1920
### (Minimum 1500 innings)

| | | Years Active | ERA |
|---|---|---|---|
| 1. | Hoyt Wilhelm | 1952–72 | 2.52 |
| 2. | Pedro Martinez | 1992– | 2.58 |
| 3. | Whitey Ford | 1950–67 | 2.75 |
| 4. | Sandy Koufax | 1955–66 | 2.76 |
| 5. | Jim Palmer | 1965–84 | 2.86 |
| 6. | Andy Messersmith | 1968–79 | 2.86 |
| 7. | Tom Seaver | 1967–86 | 2.86 |
| 8. | Greg Maddux | 1986– | 2.89 |
| 9. | Juan Marichal | 1960–75 | 2.89 |
| 10. | Rollie Fingers | 1968–85 | 2.90 |

**Only Pitchers since 1901 with Career 0.00 ERA, Minimum Nine Innings**

Tim Jones, Pittsburgh, 1977, in 10 innings had a 1–0 record and 0.00 ERA.

John Dagenhard, Boston Braves, 1943, hurled a complete-game win in his only big league start and also threw two relief innings without giving up an earned run to compile a career 0.00 ERA in 11 innings.

# On the Black

Which pitcher had the best control? It all depends on what standard you use to measure control and whether you accept that different eras require different standards. Cy Young gave up 103 bases on balls in 423 innings in 1893 and walked just 37 batters in 342 innings 10 years later. Had Young's control really improved that much by 1903, or were other factors operating? On the evidence Young definitely got sharper as his career progressed—he may even have had the best control of any pitcher in history—but it's also true that he was playing in a time that was extremely forgiving of pitchers who disdained nibbling at the corners of the plate and elected simply to come in with the ball. A very dead ball it was, scuffed up, dirt-stained and often laden with other foreign substances as well—a ball that was usually kept in play for several innings and sometimes even for an entire game. In any event, virtually all the career and season records for control were set in the early part of the 20th century.

**Best Control, Career, since 1893, Minimum 2500 Innings**

Deacon Phillippe issued 363 walks in 2607 innings, an average of 1.25 walks per nine innings. Phillippe pitched in the National League, mostly with the Pirates, from 1899 to 1911. In 1910 he walked only nine batters in 122 innings, a National League record low among pitchers in over 100 innings. Phillipe won 189 games, plus three more in the 1903 World Series when he started five games, completed them all, and relieved in two others. Almost as remarkable as his iron-man Series effort was the fact that he gave up only four walks in 50 innings.

**Best Control, Career, since 1920, Minimum 2500 Innings**

Red Lucas, 455 walks in 2543 innings. Active in the National League between 1923 and 1938, Lucas only once gave up more than 50 walks in a season. See "Pinch-Hitting Feats," page 228, for more about Lucas.

## Best Control, Career, since 1893, Left-hander

Noodles Hahn, 381 walks in 2029.1 innings, an average of 1.69 walks per nine innings. Hahn, a 22-game winner for the Reds in 1901, is also the only lefty in this century besides Steve Carlton to win 20 games for a last-place team.

## Best Control, Career, since 1920, Left-hander

Fritz Peterson, 426 walks in 2218 innings, and never more than 49 in a season.

## Best Control, Career, 300-Game Winner

Cy Young, hands down. With 1217 walks in 7357 innings—an average of only 1.49 walked per nine innings—Young begs that anyone seriously interested in determining who was the best pitcher ever examine his overall record carefully.

## Best Control, Career, 1920 through 1941, Minimum 3000 Innings

First Prize—Carl Hubbell, 724 walks in 3589 innings
Second Prize—Paul Derringer, 761 walks in 3645 innings

## Best Control, Career, 1942 through 1960, Minimum 3000 Innings

First Prize—Robin Roberts, 902 walks in 4689 innings
Second Prize—Lew Burdette, 628 walks in 3068 innings

## Best Control, Career, since 1961, Minimum 3000 Innings

First Prize—Juan Marichal, 709 walks in 3509 innings
Second Prize—Fergie Jenkins, 997 walks in 4499 innings. Jenkins is also the only pitcher to record more than 3000 K's and fewer than 1000 walks.

## Best Control Season, Minimum 250 Innings

AL—Cy Young, Boston, 1904, 29 walks in 380 innings.
NL—Babe Adams, Pittsburgh, 1920, 18 walks in 263 innings. Adams also set an NL record in 1913 when he worked 314 innings without hitting a batter. The major-league record for kindness to hitters is held by Al Crowder, who pitched 327 innings for Washington in 1932 without incurring a single

hit batsman. That same season, Crowder set a second all-time record when he went the entire year without uncorking a wild pitch. Crowder's remarkable control exhibition helped him to end the season with 15 straight wins.

## Most Consecutive Innings without Giving up a Base on Balls

AL—84⅓—Bill Fischer, Kansas City A's, 1962. Largely because of his long skein, Fischer also set an AL season record in 1962 for pitchers in over 100 innings, walking only eight batters in 128 innings.

NL—72⅓—Greg Maddux, Atlanta Braves, 2001

# Second Basemen's Records

Three names head almost everyone's list of the greatest second basemen, and all three were active between 1901 and 1919. In the new century's first decade the dominant player in the American League was Nap Lajoie. By the end of the century's second decade Rogers Hornsby was emerging as the best player in the N. L. Between their periods of dominance was Eddie Collins, viewed by many as the finest second basemen ever.

## SEASON BATTING RECORDS

| Department | National League | American League |
|---|---|---|
| Batting Average | .424, Rogers Hornsby, St. Louis, 1924 | .426, NAP LAJOIE, Philadelphia, 1901 |
| Slugging Average | .756, ROGERS HORNSBY, St. Louis, 1925 | .643, Nap Lajoie, Philadelphia, 1901 |
| Home Runs | 42, ROGERS HORNSBY, St. Louis, 1922 42, DAVEY JOHNSON, Atlanta, 1973 | 39, Alfonso Soriano, New York, 2002 |
| RBIs | 152, ROGERS HORNSBY, St. Louis, 1922 | 141, Bret Boone, Seattle, 2001 |
| Runs | 156, ROGERS HORNSBY, Chicago, 1929 | 145, Nap Lajoie, Philadelphia, 1901 |
| Hits | 250, ROGERS HORNSBY, St. Louis, 1922 | 232, Nap Lajoie, Philadelphia, 1901 |
| Doubles | 57, Billy Herman, Chicago, 1935, 1936 | 60, CHARLIE GEHRINGER, Detroit, 1936 |

| Department | National League | American League |
|---|---|---|
| Triples | 31, HEINIE REITZ, Balt., 1894 | 22, Snuffy Stirnweiss, New York, 1945 |
| | 25, Larry Doyle, N.Y. Giants, 1911* | |
| Total Bases | 450, ROGERS HORNSBY, St. Louis, 1922 | 360, Bret Boone, Seattle, 2001 |
| Bases on Balls | 148, EDDIE STANKY, Brooklyn, 1945 | 128, Max Bishop, Philadelphia, 1929, 1930 |
| Stolen Bases | 77, Davey Lopes, L.A., 1975 | 81, EDDIE COLLINS, Philadelphia, 1910 |
| Strikeouts | 168, JUAN SAMUEL, Philadelphia, 1984 | 157, Alfonso Soriano, New York, 2002 |
| Fewest Strikeouts (Minimum) 500 ABS) | 8, EMIL VERBAN, Philadelphia, 1947 | 8, Eddie Collins, Chicago, 1923 |

*Record since 1901.

Note: Davey Johnson also had one home run as a pinch hitter, giving him a total of 43 in 1973.

## Most Games, Career, at Second Base
2650—Eddie Collins, 1906–30

## Most Consecutive Games at Second Base
798—Nellie Fox, Chicago White Sox, August 7, 1955, through September 3, 1960.

# EVOLUTION OF SEASON RECORD FOR BEST FIELDING AVERAGE

| | Team | League | Year | Average |
|---|---|---|---|---|
| Ross Barnes | Chicago | National | 1876 | .910 |
| Jack Burdock | Boston | National | 1878 | .918 |
| Joe Quest | Chicago | National | 1879 | .925 |
| Davy Force | Buffalo | National | 1880 | .939[1] |
| Charlie Bastian | Philadelphia | National | 1886 | .945[2] |
| Fred Dunlap | Pittsburgh | National | 1889 | .950 |
| Charlie Bassett | New York | National | 1890 | .952 |

| | Team | League | Year | Average |
|---|---|---|---|---|
| John Crooks | Columbus | Amer. Assoc. | 1891 | .957[3] |
| Lou Bierbauer | Pittsburgh | National | 1893 | .959 |
| Heinie Reitz | Baltimore | National | 1894 | .968 |
| Bid McPhee | Cincinnati | National | 1896 | .978[4] |
| Gus Dundon | Chicago | American | 1905 | .978 |
| George Cutshaw | Pittsburgh | National | 1919 | .980 |
| Aaron Ward | New York | American | 1923 | .980 |
| Sparky Adams | Chicago | National | 1925 | .983 |
| Max Bishop | Philadelphia | American | 1926 | .987[5] |
| Max Bishop | Philadelphia | American | 1932 | .988 |
| Ski Melillo | St. Louis | American | 1933 | .991 |
| Snuffy Stirnweiss | New York | American | 1948 | .993[6] |
| Al Schoendienst | St. Louis-New York | National | 1956 | .993 |
| Jerry Adair | Baltimore | American | 1964 | .994 |
| Bobby Grich | Baltimore | American | 1973 | .995 |
| Bobby Wilfong | Minnesota | American | 1980 | .995[7] |
| Bobby Grich | California | American | 1985 | .997 |
| Bret Boone | Cincinnati | National | 1997 | .997 |

[1]Force also played a slew of games at shortstop in 1880, and his average combines his work at both spots. A weak hitter, if not the weakest ever, he relied heavily on his fielding to keep him in the league.

[2]Another extraordinarily inept hitter who got by on his fielding.

[3]The American Association consistently had poorer fielding averages than the National League during its decade as a major circuit, leading to the surmise that either the NL had better fielders—unlikely since the two leagues were about equal in every other respect—or else scorers were tougher in the AA. If the latter was the case, and I tend to think it probably was, Crooks must have been quite a good fielder.

[4]The record crept up a point or two every couple of years until Reitz and McPhee came along. McPhee had actually been around a good while by 1896 but didn't start using a glove until late in his career. Considering that his record stood for 23 years, you have to wonder if he wouldn't have come close to perfect with one of today's models.

[5]A good ballplayer whose skills weren't the sort that were highly regarded in his time. Comparable to Johnny Evers, who's in the Hall of Fame, and Nellie Fox, who recently made it.

[6]Bobby Doerr also fielded .993 in 1948, but Stirnweiss won the fielding crown that year and also became the record holder, because his average was a shade higher.

[7]Wilfong's 1980 average was .99481 in 120 games; Grich's 1973 average was .99471 in 162 games. In 1970 Ken Boswell of the Mets fielded .9956 but wasn't in enough games to qualify as the fielding leader.

## Best Career Fielding Average
.990—Ryne Sandberg, 1981–97

## Most Seasons League Leader in Fielding Averages
AL—9—Eddie Collins, last in 1924
NL—7—Red Schoendienst, last in 1958

## Most Consecutive Errorless Games
123—Ryne Sandberg, Chicago Cubs, 1989–90. Sandberg's streak ended on May 18, 1990, when he made a wild throw in a game against Houston.

## Most Consecutive Errorless Chances Accepted
582—Ryne Sandberg, Chicago Cubs, 1989–90. During his skein Sandberg broke Manny Trillo's record for consecutive errorless chances (479) and Joe Morgan's for consecutive errorless games (91).

## Most Chances Accepted, Career
14,156—Eddie Collins, 1906–30

## Most Chances Accepted, Season
1059—Frankie Frisch, St. Louis Cardinals, 1927; Frisch also set an all-time record that season when he had 641 assists.

## Most Chances Accepted, Game, Nine Innings
NL—18—Terry Harmon, Philadelphia, June 12, 1971
AL—18—Julio Cruz, Seattle, June 7, 1981, first nine innings of an 11-inning game; he handled 19 chances altogether before the game was over.

## Most Gold Glove Awards
10—Robby Alomar, last in 2001

# Triples Records

After a little more juice was added to the ball prior to the 1911 season, the scale on the hitters' side once again began to rise—but not so markedly that it can account for Owen Wilson's staggering all-time record achievement. In 1912 Wilson clubbed 36 triples, easily the most by any player in this century and 22 more than Wilson himself collected in his second-best season. There has never been a satisfactory explanation for how he did it. True, Joe Jackson of Cleveland hit 26 triples that same season, the American League record, and Detroit's Sam Crawford tied Jackson's mark just two years later, a lusty sign that the period was probably the most sanguine one in history for triples. True also that Wilson played in Forbes Field, which for many years was sculpted in such a way that balls hit between outfielders frequently grew into triples, helping the Pirates to total 110 or more three-baggers in a season seven times between 1902 and 1930, something that all the other 15 teams combined were able to do only five times. But that still doesn't begin to tell us why it was Wilson who set the record and not Honus Wagner or Fred Clarke or Tommy Leach or Max Carey, four teammates of his who were all much more prolific triples hitters over their careers than he was. To understand why, you had to be in Forbes Field that year, evidently, and even then it might not have come clear. In all likelihood, Wilson's record is just one of the many inexplicable feats that we call a fluke for the lack of a more adequate word.

**Most Career Triples by Player Active Exclusively since 1941**
177—Stan Musial, 1941–63

**Most Career Triples by Player Active since Musial Retired**
166—Roberto Clemente, 1955–72

# TOP 10 IN CAREER TRIPLES

| | Years Active | Triples |
|---|---|---|
| 1. Sam Crawford | 1899–1917 | 311 |
| 2. Ty Cobb | 1905–28 | 297 |
| 3. Honus Wagner | 1897–1917 | 252 |
| 4. Jake Beckley | 1888–1907 | 242[1] |
| 5. Roger Connor | 1880–97 | 233[2] |
| 6. Tris Speaker | 1907–28 | 223 |
| 7. Fred Clarke | 1894–1915 | 220[3] |
| 8. Dan Brouthers | 1879–1904 | 205 |
| 9. Joe Kelley | 1891–1908 | 194 |
| 10. Paul Waner | 1926–45 | 190[4] |

[1]Held the career record before Crawford broke it in 1912.
[2]Held the career record before Beckley broke it in 1904. Prior to Connor, the record belonged to Harry Stovey with 185 career triples..
[3]Clarke's career total is disputed, as are the totals of everyone on the list who played before 1900.
[4]The most career triples by a player active exclusively since 1920.

## Most Career Triples by Player Active since 1977
147—Willie Wilson, 1976–94

## Most Seasons League Leader in Triples
AL—5—Sam Crawford, last in 1915; Willie Wilson, last in 1988
NL—5—Stan Musial, last in 1951

## Most Consecutive Seasons League Leader in Triples
AL—4—Lance Johnson, 1991–94
NL—3—Garry Templeton, 1977–79

## Most Triples, Season, 1920 through 1941
NL—26—Kiki Cuyler, Pittsburgh, 1925
AL—23—Earle Combs, New York, 1927

## Most Triples, Season, 1942 through 1960
AL—23—Dale Mitchell, Cleveland, 1949
NL—20—Stan Musial, St. Louis, 1946; Willie Mays, New York Giants, 1957

**Most Triples, Season, 1961 through 1977**
  NL—17—Ralph Garr, Atlanta, 1974
  AL—15—Gino Cimoli, Kansas City A's, 1962

**Most Triples, Season, since 1977**
  AL—21—Willie Wilson, Kansas City Royals, 1985
  NL—21—Lance Johnson, New York, 1996; the most since 1930 by an NL'er.

**Fewest Triples, Season, League Leader in Triples**
  AL—8—Del Unser, Washington, 1969
  NL—10—Johnny Callison, Philadelphia, 1962; Willie Davis, Los Angeles, 1962; Maury Wills, Los Angeles, 1962; Dickie Thon, Houston, 1982; Rafael Furcal, Atlanta, 2003

**Fewest Triples, Season, 600 or More at Bats**
  AL—0—Miguel Tejada, Oakland, 2002, 662 at bats
  NL—0—Sammy Sosa, Chicago, 1998, 643 at bats

**Only Catchers Ever to Lead League in Triples**
  NL—Tim McCarver, St. Louis, 1966, led with 13 triples.
  Al—Carlton Fisk, Boston, 1972, tied Joe Rudi, Oakland, for the lead with nine triples.

**Last First Baseman to Lead League in Triples**
  NL—Stan Musial, St. Louis, 1946, led with 20 triples.
  AL—Vic Power, Kansas City A's and Cleveland, 1958, led with 10 triples.

**Last Team to Hit 100 Triples in a Season**
  NL—Pittsburgh, 1930, 119 triples
  AL—Washington, 1932, 100 triples

**Last Team to Hit More Triples Than Home Runs**
  AL—Chicago, 1949, 66 triples and 43 home runs
  NL—Houston, 1979, 52 triples and 49 home runs

**Only Player to Lead League in RBIs Two Years in a Row Without Hitting a Triple**
  Jackie Jensen, Boston Red Sox, 1958–59. Ironically, just two years earlier, in 1956, Jensen had led the American League in triples with 11.

# Pitching Records for Most Wins

Among the many records Jack Chesbro established in 1904, probably the most significant occurred when he achieved his 41st victory. Only one other pitcher in major-league history, Ed Walsh in 1908, has had a 40-win season since the mound was moved to its present 60-foot-6-inch distance from the plate. Ironically, both Chesbro and Walsh fell just short of bringing pennants to their teams by losing games on the last day of the season.

## TOP 10 IN SEASON WINS SINCE 1901

| | | Team | League | Year | Wins |
|---|---|---|---|---|---|
| 1. | Jack Chesbro | New York | American | 1904 | 41 |
| 2. | Ed Walsh | Chicago | American | 1908 | 40[1] |
| 3. | Christy Mathewson | New York | National | 1908 | 37[2] |
| 4. | Walter Johnson | Washington | American | 1913 | 36 |
| 5. | Joe McGinnity | New York | National | 1904 | 35 |
| 6. | Joe Wood | Boston | American | 1912 | 34 |
| 7. | Cy Young | Boston | American | 1901 | 33 |
| | Christy Mathewson | New York | National | 1904 | 33 |
| | Pete Alexander | Philadelphia | National | 1916 | 33 |
| 10. | Cy Young | Boston | American | 1902 | 32 |
| | Walter Johnson | Washington | American | 1912 | 32 |

[1]Disputed. Some sources say he had only 39 wins.
[2]20th-century National League record.

## TOP 10 IN SEASON WINS SINCE 1920

| | | Team | League | Year | Wins |
|---|---|---|---|---|---|
| 1. | Jim Bagby | Cleveland | American | 1920 | 31 |
| 2. | Lefty Grove | Philadelphia | American | 1931 | 31 |

| 3. | Denny McLain | Detroit | American | 1968 | 31 |
| 4. | Dizzy Dean | St. Louis | National | 1934 | 30 |
| 5. | Hal Newhouser | Detroit | American | 1944 | 29 |
| 6. | Dazzy Vance | Brooklyn | National | 1924 | 28 |
| | Dizzy Dean | St. Louis | National | 1935 | 28 |
| | Lefty Grove | Philadelphia | American | 1930 | 28 |
| | Robin Roberts | Philadelphia | National | 1952 | 28 |
| 10. | 12 with 27 wins, last done by Bob Welch, Oakland A's, 1990. | | | | |

# TEAM MILESTONE PITCHERS (SINCE 1893)

## National League

| Team | Last 30-Game Winner | Last 25-Game Winner | Last 20-Game Winner |
| --- | --- | --- | --- |
| Astros | None | None | Mike Hampton, 22 (1999) Jose Lima, 21 (1999) |
| Braves | Kid Nichols, 30 (1897) | Dick Rudolph, 27 (1914) Bill James, 26 (1914) | Russ Ortiz, 20 (2003) |
| Cardinals | Dizzy Dean, 30 (1934) | Dizzy Dean, 28 (1935) | Matt Morris, 22 (2001) |
| Cubs | None | Charlie Root, 26 (1927) | Jon Lieber, 20 (2001) |
| Diamond-backs | None | None | Randy Johnson, 24 (2002) Curt Schilling, 23 (2002) |
| Dodgers | None | Sandy Koufax, 27 (1966) | Ramon Martinez, 20 (1990) |
| Expos | None | None | Ross Grimsley, 20 (1978) |
| Giants | Christy Mathewson, 37 (1908) | Juan Marichal, 26 (1968) | John Burkett, 22 (1993) Bill Swift, 21 (1993) |
| Mets | None | Tom Seaver, 25 (1969) | Frank Viola, 20 (1990) |
| Padres | None | None | Gaylord Perry, 21 (1978) |
| Phillies | Pete Alexander, 30 (1917) | Steve Carlton, 27 (1972) | Steve Carlton, 23 (1982) |
| Pirates | Frank Killen, 30 (1896) | Burleigh Grimes, 25 (1928) | John Smiley, 20 (1991) |
| Reds | None | Bucky Walters, 27 (1939) | Danny Jackson, 23 (1988) |

# American League

| Team | Last 30-Game Winner | Last 25-Game Winner | Last 20-Game Winner |
|------|---------------------|---------------------|---------------------|
| A's | Lefty Grove, 31 (1931) | Bob Welch, 27 (1990) | Barry Zito, 23 (2002) |
| Angels | None | None | Nolan Ryan, 22 (1974) |
| Blue Jays | None | None | Roy Halladay, 22 (2003) |
| Brewers | None | None | Ted Higuera, 20 (1986) |
| Indians | Jim Bagby, 31 (1920) | Bob Feller, 26 (1946) | Gaylord Perry, 21 (1974) |
| Mariners | None | None | Jamie Moyer, 21 (2003) |
| Orioles | None | Steve Stone, 25 (1980) | Mike Boddicker, 20 (1984) |
| Rangers | None | Fergie Jenkins, 25 (1974) | Rick Helling, 20 (1998) |
| Red Sox | Joe Wood, 34 (1912) | Mel Parnell, 25 (1949) | Derrick Lowe, 21 (2002) Pedro Martinez, 20 (2002) |
| Royals | None | None | Bret Saberhagen, 23 (1989) |
| Tigers | Denny McLain, 31 (1968) | Mickey Lolich, 25 (1971) | Bill Gullickson, 20 (1991) |
| Twins | Walter Johnson, 36 (1913) | Jim Kaat, 25 (1966) | Brad Radke, 20 (1997) |
| White Sox | Ed Walsh, 40 (1908) | Red Faber, 25 (1921) | Esteban Loaiza, 21 (2003) |
| Yankees | Jack Chesbro, 41 (1904) | Ron Guidry, 25 (1978) | Andy Pettitte, 21 (2003) |

## Last Pitcher to Win 30 Games Three Years in a Row
Pete Alexander, 1915–17.

## Most Seasons League Leader in Wins
NL—9—Warren Spahn, last in 1961
AL—6—Walter Johnson, last in 1924; Bob Feller, last in 1951

## Most Seasons 30 or More Wins
Right-hander—7—Kid Nichols, 1891–94, 1896–98
Left-hander—2—Frank Killen, 1893 and 1896

## Most Seasons 20 or More Wins

Right-hander—16—Cy Young, last in 1908
Left-hander—13—Warren Spahn, last in 1963

## Most Wins, Season, Against One Team

9—Frank Smith, Chicago White Sox, versus Washington, 1904; Ed Walsh, Chicago White Sox, versus **both** the Boston Red Sox and the New York Yankees, 1908; Ed Reulbach, Chicago Cubs, versus Brooklyn, 1908; Walter Johnson, Washington Senators, versus the White Sox in 1912

## Best Pitching Duo, Season, since 1901

NL—Joe McGinnity (35) and Christy Mathewson (33) won 68 games between them for the 1904 Giants.

AL—Jack Chesbro (41) and Jack Powell (23) won 64 games between them for the 1904 Yankees.

## Best Pitching Duo, Season, since 1920

AL—Hal Newhouser (29) and Dizzy Trout (27) won 56 games between them for the 1944 Tigers.

NL—Bucky Walters (27) and Paul Derringer (25), 52 wins between them for the 1939 Reds

## Best Pitching Duo, Season, since 1961

NL—Sandy Koufax, (26) and Don Drysdale (23), 49 wins between them for the 1965 Dodgers.

AL—Bob Welch (27) and Dave Stewart (22), 49 wins between them for the 1990 Oakland A's, topping by one the 48 games Mike Cuellar and Dave McNally won between them for the 1970 Orioles.

## Best Pitching Trio, Season, since 1901

Joe McGinnity (35), Christy Mathewson (33) and Dummy Taylor (21), 89 wins among them for the 1904 New York Giants

## Best Pitching Trio, Season, since 1920

Jim Bagby (31), Stan Coveleski (24) and Ray Caldwell (20), 75 wins among them for the 1920 Cleveland Indians

## Best Pitching Trio, Season, since 1961

Mike Cuellar (24), Dave McNally (24) and Jim Palmer (20), 68 wins among them for the 1970 Baltimore Orioles

## Best Pitching Quartet, Season, since 1901

Joe McGinnity (35), Christy Mathewson (33), Dummy Taylor (21) and Hooks Wiltse (13), 102 wins among them for the 1904 New York Giants

## Best Pitching Quartet, Season, since 1920

Red Faber (23), Lefty Williams (22), Eddie Cicotte (21) and Dickie Kerr (21), 87 wins among them for the 1920 Chicago White Sox

## Best Pitching Quartet, Season, since 1961

Dave McNally (21), Mike Cuellar (20), Pat Dobson (20) and Jim Palmer (20), 81 wins among them for the 1971 Orioles

## Fewest Wins, Club Leader in Wins, World Championship Team

NL—14—John Candelaria, Pittsburgh, 1979; Brad Penny, Mark Redman and Dontrelle Willis, Florida, 2003

AL—15—Lefty Gomez and Red Ruffing, New York, 1941

## First League Champion without a 20-Game Winner

AL—Philadelphia, 1914, led by Chief Bender and Joe Bush with 17 wins each

NL—New York, 1922, led by Art Nehf with 19 wins. The Giants also won in 1923 and again in 1924 without a 20-game winner.

## First Season Neither World Series Team Had a 20-Game Winner

1975—Rick Wise led the Red Sox with 19 wins, and Gary Nolan, Jack Billingham and Don Gullett led the Reds with only 15 wins.

## First Pitcher to Win 20 Games in a Season Divided Between Two Leagues, since 1901

Joe McGinnity, 1902, 13 wins for Baltimore in the AL and then 8 more in the NL, for a total of 21, after jumping to the Giants. Pat Flaherty with the White Sox and Pirates in 1904, Hank Borowy with the Yankees and Cubs in 1945, Rick Sutcliffe with the Indians and Cubs in 1984, and Bartolo Colon with the Indians and Expos in 2002 have also done it.

## Most Wins by Pitcher on a Last-Place Team

NL—27—Steve Carlton, Philadelphia, 1972

AL—22—Nolan Ryan, California, 1974

**Most Career Wins, Relief Pitcher**
124—Hoyt Wilhelm, 1952–72

**Most Games Won, Career, From One Team**
NL—70—Pete Alexander, 1911–30, from Cincinnati
AL—66—Walter Johnson, 1907–27, from Detroit

## 300-GAME WINNERS

|     |                   | Years Active | Wins |
| --- | ----------------- | ------------ | ---- |
| 1.  | Cy Young          | 1890–1911    | 511  |
| 2.  | Walter Johnson    | 1907–27      | 417  |
| 3.  | Pete Alexander    | 1911–30      | 373  |
|     | Christy Mathewson | 1900–1916    | 373  |
| 5.  | Warren Spahn      | 1942–65      | 363  |
| 6.  | Kid Nichols       | 1890–1906    | 361  |
|     | Pud Galvin        | 1879–92      | 361  |
| 8.  | Tim Keefe         | 1880–93      | 342  |
| 9.  | Steve Carlton     | 1965–88      | 329  |
| 10. | John Clarkson     | 1882–94      | 326  |
|     | Eddie Plank       | 1901–17      | 326  |
| 12. | Don Sutton        | 1966–88      | 324  |
|     | Nolan Ryan        | 1966–93      | 324  |
| 14. | Phil Niekro       | 1964–87      | 318  |
| 15. | Gaylord Perry     | 1962–83      | 314  |
| 16. | Tom Seaver        | 1967–86      | 311  |
|     | Hoss Radbourn     | 1881–91      | 311  |
| 18. | Roger Clemens     | 1984–2003    | 310  |
| 19. | Mickey Welch      | 1880–92      | 308  |
| 20. | Early Wynn        | 1939–63      | 300  |
|     | Lefty Grove       | 1925–41      | 300  |

**Pitchers Who Won 100 or More Games in Each League (In Order Accomplished)**
1. Cy Young
2. Al Orth
3. Jim Bunning
4. Gaylord Perry
5. Fergie Jenkins
6. Nolan Ryan
7. Dennis Martinez

## Fewest Full Seasons Needed to Win 200 Games, since 1901

Pete Alexander had 190 wins after his first seven seasons, won two more in 1918 before he was inducted into the army, then had 16 wins in 1919 after he was discharged, giving him 208 wins in his first eight full seasons. Christy Mathewson had a 0–3 record in 1900, won 174 games in his first seven full seasons and had 211 wins after his eighth. Hence Mathewson achieved more wins in his first eight full seasons, but Alexander had more after his first seven seasons and probably would have had more after his eighth season, too, if his career hadn't been interrupted by military service.

## Fewest Full Seasons Needed to Win 300 Games, since 1901

12—Christy Mathewson; he had 312 wins at the end of his 12th full season

## Fewest Wins at Age 30, 300-Game Winner

31—Phil Niekro. The record was formally held by Gaylord Perry, who had only 76 wins on his 30th birthday. Early Wynn, with 83 wins when he turned 30, was the record-holder before Perry. Niekro also holds the record for the fewest wins at age 40—he had only 197—by a future 300-game winner.

# Pitching Records
# for Most Starts
# and Complete Games

In 1904 Jack Chesbro of the Yankees set a post-1893 record when he started 51 games. The modern National League record holder is the Giants' Joe McGinnity, who made 48 starts in 1903. McGinnity's record is in some ways the more remarkable because it came in the last major-league season that the schedule called for only 140 games.

**Most Games Started, Career**
815—Cy Young, 1890 through 1911. Young made 30 or more starts in 19 consecutive seasons (1891–1909), another all-time record.

**Most Games Started, League, Career**
NL—677—Steve Carlton, 1965 through 1986
AL—665—Walter Johnson, 1907 through 1927

**Most Seasons League Leader in Starts**
NL—6—Robin Roberts, 1950–55. consecutive
AL—5—Bob Feller, last in 1948; Early Wynn, last in 1959

**Most Games Started, Season, 1920 through 1941**
AL—44—George Uhle, Cleveland, 1923
NL—40—Pete Alexander, Chicago, 1920

**Most Games Started, Season, 1942 through 1960**
AL—42—Bob Feller, Cleveland, 1946
NL—42—Bob Friend, Pittsburgh, 1956

**Most Games Started, Season, 1961 through 1976**
AL—49—Wilbur Wood, Chicago, 1972. Wood also made

48 starts in 1973, as did Mickey Lolich of the Tigers in 1971. Wood's 49 starts in 1972 were the most by any pitcher since Ed Walsh made 49 for the 1908 White Sox.

NL—42—Fergie Jenkins, Chicago, 1969; Don Drysdale, Los Angeles, 1963 and 1965; Jack Sanford, San Francisco, 1963.

## Most Games Started, Season, Since 1977

NL—44—Phil Niekro, Atlanta, 1979;

AL—40—Mike Flanagan, Baltimore, 1978; Dennis Leonard, Kansas City, 1978; Jim Clancy, Toronto, 1982; Charlie Hough, Texas, 1987

## Most Consecutive Starting Assignments, No Relief Appearances

NL—534—Steve Carlton, May 17, 1971, through August 5, 1986

AL—515—Jack Morris, September 30, 1978, through 1994

ML—594—Nolan Ryan, July 30, 1974, through 1993

## Most Opening Day Starting Assignments

AL—14—Walter Johnson, all of them with Washington

NL—14—Steve Carlton, all of them with Philadelphia

—14—Tom Seaver, 10 with New York, 4 with Cincinnati

## Most Consecutive Opening Day Starting Assignments

16—Tom Seaver, 14 in the National League and two in the American League.

Chesbro also set a modern record when he completed 48 games in 1904. Two years earlier Vic Willis of the Boston Braves set the National League record when he went the route 45 times in his 46 starts.

## Most Complete Games, Season, 1920 through 1941

NL—33—Pete Alexander, Chicago, 1920; Burleigh Grimes, Brooklyn, 1923

AL—32—Red Faber, Chicago, 1922; George Uhle, Cleveland, 1926

## Most Complete Games, Season, 1942 through 1960

AL—36—Bob Feller, Cleveland, 1946

NL—33—Robin Roberts, Philadelphia, 1953

## Most Complete Games, Season, 1961 through 1976
AL—30—Catfish Hunter, New York, 1975
NL—30—Steve Carlton, Philadelphia, 1972; Fergie Jenkins, Chicago, 1971; Juan Marichal, San Francisco, 1968

## Most Complete Games, Season, since 1977
AL—28—Rick Langford, Oakland, 1980
NL—23—Phil Niekro, Atlanta, 1979

## Most Complete Games, Season, since 1901, Left-hander
NL—41—Noodles Hahn, Cincinnati, 1901; Irv Young, Boston, 1905
AL—39—Rube Waddell, Philadelphia, 1904

## Last Team with Three Pitchers Who Completed 20 or More Games
The 1980 Oakland A's registered 94 complete games, led by Rick Langford with 28, Mike Norris with 24 and Matt Keough with 20.

## Most Consecutive Complete Games
188—Jack Taylor, St. Louis Cardinals and Chicago Cubs, June 20, 1901, through August 9, 1906. On August 13, 1906, Taylor was knocked out in the third inning by the Dodgers, ending a record string of 1,727 consecutive innings without being relieved; altogether, he threw the last pitch for his team in 203 straight games in which he appeared.

## Most Seasons League Leader in Complete Games
NL—9—Warren Spahn, last in 1963
AL—6—Walter Johnson, last in 1916

## First Season League Leader Had Fewer Than 30 Complete Games
NL—1910—Three Finger Brown of the Cubs, Nap Rucker of the Dodgers and Christy Mathewson of the Giants all tied for the lead with 27 complete games.
AL—1923—George Uhle of Cleveland led with 29 complete games.

## First Season League Leader Had Fewer Than 20 Complete Games
AL—1955—Whitey Ford of the Yankess led with only 18.
NL—1957—Warren Spahn of the Milwaukee Braves led with 18; 1957 was also the first season that neither league had a pitcher who completed 20 games.

**Fewest Complete Games, League Leader in Complete Games**
   AL—7—David Wells, Toronto, 1999; Paul Byrd, Kansas City, 2002
   NL—6—Curt Schilling, Arizona, 2001

**Most Starts, Season, without Completing a Game**
   NL—37—Steve Bedrosian, Atlanta, 1985. Shipped to the Phillies in 1986, Bedrosian was sent to the bullpen.
   AL—35—Wilson Alvarez, Chicago, 1996

**Most Starts, Career, without Completing a Game**
   78—Marvin Freeman, 1986–96; several active pitchers have surpassed Freeman's mark but may still throw a complete game.

**Most Complete Games, League, Career**
   AL—531—Walter Johnson, 1907 through 1927
   NL—438—Pete Alexander, 1911 through 1930

**Most Complete Games, League, Career, Since 1920**
   NL—382—Warren Spahn, 1942 through 1965
   AL—356—Ted Lyons, 1923 through 1946

# TOP TEN IN COMPLETE GAMES, CAREER, SINCE 1893

|   | | Years active | CG |
|---|---|---|---|
| 1. | Cy Young | 1890–1911 | 642[1] |
| 2. | Walter Johnson | 1907–27 | 531 |
| 3. | Pete Alexander | 1911–30 | 438 |
| 4. | Christy Mathewson | 1900–1916 | 434 |
| 5. | Jack Powell | 1897–1912 | 422 |
| 6. | Eddie Plank | 1901–17 | 410[2] |
| 7. | Kid Nichols | 1890–1906 | 390[3] |
| 8. | Vic Willis | 1898–1910 | 388 |
| 9. | Warren Spahn | 1942–65 | 382 |
| 10. | Ted Lyons | 1923–46 | 356 |

[1]Had 107 CGs prior to 1893.
[2]The most by a left-hander.
[3]Had 141 CGs prior to 1893.

# The Great Scandals

In 1920 eight members of the Chicago White Sox were barred for life from organized baseball for their part in throwing the 1919 World Series. The eight players were Chick Gandil, Eddie Cicotte, Swede Risberg, Lefty Williams, Happy Felsch, Fred McMullin, Joe Jackson and Buck Weaver, and the order in which they are listed may also reflect their degree of guilt. Gandil, the ringleader, quit after the 1919 season and never attempted to deny or mitigate his actions. The next five players acknowledged their complicity but offered extenuating circumstances to explain their lapse from grace. Jackson admitted he took money but claimed he played his best in the Series. Weaver admitted only that he knew the fix was on and that he chose not to betray his teammates by informing on them. Although brought to trial, none of the eight players was ever convicted in court of the slightest wrongdoing. Because of testimony he gave at their trial, St. Louis Browns second baseman Joe Gedeon was also barred from the game, as were a host of former players and hangers-on. Gedeon and the Chicago Eight were neither the first nor the last players banished from the game, however. Nor were they necessarily the worst offenders. Here is a partial list of baseball's top malefactors.

### The First Great Scandal

In 1865 three players with the New York Mutuals, Thomas Devyr, Edward Duffy and William Wamsley, were accused of conspiring with gamblers to lose a game to the Brooklyn Eckfords. All three players admitted their guilt and were expelled by the Mutuals, only to be reinstated a few months later without further penalty.

### The Louisville Four

Major-league baseball in its infancy was rife with gamblers

and players suspected of dumping games. One reason the National Association collapsed was its inability to police itself, and there is ample evidence that the National League, which replaced it, improved matters only slightly. At the close of the 1877 season, NL President William Hulbert was faced with a situation he could not ignore when evidence was given to him that four Louisville players, Jim Devlin, George Hall, Al Nichols and Bill Craver, had thrown games on the team's final eastern road trip. Devlin had reputedly been approached by a gambler named McLeod and Hall simultaneously approached by his own brother-in-law. Both were urged to see to it that Louisville found a way to blow its 3½-game lead with 12 contests to play and swing the pennant to Boston. Nichols was made part of the plot and led to its unraveling when Louisville team officials, noting the deluge of telegrams he suddenly began receiving, examined their contents and discovered they were from gamblers informing him which games to lose. A case has been made that Craver wasn't one of the conspirators and was banned solely because he stood on his constitutional right not to have his mail opened without his permission.

In any event, the Louisville Four were probably not the only dishonest players in 1877—they were merely the most flagrant. In subsequent years, players under suspicion were blacklisted rather than barred, a practice that soon included not only the game's shady characters but also those who exhibited rebellious tendencies. In 1881 a formal blacklist was drawn up; on it were nine players: Mike Dorgan, Buttercup Dickerson, Emil Gross, Lipman Pike, Sadie Houck, Edward "The Only" Nolan, Bill Crowley, John Fox and Blower Brown. All except Nolan and Pike were later reinstated without undue disruption to their careers. Pike, who had first been blacklisted back in 1878 for an unrecorded offense, was 36 years old in 1881 and near the end anyway, while Nolan, who had also been blacklisted in 1878 for lying to the owner of his Indianapolis team, in disgust dropped down to the minor leagues, where he starred for years.

### The Scots Verdict

In 1904, St. Louis Cardinals pitcher Jack Taylor fell under suspicion of throwing games. Testimony was heard for and against him, and he received what sources in the period called a "Scots Verdict," meaning there was good reason to believe him to be guilty but insufficient evidence to convict him.

## The Corkscrew Brain

It belonged, Fred Lieb wrote, to Hal Chase, quite possibly the greatest fielding first baseman ever and a fine all-around player—when he wanted to be. Much has been written about Chase in recent years, all of it condemnatory and perhaps justly so, but too many sources would have you believe that Chase all by himself undermined the fabric of baseball and created the climate for the Black Sox scandal. This is ludicrous. Chase was first and foremost an opportunist. As a rookie with the Yankees in 1905, he found himself on a team that had lost the pennant the previous year on a ninth-inning wild pitch on the last day of the season, an occurrence that did not seem to overly depress team owners Frank Farrell and Big Bill Devery. Both men were gamblers by occupation and surrounded themselves with others of their breed, a combination that Chase no doubt viewed as license to do his thing. In support of this are the numerous instances when Yankees managers begged Farrell to get rid of Chase and found themselves axed instead, plus the fact that Chase was himself named manager of the club while supposedly under clouds of suspicion.

How far up into the front office and how wide on the field Chase's chicanery extended can only be guesswork now, but it is intriguing that despite his reputation for wrecking the morale of every team he played for, John McGraw hired him in 1919 and gave him the Giants first-base job. True, McGraw released him at the end of the season, along with Heinie Zimmerman and Jean Dubuc, two other questionable figures of the era, and none of the three ever played in the majors again—but where had McGraw's head been back in the spring? Did he discredit all the rumors about Chase? Had he seen Chase as still capable of being reformed? Or does the full story, for some reason, remain buried?

## The Douglas Incident

Subsequent to the Black Sox scandal, a number of players found themselves outside the barred gates of organized baseball. Among them were Gene Paulette of the Phillies, who was banned for betting on games and being foolish enough to admit it, pitchers Paul Carter and Claude Hendrix of the

Cubs, who were never formally banished but were rather declared personae non grata, and Benny Kauff, expelled in 1920 by Commissioner Landis after he was accused of being part of a stolen car ring. Three ex-big leaguers, Bill Rumler, Gene Dale and Hart Maggert, were also dismissed by Landis in 1920 for dumping Pacific Coast League games, and pitcher Ray Fisher incurred Landis's wrath when he refused to sign the contract the Reds tendered him and instead took a coaching job at the University of Michigan. When Fisher applied for reinstatement at the close of the college season, Landis refused to grant it, and Fisher, unfairly, found himself on the same list with all the crooked players who had been booted from the game in the massive effort to clean it up and restore its image. The effort seemed at an end in 1922, until pitcher Phil Douglas jumped the league-leading Giants and then sent a letter to Cardinals outfielder Les Mann, offering to make himself scarce for the rest of the season if the Cardinals would send him a little travel money. Mann, one of the most straitlaced players in the twenties, instead turned the letter over to team officials, it soon wound up on Landis's desk, and Douglas found himself out of the game.

## A Double Standard?

Rube Benton, another ex-Giants pitcher, was let go by McGraw in 1921 after admitting he bet on games. When Benton had an outstanding season with St. Paul in the American Association in 1922, the Reds tried to bring him back to the majors, but McGraw blocked the move, claiming Benton had been blacklisted. Forced by the Reds to decide the issue, Landis ruled that since Benton had never been officially expelled he was eligible to pitch for any team that would have him. So Benton, a self-confessed friend to gamblers, returned to the majors with the Reds in 1923 while Ray Fisher, whose only crime had been to reject a contract he considered to be inadequate, was left permanently outside the walls.

## The Last Major-League Player to Be Barred

In the final days of the 1924 season, with the Giants rolling to their fourth straight pennant, Giants outfielder Jimmy O'Connell sidled up to Phillies shortstop Heinie Sand before a game and offered him $500 to go easy on the Giants that day, Sand reported the bribe attempt to his manager, and the machinery was quickly set in motion that would expel both

O'Connell and Giants coach Cozy Dolan, who had allegedly put O'Connell up to approaching Sand. But few at the time believed that O'Connell, a Santa Clara graduate, had been either the instigator of the bribe offer or Dolan's unwitting dupe. There was testimony from O'Connell that several other Giants players had a hand in it and statements from them that it had all been meant as a joke. In any event, O'Connell went down alone, and Dolan, after bitterly shouting that the real story had yet to be told, then decided he wasn't going to be the one to tell it and remained mum until his death. What really happened that September afternoon in 1924? Probably no one will ever know, but, for whatever it means, it was the last scandal involving a New York Giants player, and 1924 was the last season that a club managed by John McGraw won a pennant.

### Cobb and Speaker Dodge a Bullet

In 1926 an event that threatened for a time to eclipse even the Black Sox scandal erupted when former Tigers pitcher Dutch Leonard let it be known that he had certain incriminating letters from Smokey Joe Wood regarding bets that Leonard, Wood, Tris Speaker and Ty Cobb had made on a 1919 game between the Tigers and Indians. According to Leonard, the bet was an added thought after Speaker agreed to let the Tigers win the game so that they could beat the Yankees out of second-place money. Speaker and Cobb were at first persuaded to retire in exchange for having the matter left unexplored; then they reconsidered and decided to fight the charge. When Leonard refused to appear publicly to confront them, Landis let the issue die—although neither Speaker nor Cobb, both player-managers at the time, was ever offered a manager's job again—and the popular theory was that Leonard was merely trying to retaliate against Cobb for releasing him during the 1926 season and against Speaker for not giving him a chance to catch on with the Indians. Yet the possibility is strong that if Leonard's letters had come to light a few years earlier, when Landis was mercilessly striving to rid baseball of even the smallest hint of corruption, the game might have been shorn of its two greatest stars as it was about to enter its golden era.

### Player Takes on Commissioner and Wins

In 1946 Jorge Pasquel, a wealthy customs broker in Mexico who had a financial interest in the Mexican professional league, after a chance meeting with Giants outfielder Danny Gardella at Al Roon's gymnasium in Manhattan seized upon the notion of spiriting major-league players south of the border. Soon thereafter, Gardella and several dozen other players had been induced to play in Mexico, and alarmed major-league owners looked to newly appointed commissioner Happy Chandler for help. Chandler ruled that all players who did not leave Mexico by his deadline were automatically barred from organized baseball for five years. The ban stuck until 1949 when a flurry of legal suits, most of them initiated by Gardella, made Chandler recant and take wayward players back into the fold. Gardella, a mediocre player, benefited little himself from his besting Chandler and was released after a few games. But Sal Maglie, another Mexican League renegade, became one of the National League's top pitchers.

## Most Recent Player Suspended for Gambling

Pitcher Denny McLain of the Tigers was made to sit out much of the 1970 season by Commissioner Bowie Kuhn after being implicated in a bookmaking operation. In recent years several players have been suspended for parts of a season upon being convicted of using and/or trafficking in drugs, but no one has been suspected of allowing his drug involvement to affect the honesty with which he approached the game. To date, not even Cincinnati Manager Pete Rose, who was banished in 1989 for betting on baseball games, is thought to have allowed his gambling activities to influence in any way a game upon which he wagered.

# World Series Play: 1901–19

## FRANCHISE SUMMARY

| Team | League | WS Record | Years in Series |
|------|--------|-----------|-----------------|
| Boston | American | 5–0 | 1903, 1912, 1915, 1916, 1918 |
| Cincinnati | National | 1–0 | 1919 |
| Boston | National | 1–0 | 1914 |
| Chicago | American | 2–1 | 1906, 1917, 1919 |
| Philadelphia | American | 3–2 | 1905, 1910, 1911, 1912, 1914 |
| Pittsburgh | National | 1–1 | 1903, 1909 |
| Chicago | National | 2–3 | 1906, 1907, 1908, 1910, 1918 |
| New York | National | 1–4 | 1905, 1911, 1912, 1913, 1917 |
| Philadelphia | National | 0–1 | 1915 |
| Brooklyn | National | 0–1 | 1916 |
| Detroit | American | 0–3 | 1907, 1908, 1909 |

### Yearly Highlights

1903—Boston (AL) defeated Pittsburgh (NL) 5 games to 3

The first "World Series" since 1890 and the first between the NL and the AL was a five-of-nine affair, Boston winning despite yeoman's work by the Pirates' Deacon Phillippe, who pitched five complete games and had three wins. Boston was led by Bill Dinneen, who won three of his four starts. Philippe was called on so often because Sam Leever had injured his shoulder in a trapshooting tournament prior to the Series, and another Pirates pitcher, Ed Doheny, was committed to a mental hospital. Jimmy Sebring of the Pirates was the batting star, starting a Series tradition wherein lightly regarded players were often the ones to shine most brilliantly. The teams hit a record 25 triples between them due to a ground rule that any ball going into the overflow crowds that ringed the outfield rated three bases. Members of the Pirates received a larger Series share than the winning Red Sox because Pittsburgh owner Barney Dreyfuss gave all of the club's take to his players while Boston owner Henry Killilea pocketed his portion and then sold the team to John Taylor, son of the owner of the *Boston Globe*.

**1905—New York (NL) defeated Philadelphia (AL) 4 games to 1**

There was no World Series in 1904, largely because Giants manager John McGraw and team owner John Brush feared the Yankees would win the AL pennant and were loath to risk their supremacy against a rival New York team. The Giants made this decision in July while the Yankees were leading the AL and then were stuck with it when Yankees ace Jack Chesbro, on the last day of the season, wild-pitched home the run that handed Boston the game and the pennant. In October of 1904, Brush issued an announcement that if the Giants won again in 1905 they would play the AL champ, regardless of who it was. When the Giants repeated, Christy Mathewson, their star pitcher and a Bucknell graduate, found himself pitted against the A's Eddie Plank of Gettsyburg College. It was the first time two college grads faced each other in a Series, and the Giants prevailed easily, with all five contests ending in shutouts, three of them pitched by Mathewson.

**1906—Chicago (AL) defeated Chicago (NL) 4 games to 2**

The Cubs were 26–3 in August and 24–5 down the stretch to finish with a 50–8 surge that gave them a record 116 victories. Against their vaunted pitching staff, the White Sox, known at "The Hitless Wonders," seemed hopelessly overmatched. But after holding the Sox to 6 runs in the first four games, Cubs pitchers gave up 16 runs in the last two contests. Ed Walsh of the triumphant Sox struck out 12 batters in Game Three, a Series nine-inning record that stood until 1929.

**1907—Chicago (NL) defeated Detroit (AL) 4 games to 0**

The first game ended in a 12-inning deadlock after the Cubs scored the tying run in the ninth on a passed ball. The Cubs then swept the next four games.

1908—Chicago (NL) defeated Detroit (AL) 4 games to 1

In the first Series that matched repeat pennant winners, the Cubs again won easily as Orval Overall and Three Finger Brown each won two games and allowed only two earned runs between them.

1909—Pittsburgh (NL) defeated Detroit (AL) 4 games to 3

It was the first Series to go the distance. In his third and final try to win a World Championship, Ty Cobb of the Tigers once again came up on the short end. Pirates rookie Babe Adams became the second pitcher to win three games in a seven-game Series, and Pittsburgh stole 18 bases, breaking the Series record of 16 set in 1907 by the Cubs.

1910—Philadelphia (AL) defeated Chicago (NL) 4 games to 1

Jack Coombs of the A's won three games and hit .385. The Cubs won Game Four after a last-ditch ninth inning rally to avert a Series sweep.

1911—Philadelphia (AL) defeated New York (NL) 4 games to 2

Home Run Baker earned his nickname by hitting two key four-baggers in the Series. Giants second baseman Larry Doyle, carrying the winning run in Game Five, missed home plate on his slide, but none of the A's noticed, and home plate umpire Bill Klem rightfully held silent. The A's lapse became unimportant when they won Game Six 13–2.

1912—Boston (AL) defeated New York (NL) 4 games to 3

The first Series played in Fenway Park and the first truly great one. Art Irwin, who played with Providence in the 1884 World Series, attended the opener and lamented that he'd been born too soon when he saw the size of the crowd. The Series was decided in the bottom of the 10th inning of the seventh game when the Red Sox, trailing 2–1, scored two runs after Giants outfielder Fred Snodgrass muffed a fly ball, Christy Mathewson issued an uncharacteristic walk to weak-hitting Steve Yerkes, Tris Speaker singled home the tying run after Fred Merkle and Chief Meyers of the Giants let his pop foul drop between them, Duffy Lewis was intentionally walked, and Larry Gardner then brought Yerkes home with the Series-ending run on a sacrifice fly. The overall hitting star was Buck Herzog of the Giants with 12 hits, while Joe Wood, who won three games for the Red Sox, topped all pitchers.

**1913—Philadelphia (AL) defeated New York (NL) 4 games to 1**

Home Run Baker was again the hitting star, rapping his third Series four-bagger. Chief Bender of the A's won two complete games despite being hit hard while Christy Mathewson, in his final Series, lost the last game 3–1 to Eddie Plank.

**1914—Boston (NL) defeated Philadelphia (AL) 4 games to 0**

The only team to win a pennant after being in last place on July 4, the Braves were accorded little chance in the Series. But they swept the A's behind pitchers Bill James and Dick Rudolph, who won two games apiece and allowed only one earned run between them. The Braves, who played in decrepit South End Grounds, borrowed Fenway Park for the Series. A year later the Red Sox borrowed brand-new Braves Field, which was larger than Fenway.

**1915—Boston (AL) defeated Philadelphia (NL) 4 games to 1**

Babe Ruth made his first Series appearance, as a pinch hitter, in Baker Bowl, where 400 extra seats were put in right field, reducing the park's dimensions and enabling Red Sox outfielder Harry Hooper to bounce two balls into the temporary seats in Game Five—hits that would now be ground-rule doubles that then counted as home runs. The Phils, in a sense, were the victims of their own greed, losing their fourth Series game in a row by one run when Hooper's second park-created homer came in the ninth inning.

**1916—Boston (AL) defeated Brooklyn (NL) 4 games to 1**

In the longest Series game in history—Game Two on October 9—it took Babe Ruth 14 innings to beat Sherry Smith of the Dodgers 2–1. The following day Jack Coombs edged Carl Mays, 4–3, to give Brooklyn its only win.

**1917—Chicago (AL) defeated New York (NL) 4 games to 2**

In Game Four, Benny Kauff became the first National Leaguer to hit two homers in a Series game; Patsy Dougherty of Boston had been the first American Leaguer, in 1903. Heinie Zimmerman of the Giants was tagged the Series goat when Eddie Collins was trapped off third base in the fourth inning of the sixth game but darted past Giants catcher Bill Rariden, leaving Zimmerman to chase Collins helplessly across the plate when neither pitcher Rube Benton nor first baseman Walter Holke covered home. Red Faber of the White Sox won three games and lost one, making him the only pitcher ever to post four decisions in a seven-game Series.

**1918—Boston (AL) defeated Chicago (NL) 4 games to 2**

In anticipation of big crowds that never materialized, the Cubs borrowed Comiskey Park from the White Sox. George Whiteman of the Red Sox hit .250 and knocked in only one run but is still remembered as one of the Series heroes, whereas Cubs second baseman Charlie Pick, who, like Whiteman, came up from the minors in midseason and played only because his team was short-handed, isn't remembered at all despite batting .389 and leading both clubs with seven hits. The Red Sox scored only nine runs in the Series and hit just .186 but won because Carl Mays and Babe Ruth held the Cubs to only four runs and won two games each.

**1919—Cincinnati (NL) defeated Chicago (AL) 5 games to 3**

Aiming for increased gate receipts to make up for the short—140-game—regular-season schedule, the National Commission, comprising the two league presidents, Ban Johnson and John Heydler, plus Garry Herrmann, president of the Reds, expanded the Series to a best-five-of-nine format but could have halted proceedings after the first game because the verdict was already self-evident to many in attendance. The signal that the Series was fixed came in the bottom of the first inning when Eddie Cicotte of the White Sox deliberately plunked Reds leadoff hitter Morrie Rath in the back. Joe Jackson, one of the fixers, led all batters with 12 hits and a .375 average, giving credence to his lifelong contention that he promised his worst to gamblers but played his best.

# SECTION 3

# Famous Firsts:
# 1920–41

**1920**—The pall that hangs over baseball after the 1919 World Series leads officials to abolish the spitball and all other pitches that involve applying foreign substances to the ball in an effort to sanitize the game and increase hitting. A select few pitchers are exempted from the abolition and allowed to continue throwing spitters until their careers are over.

**1920**—The Bill Doak fielder's glove is introduced by the Rawlings Sporting Goods Company of St. Louis. In contrast to the old pancake glove, it has a natural pocket whose size can be adjusted by leather laces.

**1920**—Cleveland shortstop Ray Chapman becomes the first player to die as a result of an injury incurred in a major-league game when he succumbs after Carl Mays of the Yankees beans him with a submarine pitch on August 16 in a game at the Polo Grounds.

**1921**—On August 25, Harold Arlen, the voice of radio station KDKA in Pittsburgh, broadcasts the first baseball game over the air, from Philadelphia, the Pirates winning 8–5 over the Phillies. In the fall of that year KDKA installs a wire between Pittsburgh and New York, which Grantland Rice uses to issue sporadic reports from the Polo Grounds, where the World Series is being played between the Yankees and Giants. Another radio station, WJZ in Newark, New Jersey, is even more ambitious and manages to broadcast the Series in its entirety by relay as Sandy Hunt of the *Newark Sunday Call* reports play-by-play action from his seat in the Polo Grounds to the WJZ radio shack, where Tommy Cowan then repeats Hunt's account to station listeners.

**1921**—American League pitcher Al Sothoron sets a post-deadball era record when he works the entire season—178 innings—without surrendering a home run.

**1921**—Eppa Rixey of the Reds gives up only one homer in 301 innings—an NL post-deadball record.

**1922**—The Williams shift is introduced—not to frustrate Ted Williams, who's only about four years old at the moment, but rather to combat lefty pull-hitters Ken Williams of the Browns and Cy Williams of the Phillies.

**1922**—George Uhle of the Indians wins 22 games with a 4.07 ERA, the first pitcher since 1901 to achieve 20 victories despite allowing over four runs a game.

**1922**—White Sox owner Charlie Comiskey, anxious to shed his miserly image, forks over $125,000 to the San Francisco Seals for the contract of third baseman Willie Kamm, the first $100,000 purchase of a minor leaguer.

**1923**—The Giants buy pitcher/first baseman Jack Bentley from the Baltimore club in the International League for $65,000, but Bentley refuses to report unless he's given a piece of his sale price. The first minor leaguer to demand a cut of the action, Bentley finally relents—but the suspicion will always linger that the Giants secretly gave him signing money after extracting a pledge from him to deny it.

**1923**—Graham McNamee, the first famous baseball announcer, begins his career. Although not terribly knowledgeable about baseball McNamee has personality—or what in later years is called "charisma." By profession a singer, McNamee obtains his first radio job on a lunch break while serving on jury duty and shortly thereafter is heard for the first time over the air on WEAF in New York, a forerunner of WNBC. From the start it is obvious that McNamee's enthusiastic cultivated delivery gives his audience the feeling that it is part of whatever he is describing, and he is the natural choice to handle the microphone when WEAF decides to broadcast the 1923 World Series.

**1924**—WMAQ of Chicago broadcasts the home games of both the Cubs and the White Sox, with Hal Totten the voice. Totten is later joined by Pat Flaherty.

**1925**—The American League permits resin bags to counteract somewhat the ruinous effect that banning foreign substances has had on pitchers.

**1929**—The Indians and the Yankees become the first teams to put numbers on the backs of their uniforms and leave them there. On May 13, at League Park in Cleveland, fans for the first time are treated to the sight of two teams wearing numbered uniforms and get an additional charge when Willis Hudlin beats the Yankees 4–3. Two years later the American League makes numbered uniforms mandatory for all teams.

**1929**—On July 5, the Giants use the first public address system in a major-league park for a game against Pittsburgh.

**1929**—Cincinnati's Harry Hartman becomes the first radio announcer to say "Going, going, gone," whenever a fair-hit ball is headed over the wall.

**1932**—Jack Graney, former Cleveland outfielder and the first major-league player to hit a home run off Babe Ruth, in 1914, starts as the voice of the Indians, a job he will hold until his retirement after the 1954 World Series. Since announcers in the early days of radio don't travel with teams, Graney becomes a master at re-creating road games, play-by-play reports of which he receives by wire. (In the late 1950s, long after most other teams have begun putting their announcers on the scene, Waite Hoyt and Les Keiter, the twin voices of the Cincinnati Reds, will still be re-creating away games.) To Graney falls the honor of being the first ex-major-leaguer to become a play-by-play announcer, with Hoyt not far behind him—but the first future Hall of Famer to hold down the job is Harry Heilmann, the longtime voice of the Detroit Tigers.

**1932**—The Kessler brothers provide a harbinger of what fans in Philadelphia will be like in another few decades when they heap so much abuse on A's third baseman Jimmy Dykes that manager-owner Connie Mack finally gives Dykes a break and sells him to the White Sox.

**1933**—Washington deals first baseman Joe Judge to Brooklyn, ending the record 18 consecutive years that Judge and Senators outfielder Sam Rice had been road roommates.

**1934**—On Sunday, April 29, the Pirates entertain the Reds in Forbes Field and beat them 9–5 as Pittsburgh becomes the last major-league city to lift its blue laws and host a Sunday game.

**1934**—Burleigh Grimes wins his 270th and final victory on May 30 when he beats Washington 5–4 while pitching in a relief role for the Yankees. Grimes's win is the last in major-league history by a pitcher legally permitted to throw a spitball.

**1934**—A few members of the Cincinnati Reds fly to a game in Chicago, the first major-league team to travel together by air.

**1935**—William Wrigley of the Cubs becomes the first owner to allow all his team's games to be broadcast.

**1935**—Augie Galan of the Cubs sets a major-league record

when he becomes the first player to play an entire 154-game season without grounding into a double play.

**1938**—The Giants, Dodgers and Yankees for the first time allow their home games to be broadcast on a regular basis. The Yankees hire Mel Allen and team him with Arch McDonald.

**1938**—Ernie Lombardi of the Reds grounds into 30 double plays, a National League record.

**1939**—The *Reach Baseball Guide* merges with the *Spalding Baseball Guide*. The two publish under the *Spalding-Reach Baseball Guide* name through 1941, then both bow out after over half a century in the business as the *Sporting News* takes over the publication of the annual guide.

**1939**—The 25-player limit, reduced to 23 in the depression, is restored and, with the exception of the 1946 season when teams are allowed to carry more players to accommodate returning service vets, remains unchanged until 1986 when the owners, locked in a power struggle with the players' union, cut back to 24-man rosters.

**1939**—On May 17, W2XBS of New York televises a college contest between Princeton and Columbia, the first baseball game ever to appear on the new video device. On August 26 of that same year, also over W2XBS, the first major-league game is telecast when a TV camera is lugged into Ebbets Field, where the Dodgers are hosting the Reds.

**1939**—Lou Gehrig becomes the first player to have his uniform number retired. By 2004 the Yankees will have permanently removed 16 numbers from circulation.

**1941**—The Dodgers become the first team to wear plastic batting helmets after Pee Wee Reese and Pete Reiser are idled by beanings.

**1941**—The Tigers give $52,000 to University of Michigan student Dick Wakefield, making him the first big "bonus baby."

**1941**—On March 8, Phillies pitcher Hugh Mulcahy becomes the first major-leaguer to be drafted in the prelude to World War II; Tigers outfielder Hank Greenberg becomes the second after playing 19 games. Within two years over 100 major leaguers are involved in the war effort, but only two, Elmer Gedeon and Harry O'Neill, are killed in action.

# Total Bases Records

In 1921 Babe Ruth set an all-time major-league record when he collected 457 total bases. The following year Rogers Hornsby amassed 450 total bases, setting the National League mark. Since 1930 no player has seriously threatened either record.

## TOP 10 IN TOTAL BASES, SEASON

|  | Year | Team | League | Total Bases |
|---|---|---|---|---|
| 1. Babe Ruth | 1921 | New York | American | 457 |
| 2. Rogers Hornsby | 1922 | St. Louis | National | 450 |
| 3. Lou Gehrig | 1927 | New York | American | 447 |
| 4. Chuck Klein | 1930 | Philadelphia | National | 445 |
| 5. Jimmie Foxx | 1938 | Boston | American | 438 |
| 6. Stan Musial | 1948 | St. Louis | National | 429 |
| 7. Sammy Sosa | 2001 | Chicago | National | 425 |
| 8. Hack Wilson | 1930 | Chicago | National | 423 |
| 9. Chuck Klein | 1932 | Philadelphia | National | 420[1] |
| 10. Lou Gehrig | 1930 | New York | American | 419 |
| Luis Gonzalez | 2001 | Arizona | National | 419 |

[1]The only player to have two seasons with 420 or more total bases.

**Most Total Bases, Season, 1901 through 1919**
    AL—367—Ty Cobb, Detroit, 1911
    NL—325—Cy Seymour, Cincinnati, 1905

**Most Total Bases, Season, 1942 through 1960**
    NL—429—Stan Musial, St. Louis, 1948
    AL—376—Mickey Mantle, New York, 1956

**Most Total Bases, Season, 1961 through 1976**
NL—382—Willie Mays, San Francisco, 1962
AL—374—Tony Oliva, Minnesota, 1964

**Most Total Bases, Season, 1977 through 1993**
AL—406—Jim Rice, Boston, 1978
NL—338—George Foster, Cincinnati, 1977

**Most Total Bases, Season, since 1994**
NL—425—Sammy Sosa, Chicago, 2001
AL—399—Albert Belle, Chicago, 1998

**Fewest Total Bases, Season, League Leader in Total Bases**
NL—237—Honus Wagner, Pittsburgh, 1906
AL—260—George Stone, St. Louis, 1905

**Most Seasons 400 or More Total Bases**
AL—5—Lou Gehrig, last in 1936
NL—3—Chuck Klein, last in 1932

**Most Seasons 300 or More Total Bases**
NL—15—Hank Aaron, last in 1971
AL—13—Lou Gehrig, 1926 through 1938 consecutive

## TOP 10 IN TOTAL BASES, CAREER

|  | Years Active | Total Bases |
|---|---|---|
| 1. Hank Aaron | 1954–76 | 6856[3] |
| 2. Stan Musial | 1941–63 | 6134[2] |
| 3. Willie Mays | 1951–73 | 6066 |
| 4. Ty Cobb | 1905–28 | 5856[1] |
| 5. Babe Ruth | 1914–35 | 5793 |
| 6. Pete Rose | 1963–86 | 5752 |
| 7. Carl Yastrzemski | 1961–83 | 5539 |
| 8. Eddie Murray | 1977–97 | 5387 |
| 9. Frank Robinson | 1958–76 | 5373 |
| 10. Barry Bonds | 1986– | 5253 |

[1]The first player to collect 5000 total bases.
[2]Broke Cobb's career total bases record in 1962.
[3]Broke Musial's career total bases record in 1972.

## Fewest Total Bases, Season, Minimum 500 Plate Appearances

NL—117—Leo Durocher, St. Louis, 1937

AL—115—Hunter Hill, St. Louis-Washington, 1904. A member of one of the worst teams in history, the 1904 Senators, Hill retained his third base job despite posting a .197 BA and a .224 SA.

## Most Total Bases, Game

NL—18—Joe Adcock, Milwaukee Braves, July 31, 1954, against Brooklyn in Ebbets Field; four home runs and a double.

AL—16—Held by several players. The first to do it was Ty Cobb, who hit three home runs, two singles and a double in six at bats against the St. Louis Browns in Sportsman's Park on May 5, 1925. The next day Cobb hit two more homers, making him the first player since Cap Anson in 1884 to hit five home runs in two games.

# Record Slugging Averages

Once again we find the same two names at the head of the class. In 1920 Babe Ruth compiled a 20th-century record .847 slugging average when he clubbed 54 home runs in only 458 at bats. Five years later Rogers Hornsby slugged at a .756 clip to set the National League record.

**Highest Slugging Average, Season, 1901 through 1919**
AL—.657—Babe Ruth, Boston, 1919
NL—.571—Heinie Zimmerman, Chicago, 1912

**Highest Slugging Average, Season, 1941 through 1960**
AL—.731—Ted Williams, Boston, 1957; the last player to slug .700 in a strike-free season prior to 1996
NL—.702—Stan Musial, St. Louis, 1948

**Highest Slugging Average, Season, 1961 through 1976**
AL—.687—Mickey Mantle, New York, 1961
NL—.669—Hank Aaron, Atlanta, 1971

**Highest Slugging Average, Season, 1977 through 1993**
NL—.677—Barry Bonds, San Francisco, 1993
AL—.664—George Brett, Kansas City, 1980

**Highest Slugging Average, Season, since 1994**
NL—.863—Barry Bonds, San Francisco, 2001
AL—.730—Mark McGwire, Oakland, 1996

**Most Seasons League Leader in Slugging Average**
AL—13—Babe Ruth, last in 1931
NL—9—Rogers Hornsby, last in 1929

**Highest Slugging Average, Season, by Runner-up to League Leader**

AL—.765—Lou Gehrig, New York, 1927; second to Babe Ruth who slugged .777

NL—.687—Chuck Klein, Philadelphia, 1930; second to Hack Wilson, Chicago, who slugged .723

**Lowest Slugging Average, Season, League Leader in Slugging Average**

NL—.436—Hy Myers, Brooklyn, 1919

AL—.466—Elmer Flick, Cleveland, 1905

**Lowest Slugging Average, Season, since 1920, League Leader in Slugging Average**

AL—.476—Snuffy Stirnweiss, New York, 1945

NL—.521—Johnny Mize, New York Giants, 1942

**Lowest Slugging Average, Season, since 1961, League Leader in Slugging Average**

AL—.502—Reggie Jackson, Baltimore, 1976

NL—.536—Will Clark, San Francisco, 1991

**Lowest Slugging Average, Season, Minimum 400 at Bats**

19th Century—.197—Jim Lillie, Kansas City, National League, 1886, 416 at bats and 82 total bases

20th Century—.206—Pete Childs, Philadelphia, National League, 1902, 403 at bats and 83 total bases

**Lowest Slugging Average, Season, since 1901, Minimum 500 at Bats**

AL—.240—Jim Levey, St. Louis, 1933; 529 at bats and 127 total bases

NL—.242—Al Bridwell, Boston, 1907; 509 at bats and 123 total bases

**Smallest Differential between Slugging Average and Batting Average, Season, since 1901, Minimum 500 at Bats**

NL—19 points—Spike Shannon, St. Louis and New York Giants, 1906; .256 batting average and .275 slugging average

AL—22 points—Hunter Hill, St. Louis and Washington, 1904; .204 batting average and .226 slugging average

**Special Mention**

Only one player in major-league history, Roger Metzger, was a league leader more than once in an extra-base hit department and yet retired with a career slugging average that was under .300. Metzger tied for the National League in triples in 1972, then led alone in 1974 before an amputated finger forced him to quit in 1980 with a .231 career batting average and a .293 career slugging average.

# THE 10 HIGHEST CAREER SLUGGING AVERAGES

|  | | Years Active | SA |
|---|---|---|---|
| 1. | Babe Ruth | 1914–35 | .690 |
| 2. | Ted Williams | 1939–60 | .634 |
| 3. | Lou Gehrig | 1923–39 | .632 |
| 4. | Jimmie Foxx | 1925–45 | .609 |
| 5. | Hank Greenberg | 1930–47 | .605 |
| 6. | Mark McGwire | 1986–2001 | .588 |
| 7. | Joe DiMaggio | 1938–51 | .579 |
| 8. | Rogers Hornsby | 1915–37 | .577 |
| 9. | Johnny Mize | 1936–53 | .562 |
| 10. | Stan Musial | 1941–63 | .559 |

**Highest Career Slugging Average, Player Active Primarily between 1901 and 1919**

.517—Joe Jackson, 1908–20

**Highest Career Slugging Average, Player Active Primarily between 1942 and 1960**

.559—Stan Musial, 1941–63

**Highest Career Slugging Average, Player Active Primarily after 1961**

.557—Willie Mays, 1951–73

**Highest Career Slugging Average, Player with under .300 Career Batting Average, Prior to Mark McGuire**

First Place—.557—Mickey Mantle, 1951–68; .298 batting average. Mantle ranks 12th on the career list

Second Place—.548—Ralph Kiner, 1946–55; .279 batting average

**Lowest Career Slugging Average, Player with .300 Career Batting Average**
.355—Patsy Donovan, 1890–1907; .301 batting average.

Among players with 2,000 hits, Donovan also has the second-fewest extra-base hits. Of his 2,253 hits, .868 percent of them were singles. Maury Wills, with a single percentage of .874, ranks first in fewest extra-base hits.

## TOP 10 SLUGGING AVERAGES
## AMONG ACTIVE PLAYERS

### (Minimum 3000 at bats)

|  | | First Year | SA |
|---|---|---|---|
| 1. | Todd Helton | 1997 | .616 |
| 2. | Barry Bonds | 1986 | .602 |
| 3. | Manny Ramirez | 1993 | .598 |
| 4. | Vladimir Guerrero | 1996 | .588 |
| 5. | Alex Rodriguez | 1994 | .581 |
| 6. | Mike Piazza | 1992 | .572 |
| 7. | Frank Thomas | 1990 | .568 |
|  | Jim Thome | 1991 | .568 |
| 9. | Larry Walker | 1989 | .567 |
| 10. | Brian Giles | 1995 | .563 |
|  | Juan Gonzalez | 1989 | .563 |

# Long Day's Journey

The 1920 season was less than a month old when a reminder was served that even though the deadball era was over a whiff of it still lingered. On May 1, in Boston, the Brooklyn Dodgers hooked up in a 26-inning 1–1 tie with the Braves that will probably always stand as both the longest game in major-league history and the longest game not played to a decision. What made the game most seem like a throwback to an earlier time, however, was not its extraordinary length but the fact that both starting pitchers, Leon Cadore of the Dodgers and Joe Oeschger of the Braves, went all the way. The following day the Dodgers played 13 innings against the Phillies and then went into overtime again on May 3 against the Braves, losing to them 2–1 in 19 innings. Brooklyn's three-game total of 58 innings played—the equivalent of six and a half games—is a record that has never been even remotely challenged.

**Longest Game Played to a Decision, Same Day**

NL—25 innings—St. Louis 4, New York Mets 3, September 11, 1974; also the longest night game in major-league history

AL—24—innings—Philadelphia 4, Boston 1, September 1, 1906. Both Jack Coombs of the A's and Joe Harris of the Red Sox went all the way. Harris, rarely the recipient of any support from his teammates, had a dreadful 3–21 record and .087 winning percentage in 1906, the second-worst performance since 1901 by a 20-game loser, behind only Jack Nabors who was 1–20 in 1916.

**Longest 1–0 Game, since 1901**

24 innings—Houston 1, New York Mets 0, April 15, 1968

**Most Innings without Scoring, One Day**

27—St. Louis Cardinals, July 2, 1933, lost the first game of a double-header 1–0 to Carl Hubbell and the New York Giants in 18 innings, then were blanked 1–0 again in the nightcap by Roy Parmalee.

## Longest Day's Work to No Avail
On May 31, 1964, the New York Mets lost a double-header to San Francisco that consumed an all-time record 10½ hours; the nightcap, in addition, lasted 23 innings.

## Longest Game in Organized Baseball History
33 innings—Pawtucket 3, Rochester 2, International League, April 19, 1981. The game was suspended at 4:07 A.M. after 32 innings with the score 2–2, then completed that night, with Pawtucket pushing across the winning run almost as soon as the game was resumed. The longest game that was not interrupted by suspension was played on June 14, 1966, between Miami and St. Petersburg of the Class A Florida State League, Miami, managed by Billy DeMars, winning 4–3 in 29 innings over Sparky Anderson's St. Pete Club.

## Last Team to Play Two Opponents in One Day
Rainouts in 2000 forced the Indians into a situation whereby they had to entertain the division-winning Chicago White Sox on the afternoon of September 25 at Jacobs Field, then shower, change uniforms and return to the field that night to drop a very costly 4–2 decision to the lowly Minnesota Twins.

## Most Days in a Row, since 1901, Playing No Opponents
10—Philadelphia Phillies, 1909. On August 19 a prolonged spell of poor weather in the East resulted in the Phillies being rained out for the 10th straight day.

## Only Tripleheader in Which All Three Games Went the Full Nine Innings
September 1, 1890—Brooklyn Bridegrooms (NL) versus Pittsburgh Innocents (NL). The Bridegrooms swept the triple bill—10–9, 3–2, and 8–4—and went on to win the National League pennant that season. Not surprisingly, Pittsburgh finished in the cellar, 66½ games behind Brooklyn.

# Iron-Man Pitchers

On June 19, 1927, Jack Scott of the Phillies pitched both ends of a double-header against the Reds, winning the first game 3–1 and then losing the nightcap 3–0. Thirty-five at the time, Scott became the oldest major-league player ever to pitch two complete games in one day. No one realized then that he would also be the last major-league player to do it.

**First Pitcher to Win Two Complete Games in One Day**
Candy Cummings, Hartford, beat Cincinnati 14–4 and 8–4 on September 9, 1876.

**First Pitcher to Win Two Complete Games in One Day, Mound at its Present Distance**
Cy Seymour of the New York Giants, while beating Louisville 6–1 and 10–6 on June 3, 1897, became the first pitcher to win a doubleheader after the mound was moved to 60 feet 6 inches from the plate. The second game was called after seven innings.

**First Pitcher to Pitch Two Complete Games in One Day, since 1901**
Joe McGinnity of the Baltimore Orioles worked both ends of a doubleheader twice in 1901, splitting on each occasion. On August 1, 1903, McGinnity became the first pitcher in this century to win both ends of a doubleheader. With the Giants by then, he won two more complete-game doubleheaders before the month was out, the last on August 31.

**Only Pitcher since 1901, Besides McGinnity, to Win Two Complete Games in One Day More Than Once**
Pete Alexander of the Phillies in 1916 and again in 1917

## Only Pitcher Since 1901, Besides McGinnity, to Pitch More Than Two Complete-Game Doubleheaders

Mule Watson did it twice with the Philadelphia A's in 1918 and a third time in 1921 with the Boston Braves. His record for the six games was three wins, two losses and one tie.

## Only Pitcher to Hurl Two Complete-Game Shutouts in One Day

Ed Reulbach of the Cubs, in the thick of the 1908 pennant race, beat Brooklyn 5–0 and 3–0 on September 26.

## Only Pitcher to Be Involved in Two Complete-Game 1-0 Decisions in One Day

On July 31, 1915, Dave Davenport, pitching for the St. Louis Terriers in the Federal League, beat Buffalo 1–0 and then lost the second game of the twin bill 1–0. Davenport gave up only five hits that day—and just one in the game he lost.

## Last Pitcher to Win Two Complete Games in One Day

Emil Levsen, Cleveland, beat the Boston Red Sox 6–1 and 5–1 on August 28, 1926. Levsen did it without striking out a batter in either game. Johnny "Stud" Stuart of the St. Louis Cardinals also pitched a double-header win against the Boston Braves in 1923 without registering a single strike-out that day. Stuart's performance enabled rookie Harry McCurdy, who caught both games, to set a major-league mark when he completed the twin bill without handling a single chance.

## First Pitcher to Lose Two Complete Games in One Day

Dave Anderson of Pittsburgh lost two of the three games the Innocents dropped in their tripleheader loss to the Brooklyn Bridegrooms on September 1, 1890.

## Only Pitcher in This Century to Lose Two Complete Games in One Day

Wiley Piatt, Boston Braves, lost 1–0 and 5–3 to Pittsburgh on June 25, 1903.

## Closest Any Pitcher Has Come since 1927 to Hurling Two Complete Games in One Day

On September 6, 1950, Don Newcombe of the Brooklyn Dodgers started both ends of a doubleheader against the league-leading Phillies. Newcombe shut out the Phils 2–0 in the opener but left in the sixth inning of the nightcap, trailing 2–0.

## Last Pitcher to Start Both Ends of a Doubleheader

Wilbur Wood, Chicago White Sox, on July 20, 1973, against the Yankees. He was knocked out in both games and wound up with two losses that day.

# No-Hitters and Perfect Games

On April 30, 1922, Charlie Robertson of the White Sox became the first pitcher in major-league history to hurl a perfect game on the road when he beat Detroit 2–0 at Navin Field. It was the fourth perfect game in the American League since 1904, but after Robertson's masterpiece there was a 34-year drought before Don Larsen of the Yankees pitched a perfect game in the 1956 World Series.

## CHRONOLOGY OF FULL-LENGTH PERFECT GAMES

| | |
|---|---|
| June 12, 1880 | Lee Richmond; Worcester defeated Cleveland (NL) 1–0. |
| June 17, 1880 | Monte Ward; Providence defeated Buffalo (NL) 5–0. |
| May 5, 1904 | Cy Young; Boston defeated Philadelphia (AL) 1–0. |
| October 2, 1908 | Addie Joss; Cleveland defeated Chicago (AL) 1–0.[1] |
| April 30, 1922 | Charlie Robertson; Chicago defeated Detroit (AL), 2–0. |
| October 8, 1956 | Don Larsen; New York (AL) defeated Brooklyn (NL) 2–0.[2] |
| May 29, 1959 | Harvey Haddix; Pittsburgh lost to Milwaukee (NL), 1–0 in 13 innings.[3] |
| June 21, 1964 | Jim Bunning; Philadelphia defeated New York Mets (NL) 6–0. |
| September 9, 1965 | Sandy Koufax; Los Angeles defeated Chicago (NL) 1–0. |
| May 8, 1968 | Catfish Hunter; Oakland defeated Minnesota (AL) 4–0. |

| May 15, 1981 | Len Barker; Cleveland defeated Toronto (AL) 3–0. |
| September 30, 1984 | Mike Witt; California defeated Texas (AL) 1–0. |
| September 16, 1988 | Tom Browning, Cincinnati, defeated Los Angeles (NL) 1–0. |
| July 28, 1991 | Dennis Martinez, Montreal, defeated Los Angeles (NL) 2–0. |
| July 28, 1994 | Kenny Rogers, Texas, defeated California (AL) 4–0. |
| May 17, 1998 | David Wells, New York, defeated Minnesota (AL) 4–0. |
| July 18, 1999 | David Cone, New York, defeated Montreal (NL) 6–0 |

[1]Probably the greatest clutch pitching job ever. Cleveland and Chicago were locked, along with Detroit, in the closest pennant race in American League history when Joss took the mound that day; his opponent was 40-game winner Ed Walsh.

[2]Larsen beat Sal Maglie in his perfect game; the last batter he faced, pinch hitter Dale Mitchell, took a called third strike on a 3–2 count.

[3]Haddix's gem was recognized at the time as a perfecto and hence is included. Major league baseball no longer recognizes it, though, which is why Pedro Martinez's nine-inning perfecto, ruined in the 10th, on June 3, 1995, is not included here.

## Close But No Cigar Award

On September 2, 2001, Mike Mussina lost his bid to become the third Yankee hurler in four years to toss a perfect game when Carl Everett of the Red Sox hit a two-out, two-strike pinch single in the bottom of the ninth, but many other pitchers on the brink of immortality have also suffered crushing disappointments.

First Prize—Hooks Wiltse. Hurling for the Giants on July 4, 1908, Wiltse had a perfect game with two out in the ninth inning of a scoreless contest and two strikes on his mound opponent, George McQuillan of the Phils. Wiltse then nicked McQuillan with a pitch to spoil his perfecto, although he did win 1–0 in ten innings.

Second Prize—Milt Pappas. On September 2, 1972, Pappas, working for the Cubs, was one pitch away from a perfect game when he walked San Diego pinch hitter Larry Stahl on a 3–2 count.

Third Prize—In 1958 Billy Pierce of the White Sox had a

1–0 lead over Washington and was one out away from a perfect game, the first by an American League left-hander, when pinch hitter Ed Fitzgerald stroked an opposite-field double.

Fourth Prize—Tommy Bridges of the Tigers shut out Washington 13–0 on August 15, 1932, but lost a perfect game with two out in the ninth inning when pinch hitter Dave Harris hit a bloop single.

Fifth Prize—In 1983 another Tigers pitcher, Milt Wilcox, saw his try for a perfect game slip away when Jerry Hairston of the White Sox singled with two out in the ninth inning.

On June 15, 1938, in the initial night game played at Ebbets Field, Johnny Vander Meer of the Reds no-hit the Dodgers 6–0 four days after he'd held the Braves hitless. Vander Meer's back-to-back gems were the first no-hitters in the National League since 1934 and made him the first player to pitch consecutive no-hitters as well as the first to throw two in the same season. Fifteen years earlier an American League pitcher, Howard Ehmke with the last-place Red Sox, narrowly missed earning the dual distinction that fell to Vander Meer. Ehmke no-hit the Athletics on September 7, 1923, and then lost his chance at a second straight no-hitter four days later when the official scorer called a ground ball that was misplayed by the Red Sox third baseman a single. The muffed grounder turned out to be the only hit off Ehmke, but the scorer might have only been trying to even up the breaks. While Ehmke had a valid argument that he'd been cheated out of a second no-hitter, he could not deny that his first one was a gift from Athletics pitcher Slim Harriss, who doubled off the right-field wall early in the game but was called out for missing first base.

## Pitcher Who Came the Closest After 1938 to Equaling Vander Meer's Feat

Ewell Blackwell of the Reds no-hit the Braves 6–0 on June 18, 1947. Following the same patterns as Vander Meer, he started against the Dodgers four days later and was working on a second consecutive no-hitter when Eddie Stanky singled with one out in the ninth inning.

## Second Pitcher to Throw Two No-Hitters in a Season

Allie Reynolds, New York Yankees, 1951. Three other pitchers have also done it—Virgil Trucks, Detroit Tigers, 1952; Jim Maloney, Cincinnati Reds, 1965; and Nolan Ryan,

California Angels, 1973. Trucks, who had only a 5–19 record for the season, won both his no-hitters by a 1–0 score and also hurled a 1–0 one-hit victory over Washington that year that was marred only by leadoff batter Eddie Yost's single on the first pitch of the game.

### First Pitcher to Hurl Three Career No-Hitters
Larry Corcoran, Chicago White Stockings, 1880, 1882 and 1884

### First Pitcher to Hurl Four Career No-Hitters
Sandy Koufax, Los Angeles Dodgers, threw no-hitters in four consecutive seasons (1962–65), the last one a perfect game.

### First Pitcher to Hurl Seven Career No-Hitters
Nolan Ryan (7), California Angels, 1973 (2), 1974, 1975; Houston Astros, 1981; and Texas Rangers, 1990, 1991

### First Pitcher to Hurl Two No-Hitters after 1901
Christy Mathewson, New York Giants, 1901 and 1905

### First Pitcher to Hurl Three No-Hitters after 1901
Bob Feller, Cleveland Indians, 1940, 1946 and 1951. Feller won all three of his no-hitters by one run and also pitched a record 12 complete-game one-hitters.

### First Major-League No-Hitter
It depends on what you believe was the first major league. On July 28, 1875, a couple of months before the National Association concluded its final season, Philadelphia's Joe Borden, aka Joe Josephs, no-hit Chicago 4–0. The following year, in the National League's first season, George Bradley of St. Louis no-hit Hartford 2–0 on July 28.

### Only Pitcher since 1893 to Hurl a No-Hitter in His First Start
Bobo Holloman, St. Louis Browns, held the Philadelphia A's hitless on May 6, 1953; it was his only complete game in the majors. Before the mound was moved to its present distance from the plate, Ted Breitenstein of the American Association St. Louis Browns, in 1891, and Bumpus Jones of the Cincinnati Reds, in 1892, also threw no-hitters in their first starts. On April 14, 1967, Red Sox rookie Bill Rohr, pitching in his first major-league game, saw his no-hit bid in Yankee

Stadium disappear when Elston Howard of the Yankees singled with two out in the ninth inning, Similarly, Padres yearling Jimmy Jones lost a no-hitter in his first major-league game on September 22, 1986, when Bob Knepper of the Astros, Jones's mound opponent, tripled for the lone hit the rookie surrendered in his 5–0 win.

## Most Famous No-Hit Game

A close call among several possible choices, but most pitching aficionados vote for the double no-hit duel on May 2, 1917, between the Reds' Fred Toney and Hippo Vaughn of the Cubs, won 1–0 by Toney in the 10th inning when Jim Thorpe drove in the winning run. The only other two double no-hit games in organized baseball history occurred in the minor leagues. The first came in 1952 in a Pony League game between Bradford and Batavia, and the second happened in 1992 when Andy Carter of the Clearwater Phillies in the Florida State League topped Scott Bakkum of the Winter Haven Red Sox, 1–0.

## First American League No-Hitter

On May 9, 1901, Cleveland's Earl Moore no-hit the White Sox for nine innings but lost 4–2 in the 10th, making him also the first pitcher in this century to lose a no-hit game.

## First Pitcher to Hurl a No-Hitter In Each League after 1900

Tom Hughes, Boston Braves, pitched a no-hitter against Pittsburgh in 1916 six years after he'd pitched a nine-inning no-hitter for the Yankees before losing 5–0 to Cleveland in the 11th. Jim Bunning was the second pitcher to throw a no-hitter in each league; Nolan Ryan was the third and most recent to do it.

## Only Teammates to Pitch No-Hitters on Consecutive Days

In 1917 two St. Louis Browns pitchers, Ernie Koob and Bob Groom, no-hit that year's World Champion, the White Sox, on consecutive days—May 5 and May 6—but not in consecutive games; Groom's no-hitter came in the second half of a double-header. Less than a month earlier, on April 14, 1917, Eddie Cicotte of the White Sox had no-hit the Browns 11–0. After May, the White Sox went the rest of the year without being involved in any more hitless games, but they still remain the only World Champion to be victimized twice in a season by no-hitters.

## Only No-Hitters Lost in Nine Innings

NL—On April 23, 1964, Ken Johnson of Houston became the only pitcher ever to lose a complete-game no-hitter in nine innings when he was beaten 1–0 by the Reds.

AL—On April 30, 1967, Steve Barber of the Orioles carried a no-hitter into the ninth inning against the Tigers, then was relieved by Stu Miller, who lost the game 2–1 on an error by shortstop Mark Belanger.

## Only Fans to See Their Team No-Hit Twice in Three Years and Yet Win Both Games

On May 26, 1956, Milwaukee fans watched Johnny Klippstein, Hersh Freeman and Joe Black of the Reds combine to no-hit the Braves through nine innings before losing in the tenth. Exactly three years later, on May 26, 1959, County Stadium hosted another no-hitter—indeed, the first perfect game in the National League since 1880—when the Pirates' Harvey Haddix held the Braves without a base runner for 12 innings before losing 1–0 in the 13th.

## Only Opening Day No-Hitters

NL—Red Ames, New York Giants, lost 3–0 to the Dodgers in 13 innings on April 15, 1909, after holding them hitless until the 10th inning.

AL—Bob Feller, Cleveland, defeated Chicago 1–0 on April 16, 1940.

## First Independence Day No-Hitters

NL—Hooks Wiltse, New York Giants, defeated Philadelphia 1–0 in 10 innings on July 4, 1908.

AL—George Mullin, Detroit, defeated St. Louis 7–0 on July 4, 1912, which also happened to be his 32nd birthday.

## Only No-Hitters to Clinch Titles

AL—Allie Reynolds, New York, 8–0 over Boston on September 28, 1951.

NL—Mike Scott, Houston, 2–0 over San Francisco on September 25, 1986.

## Pitcher Receiving the most Support While Throwing a No-Hitter

Frank Smith, Chicago White Sox, defeated Detroit 15–0 on September 6, 1905. Twenty years later, on September 19, 1925, Ted Lyons of the White Sox, about to put the final touch on a 17–0 no-hitter against Washington, instead became the first of many pitchers to fall prey to a Senators pinch hitter when Bobby Veach singled with two out in the ninth inning.

### First No-Hitter by Pitcher With Expansion Team

AL—Bo Belinsky, Los Angeles, defeated Baltimore 2–0 on May 5, 1962.

NL—Don Nottebart, Houston, defeated Philadelphia 4–1 on May 17, 1963.

# FIRST NO-HITTER FOR EACH TEAM AFTER 1900

## (Present Franchise Location Only)
## National League

| Team | Pitcher | Date | Opponent | Score |
|------|---------|------|----------|-------|
| Arizona | None | | | |
| Atlanta | Phil Niekro | August 7, 1973 | San Diego | 9–0[1] |
| Chicago | Bob Wicker | June 11, 1904 | New York | 1–0, 12 innings |
| Cincinnati | Fred Toney | May 2, 1917 | Chicago | 1–0, 10 innings |
| Colorado | None | | | |
| Florida | Al Leiter | May 11, 1996 | Colorado | 11–0 |
| Houston | Don Nottebart | May 17, 1963 | Philadelphia | 4–1 |
| Los Angeles | Sandy Koufax | June 30, 1962 | New York | 5–0[2] |
| Milwaukee | Juan Nieves | April 15, 1987 | Baltimore | 7–0 |
| Montreal | Bill Stoneman | April 17, 1969 | Philadelphia | 7–0 |
| New York | None | | | |
| Philadelphia | Chick Fraser | September 18, 1903 | Chicago | 10–0 |
| Pittsburgh | Nick Maddox | September 20, 1907 | Brooklyn | 2–1[3] |
| St. Louis | Jesse Haines | July 17, 1924 | Boston | 5–0 |
| San Diego | None | | | |
| San Francisco | Juan Marichal | June 15, 1963 | Houston | 1–0[4] |

[1]Frank Pfeffer pitched the first Boston Braves no-hitter, beating Cincinnati 6–0 on May 8, 1907; Jim Wilson pitched the first Milwaukee Braves no-hitter, beating Philadelphia 2–0 on June 12, 1954.

[2]Mal Eason pitched the first Brooklyn Dodgers no-hitter, beating St. Louis 2–0 on July 20, 1906.

[3]Maddox's no-hitter was the last by a Pittsburgh pitcher at home until John Candaleria no-hit Los Angeles 2–0 on August 9, 1976, at Three Rivers Stadium. No Pirate ever pitched a no-hitter at Forbes Field (1909–70)—nor, for that matter, did any pitcher for a visiting team.

[4]Christy Mathewson pitched the first New York Giants no-hitter, beating St. Louis 5–0 on July 15, 1901.

**Most One-Hitters, Season**
  4—Pete Alexander, Philadelphia, 1915. Alexander never pitched a no-hitter.

**Special Mention**
  Jim Barr also never pitched a no-hitter, but he once did something far more extraordinary. With the Giants in 1972, he retired a record 41 batters in a row over the course of two games before surrendering a double to Bernie Carbo of the Cardinals.

# American League

| Team | Pitcher | Date | Opponent | Score |
|------|---------|------|----------|-------|
| Baltimore | Hoyt Wilhelm | September 2, 1958 | New York | 1–0[1] |
| Boston | Cy Young | May 5, 1904 | Philadelphia | 3–0[2] |
| California | Bo Belinsky | May 5, 1962 | Baltimore | 2–0 |
| Chicago | Nixey Callahan | September 20, 1902 | Detroit | 3–0 |
| Cleveland | Earl Moore | May 9, 1901 | Chicago | 2–4, 10 innings |
| Detroit | George Mullin | July 4, 1912 | St. Louis | 7–0 |
| Kansas City | Steve Busby | April 27, 1973 | Detroit | 3–0 |
| Minnesota | Jack Kralick | August 26, 1963 | Kansas City | 1–0[3] |
| New York | Tom Hughes | August 30, 1910 | Cleveland | 0–5, 11 innings |
| Oakland | Catfish Hunter | May 8, 1968 | Minnesota | 4–0[4] |
| Seattle | Randy Johnson | June 2, 1990 | Detroit | 2–0 |
| Tampa Bay | None | | | |
| Texas | Jim Bibby | July 7, 1973 | Oakland | 6–0[5] |
| Toronto | Dave Stieb | September 2, 1990 | Cleveland | 3–0 |

[1]Earl Hamilton pitched the first St. Louis Browns no-hitter, beating Detroit 5–1 on August 30, 1912.
[2]Perfect game. Young's mound opponent that day was Rube Waddell.
[3]Walter Johnson pitched the first Washington Senators no-hitter, beating Boston 1–0 on July 1, 1920.
[4]Perfect game. Weldon Henley pitched the first Philadelphia A's no-hitter, beating St. Louis 6–0 on July 22, 1905. No A's pitcher threw a no-hitter while the franchise was in Kansas City.
[5]The franchise's first no-hitter. No member of the expansion Washington Senators ever threw one.

# Record-breaking Scorers

In 1939 third baseman Red Rolfe of the New York Yankees set a 20th-century record when he scored in 18 consecutive games (Cleveland's Kenny Lofton tied Rolfe's mark in 2000, the final year of the century); the all-time record is held by Billy Hamilton of the Philadelphia Phillies, who scored in 24 straight games in 1894. Rolfe was typical of a kind of player who flourished in the 1930s when runs were scored at a record rate, especially by the Yankees, but would have been only a footnote in any other era. Between 1934 and 1941 Rolfe scored 846 runs—an average of 105.8 per year—without ever having more than 14 home runs, 90 walks or 80 RBIs in a season. Moreover, his batting average during that span was under .300.

**Most Runs, Season, since 1901**
    AL—177—Babe Ruth, New York, 1921
    NL—158—Chuck Klein, Philadelphia, 1930

**Most Runs, Season, 1901 through 1919**
    AL—147—Ty Cobb, Detroit, 1911
    NL—139—Jesse Burkett, St. Louis, 1901

**Most Runs, Season, 1942 through 1960**
    AL—150—Ted Williams, Boston, 1949
    NL—137—Johnny Mize, New York Giants, 1947

**Most Runs, Season, 1961 through 1976**
    NL—137—Billy Williams, Chicago, 1970
    AL—132—Mickey Mantle and Roger Maris, New York, 1961

## Most Runs, Season, since 1977
NL—152—Jeff Bagwell, Houston, 2000
AL—146—Rickey Henderson, New York, 1985

## Most Years League Leader in Runs
AL—8—Babe Ruth, last in 1928
NL—5—George Burns, last in 1920; Rogers Hornsby, last in 1929; Stan Musial, last in 1954

## Most Years 150 or More Runs, since 1901
AL—6—Babe Ruth, last in 1930
NL—2—Chuck Klein, last in 1932

## Only Player to Score Six Runs in a Game Twice
Mel Ott, New York Giants, August 4, 1934, and again on April 30, 1944. The all-time record for the most runs scored in a game is seven, on August 15, 1886, by Guy Hecker of the Louisville Eclipse team in the American Association.

## Highest Percentage of Team's Runs Scored, Season
AL—.199—Burt Shotton, St. Louis, 1913, scored 105 of the Browns' 528 runs.
NL—.196—Tim Raines, Montreal, 1983, scored 133 of the Expos' 677 runs.

## Fewest Runs, Season, League Leader in Runs
NL—89—Gavvy Cravath, Philadelphia, 1915
AL—92—Harry Davis, Philadelphia, 1905

## CAREER TOP 10 IN RUNS

|  | | Years Active | Runs |
|---|---|---|---|
| 1. | Rickey Henderson | 1979– | 2295 |
| 2. | Ty Cobb | 1905–28 | 2246 |
| 3. | Babe Ruth | 1914–35 | 2174 |
|  | Hank Aaron | 1954–76 | 2174 |
| 5. | Pete Rose | 1963–86 | 2165 |
| 6. | Willie Mays | 1951–73 | 2062 |

|  | Years Active | Runs |
|---|---|---|
| 7. Stan Musial | 1941–63 | 1949 |
| 8. Barry Bonds | 1986– | 1941 |
| 9. Lou Gehrig | 1923–39 | 1888[1] |
| 10. Tris Speaker | 1907–28 | 1881[2] |

[1] In the 14 full seasons he played—1925-38—Gehrig averaged 134 runs per year.
[2] Tenth on the career list, although he was never a league leader in runs.

# The Three Most Interesting Teams between 1920 and 1941

## 1921 NEW YORK YANKEES
### W-98 L-55
### Manager: Miller Huggins

**Regular Lineup**—1B, Wally Pipp; 2B, Aaron Ward; 3B, Home Run Baker; SS, Roger Peckinpaugh; RF, Bob Meusel; CF, Elmer Miller; LF, Babe Ruth; C, Wally Schang; P, Carl Mays; P, Waite Hoyt; P, Bob Shawkey.

The first Yankees team to win a pennant and the first club in the 20th century to post a slugging average above .450, they also had the league's best pitching staff and could even run when necessary. Ruth, Meusel and Pipp, the three top RBI men, all tied for the club lead in stolen bases with 17, not a bad figure in 1921—only three players in the AL had as many as 25. Yankees pitchers led the AL with a 3.83 ERA and 481 strikeouts, the first number reflecting the sudden surge in run production, the latter number indicating that even with the increase in scoring batters weren't as yet swinging from the heels. Mays topped the AL with 27 wins a year after the Chapman tragedy. On the club also was Shotgun Rogers, who had killed John Dodge, a former major-league infielder, with a pitch in a 1916 Southern Association game.

# 1930 PHILADELPHIA PHILLIES
## W-52 L-102
## Manager: Burt Shotton

**Regular Lineup**—1B, Don Hurst; 2B, Fresco Thompson; 3B, Pinky Whitney; SS, Tommy Thevenow; RF, Chuck Klein; CF, Denny Sothern; LF, Lefty O'Doul; C, Spud Davis; P, Phil Collins; P. Ray Benge; P, Les Sweetland; P, Claude Willoughby; P, Hap Collard; P, Hal Elliott.

Spearheaded by Klein and O'Doul, the Phils scored 944 runs and had a .315 batting average. Yet they finished last, attributable mostly to their grisly pitching staff, which was the worst in this century. Collins posted a fine 16–11 record and Benge finished at 11–15, but the rest of the Phillies hurlers had a combined 25–76 mark and surrendered over 7.5 runs a game. Sweetland, Willoughby and Elliott were the leading culprits (see "Astronomical ERAs" for more about them), but Collard was only a notch better. Dead last in every pitching department except strikeouts, the 1930 Phillies allowed 1199 enemy base runners to cross the plate, a record that will almost surely never be broken. A year later the Phils still had the poorest pitching in the league but improved to sixth place when some of the rabbit was siphoned from the ball, reducing the number of runs they surrendered to 828. Twenty years later Shotton repaid Phillies fans for their patience with his efforts in 1930 by mismanaging a Brooklyn Dodgers team that lost the pennant to the Phils on the last day of the season.

# 1936 CLEVELAND INDIANS
## W-80 L-74
## Manager: Steve O'Neill

**Regular Lineup**—1B, Hal Trosky; 2B, Roy Hughes; 3B, Bad News Hale; SS, Bill Knickerbocker; RF, Roy Weatherly; CF, Earl Averill, LF, Joe Vosmik; C, Billy Sullivan; P, Johnny Allen; P, Mel Harder; P, Oral Hildebrand; P, Denny Galehouse; P, Lloyd Brown.

The Indians led the AL with a .304 batting average, had the league's RBI leader in Trosky, got a .351 season from catcher Sullivan, a .378 season from Averill, and 20 wins from Allen—yet finished in fifth place, albeit one game short of the best ever AL record for a second division team. The reasons they faltered were obvious; Harder, who posted 223 career wins, had an off year with a 15–15 record and a 5.17 ERA, and Joe Vosmik, after losing the 1935 batting crown on his last at bat of the season, sagged to a .287 mark. Apart from Harder and Vosmik, the team got good numbers from all its regulars and seemed only to be waiting on the development of a 17-year-old rookie phenom Bob Feller to make its move. By 1938 Feller was ready, but the Indians, it turned out, had peaked two years too early. They would not contend until 1940 and then only for that one season before once again falling back into the pack.

# MVP Award Winners

Between 1911 and 1914 the Chalmers Award, in the form of a new car, was given each season to the most valuable players in both leagues but was stopped largely because the rules stipulated that no player could win it twice. From 1922 through 1928 the American League gave a most valuable player award, with the voting limited to eight players, one from each team, and the National League followed suit, beginning in 1924 and continuing through 1929. But the league awards never quite managed to capture public fancy, and the concept of choosing a most valuable player was shelved until 1931 when the Baseball Writers Association of America revived it. They have selected two Most Valuable Players, one in each league, ever since.

**First BWAA Most Valuable Player Award Winner**
   AL—Lefty Grove, Philadelphia
   NL—Frankie Frisch, St. Lous

**First Player to Win Two MVP Awards**
   AL—Jimmie Foxx, Philadelphia, 1932 and 1933; also the first to win consecutive MVP Awards
   NL—Carl Hubbell, New York Giants, 1933 and 1936

**First Player to Win Three MVP Awards**
   AL—Jimmie Foxx, Philadelphia, Boston, 1932, 1933 and 1938
   NL—Stan Musial, St. Louis, 1943, 1946 and 1948

**First Player to Win Five MVP Awards**
   NL—Barry Bonds, Pittsburgh, San Francisco, 1990, 1992, 1993, 2001, 2002 and 2003

**First Player on a Second-Division Team to Win an MVP Award**
   NL—Hank Sauer, Chicago, 1952; the Cubs finished fifth.
   AL—None

**First Player to Win MVP Award and Cy Young Award in Same Season**
   NL—Don Newcombe, Brooklyn, 1956
   AL—Denny McLain, Detroit, 1968

**Youngest Player to Win MVP Award**
   AL—Vida Blue, Oakland, 1971; 22 years old.
   NL—Johnny Bench, Cincinnati, 1970; 22 years old.

**Oldest Player to Win MVP Award**
   NL—Willie Stargell, Pittsburgh; 39 years old
   AL—Spud Chandler, New York, 1943; 36 years old

**First Catcher to Win MVP Award**
   AL—Mickey Cochrane, Detroit, 1934
   NL—Gabby Hartnett, Chicago, 1935

**First Shortstop to Win MVP Award**
   NL—Marty Marion, St. Louis, 1944
   AL—Lou Boudreau, Cleveland, 1948

**First Third Baseman to Win MVP Award**
   NL—Bob Elliott, Boston, 1947
   AL—Al Rosen, Cleveland, 1953

**First Relief Pitcher to Win MVP Award**
   NL—Jim Konstanty, Philadelphia, 1950
   AL—Rollie Fingers, Milwaukee, 1981

**Only Second Baseman to Win Two MVP Awards**
   Joe Morgan, Cincinnati, 1975 and 1976

**Only Third Baseman to Win Two or More MVP Awards**
   Mike Schmidt, Philadelphia Phillies, (3) 1980, 1981 and 1986.

**Only Shortstops to Win Two MVP Awards**
   Ernie Banks, Chicago Cubs, 1958 and 1959
   Cal Ripken, Jr., Baltimore, 1983 and 1991

**Only Player to Win MVP Awards in Both Leagues**
Frank Robinson, Cincinnati (NL), 1961; Baltimore (AL), 1966.

**Only Pitcher to Win Consecutive MVP Awards**
Hal Newhouser, Detroit, 1944 and 1945.

**Only Rookie to Win MVP Award**
Fred Lynn, Boston Red Sox, 1975

**First Unanimous Selection for MVP Award**
AL—Hank Greenberg, Detroit, 1938
NL—Orlando Cepeda, St. Louis, 1967

**Teams That Have Never Had an MVP Award Winner**
NL—New York Mets, Montreal, Florida and Arizona
AL—Toronto and Tampa Bay. No St. Louis Browns player ever won an MVP Award before the franchise moved to Baltimore, nor did any player on either the original or the expansion Washington Senators.

**Teams with the Most MVP Winners**
AL—19—New York; but only two—Thurman Munson in 1976 and Don Mattingly in 1985—since 1963
NL—14—St. Louis

# All-Star Game Feats

In 1933 Arch Ward of the *Chicago Tribune* hit upon the notion of holding a major-league all-star game as an adjunct to the World's Fair in Chicago that year, and it has been an annual event ever since with the exception of 1945, the final year of World War II.

**First All-Star Game Home Run**
   AL—Babe Ruth, New York, in the very first game, July 6, 1933, at Comiskey Park
   NL—Frankie Frisch, St. Louis, also in the inaugural game

**First All-Star Game Won, League**
   AL—1933 at Comiskey Park, by a 4–2 score
   NL—1936 at Braves Field, by a 4–3 score. A record-low crowd of 25,556 attended after a story was circulated around Boston that the game was sold out when in fact there were still plenty of seats available.

**First Pitcher to Win Two All-Star Games**
   AL—Lefty Gomez, New York, 1933 and 1935. Gomez won a record third game in 1937 and then was the losing pitcher the following year, giving him an additional record of four decisions in All-Star play.
   NL—Bob Friend, Pittsburgh, 1956 and 1960 (first game)

**First Player to Hit Two Home Runs in All-Star Competition**
   NL—Frankie Frisch, St. Louis, 1933 and 1934
   AL—Lou Gehrig, New York, 1936 and 1937

**First Player to Hit Two Home Runs in One Game**
   Arky Vaughan, Pittsburgh, 1941 at Briggs Stadium, Detroit

## First Player to Get Four Hits in One Game

Joe Medwick, St. Louis Cardinals, 1937 at Griffith Stadium, Washington

## Longest Pitching Stint in an All-Star Game

Lefty Gomez of the Yankees went six innings as the starting pitcher for the American League in 1935, at Cleveland, as the AL won 4–1. The rules then did not limit pitchers to three innings.

## Most Memorable Single Feat in All-Star Play

Probably Carl Hubbell's five consecutive strikeouts at the Polo Grounds in 1934. Hubbell opened the game by giving up a single to Charlie Gehringer and a walk to Heinie Manush. Then he fanned Babe Ruth, Lou Gehrig and Jimmie Foxx to end the first inning and began the second inning by whiffing Al Simmons and Joe Cronin. Hubbell's record for consecutive strikeouts in an All-Star Game was tied in 1986 by Fernando Valenzuela, who fanned Don Mattingly, Cal Ripken, Jesse Barfield, Lou Whitaker and Ted Higuera in order.

## Most Serious Injury in All-Star Play

NL—Dizzy Dean's broken toe, suffered when Earl Averill of Cleveland hit a line drive off Dean's foot in the first inning of the 1937 game. Dean pitched three innings before giving in to the injury, then tried to come back from it too soon, hurt his arm and was never the same pitcher.

AL—Ted Williams's broken elbow, sustained when he crashed into the left-field wall in the first inning of the 1950 game at Comiskey Park. The injury kayoed Williams until late in the season, and without him the Red Sox lost the pennant by four games.

## Most Exciting All-Star Game

The 1950 game gets my vote for several reasons. Not only was it the first extra-inning game and the first one televised, but when Red Schoendienst homered in the top of the 14th inning to win 4–3 for the NL, it seemed to have an odd impact on the American League that has lasted ever since. Prior to 1950, the AL held a 12–4 lead in games; by 1964 the NL had caught up. A year later the NL took the lead for the first time in games won and is now ahead 39 to 29 with 2 ties.

## Second Most Exciting Game

The 1957 game at Sportsman's Park, won by the AL 6–5. After scoring three runs in the top of the ninth inning, the AL led 6–2, but the NL came back with three runs in the bottom half and had the tying run on base when Minnie Minoso speared Gil Hodges's line drive to end the game.

## Highest-Scoring Game

The 1954 game at Cleveland Stadium won by the AL 11–9. You won't get much of an argument from my corner if you vote this also the most exciting game.

## Most Lop-sided Game

The 1946 game at Fenway Park, won by the AL 12–0 as Ted Williams hit two home runs, compiled a record 10 total bases and five RBIs, also a record, later tied by Al Rosen in the 1954 game.

## Last Time Prior to 1989 AL Won Two Games in a Row

In 1958 at Baltimore. The following year two games were played, an experiment that lasted until 1962; in that four-year span the NL won five of the eight games with one a tie, in 1961 at Fenway Park, when rain began falling after the ninth inning with the score knotted 1–1.

## First Indoor Game

In 1968 at the Astrodome. It was also the first 1–0 game and the only game in which no player had an RBI. The NL's winning run scored in the bottom of the first inning as Willie McCovey of the Giants hit into a double play.

## First Game Played Outside the United States

In 1982 at Montreal, won by the NL, 4–1.

## Last of the 16 Teams that Existed in 1933 to Host a Game

The Philadelphia Phillies. The 1943 game was played in Shibe Park, their home ground, but the Athletics were the hosts. By the time the Phillies finally got the honor in 1952 both the White Sox and Tigers had hosted two games. To add to the grief of Phillies fans, who'd waited nearly 20 years to see their club in the host's role, rain forced the game to be called after five innings.

## Best Pitcher in All-Star Play
AL—Mel Harder, Cleveland, appeared in four games, a total of 13 innings, without allowing an earned run.

NL—Juan Marichal, San Francisco, in 18 innings of All-Star play gave up only one earned run.

## Most Career Strikeouts by Pitcher in All-Star Play
19—Don Drysdale, Los Angeles.

## Most All-Star Appearances
24—Stan Musial, Willie Mays and Hank Aaron

## Most Career Hits in All-Star Play
23—Willie Mays

## Most Career Home Runs in All-Star Play
6—Stan Musial

## Most Career Total Bases in All-Star Play
40—Stan Musial and Willie Mays

## Most Career RBIs in All-Star Play
12—Ted Williams

## First Player to Win Two All-Star Game MVP Awards
Willie Mays, 1963 and 1968

## Most Recent Player to Win Two All-Star Game MVP Awards
Cal Ripken, 1991 and 2001

## Most Recent Player to Win All-Star Game MVP Award Playing for Losing Team
Carl Yastrzemski, 1970, when the AL lost 5–4 in 12 innings. Altogether there have been seven extra-inning All-Star Games, and the NL has won all seven.

# Shortstops' Records

I'm probably going to make myself even more unpopular with sabermetricians when I say that there is no way we are ever going to be able to gauge which shortstop had the greatest range, the best arm or the surest glove. Statistics alone can't give us any of these answers, and no one has had the fortune to see all of the contenders for the title of best-ever play, let alone play under conditions similar enough to allow meaningful comparisons to be made. But statistics do tell us that two of the top-hitting shortstops of all time were Luke Appling and Arky Vaughan, and that both were active in the 1930s. Appling and Vaughan were not just offensive standouts, however. Both were also among the best glovemen of the era, and Vaughan regularly led the NL in double plays and assists. By the time World War II began they had been joined by five outstanding young shortstops—Lou Boudreau, Marty Marion, Pee Wee Reese, Eddie Miller and Phil Rizzuto—perhaps the most massive gathering of fielding talent at the position in history. These five men would sweep the vast majority of fielding honors in both leagues during the 1940s, and three of them would win Most Valuable Player Awards.

## SEASON BATTING RECORDS

| Department | National League | American League |
| --- | --- | --- |
| Batting Average | .401, HUGHIE JENNINGS, Baltimore, 1896<br>.385, Arky Vaughan, Pittsburgh, 1935* | .388 Luke Appling, Chicago, 1936 |
| Slugging Average | .614 Ernie Banks, Chicago, 1958 | .631 ALEX RODRIGUEZ, Seattle, 1996 |

| Department | National League | American League |
|---|---|---|
| Home Runs | 47, Ernie Banks, Chicago, 1958 | 57, ALEX RODRIGUEZ, Texas, 2002 |
| RBIs | 143, Ernie Banks, Chicago, 1959 | 159, VERN STEPHENS, Boston 1949 |
| Runs | 159, HUGHIE JENNINGS, Baltimore, 1895<br>132, Pee Wee Reese, Brooklyn, 1949* | 141, Alex Rodriguez. Seattle, 1996 |
| Hits | 211, Garry Templeton, St. Louis, 1978 | 219, DEREK JETER, New York, 1999 |
| Doubles | 54, Mark Grudzielanek, Montreal, 1997 | 56, NOMAR GARCIAPARRA, Boston, 2002 |
| Triples | 24, ED MCKEAN, Cleveland, 1893<br>20, Honus Wagner, Pittsburgh, 1912* | 21, Bill Keister, Baltimore, 1901 |
| Total Bases | 379, Ernie Banks, Chicago, 1958 | 393, ALEX RODRIGUEZ, Texas, 2001 |
| Stolen Bases | 104, MAURY WILLS, Los Angeles, 1962 | 62, Bert Campaneris, Oakland, 1968 |
| Bases on Balls | 118, Arky Vaughan, Pittsburgh, 1936 | 149, EDDIE JOOST, Philadelphia, 1949 |
| Strikeouts | 188, JOSE HERNANDEZ, Milwaukee, 2002 | 149, Alex Gonzalez, Toronto, 2001 |
| Fewest Strikeouts | 5, Charlie Hollocher, Chicago, 1922 | 4, JOE SEWELL, Cleveland, 1925 |

*Record since 1901

## Most Games, Career, at Shortstop
2581—Luis Aparicio, 1956–73

## Most Consecutive Games at Shortstop
2216—Cal Ripken, Jr., July 1, 1982 through July 15, 1996, after which he was moved temporarily to third base, but his consecutive-games-played streak eventually reached 2632.

## Best Career Fielding Average
.983—Omar Vizquel, 1989–

# EVOLUTION OF SEASON RECORD FOR BEST FIELDING AVERAGE

|  | Team | League | Year | Average |
|---|---|---|---|---|
| Johnny Peters | Chicago | National | 1876 | .932 |
| George Wright | Boston | National | 1878 | .947[1] |
| George Davis | Chicago | American | 1902 | .951[2] |
| Tommy Corcoran | Cincinnati | National | 1905 | .952 |
| Terry Turner | Cleveland | American | 1906 | .960 |
| Terry Turner | Cleveland | American | 1910 | .973[3] |
| Everett Scott | Boston | American | 1919 | .976[4] |
| Eddie Miller | Boston | National | 1942 | .983[5] |
| Ernie Banks | Chicago | National | 1959 | .985 |
| Larry Bowa | Philadelphia | National | 1971 | .987 |
| Ed Brinkman | Detroit | American | 1972 | .990 |
| Larry Bowa | Philadelphia | National | 1979 | .991 |
| Tony Fernandez | Toronto | American | 1989 | .992 |
| Cal Ripken | Baltimore | American | 1990 | .996 |
| Mike Bordick | Baltimore | American | 2002 | .998 |

[1]Though documented; many of the relatively high fielding averages in the National League's early years are suspect, Wright's among them. Official scorers of that period were notoriously uneven. Testimony to this is that despite continuous improvements in gloves and overall playing conditions Wright's mark stood unchallenged, even by Wright himself, until 1895 when Hughie Jennings of Baltimore became only the second shortstop to field .940 or better.

[2]Seldom mentioned anymore by historians, Davis was not only a fine fielder but also at one time held the record for most career hits by a switch hitter.

[3]Turner's 1910 mark includes games he played at other infield positions. Even so, he was undoubtedly one of the top fielders of his era, good enough to be the only player ever to hold simultaneously a season record for the best fielding average at two different positions—shortstop and third base.

[4]Scott's record, long forgotten, can now be seen to have been a quantum leap; he also fielded just a hair lower in 1918.

[5]Lou Boudreau fielded .983 in 1944, but injuries kept him from playing in enough games to qualify as a record breaker.

## Most Seasons League Leader in Fielding Average

AL—8—Everett Scott, 1916 through 1923 consecutive; Lou Boudreau, last in 1948; Luis Aparicio, 1959 through 1966 consecutive.

NL—8—Ozzie Smith, last in 1994

## Most Consecutive Errorless Games
110—Mike Bordick, Baltimore, April 11, 2002, through close of 2002 season; ended April 2, Opening Day, 2003

## Most Consecutive Errorless Chances
During his record errorless games streak of 110, Bordick also set a new mark for errorless chances at 544.

## Most Chances Accepted, Career
12,564—Luis Aparicio, 1956–73

## Most Chances Accepted, Season
984—Dave Bancroft, New York Giants, 1922

## Most Chances Accepted, Game, Nine Innings, since 1902
19—Eddie Joost, Cincinnati Reds, May 7, 1941

## Most Consecutive Games, No Chances accepted
3—Tommy Tresh, New York Yankees, August 30, August 31 and September 1, 1968

## Most Assists, Season
621—Ozzie Smith, San Diego Padres, 1980

## Most Assists, Game, Nine Innings, since 1901
14—Tommy Corcoran, Cincinnati Reds, August 7, 1903

## Most Seasons League Leader in Assists
AL—7—Luke Appling, last in 1946; Luis Aparicio, last in 1968; Cal Ripken, Jr., last in 1993
NL—8—Ozzie Smith, last in 1989

## Most Double Plays, Season
AL—147—Rick Burleson, Boston, 1980
NL—137—Bobby Wine, Montreal, 1970

## Most Years League Leader in Double Plays
AL—7—Cal Ripken, Jr., last in 1994

NL—5—Mickey Doolan, last in 1913; Dick Groat, last in 1964; Ozzie Smith, last in 1991

**Most Gold Glove Awards**
13—Ozzie Smith, 1980–92 consecutive

# Astronomical ERAs

The law that for every action there is an equal and opposite reaction applies not only in physics but also in baseball. While slugging statistics and scoring totals were soaring in the 1920s and 1930s so were pitchers' ERAs. In 1930 Remy Kremer of the Pirates became the first pitcher in major-league history to win 20 games despite allowing over five earned runs (5.02) per each nine innings he worked. Before the decade was out Bobo Newsom had won 20 games with an even higher ERA, and Roxie Lawson of the Tigers had somehow managed to achieve an 18–7 record and a dazzling .720 winning percentage in 1937 on a 5.27 ERA. But Kremer, Newsom and Lawson were stingy with enemy batters compared to three other pitchers in the 1930s who posted the three worst season ERAs since 1901 among hurlers in 150 or more innings.

**The Terrible Trio**
   First Prize—Les Sweetland, Philadelphia Phillies, 1930; 7.71 ERA in 167 innings
   Second Prize—Claude Willoughby, Philadelphia Phillies, 1930; 7.59 ERA in 153 innings
   Third Prize—Jim Walkup, St. Louis Browns, 1937; 7.36 ERA in 150 innings

**Highest ERA, Season, since 1942, ERA Qualifier**
   Jim Deshaies, Minnesota Twins, 1994, 7.39 ERA in 130.1 innings. Deshaies' ERA in the truncated 1994 campaign set a new AL record for the worst ERA by a pitcher in enough innings to qualify for the loop ERA crown.

**Highest ERA, Season, 1901 through 1919, 150 Innings**
   5.30—Orlie Weaver, Chicago Cubs and Boston Braves, 1911; 165 innings

**Highest ERA, Season, Prior to 1901, Minimum 10 Starts**
  10.32—Bill Stecher, Philadelphia, American Association, 1890

**Highest ERA, Season, since 1901, Minimum 10 Starts**
  10.64—Roy Halladay, Toronto, 2000. In Halladay's 67.2 innings, hitters ripped him for a .357 BA and a .439 OBP. Somehow he still managed to win four games in 11 decisions.

**Highest ERA, Season, League Leader in ERA**
  AL—3.20—Early Wynn, Cleveland, 1950
  NL—3.08—Bill Walker, New York Giants, 1929

**Highest ERA, Season 20-Game Winner**
  1893–1900—4.92—Kid Carsey (24–16), Philadelphia, 1895
               Brickyard Kennedy (24–20), Brooklyn, 1894, Clark Griffith (21–11), Chicago, 1894
  1901–19—3.83—Henry Schmidt (22–13), Brooklyn, 1903
  1920–41—5.08—Bobo Newsom (20–16), St. Louis Browns, 1938
  1942–60—4.07—Lew Burdette (21–15), Milwaukee Braves, 1959
  1961–76—4.08—Jim Merritt (20–12), Cincinnati Reds, 1970
  1977–93—4.04—Jack Morris (21–6), Toronto Blue Jays, 1992
  1994–2001—4.41—Rick Helling (20–7), Texas Rangers, 1998

# HALL OF FAME PITCHERS WITH THE HIGHEST CAREER ERAS

|  | Years Active | Wins | ERA |
|---|---|---|---|
| 1. Red Ruffling | 1924–47 | 273 | 3.80 |
| 2. Ted Lyons | 1923–46 | 260 | 3.67 |
| 3. Jesse Haines | 1918–37 | 210 | 3.64 |
| 4. Herb Pennock | 1912–34 | 241 | 3.61 |
| 5. Waite Hoyt | 1918–38 | 237 | 3.59 |

## Highest Career ERA, 200-Game Winner

4.36—Earl Whitehill, 1923–39. Lew Burdette has never revealed whom he chose as his model when he was learning to pitch, but Whitehill would be a good guess. In 3566 innings he gave up 3917 hits and 1431 walks while striking out only 1350 batters. Yet he won 218 games and lost only 185.

## Winner of the "Where Did He Go Wrong?" Award

Russ Van Atta. As a rookie with the 1933 Yankees, Van Atta pitched a shutout in his first major-league start and finished with a 12–4 record. Traded to the Browns in 1935, he twice led the American League in mound appearances and lasted until 1939 solely, it would seem, in the hope that he'd recover his early form. But Van Atta only got worse and worse. By the time he retired he'd absorbed so many fearful shellings that he had a 5.60 career ERA, the third highest in history among pitchers in over 700 innings. Whatever the Browns' strategy was in those years, it apparently didn't include molding a decent pitching staff. While they were clinging to Van Atta and Jim Walkup, they cut people like Fay Thomas, who won seven games in 1935 on a respectable (for the Browns) 4.78 ERA and all during the 1930s was regarded as one of the top pitchers in the minors.

## Winner of the "Team That Never Learned How to Pick Them" Award

The Browns. In their 52-year history they never had a single ERA leader, and in 1951 they contrived to put together a mound staff that for a time had on it possibly the two worst pitchers ever—Sid Schacht and Irv Medlinger. Schacht, mainly a relief pitcher, worked in 19 games in 1950–51, gave up 44 hits and 21 walks in 22 innnings and left with a 14.34 ERA, the 20th-century high among pitchers in more than 20 innings, Medlinger, who had a 13.83 ERA in 14 innings, is fourth among 20th-century pitchers who worked more than 12 innings.

## The All-Time Worst Career ERAs

100 Innings—8.86—Andy Larkin, 105.2 innings (1996, 1998–2000)

8.30—John McDougal, 125 innings (1895–96)

7.69—Mark Holzemer, 100.2 innings (1993, 1995–98, 2000)

7.60—Bill Rhodes, 152 innings (1893)
7.39—David Wainhouse, 104.2 innings (1991, 1993, 1996–2000)
7.20—Jake Boyd, 136 innings (1894–96)

250 Innings—6.99—Bill Kissinger, 319 innings (1895–97)
6.95—Hal Elliott, 322 innings (1929–32)

400 Innings—6.74—Jim Walkup, 462 innings (1934–39)
6.10 Les Sweetland, 741 innings (1927–31)

800 Innings—5.84—Claude Willoughby, 841 innings (1925–31)
5.45—Les German, 859 innings (1890, 1893–97)

1000 Innings—5.11—Mike Sullivan, 1123 innings (1889–99)
5.04—Willie Blair, 1274 innings (1990–2000)
5.02—Chief Hogsett, 1222 innings (1929–44)
5.01—Roy Mahaffey, 1056 innings (1926–36)
4.97—Jack Knott, 1557 innings (1933–46)
4.95—Kid Carsey, 2222 innings (1891–1901)
4.94—Buck Ross, 1365 innings (1936–45)
4.91—Alex Ferguson, 1236 innings (1918–29)

# The Hall of Fame

In the mid-1930s Ford Frick, then the National League president, was the prime mover behind the sentiment that a Hall of Fame to commemorate the game's greatest players should be opened in 1939, marking the centennial season for those who believed the Mills Commission's report that Abner Doubleday invented baseball. Acting on Frick's lead, Henry Edwards, secretary of the American League Service Bureau, polled the 226 members of the Baseball Writers Association of America for their choices from a list of 33 players. Two-thirds of the ballots cast were needed for selection. Ty Cobb led with 222 votes, Babe Ruth and Honus Wagner both had 215, Christy Mathewson had 205, and Walter Johnson received 189 votes. Before 1939 two more pollings were done, resulting in the selection of Nap Lajoie, Tris Speaker, Eddie Collins, George Sisler, Cy Young, Willie Keeler, Peter Alexander and Lou Gehrig (by special election) as well as 13 pre-1900 figures chosen by the Centennial Commission and the Committee on Old-Timers. These 26 immortals had their plaques installed in the Hall of Fame in a special induction ceremony in 1939 and have been joined in the years since by a long list. Although exceptions have been made in special cases, the three original criteria for selection have remained constant. A player must be active at least 10 seasons, must be retired at least 5 and must receive at least 75 percent of the vote.

In 1971 a Special Negro League Committee was formed to select players from the defunct Negro Leagues. Names followed by (NL) designate Negro League players who never played in the majors. Starred names belong to figures who were selected to the Hall of Fame as non-players.

**Members of the Hall of Fame**

**1936** Ty Cobb, Honus Wagner, Babe Ruth, Christy Mathewson, Walter Jonson

**1937** Nap Lajoie, Tris Speaker, Cy Young, Morgan Buckley,* Ban Johnson,* Connie Mack, John McGraw, George Wright

**1938** Pete Alexander, Alexander Cartwright,* Henry Chadwick*

**1939** George Sisler, Eddie Collins, Willie Keeler, Lou Gehrig, Cap Anson, Charlie Comiskey, Candy Cummings, Buck Ewing, Hoss Radbourn, Al Spalding

**1942** Rogers Hornsby

**1944** Judge K. M. Landis*

**1945** Roger Bresnahan, Dan Brothers, Fred Clarke, Jimmy Collins, Ed Delahanty, Hugh Duffy, Hughie Jennings, Mike Kelly, Jim O'Rourke, Wilbert Robinson

**1946** Jesse Burkett, Frank Chance, Jack Chesbro, Johnny Evers, Clark Griffith, Tom McCarthy, Joe McGinnity, Eddie Plank, Joe Tinker, Rube Waddell, Ed Walsh

**1947** Carl Hubbell, Frank Frisch, Mickey Cochrane, Lefty Grove

**1948** Herb Pennock, Pie Traynor

**1949** Charlie Gehringer, Three Finger Brown, Kid Nichols

**1951** Mel Ott, Jimmie Foxx

**1952** Harry Heilmann, Paul Waner

**1953** Dizzy Dean, Al Simmons, Ed Barrow,* Chief Bender, Tom Connolly,* Bill Klem,* Bobby Wallace, Harry Wright*

**1954** Rabbit Maranville, Bill Dickey, Bill Terry

**1955** Joe DiMaggio, Ted Lyons, Dazzy Vance, Gabby Hartnett, Frank Baker, Ray Schalk

**1956** Hank Greenberg, Joe Cronin

**1957** Sam Crawford, Joe McCarthy*

**1959** Zack Wheat

**1961** Max Carey, Billy Hamilton

**1962** Bob Feller, Jackie Robinson, Bill McKechnie,* Edd Roush

**1963** John Clarkson, Elmer Flick, Sam Rice, Eppa Rixey

**1964** Luke Appling, Red Faber, Burleigh Grimes, Miller Huggins, Tim Keefe, Heinie Manush, John Ward

**1965** Pud Galvin

**1966** Ted Williams, Casey Stengel

**1967** Red Ruffing, Branch Rickey,* Lloyd Waner

**1968** Joe Medwick, Kiki Cuyler, Goose Goslin

**1969** Stan Musial, Roy Campenella, Stan Coveleski, Waite Hoyt

**1970** Lou Boudreau, Earle Combs, Ford Frick,* Jesse Haines

**1971** Jake Beckley, Dave Bancroft, Chick Hafey, Harry Hooper, Joe Kelley, Rube Marquard, George Weiss,* Satchel Paige

**1972** Sandy Koufax, Yogi Berra, Early Wynn, Lefty Gomez, Will Harridge,* Ross Youngs, Josh Gibson (NL), Buck Leonard (NL)

**1973** Warren Spahn, Billy Evans,* George Kelly, Mickey Welch, Monte Irvin, Roberto Clemente

**1974** Mickey Mantle, Whitey Ford, Jim Bottomley, Jocko Conlan,* Sam Thompson, Cool Papa Bell (NL)

**1975** Ralph Kiner, Earl Averill, Bucky Harris,* Billy Herman, Judy Johnson (NL)

**1976** Robin Roberts, Bob Lemon, Roger Connor, Fred Lindstrom, Cal Hubbard,* Oscar Charleston (NL)

**1977** Ernie Banks, Amos Rusie, Joe Sewell, Al Lopez,* Martin Dihugo (NL), John Henry Lloyd (NL)

**1978** Eddie Mathews, Addie Joss, Larry MacPhail*

**1979** Willie Mays, Warren Giles,* Hack Wilson

**1980** Al Kaline, Duke Snider, Chuck Klein, Tom Yawkey*

**1981** Bob Gibson, Johnny Mize, Rube Foster (NL)

**1982** Hank Aaron, Frank Robinson, Travis Jackson, Happy Chandler*

**1983** Brooks Robinson, Juan Marichal, George Kell, Walter Alston*

**1984** Luis Aparicio, Harmon Killebrew, Don Drysdale, Rick Ferrell, Pee Wee Reese

**1985** Hoyt Wilhelm, Lou Brock, Enos Slaughter, Arky Vaughan

**1986** Willie McCovey, Bobby Doerr, Ernie Lombardi

**1987** Billy Williams, Catfish Hunter, Ray Dandridge (NL)

**1988** Willie Stargell

**1989** Johnny Bench, Carl Yastrzemski, Red Schoendienst, Al Barlick*

**1990** Joe Morgan, Jim Palmer

**1991** Rod Carew, Gaylord Perry, Fergie Jenkins, Tony Lazzeri, Bill Veeck*

**1992** Rollie Fingers, Tom Seaver, Hal Newhouser, Bill McGowan*

**1993** Reggie Jackson

**1994** Steve Carlton, Leo Durocher*, Phil Rizzuto

**1995** Mike Schmidt, Richie Ashburn, Vic Willis, William Hulbert*

**1996** Ned Hanlon*, Earl Weaver*, Jim Bunning, Bill Foster (NL)

**1997** Nellie Fox, Phil Niekro, Tommy LaSorda*, Willie Wells (NL)

**1998** Don Sutton, Larry Doby, Bullet Rogan (NL)

**1999** Nolan Ryan, George Brett, Robin Yount, Frank Selee*, Smoky Joe Williams (NL), Nestor Chylak*, Orlando Cepeda

**2000** Carlton Fisk, Tony Perez, Bid McPhee, Sparky Anderson*, Turkey Stearnes (NL)

**2001** Kirby Puckett, Dave Winfield, Bill Mazeroski, Hilton Smith (NL)

**2002** Ozzie Smith

**2003** Eddie Murray, Gary Carter

**2004** Paul Molitor, Dennis Eckersley

# Individual Batting and Pitching Streaks

A significant majority of the great batting and pitching streaks occurred between 1920 and 1941. Foremost among them is probably Joe DiMaggio's hitting streak in 1941, which began inauspiciously on May 15 when DiMaggio collected a meager single off Eddie Smith of the White Sox. Two months later the streak reached 56 games after DiMaggio rapped a double and two singles against Al Milnar and Joe Krakauskas of the Indians. The following night, on July 17, at Cleveland Stadium, DiMaggio was stopped by Al Smith and Jim Bagby but more by third baseman Ken Keltner and shortstop Lou Boudreau. Keltner converted two hard shots down the third-base line into outs, and in DiMaggio's last at bat, in the eighth inning, Boudreau fashioned a double play out of a smash that DiMaggio later said was among the hardest balls he ever hit. During his 56-game streak DiMaggio hit .408 with 91 hits in 223 at bats. That same year Ted Williams of the Boston Red Sox lost the MVP Award to DiMaggio although he hit .406 for the entire season.

**Longest National League Hitting Streak**
44 games—Pete Rose, Cincinnati, 1978; stopped on August 1 by Larry McWilliams and Gene Garber of the Atlanta Braves.

Willie Keeler, Baltimore, 1897. Prior to Keeler's 44-game streak, the record was held by Bill Dahlen of the Chicago White Stockings, who hit safely in 42 straight games in 1894, breaking George Davis's year-old mark of 33 games. Dahlen's streak ended on August 7 against Cincinnati in a game in which the White Stockings made 20 hits, five each by Bill Lange and Cap Anson, who preceded and followed Dahlen in the Chicago batting order. According to some record books, Dahlen began a 28-game streak the next day, meaning that he narrowly missed putting together a 71-game skein, but the second streak is still the subject of dispute.

## Most Consecutive Base Hits, No Bases on Balls Intervening
AL—12—Walt Dropo, Detroit, July 14 and 15, 1952
NL—10—Jake Gettman, Washington, September 10 and 11, 1897; Ed Konetchy, Brooklyn, June 28, June 29 and July 1, 1919

## Most Consecutive Games Hitting at Least One Home Run
NL—8—Dale Long, Pittsburgh, May 19 through May 28, 1956
AL—8—Don Mattingly, New York, July 8 through July 18, 1987
—8—Ken Griffey, Jr., Seattle, July 20 through July 28, 1993

## Most Consecutive Games Collecting at Least One RBI
NL—17—Ray Grimes, Chicago, 1922. For many years Grimes's mark went unrecognized because a back injury sidelined him for a nine-day stretch during the streak.
AL—13—Taft Wright, Chicago, 1941.
—13—Mike Sweeney, Kansas City, 1999.

## Most Consecutive Games Played
2632—Cal Ripken, Baltimore. Ripken began his streak on May 30, 1982, and ended it voluntarily on September 20, 1998, against Lou Gehrig's old team, the Yankees. Ripken's record skein was amazingly uneventful; there was never really a moment when his string seemed in danger of ending. Gehrig's former-record 2130-game skein was very different. It began on June 1, 1925, when he pinch-hit for shortstop Pee Wee Wanninger; continued because regular first baseman Wally Pipp was beaned in batting practice by Charlie Caldwell (who later earned fame for a streak of his own when he coached Princeton to two straight undefeated football seasons); seemed destined for an early end on July 5, 1925, until Fred Merkle fainted from the heat in the ninth inning after playing the whole game at first base for the Yankees; took a small detour on September 28, 1930, when Gehrig played left field while Babe Ruth pitched and Harry Rice played first base; aroused only mild attention until 1933 when Gehrig surpassed the previous record of 1,307 games set by former Yankees

shortstop Everett Scott (whose own streak ended when he was replaced by Pee Wee Wanninger, the man Gehrig pinch-hit for to start his skein); came within a hair of being terminated in 1934 when Gehrig was beaned in a midseason exhibition game; and seemed definitely over a month later when he had to be carried off the field after suffering a back injury, only to see him penciled in the lineup the following day at shortstop and then replaced by a pinch runner after leading off the game with a single. The streak finally ended on May 2, 1939, when Gehrig, already showing the debilitating effects of the neuromuscular disease that just two years later would claim his life, removed himself from the lineup, allowing Babe Dahlgren to play the entire game at first base. Steve Garvey holds the National League record, playing in 1207 consecutive games before a thumb injury ended his string on July 30, 1983.

## Most Consecutive Wins by a Pitcher, League

NL—24—Carl Hubbell, New York Giants, 1936–37
AL—20—Roger Clemens, Toronto-New York, 1998–99.

## Most Consecutive Wins by a Pitcher, Season, League

NL—19—Tim Keefe, New York Giants, 1888
Rube Marquard, New York Giants, 1912. On July 3, 1912, after beating Brooklyn 2–1, Marquard had an incredible 19–0 record, which by modern rules would have been 20–0 since he came on in relief in the top of the ninth inning of a game in which the Giants were trailing and then saw them come back and win in their final turn at bat.
AL—16—Walter Johnson, Washington, 1912
Joe Wood, Boston, 1912; beating Johnson on September 1 to tie Johnson's brand-new record
Lefty Grove, Philadelphia, 1931; missing his chance for an AL season-record 17th straight win when he lost 1–0 to the Browns on August 23, after left-fielder Jimmy Moore, spelling Al Simmons, who took the day off, misplayed a fly ball, leading to the game's only run.
Schoolboy Rowe, Detroit, 1934
Roger Clemens, New York, 2001

## Most Consecutive Wins by a Pitcher in His Home Park

20—Lefty Grove, Boston Red Sox, May 3, 1938, through May 12, 1941. In the process Grove forever buried the notion that a southpaw could not win in Fenway Park.

## Most Consecutive Wins by a Relief Pitcher

22—Roy Face, Pittsburgh Pirates, 1958–59. Face was only two short of Hubbell's alltime-record 24 straight wins when he lost his next-to-last decision in 1959 after getting off to a 17–0 start.

## Most Consecutive Wins by a Pitcher with a Last-Place Team

15—Steve Carlton, Philadelphia Phillies, 1972. Carlton's record streak helped make him a 27-game winner with a team that won only 59 games.

# World Series Play:
# 1920–41

## FRANCHISE SUMMARY

| Team | League | WS Record through 1941 | Last year in WS |
|------|--------|------------------------|-----------------|
| Boston | American | 5–0 | 1918 |
| Cleveland | American | 1–0 | 1920 |
| Boston | National | 1–0 | 1914 |
| New York | American | 9–3 | 1941 |
| Cincinnati | National | 2–1 | 1940 |
| Chicago | American | 2–1 | 1919 |
| Philadelphia | American | 5–3 | 1931 |
| St. Louis | National | 3–2 | 1934 |
| Pittsburgh | National | 2–2 | 1927 |
| New York | National | 4–8 | 1937 |
| Washington | American | 1–2 | 1933 |
| Chicago | National | 2–7 | 1938 |
| Detroit | American | 1–5 | 1940 |
| Philadelphia | National | 1–1 | 1915 |
| Brooklyn | National | 0–3 | 1941 |

**Yearly Highlights**
1920—Cleveland (AL) defeated Brooklyn (NL) 5 games to 2

Indians player-manager Tris Speaker platooned at three positions—first base, left field and right field—and got a trio of wins from Stan Coveleski, the last pitcher until 1946 to win three in a Series. The Indians also received the first Series grand-slam homer from Elmer Smith, the first Series homer by a pitcher from Jim Bagby, and Bill Wambsganss' unassisted triple play, the only one in Series history. Cleveland won the pennant despite losing the AL's premier shortstop, Ray Chapman, who was killed by a Carl Mays pitch in August.

1921—New York (NL) defeated New York (AL) 5 games to 3

The first Subway Series and also the last Series played on a best-five-of-nine format. Waite Hoyt of the Yankees pitched three complete games without allowing an earned run but lost one of them, the Series finale, on an error by shortstop Roger Peckinpaugh. In Game Three, the Giants pounded a Series-record 20 hits while winning 13–5.

1922—New York (NL) defeated New York (AL) 4 games to 0

When the best the Yankees could do was a tie in Game Two, manager Miller Huggins was nearly fired, and John McGraw and his Giants seemed to have permanently ce-mented the Yankees into place as the city's second-best team. Of Babe Ruth, who hit only .118 in the Series, sports-writer Joe Vila wrote: "The exploded phenomenon didn't surprise the smart fans who long ago realized that he couldn't hit brainy pitching. Ruth, therefore, is no longer a wonder. The baseball public is onto his real worth as a batsman and in the future, let us hope, he will attract just ordinary attention."

1923—New York (AL) defeated New York (NL) 4 games to 2

Casey Stengel hit two game-winning homers for the Giants, the first one inside the park, but Ruth, just a year after Vila's put-down, broke out of his Series slump with a vengeance, hitting .368 and hammering three homers.

1924—Washington (AL) defeated New York (NL) 4 games to 3

The most exciting Series to date. Washington won the de-ciding game in 12 innings, Walter Johnson getting the victory in relief. The winning run came home when Earl McNeely's ground ball hit a pebble and bounced over Giants third base-man Fred Lindstrom's head. In McGraw's last Series game he was outfoxed by Senators manager Bucky Harris, who started right-hander Curly Ogden, allowed him to pitch to just two batters and then brought in lefty George Mogridge, sad-dling the Giants with a lineup of left-handed hitters.

1925—Pittsburgh (NL) defeated Washington (AL) 4 games to 3

In the eighth inning of Game Three, with the Senators leading 4–3 and two out, Earl Smith of the Pirates hit a drive headed into the temporary right-centerfield seats in Griffith Stadium, but Sam Rice dove over the wall and came out of the crowd clutching the ball. Second base umpire Rigler signaled the catch, but many observers felt that Rice had wrestled the ball out of a fan's hand. On his way to becoming the Series hero when he also led both teams with 12 hits, Rice saw his dream fade when the Pirates, down three games to one, pulled out the next two contests and then rallied to win the seventh game, getting 15 hits and nine runs off Walter Johnson, who was making his last Series appearance. Roger Peckinpaugh, the AL's MVP in 1925, once again became the Series goat when he made eight errors.

1926—St. Louis (NL) defeated New York (AL) 4 games to 3

For the third year in a row the Series went the full seven games. The deciding clash was played in a steady drizzle at Yankee Stadium. Pitching in relief, Pete Alexander struck out the Yankees' Tony Lazzeri with the bases loaded and two out in the seventh inning, preserving a 3–2 Cardinals lead. The Series ended when Babe Ruth was caught trying to steal second base with two out in the ninth inning.

1927—New York (AL) defeated Pittsburgh (NL) 4 games to 0

Herb Pennock of the Yankees had a perfect game going in Game Three until Pie Traynor ended it with one out in the eighth. Ruth and Lou Gehrig between them knocked in 11 runs while the Pirates scored only 10.

1928—New York (AL) defeated St. Louis (NL) 4 games to 0

Ruth set several Series records as he hit three homers and batted .625 while Gehrig knocked home nine runs against a Cardinals pitching staff that had a 6.09 Series ERA.

1929—Philadelphia (AL) defeated Chicago (NL) 4 games to 1

Howard Ehmke broke Ed Walsh's Series record when he fanned 13 Cubs in the opener. The Cubs led 8–0 in the seventh inning of Game Four but lost 10–8 as the A's put on the most amazing one-inning rally in Series history.

**1930—Philadelphia (AL) defeated St. Louis (NL) 4 games to 2**

Al Simmons and Jimmie Foxx both had a good Series, but it was the pitching of Lefty Grove and George Earnshaw, each of whom won two games, that beat the Cards.

**1931—St. Louis (NL) defeated Philadelphia (AL) 4 games to 3**

The Cards were led by Pepper Martin, who hit .500 and stole five bases, and Bill Hallahan, who recorded two wins and saved the seventh game.

**1932—New York (AL) defeated Chicago (NL) 4 games to 0**

Ruth may or may not have "called" his shot in Game Three, but in any event it was his second homer of the game and last in Series play. It came in the fifth inning of a 4–4 game, against Charlie Root, on an 0–2 pitch, a high inside change-up. The homer overrode Gehrig's overall Series effort of three homers and eight RBIs.

**1933—New York (NL) defeated Washington (AL) 4 games to 1**

In their first Series, Carl Hubbell and Mel Ott of the Giants were the pitching and hitting stars. Hubbell won two games without giving up an earned run, and Ott slugged two homers, the second bringing home the deciding run in the 10th inning of the final game.

**1934—St. Louis (NL) defeated Detroit (AL) 4 games to 3**

In the sixth inning of the final game, Joe Medwick of the Cardinals slid hard into Tigers third baseman Marv Owen, nearly triggering a riot in Briggs Stadium. When Detroit fans pelted Medwick with fruit and vegetables as he tried to take his left-field post in the bottom of the inning, Commissioner Landis ordered him removed from the game for his own protection. The Cardinals were ahead at the time 9–0 and didn't protest Landis's decision, but if the score had been closer, one wonders whether Landis would not have been forced to declare the first forfeit in Series history.

**1935—Detroit (AL) defeated Chicago (NL) 4 games to 2**

Lon Warneke's two fine pitching efforts were all the Cubs could point to, as the Tigers made do without Hank Greenberg, who was injured early in the Series.

**1936—New York (AL) defeated New York (NL) 4 games to 2**

After losing the opener 6–1 to Carl Hubbell, the Yankees scored 42 runs in the next five games, including a record 18 in Game Two.

**1937—New York (AL) defeated New York (NL) 4 games to 1**

Hubbell's win in Game Four was all that prevented the Yankees from sweeping.

**1938—New York (AL) defeated Chicago (NL) 4 games to 0**

Stan Hack of the Cubs hit .471 to lead all Series batters. The rest of the accolades once again belonged to the Yankees.

**1939—New York (AL) defeated Cincinnati (NL) 4 games to 0**

The Reds hung tough before losing the opener 2–1 in the ninth inning and took the Yankees to 10 innings before dropping Game Four but managed only 12 singles in the other two contests.

**1940—Cincinnati (NL) defeated Detroit (AL) 4 games to 3**

Two complete-game victories by both Bucky Walters and Paul Derringer sparked the Reds to their first untainted World Championship.

**1941—New York (AL) defeated Brooklyn (NL) 4 games to 1**

In Game Three, Fred Fitzsimmons of the Dodgers blanked the Yankees for seven innings before a line drive off the bat of Yankees pitcher Marius Russo broke his kneecap and forced him to leave the game. The Dodgers ultimately lost 2–1 and then dropped Game Four in the ninth inning when Tommy Henrich fanned for what should have been the final out of a 4–3 Dodgers victory, only to have the third strike elude catcher Mickey Owen and Henrich reach first base. Before the Yankees were retired they scored four runs and broke open the most competitive Series they had been in since 1926.

# SECTION 4

# Famous Firsts:
# 1942–60

**1942**—Ted Lyons sets a post deadball era record when he makes 20 starts and completes all 20 games.

**1943**—To save on rubber, which is in short supply during the war, a new balata baseball is manufactured and used. It results in no home runs being hit in the first 11 games of the season and shutouts in 11 of the first 29 games. Finally, the balls left over from 1942 are brought out of the closet while balls with a better quality of rubber cement are rushed into production.

**1944**—On July 20, in a game against the Yankees, Nels Potter of the Brown becomes the first pitcher ever to be ejected expressly for violating the spitball rule.

**1945**—The Washington Senators miss becoming the first team in modern history to vault from last place to a pennant the following year when they lose on the final day of the season to the A's in extra innings on a fly ball that outfielder Bingo Binks, who's neglected to don sunglasses after the sun breaks through late in the day, loses in the brightness.

**1945**—The National League's leader in pitching wins, leader in pitching losses, runner-up in stolen bases and the Red Sox leader in saves all have the same last name—Barrett—and no two of them are related.

**1947**—Pitcher Bill Voiselle of the Braves, who resides in Ninety-Six, North Carolina, becomes the first player to wear the name of his hometown on the back of his uniform when he appears on the field bearing number 96.

**1947**—Bonus baby Joe Tepsic stings the Dodgers and quits rather than be sent to the minors after spending the 1946 season with the club.

**1947**—"Howling Hilda" Chester, now at her peak, lets other Dodgers fans know how she feels about Tepsic's betrayal. With her ringing cow bells and shouts to Dodgers players until they wave to her in her seat in the Ebbets Field bleachers, Chester prefers the sobriquet "Queen of the Bleachers" to "Howling Hilda." Before each game she can be seen carrying a banner with her name on it and earning the price of admission by selling songsheets at the corner of DeKalb Avenue and Flatbush Extension. When the Dodgers are out of town, she bides her time by selling newspapers in downtown Brooklyn. Chester has her counterparts in Mary Ott, the "Horse Lady of St. Louis," who for 25 years has been the scourge of umpires and visiting players to Sportsman's Park, and "Megaphone Lolly" Hopkins in Boston. Hopkins, however, is considerably more genteel than Ott and much less partisan than Chester; she bestows her cheers not only on Braves and Red Sox players but also on players from visiting teams should they happen to do something that pleases her.

**1948**—There are no Hildas or Lollys or Marys in Cleveland, but there is Joe Early, a night watchman, who writes to Indians owner Bill Veeck, asking how come players are always honored—why not a fan every now and then? Why not indeed, responds Veeck, and he has a special night for Early at which Early receives an outhouse, a backfiring Model T and some weird animals, plus a Ford convertible, luggage, a refrigerator, a washing machine, a watch, a stereo, clothes and lots more. Between Veeck's promotions and the first Cleveland pennant-winner in 28 years, the Indians draw 2,620,627 and shatter every all-time attendance record.

**1949**—Mel Allen is first heard to utter the line that made him famous, "How about that?" when Joe DiMaggio returns to the New York lineup after being disabled by a bone spur and cracks a hit his first time up. Another colorful bit of work from that same era, though never heard nationally, comes from Pittsburgh's Rosie Rosewell, who says, each time Ralph Kiner cranks one out of Forbes Field, "Open the window, Aunt Minnie, here it comes!" pauses a moment, and then shatters a light bulb over the air.

**1951**—Bill Veeck, now the owner of the Browns, hires Eddie Gaedel, a three-foot-seven-inch midget, and uses him as a pinch hitter for leadoff man Frank Saucier in the bottom of the first inning of a game on August 19 against Detroit. Pitcher Bob Cain of the Tigers, after he realizes it isn't a gag and stops laughing, walks Gaedel on four pitches. American League president Will Harridge is appalled when he learns of Veeck's latest innovation and orders Gaedel's at-bat stricken from the record book until it's pointed out to him by Veeck that the game's stats will thereupon make it seem that Cain pitched to no one.

**1951**—Russ Hodges utters the most famous single line ever mouthed by a play-by-play announcer when he ecstatically shouts, shrieks and sobs, "The Giants win the pennant!" over and over again after Bobby Thomson's three-run homer abruptly ends the National League pennant playoff series between the Giants and the Dodgers.

**1953**—Paul Pettit, the Pirates' $100,000 bonus baby, posts a 7.11 ERA but manages to win a game, for which the Pirates are grateful. Cleveland's $100,000 bonus baby, Billy Joe Davidson, in contrast, never even throws a single pitch in a major-league game.

**1954**—The sacrifice fly rule, tinkered with for years, sometimes in effect and other times not, is once again adopted and this time remains on the books; a batter who hits a run-scoring fly ball is henceforth not charged with time at bat.

**1954**—Players for the first time are no longer allowed to leave their gloves on the playing field while their team is at bat.

**1950s**—Warning tracks are at last required in the outfields of all major-league parks. Padded fences, however, will not be mandatory until the 1970s.

**1956**—Robin Roberts of the Phillies is tagged for a National League record 46 home runs on his way to surrendering an all-time career record 502 homers.

**1957**—The American League makes batting helmets mandatory. Prior to this many players have already begun wearing them.

**1957**—Pedro Ramos of the Senators surrenders 43 home runs, a new American League season record.

**1960**—Jerry Holtzman of the *Chicago Sun Times* helps initiate the crediting of "saves" to relief pitchers.

**1960**—White Sox owner Bill Veeck is the first to put names on the backs of his team's uniforms. Veeck also unveils an exploding scoreboard in Comiskey Park. On the other hand, Veeck's crosstown rival, the Chicago Cubs, calmly ally themselves with the Red Sox and remain the last clubs to have a manually operated scoreboard until 1986, when the Oakland A's turn back the clock and convert their scoreboard to a human-run operation.

# Batting Title
# Record Holders

Ted Williams and Stan Musial were unquestionably the elite hitters in their respective leagues during the period between 1942 and 1960. The last two players to retire with career averages above .330, they each set numerous offensive records, not the least of which are their league marks for the longest span of time between their first and last batting titles. Williams took his initial American League crown in 1941 and his final crown an all-time record 17 years later; Musial holds the National League record with a 14-year spread between his first triumph in 1943 and his last in 1957.

## Most Batting Titles Won
AL—12—Ty Cobb, last in 1919
NL—8—Honus Wagner, last in 1911
        Tony Gwynn, last in 1997

## Other Players Who Won Four or More Batting Titles
7—Rod Carew (AL), last in 1978
    Stan Musial (NL), last in 1957
    Rogers Hornsby (NL), last in 1928
6—Ted Williams (AL), last in 1958
5—Wade Boggs (AL), last in 1988
4—Bill Madlock (NL), last in 1983
    Roberto Clemente (NL), last in 1967
    Harry Heilmann (AL), last in 1927

## Most Batting Titles Won Prior to 1901
5—Dan Brouthers led the National League in 1882, 1883, 1889, and 1892 and the American Association in 1891. The only other players ever to lead two different major leagues batting were Pete Browning, who won the American Association batting crown in 1882 and 1885 and the Players League

batting crown in 1890, and Ed Delahanty, National League in 1899 and American League in 1902.

## Most Consecutive Batting Titles Won
AL—9—Ty Cobb, 1907–15
NL—6—Rogers Hornsby, 1920–25

## Youngest Batting Title Winner
AL—Al Kaline, Detroit, 1955; 20 years old
NL—Pete Reiser, Brooklyn, 1941; 22 years old

## Oldest Batting Title Winner
AL—Ted Williams, Boston, 1958; 40 years old
NL—Barry Bonds, San Francisco, 2002; 38 years old

## Oldest Player to Win His First Batting Title
NL—Barry Bonds, San Francisco, 2002; 38 years old
AL—Charlie Gehringer, Detroit, 1937; 34 years old

## Most Batting Title Winners, Team
NL—24—Pittsburgh; won by 10 different players; last winner was Bill Madlock in 1983.

AL—24—Boston, six won by Ted Williams, five by Wade Boggs, three by Carl Yastrzemski, two by both Nomar Garciaparra and Pete Runnels and one each by seven other players.

## Fewest Batting Title Winners, Team
NL—0—New York Mets; Houston; Florida; Arizona; Milwaukee
AL—0—A's while in Oakland; Tampa Bay

## Most Seasons Since Last Batting Title Winner, Team
AL—51—Oakland–Kansas City–Philadelphia A's. The franchise's last winner was Ferris Fain in 1952.

NL—45—Philadephia; last winner was Richie Ashburn in 1958.

## Only Third Baseman to Win More Than One Batting Title
NL—4—Bill Madlock, 1975, 1976, 1981, and 1983
AL—5—Wade Boggs, 1983, 1985, 1986, 1987, 1988
—3—George Brett, 1976, 1980, and 1990

## Last Shortstop Prior to 1996 to Win a Batting Title

AL—Lou Boudreau, Cleveland, 1944

NL—Dick Groat, Pittsburgh, 1960. Only three shortstops have won NL batting titles since 1901—Honus Wagner, Arky Vaughan and Groat—and all three played for the Pirates.

## Only Catchers to Win a Batting Title

NL—Bubbles Hargrave, Cincinnati, 1926

Ernie Lombardi, Cincinnati, 1938, and Boston, 1942

AL—None.

## Only Pitcher Ever to Win a Batting Title

Guy Hecker, Louisville (AA), 1886. Hecker was one of a kind. Nicknamed "The Big Blond," he didn't begin his professional career until he was in his mid-twenties and played only nine seasons in the majors after his belated start. But he packed so many extraordinary feats into his brief career that he could occupy a full page in the all-time record book by himself. As a rookie with Louisville in 1882, Hecker authored a no-hitter, only the second in American Association history, which was further distinguished by the fact that his teammates made six errors behind him. Two years later he won 52 games for Louisville, an Association record. In 1886 Hecker slipped to only 27 wins but hit .341, edging out teammate Pete Browning for the AA batting crown by one point. That same season, in a game against Baltimore on August 15, Hecker hit three home runs, the only AA player ever to do so, and in addition crossed the plate seven times, an all-time one-game record. Now the possessor of batting, slugging and pitching marks that can never be surpassed, Hecker was still not done. Versatile enough to play elsewhere when he wasn't pitching, he set the unsurpassable *fielding* record on October 9, 1887, when he became the first player in major-league history to play an entire game at first base without handling a single chance.

## Most Recent Batting Title Winner to Repeat the Following Season

NL—Larry Walker, Colorado, 1998–99

AL—Nomar Garciaparra, 1999–2000

## Most Recent Player to Win a Batting Title without Hitting a Home Run

AL—Rod Carew, Minnesota, 1972
NL—Zack Wheat, Brooklyn, 1918

## Fewest Base Hits by a Batting Title Winner

NL—102—Ernie Lombardi, Boston, 1942
AL—127—Ty Cobb, Detroit, 1914

## Biggest Leap in Average from Previous Season by Batting Title Winner (qualifiers only)

NL—97 points—Carl Furillo, Brooklyn, 1953; hit .247 in 1952, .344 in 1953
AL—85 points—Mickey Vernon, Washington, 1946; hit .268 in 1943, .353 in 1946 after losing two years to military service.

## Biggest Drop in Average Season after Winning Batting Title

AL—118 points—Norm Cash, Detroit, 1962; hit .362 in 1961, .243 in 1962
NL—99 points—Willie McGee, St. Louis, 1986; hit .353 in 1985, .254 in 1986

## Most Discouraging Season after Winning Batting Title

NL—Rico Carty, Atlanta, 1971. Carty hit .366 to win the NL batting title in 1970, then missed all of 1971 after suffering a severe knee injury.
AL—George Sisler, St. Louis, 1923. After Sisler won the AL batting crown in 1922; sinus trouble idled him in 1923.

## Only Players to Win Two Batting Titles with Averages Below Their Career Averages

Ty Cobb, Detroit, 1906 (.350), 1907 (.324); .367 career average
Ted Williams, Boston Red Sox, 1947 (.343), 1958 (.328); .344 career average

## Multiple Batting Title Winners Who Retired with Career Averages Below .300

AL—Carl Yastrzemski, Boston, 1963, 1967, and 1968; .285 career average
Pete Runnels, Boston, 1960 and 1962; .291 career average

Ferris Fain, Philadelphia, 1950 and 1951; .290 career average

Mickey Vernon, Washington, 1946 and 1953; .286 career average

NL—Tommy Davis, Los Angeles, 1962 and 1963; .294 career average

Dave Parker, Pittsburgh, 1977 and 1978; .290 career average

## Highest Batting Average to Win Batting Title, since 1901
AL—.426—Nap Lajoie, Philadelphia, 1901
NL—.424—Rogers Hornsby, St. Louis, 1924

## Highest Batting Average Failing to Win Batting Title, since 1901
AL—.408—Joe Jackson, Cleveland, 1911; runner-up to Ty Cobb's .420. Cobb's .401 average in 1922, second to George Sisler's .420, is the only other .400 season in this century that failed to win a batting crown.

NL—.393—Babe Herman, Brooklyn, 1930; runner-up to Bill Terry's .401

## Lowest Average to Win Batting Title
AL—.301—Carl Yastrzemski, Boston, 1968
NL—.313—Tony Gwynn, San Diego, 1988

## Closest Batting Title Races
First place—Snuffy Stirnweiss of the Yankees won the AL batting crown in 1945 by less than a thousandth of a point, hitting .30854 to Tony Cuccinello's .30845. After missing the batting title by the narrowest margin in history, Cuccinello was released by the White Sox and never again played in the majors.

Second Place—George Kell, Detroit, won the AL batting crown in 1949 by .00016 of a point over Ted Williams, Boston Red Sox.

Third Place—Albert Pujols, St. Louis Cardinals, won the NL batting crown in 2003 by .00022 of a point over Todd Helton of the Colorado Rockies.

Fourth Place—Chick Hafey, St. Louis Cardinals, won the NL batting crown in 1931 by .00028 of a point over Bill Terry, New York Giants. Both hit .349 when their averages were rounded off. In third place with a .348 average was Jim Bottomley of the Cardinals.

## Most Disputed Batting Title

First Place—For 70 years Ty Cobb was credited with winning the 1910 AL batting title by a single point—.385 to .384—over Nap Lajoie of Cleveland despite efforts on Lajoie's behalf by St. Louis Browns manager Jack O'Connor and coach Harry Howell, who instructed rookie third baseman Red Corriden to play deep each time Lajoie batted in a doubleheader on the last day of the season. Corriden's positioning allowed Lajoie to beat out eight bunts and resulted in both O'Connor and Howell being barred from future major-league jobs. In 1981 the *Sporting News* discovered that Lajoie had won after all—.384 to .383—because Cobb received double credit for a 2-for-3 game, and two hitless at bats were omitted from his statistics. The *Sporting News* is right, yet it's also true that Lajoie's season-ending flurry of hits was tainted. Your choice who the real winner was.

Second Place—In 1976 George Brett of the Kansas City Royals won the AL batting title over teammate Hal McRae when outfielder Steve Brye of the Minnesota Twins allowed a fly ball Brett hit on his last at bat of the season to fall safely. Brye made only a token attempt to deny he'd deliberately engineered Brett's batting title win and justified his machinations by claiming that Brett, a third baseman, was more deserving of the crown than McRae, a designated hitter. Again, your choice who really won.

# Handicapped Players

In 1945 the St. Louis Browns purchased Pete Gray, the MVP the previous year in the Southern Association. Gray, who had only one arm, played 77 games for the 1945 Browns, a remarkable achievement for a man missing a limb, but it was surpassed in 1989 when rookie Jim Abbott, lacking the use of his right arm owing to a birth defect, leaped from the Michigan University campus to win 12 games for the Angels.

**Most Successful One-Armed Player, prior to Abbott**
Hugh "One Arm" Daily. Daily pitched in the National League, Union Association and American Association from 1882 to 1887. In 1883, pitching for Cleveland, he led the National League in bases on balls and threw a no-hitter against Philadelphia; the following year he led all Union Association hurlers in strikeouts. No known photographs of Daily in action have survived, but we know it was his left arm that was lacking and that, since he was a pitcher, he couldn't have worn a glove while in the field. Reportedly, Daily fielded hard-hit balls by first blocking them with a pad attached to his truncated left forearm.

**Major-League Pitcher Overcoming the Greatest Handicap**
Bert Shepard, a former minor-league pitcher, lost a leg after being shot down over Germany in World War II while serving as an Army Air Corps pilot. Outfitted with an artificial leg, he was signed as a coach by the Washington Senators in 1945. After pitching in several exhibition games, he made a relief appearance on August 14 in the regular-season game against the Red Sox and gave up only one run in five innings. Shepard, who came to bat three times during his relief stint, also classifies as the hitter overcoming the greatest handicap. In

1948, while managing the Class B Waterbury, Connecticut, club, he played several games at first base.

## Most Successful Handicapped Pitcher, since 1901

Luther "Dummy" Taylor, a deaf-mute, won 21 games for the New York Giants in 1904 and 116 games over a nine-year career. One of only two deaf-mutes to play in the majors, after leaving baseball Taylor worked as a housefather at the Illinois School for the Deaf in Jacksonville, where he helped Dick Sipek, who was partly deaf, to become a good enough outfielder to play with the Cincinnati Reds in the middle 1940s.

## Most Successful Handicapped AL Pitcher, prior to Abbott

Many players have had lengthy major-league careers despite missing toes and fingers, two Hall of Famers, Three Finger Brown and Red Ruffing, among them; Gray, Shepard and Daily were the only three who managed to play without a limb. But another Daley—Buddy Daley—pitched in the American League for 10 years with nearly as great a handicap. Daley had a withered right arm, the result of an injury incurred at birth, but was still able to win 60 games, plus one in the 1961 World Series.

## Smallest Player

Eddie Gaedel, the midget Bill Veeck hired in 1951, stood three feet seven inches and weighed 67 pounds. Prior to Gaedel, there were a goodly number of fringe players who barely topped the five-foot mark, but the smallest player to play a full season in the majors was probably Cub Stricker listed as having been only five feet, three inches. The smallest player to become a star was Dummy Hoy, who was five foot four inches and weighed 148 pounds. Hoy was easily the most successful handicapped player of all time; not only was he diminutive but he was a deaf-mute. His dual handicap kept him from making the major leagues until he was given a chance in 1888 by Washington at age 26. He went on to play 14 seasons and compile over 2000 hits. Among the many other successful small players were Harry Chappas, five feet, three inches; Hugh Nicol, five feet, four inches; Davy Force, five feet, four inches; Willie Keeler, five feet, four-and-a-half inches; Sparky Adams, five feet, four-and-a-half inches; Freddy Patek, five feet, five inches; Albie Pearson, five feet, five inches; and Bobby Shantz, five feet, six inches but only 139 pounds. Special mention: Ernie Oravetz, an outfielder with the Washington Senators for two years in the 1950s, was not only five feet, four inches but also wore glasses.

## Tallest Player Prior to Randy Johnson

Johnny Gee, who won seven games in the National League between 1939 and 1946, was six feet, nine inches—an inch taller than Gene Conley, the most successful tall player. Conley won 91 games for the Braves, Phillies and Red Sox in the 1950s and early 1960s. At one point in his career Conley also played with the NBA Boston Celtics during the winter months.

## First Player to Wear Glasses

Will White, pitcher, 1877–86, and a 229-game winner

## First Player in the 20th Century to Wear Glasses

Lee Meadows, St. Louis Cardinals, 1915

## First Player Other Than a Pitcher to Wear Glasses

George Toporcer, St. Louis Cardinals, 1921

## First Catcher to Wear Glasses

Clint Courtney, New York Yankees, 1951

## First Winner of Most Valuable Player Award to Wear Glasses

NL—Jim Konstanty, Philadelphia, 1950
AL—Dick Allen, Chicago, 1972

## First League Leader in a Major Hitting Department to Wear Glasses

NL—Chick Hafey, St. Louis, 1931, won the batting title.
AL—Bob Dillinger, St. Louis, 1948, had the most base hits.

## First 20-Game Winner to Wear Glasses, since 1901

NL—Lee Meadows, Pittsburgh, 1926 (20–9)
AL—Mel Harder, Cleveland, 1934 (20–12)

# Firsts by Black Players

The first black professional baseball player, according to most sources, was John Jackson, who played under the name of Bud Fowler with the Newcastle, Pennsylvania, club in 1872. During the next two decades a number of other black players made their marks in the minor leagues. The two best probably were second baseman Frank Grant, who broke in with Buffalo in the International League in 1886 and was called the "Black Fred Dunlap," and George Stovey, the leading pitcher in the International League in the mid-1880's. Grant and Stovey would have both undoubtedly played in either the American Association or the National League, along with many other black players who were their contemporaries, had they not encountered a latent prejudice that emerged and soon permeated all of organized baseball when the Toledo American Association club hired the Walker brothers in 1884.

### First Black Major-League Player

Probably catcher Fleet Walker with Toledo in 1884, followed shortly thereafter by his younger brother Weldy, an outfielder. Fleet actually made his professional debut with Toledo a year earlier when the team was in the Northwestern League. In 50 games he batted .251, and the following season, facing stronger AA pitching, raised his average to .263, a highly respectable showing for a catcher in an era when many backstoppers hit below .200. The Walkers first attracted the attention of Toledo manager Charlie Morton while they were playing for Oberlin College. Welday did little in the few major-league games he played, but Fleet was good enough to keep another rookie catcher, Deacon McGuire, on the bench for much of the 1884 season. McGuire would go on to become the first player to catch in over 1500 major-league games, while Walker's big-league experience would last only a few months. Not all historians agree, however, that the Walkers were the first black major leaguers. In 1882 the Providence Grays signed catcher Sandy Nava and used him for the next three seasons to spell their regular backstopper Barney Gilligan. Nava, possibly the second native San Franciscan to play in the majors, explained his dark complexion by saying he was Cuban. Whether or not Nava was actually black is impossible to determine now, but it may be significant that when prejudice began mushrooming later in the decade he was phased out of the major leagues.

### First Professional Black Player in the 20th Century

Technically, it was Jimmy Claxton, who pitched briefly in 1916 for the Oakland Oaks in the Pacific Coast League, but once again there is lots of room for debate. In 1901 John McGraw tried to sign Charlie Grant, a black second baseman, to a contract with the Baltimore Orioles, who were about to begin their fledgling season in the American League. To circumvent the issue of Grant's color, McGraw presented him as Tokohama, a full-blooded Cherokee Indian, after he saw a creek with that name on a wall map in the Hot Springs, Arkansas, hotel where the Orioles were staying during spring training. But White Sox owner Charlie Comiskey, among others, saw through the hoax and blocked Grant's signing. A few years later, as manager of the New York Giants, McGraw attempted to hire a Cuban pitcher named Jose Mendez, but Mendez's nickname alone—"the Black Matty"—unified rival National League clubs against McGraw's integration effort. In 1911, however, the Cincinnati Reds successfully managed to sign two light-skinned Cubans named Rafael Almeida and Armando Marsans. Almeida failed to stick, but Marsans proved to be a pretty good outfielder and paved the way for other clubs, the Washington Senators in particular, to import more Cuban players. All of course were light-skinned, but there have been numerous light-skinned Latin players who, since the color line was finally broken, have acknowledged their ancestry was at least partially black. So it's safe to say, I think, that one or two black players besides the Walkers—and one hopes a lot more than that—found ways before 1946 to get past the color barrier.

### First Black American Player Officially Accepted by Organized Baseball in the 20th Century

Jackie Robinson in 1946 with the Montreal Royals, Brooklyn's International League farm club. In his first game in organized baseball, on April 18, 1946, at Roosevelt Stadium in Jersey City, Robinson collected three singles and a home run off Jersey City's Phil Oates.

### First Black American to Play in the National League
Jackie Robinson. He made his major-league debut with Brooklyn on April 15, 1947, against the Boston Braves, went hitless, and was 0-for-20 after his first five games. Robinson ended the 1947 season with a .297 batting average, led the National League in stolen bases, and was named Rookie of the Year.

### First Black American to Play in the American League
Larry Doby, Cleveland, 1947. Used mainly at second base and as a pinchhitter, Doby hit only .156 in 29 games. Moved to center field the following spring, he hit .301 and sparked the Indians to their first pennant since 1920.

### First Black American to Pitch in the National League
Dan Bankhead, Brooklyn, 1947. Used as a reliever in four games, he had an 0–0 record but homered in his first major-league at bat. In the fall he became the first black pitcher to play in a World Series—though not the first to pitch in one—when he got into a game as a pinch runner.

### First Black American to Pitch in the American League
Satchel Paige, Cleveland, 1948. Paige was also the first black to win a game and the first to pitch a shutout, both occurring in his first major-league start. On October 10, 1948, he became, in addition, the first black to pitch in a World Series game when he worked two-thirds of an inning in relief.

### First Black Pitcher to Win a World Series Game
Joe Black, Brooklyn, started and won the first game of the 1952 Series.

### First Black Pitcher to Throw a No-Hitter
Sam Jones, Chicago Cubs, May 12, 1955, against Pittsburgh

### First Black Pitcher to Win 20 Games in a Season
NL—Don Newcombe, Brooklyn, 1955 (20–5)
AL—Mudcat Grant, Minnesota, 1965 (21–7)

**First Black Manager**
AL—Frank Robinson, Cleveland, 1975
NL—Frank Robinson, San Francisco, 1981

**First Black to Be a League Leader in Fielding Average**
NL—Jackie Robinson, Brooklyn, 1948, led all second basemen with a .980 FA.
AL—Vic Power, Kansas City A's, 1957, led first basemen with a .998 FA.

**First Black Umpire**
Emmett Ashford, American League, 1965. Ashford retired in 1970 and died of a heart attack in 1980.

## YOUR FAVORITE TEAM'S FIRST BLACK PLAYERS

(Teams in Existence Prior to 1961)

| Team | First Black Player | Second Black Player | First Black Regular |
|------|--------------------|--------------------|--------------------|
| Brooklyn Dodgers | Jackie Robinson, 1947 | Dan Bankhead, 1947 | Jackie Robinson, 1947 |
| Cleveland Indians | Larry Doby, 1947 | Satchel Paige, 1948 | Larry Doby, 1948 |
| St. Louis Browns | Hank Thompson, 1947 | Willard Brown, 1947 | Satchel Paige, 1952 |
| New York Giants | Hank Thompson, 1949 | Monte Irvin, 1949 | Hank Thompson, 1950 |
| Boston Braves | Sam Jethroe, 1950 | Luis Marquez, 1951 | Sam Jethroe, 1950 |
| Chicago White Sox | Minnie Minoso, 1951 | Sam Hairston, 1951 | Minnie Minoso, 1951 |
| Philadelphia A's | Bob Trice, 1953 | Vic Power, 1954 | Vic Power, 1954 |
| Chicago Cubs | Ernie Banks, 1953 | Gene Baker, 1953 | Banks and Baker, 1954 |
| Pittsburgh Pirates | Curt Roberts, 1954 | Sam Jethroe, 1954 | Curt Roberts, 1954 |
| St. Louis Cards | Tom Alston, 1954 | Brooks Lawrence, 1954 | Curt Flood, 1958 |
| Cincinnati Reds | Nino Escalera, 1954 | Chuck Harmon, 1954 | Frank Robinson, 1956 |
| Washington Senators | Carlos Paula, 1954 | Joe Black, 1957 | Carlos Paula, 1954 |

| Team | First Black Player | Second Black Player | First Black Regular |
|---|---|---|---|
| New York Yankees | Elston Howard, 1955 | Harry Simpson, 1957 | Elston Howard, 1959 |
| Philadelphia Phillies | John Kennedy, 1957 | Chuck Harmon, 1957 | Pancho Herrera and Tony Taylor 1960 |
| Detroit Tigers | Ozzie Virgil, 1958 | Larry Doby, 1958 | Jake Wood, 1961 |
| Boston Red Sox | Pumpsie Green, 1959 | Earl Wilson, 1959 | Willie Tasby, 1960 |

*Note:* The St. Louis Browns, the third team to integrate, never had a black regular until after the franchise moved to Baltimore (Bob Boyd, 1956). Paige, who had a 12–10 record in 138 innings in 1952, was the first black to see more than token action with the team.

Thompson and Irvin debuted in the same game with the Giants in 1949; ditto Escalera and Harmon with the Reds in 1954.

Some Sources credit Hairston with being the White Sox first black player in July 1951; by then, however, Minoso had already been with the team for several weeks.

# FIRST BLACK LEAGUE LEADERS
## Batting

| Department | National League | American League |
|---|---|---|
| Batting Average | Jackie Robinson, Brooklyn, 1949 | Tony Oliva, Minnesota, 1964 |
| Slugging Average | Willie Mays, N.Y. Giants, 1954 | Larry Doby, Cleveland, 1952 |
| Home Runs | Willie Mays, N.Y. Giants, 1955 | Larry Doby, Cleveland, 1952 |
| RBIs | Monte Irvin, N.Y. Giants, 1951 | Larry Doby, Cleveland, 1954 |
| Stolen Bases | Jackie Robinson, Brooklyn, 1947 | Minnie Minoso, Chicago, 1951 |
| Hits | Willie Mays, S.F. Giants, 1960 | Minnie Minoso, Cleveland, 1960 |
| Runs | Frank Robinson, Cincinnati, 1956 | Larry Doby, Cleveland, 1952 |

| Department | National League | American League |
|---|---|---|
| Doubles | Hank Aaron, Milwaukee, 1955 | Minnie Minoso, Chicago, 1957 |
| Triples | Hank Thompson N.Y. Giants, 1952 | Minnie Minoso, Chicago, 1951 |
| Bases on Balls | Jim Gilliam, Los Angeles, 1959 | Dick Allen, Chicago, 1972 Roy White, New York, 1972 |
| Strikeouts | Pancho Herrera, Philadelphia, 1960 | Larry Doby, Cleveland, 1952 |
| Total Bases | Willie Mays, N.Y. Giants, 1955 | Tony Oliva, Minnesota, 1964 |

## Pitching

| | | |
|---|---|---|
| Wins | Don Newcombe, Brooklyn, 1956 | Mudcat Grant, Minnesota, 1965 |
| Losses | Sam Jones, Chicago, 1955 | Orlando Pena, Kansas City A's, 1963 |
| Winning Pct. | Don Newcombe, Brooklyn, 1955 | Mudcat Grant, Minnesota, 1965 |
| Shutouts | Bob Gibson, St. Louis, 1962 | Mudcat Grant, Minnesota, 1965 |
| Strikeouts | Don Newcombe, Brooklyn, 1951 | Al Downing, New York, 1964 |
| ERA | Sam Jones, San Francisco, 1959 | Luis Tiant, Cleveland, 1968 |
| Bases on Balls | Sam Jones, Chicago, 1955 | Earl Wilson, Boston, 1963 |
| Complete Games | Juan Marichal, San Francisco, 1964 | Fergie Jenkins, Texas, 1974 |

## Awards

| | | |
|---|---|---|
| Rookie of the Year | Jackie Robinson, Brooklyn, 1947 | Tony Oliva, Minnesota, 1964 |
| Most Valuable Player | Jackie Robinson, Brooklyn, 1949 | Elston Howard, New York, 1963 |
| Cy Young | Don Newcombe, Brooklyn, 1956 | Vida Blue, Oakland, 1971 |

# The Four Most Interesting Teams between 1942 and 1960

## 1946 BROOKLYN DODGERS
## W–96 L–60
## Manager: Leo Durocher

**Regular Lineup**—1B, Ed Stevens; 2B, Eddie Stanky; 3B, Cookie Lavagetto; SS, Pee Wee Reese; RF, Dixie Walker; CF, Carl Furillo; LF, Pete Reiser; C, Bruce Edwards; P, Joe Hatten; P, Kirby Higbe; P, Vic Lombardi; P, Hank Behrman; P, Hugh Casey.

With only one regular, Walker, hitting .300 and Higbe's 17 wins leading the pitching staff, the Dodgers nevertheless succeeded in ending the regular season tied with the heavily favored Cardinals. They were swept in the two-of-three pennant playoff series yet seemed on the verge of replacing the Cards as the NL's next great dynasty, especially when they won the flag in 1947. And while it's true that the Dodgers did win five more pennants in the next decade, many observers felt they perennially seemed to fall short of expectations—one game short each season, to be exact. The 1946 club set a painful pattern; it was the first of three Dodgers teams in a six-year period to lose the pennant by dint of dropping its last game of the season. Moreover, of the six World Series the Dodgers participated in between 1947 and 1956, they lost five of them, all to the Yankees. Had the Dodgers defeated the Cards in 1946 and thereupon started off their reign as the NL's top team by proving to themselves that they could win the big game, it is conceivable that they would have won 9 pennants in the next 11 years rather than 6, and that they, and not the Yankees, would have been the era's dominant club.

## 1950 BOSTON RED SOX
### W–94 L–60
### Manager: Joe McCarthy/Steve O'Neill

**Regular Lineup**—1B, Walt Dropo; 2B; Bobby Doerr; 3B Johnny Pesky; SS, Vern Stephens; RF, Al Zarilla; CF, Dom DiMaggio; LF, Ted Williams; C. Birdie Tebbetts; P. Mel Parnell; P, Ellis Kinder; P, Joe Dobson; P, Chuck Stobbs.

This team ought to have won its third consecutive pennant but instead ended up with three hairline misses, losing in 1948 to the Indians in a pennant playoff game, to the Yankees in 1949 by dropping the last two games after leading by one game with two to go, and to the Yankees again in 1950 despite hitting .302 as a unit and scoring 1027 runs, both figures records for the era. Analysts pointed to the disabling broken elbow Ted Williams sustained in the All-Star Game as the reason the Sox came up short in 1950, yet it's hard to see how they could have needed more hitting. What did them in was a dreadful 4.88 staff ERA—nearly a run worse than in 1949—and an AL-high 748 bases on balls. Mel Parnell, with an 18–10 record, was the only pitcher whose ERA was under 4.00, but even Parnell failed to match his 1949 performance, when he won 25 games. The most exciting post-World War II offensive show, the Sox featured a utilityman, Billy Goodman, who wasn't good enough to crack the regular lineup even though he won the AL batting crown with a .354 average. It was sad to see them fade. The 1950 season was both their last gasp and McCarthy's; he quit in mid-campaign, the team slipped to distant third in 1951 and then started tumbling swiftly toward mediocrity. Those who loved hitting in those years still talk wistfully about the classic Series matchup they never got to see—the Rex Sox versus the Dodgers.

## 1956 CINCINNATI REDS
### W–91 L–63
### Manager: Birdie Tebbetts

**Regular Lineup**—1B, Ted Kluszewski; 2B, Johnny Temple; 3B, Ray Jablonski; SS, Roy McMillan; RF, Wally Post; CF, Gus Bell; LF, Frank Robinson; C, Ed Bailey; P, Brooks Lawrence; P, Johnny Klippstein; P. Joe Nuxhall; P, Art Fowler; P, Hal Jeffcoat; P, Hersh Freeman.

McMillan hit three home runs and Temple hit just two, but the rest of the team clubbed 216, spurring Reds fans to vote the entire starting lineup to the All-Star team the following year, and who can argue that their chauvinism was all that wrongheaded? Had Bell hit one more four-bagger, the Reds would have been the first team in history to have four 30-homer men; as it was, they tied the 1947 Giants' record for the most home runs in a 154-game season. Weak pitching did them in—what else?—but the Big Red Machine in the 1970s was pallid in comparison to this team. The most comparable club in recent history was the 1963 Twins.

## 1959 MILWAUKEE BRAVES
### W–86 L–70
### Manager: Fred Haney

**Regular Lineup**—1B, Joe Adcock; 2B, Felix Mantilla; 3B, Eddie Mathews; SS, Johnny Logan; RF, Hank Aaron; CF, Billy Bruton; LF, Wes Covington; C, Del Crandall; P. Warren Spahn; P, Lew Burdette; P, Bob Buhl; P, Joey Jay; P, Don McMahon.

Not a great team in any sense but good enough to have easily won its third consecutive pennant if Red Schoendienst hadn't been idled for the entire season by tuberculosis. Minus Schoendienst, the Braves tried seven players at second base before going with 35-year-old Bobby Avila in the stretch drive. Avila had been on the downside of the hill for about five years by then and played his last innings in the two-game pennant playoff loss to the Dodgers. Equally responsible for the Braves' also-ran status, though not as well publicized, was Haney's stubborn insistence of platooning lefty Frank Torre at first base with righty Joe Adcock. Torre hit .228 and had one homer; Adcock batted .292 and clubbed 25 homers. No one could fault Haney for the loss of Schoendienst, but his Adcock-Torre experiment played a large hand in his being replaced at the close of the season by Chuck Dressen.

# Minor League
# Feats and Firsts

The first minor league was the International Association, formed in 1877. A second minor-league circuit, the League Alliance, also tried to get off the ground that same year but failed to complete its schedule. In 1879 the Western League, the first minor league to endure for a substantial length of time, was founded by Ted Sullivan. Five years later the International League, the oldest minor league still in existence, began as the Eastern League. By 1903 there were 19 minor leagues, and ten years later the total had climbed to 40. In 1949, the peak of what is now seen to have been the golden age of organized baseball, there were 59 minor leagues in operation. Many were forced to close their doors, however, when major-league teams began televising games into their areas. Even the relatively stable Triple A leagues underwent severe upheavals once the two major leagues began transferring franchises in the 1950s and placed teams in Milwaukee, Kansas City, Baltimore, San Francisco and Los Angeles, all former AAA bastions. Major-league expansion in the 1960s and 1970s removed several more Triple A strongholds from minor-league circuits. In 1996 there were 15 minor leagues, with four of them organized exclusively for first-year professional players, and 9 independent leagues.

### First Minor-League Pennant Winner
The Tecumseh club of London, Ontario, which won the 1877 International Association flag with a team batting average of .191; St. Paul was leading the League Alliance that same year when it disbanded.

### Biggest Crowd to See a Minor-League Game
In 1982, 65,666 fans turned out for an American Association game between Denver and Omaha. The previous record

had been held by the Miami Marlins, who drew 57,000 to the Orange Bowl on August 7, 1956, to watch Satchel Paige beat Columbus in an International League game. In 1941 the Jersey City Giants of the IL set a record when they sold 65,391 tickets for their home opener at Roosevelt Stadium, but since the park held only 40,000 all ticket buyers could not, and obviously did not, attend the game.

## First Minor-League Team to Draw 1 Million Fans in a Season

The Louisville Redbirds in 1983 had a total attendance of 1,052,438.

## Best Minor-League Team Ever

By almost unanimous consensus the 1919–25 Baltimore Orioles, who won an organized-baseball record seven pennants in a row after losing their star southpaw Ralph Worrell, who won 25 games in 1918 at age 19 and then perished in the flu epidemic. In 1919 the Orioles featured Max Bishop at second base; 23-year-old coal miner Joe Boley at shortstop; Fritz Maisel, down from the majors, at third base; Merwin Jacobson in center field; and Otis Lawry, the International League's top hitter with a .364 average. A year later Jacobson led the IL with a .404 mark, the league's highest average since 1897, and 20-year-old Lefty Grove was purchased from Martinsburg in the Blue Ridge League to augment an already solid mound staff that was led by Harry Frank, Jack Ogden and Jack Bentley. The 1920 Orioles won the IL flag by a record 26½ games and demolished St. Paul in the Little World Series.

In 1921 the Orioles won 119 games in a 168-game season and a record 27 games in a row. The team easily triumphed again in 1922 as owner-manager Jack Dunn continued to resist offers from major-league teams for his stars like Grove and Bishop, although he did auction off Jack Bentley to the Giants for $65,000 at the end of the season.

Good as Grove was, however, the club's best pitcher in 1923 was Rube Parnham with a 33–7 record and a season-ending string of 20 wins in a row. Parnham had earlier pitched briefly with the Philadelphia A's, but several other Orioles stars like outfielder Clarence Pitt, the IL's top hitter in 1923, and first baseman Clayton Sheedy, never got a major-league opportunity at all, in part because of Dunn's refusal to let go of his players until his price was met. At the conclusion of the 1923 season, with rival IL clubs tiring of the Orioles' dominance and pressing league officials to end the circuit's hold-out against the major-league draft system that embraced the rest of organized baseball, Dunn finally agreed to sell Max Bishop to the A's for $25,000 but held on to Joe Boley until 1927 when the A's forked over $65,000. By then Boley was 31 years old and on the downside of his career.

Lefty Grove was more fortunate; he went to the A's for $100,600 after a 26–6 season in 1924. In his five years with the Orioles, Grove won 108 games and lost only 36, giving him a combined major- and minor-league record of 411 wins and 190 losses, easily the highest winning percentage in organized baseball history. Preparing for Grove's departure, the Orioles signed 24-year-old amateur pitching star George Earnshaw late in the 1924 season and kept him until the spring of 1928 when he too was sold to the A's—for $70,000. In 1925 Earnshaw, Jack Ogden and Tommy Thomas still gave the Orioles the most formidable pitching staff in the minors and spurred the club to its seventh straight pennant with help from outfielders Maurice Archdeacon and Twitchy Dick Porter, the IL's batting champ in 1924 and again in 1927. Earnshaw, Ogden and Thomas were all in the majors by the 1928 season, but Dunn clung to Porter until a few weeks before his death in October of 1928 when Porter was finally sold to Cleveland for $40,000. By the time Porter left the Orioles he was 28 years old.

A few last comments. Great as the Orioles were, they had one glaring weakness. At no time during their seven-year reign could Dunn manage to land a top-flight catcher. On that count, and that count alone, the team was below major-league caliber. Many observers believed that in all other respects the Orioles were better than most of the teams in the majors. The best evidence of that was that the A's, who wound up with the majority of Dunn's stars, emerged as the game's strongest team by the end of the decade.

Now, to answer your two questions. How did Connie Mack corral so many of those great Orioles? Well, it didn't hurt that he and Dunn were both Irish. The more interesting question is how did the A's come up with all that dough in the mid-1920s after suffering a long series of last-place clubs that drew hardly any fans at all and then, despite winning three pennants in a row, fall on such hard times by the early 1930s that Mack had to sell almost all of his purchased Orioles? There was a depression on, sure, but was that the whole story? It would take space that I don't have to spare in this book and a grasp of Mack's rather strange psychological makeup that no one may ever have to tell you why I don't think it was.

## Second-Best Minor-League Team Ever

Ironically, while the Orioles were dashing to seven straight International League pennants, the Fort Worth Panthers of the Texas League won seven consecutive percentage championships between 1919 and 1925, losing the pennant only in 1919 in a split-season playoff to the Shreveport Gassers, the first-half winner, and then sweeping both halves of the league race for the next six years. Managed by Jake Atz, the "Cats" featured first baseman Clarence "Big Boy" Kraft, who collected 55 homers in 1924 (at the time a minor-league record) and 196 RBIs, still a Texas League record, then retired and was replaced in 1925 by Ed Konetchy, a former longtime major-league star. Atz's top moundsmen were Paul Wachtel, who won a Texas League-record 232 games, and Joe Pate. Many of the Cats stars saw big-league duty at some point in their careers, but apart from Konetchy only pitcher Wilcy Moore and infielders Jackie Tavener and Topper Rigney were significant performers in the majors.

## Worst Minor League Team Ever

In 1926 Reading of the International League posted a 31–129 record and .194 winning percentage while finishing an organized baseball-record 75 games behind pennant-winning Toronto.

## Most Recent Minor-League Team that Staked a Legitimate Claim to Being Major League

In 1945 Paul Fagan bought a one-third interest in the San Francisco Seals from owner Charlie Graham and immediately vowed to bring major-league baseball to San Francisco and soon—as soon, the fact was, as he succeeded in having the Pacific Coast League certified as a third major league. Fagan, the scion of a San Francisco banking family, was at first viewed as a crackpot by members of the major-league establishment, but his vision suddenly took on a frightening tinge of reality when he began implementing it. Fagan believed that the path to big-league recognition lay in getting all PCL teams to stop selling their star players to major-league clubs and start paying them big-league salaries. Accordingly, he saw to it that the 1946 Seals were better paid than many of their major-league counterparts and arranged for them to travel first class and stay in the best hotels. His reward in 1946 was a new minor-league attendance record, and San Francisco's reward was a Seals pennant behind pitcher Larry Jansen's 30–6 season and the stellar work of second baseman Hugh Luby, the PCL's Most Valuable Player that year, and first baseman Ferris Fain. Fagan's plan collapsed when other PCL club owners refused to match his largesse and undermined him by arranging working agreements with major-league teams that cemented the PCL's minor-league status, but for that one year the Seals looked, traveled, played and were paid like major leaguers. Ferris Fain, for one, balked when he was sold to the Philadelphia A's because he would have to take a cut in salary.

### Number of Home Runs Babe Ruth Hit in the Minor Leagues

Just one. It came in 1914 while he'd been sold earlier in the year by Baltimore. Ruth was the first great star that Jack Dunn auctioned to a major-league club. Dunn had hoped to hang onto Ruth awhile longer but encountered money problems when the Federal League put a team in Baltimore to compete with the Orioles. Why did Ruth go to the Boston Red Sox instead of Philadelphia like so many of Dunn's latter-day stars? Actually Ruth came very close to winding up with the A's. Connie Mack was given first crack at him but declined, and Dunn then contacted Boston owner Joe Lannin, who also happened to be Irish, as was the Red Sox player-manager, Bill Carrigan. John McGraw, of the same persuasion, felt betrayed when Dunn sold Ruth without first offering the Babe to the Giants.

### All-time Organized-Baseball Record for Most Home Runs in an Inning

3—Gene Rye, Waco, Texas League, May 6, 1930, against Beaumont; Waco scored 18 runs in the inning and won 22–4. Rye, whose real name was Mercantelli, appeared briefly with the Boston Red Sox the following year and went 7-for-39, all singles.

### Organized Baseball Record for Best Season by a Pitcher

Bob Riesener had a perfect 20–0 record in 1957 for Alexandria in the Evangeline League; in 1949, 40-year-old right-hander Orie Arntzen of Albany in the Eastern League posted a 25–2 record and was voted the Minor League Player of the Year by the *Sporting News;* but many consider Bill Kennedy's 1946 season with Rocky Mount in the Coastal Plains League to be the most awesome year ever by a minor-league hurler. Kennedy, who later had an eight-year major-league career, mainly as a reliever, had a 28–3 record, with 456 strikeouts and a 1.03 ERA in 280 innings.

## Longest Hitting Streak in Organized Baseball History

Joe DiMaggio went on a 61-game tear for the San Francisco Seals in 1933 as a prelude to his major-league 56-game record, but the all-time record belongs to outfielder Joe Wilhoit of Wichita in the Western League, who in 1919 hit in 69 straight games. Wilhoit had earlier played four seasons in the majors and hoped his skein would earn him a return ticket, but it didn't happen.

## Organized Baseball Record for Highest Season Batting Average (USA leagues only)

.441—Bob Schmidt, Duluth, Northern League, 1939

## Organized Baseball Record for Most Home Runs in a Season

72—Joe Bauman, Roswell Rockets, Longhorn League, 1954. Bauman, a 32-year-old first baseman, also had 224 RBIs, hit an even .400 and had a .916 slugging average.

## Organized Baseball Record for Most RBIs in a Season

254—Bob Crues, Amarillo, West Texas–New Mexico League, 1948. In addition, Crues hit .404 and had 69 home runs.

## Organized Baseball Record for Most Home Runs in a Game

8—Nig Clarke, Corsicana, Texas League, June 15, 1902. That day Corsicana and Texarkana moved their game to Ennis and played in the morning to circumvent the Sunday blue laws then in force. In the tiny Ennis park, Corsicana eked out a 51–3 win as Clarke went 8-for-8, all four-baggers. The class of the Texas League at the time, Corsicana posted a record 27 straight wins in 1902, led by Clarke, who later made the major leagues as a catcher with Cleveland.

## Organized Baseball Record for Best Single-Game Performance by a Pitcher

On May 13, 1952, Ron Necciai, pitching for Bristol, a Pittsburgh farm club in the Class D Appalachian League, threw a no-hitter and struck out 27 batters in a nine-inning game. That same summer a teammate of his, Bill Bell, threw three no-hitters, two of them back-to-back. By the end of the 1952 season Pittsburgh owner Branch Rickey, groping for ways to bolster the last-place Pirates, had rushed both Necciai and Bell up to the majors, where they were hit hard, lost confidence and never recovered it.

## Best Minor-League Player Prior to World War II

Plenty of grist for argument here, but I recommend Ike Boone, who won five minor league batting titles in four different circuits—the Southern Association in 1921, the Texas League in 1923, the Pacific Coast League in 1929 and the International League in 1931 and 1934. With the San Francisco Mission Reds in 1929, Boone hit .407 and had 55 homers and 323 hits, leading the Pacific Coast League in all these departments; in addition, he collected 553 total bases, an all-time organized-baseball season record. A year later Boone was hitting .448 for the Mission Reds after 83 games when he was acquired by Brooklyn. Boone was among the rare minor-league *wunderkinds* who hit nearly as well in the majors—.319 in 356 games and .330-plus in his only two seasons as a regular. The rap against him was that he was slow afoot and a lackadaisical outfielder, the same rap borne by Smead Jolley and, to a lesser extent, Buzz Arlett, two PCL contemporaries of Boone's who many contend were his superiors. Another PCL star of the same vintage, Ox Eckhardt, was lightly regarded by major-league scouts because he fashioned his astronomical minor-league batting average by hitting to the opposite field rather than with power.

## Best Minor League Player since World War II

Rocky Nelson gets my vote. Unlike Boone, Arlett and Jolley, who hit well when given opportunities in the majors, and Eckhardt, who never got a real opportunity, Nelson was given chance after chance in the late 1940s and early 1950s but flopped so many times that it seemed inevitable he would finish out his career in the International League, where he won two Triple Crowns. But then Pittsburgh gave him one last shot in 1959 at age 34, and he responded with two good seasons while sharing first base with Dick Stuart, another minor-league sensation no one really believed would ever produce in the majors.

### Career Home Run Leader, American Association

Bunny Brief, 256. Brief also led the PCL in 1916 with 33 homers. In 569 major-league at bats, he hit .223 and had only five homers.

### Career Home Run Leader, International League

Ollie Carnegie, 258. Frozen for years in the high minors, Carnegie never played a single game in the majors.

### Career Home Run Leader, Pacific Coast League

Buzz Arlett, 251. Arlett began as a pitcher with the Oakland Oaks and still holds the PCL record for the most putouts in a season by a pitcher, one of the many paradoxes in a career that was restricted to the minors for all but one year supposedly because of weak glovework. Like Brief, Arlett cut a swath in more than one Triple A league. In 1932 he twice hit four home runs in a game for Baltimore and led the International League with 54 homers and 144 RBIs. For how he did in his lone year in the majors, see both "Rookie Records" and "Final Season Records."

## MINOR LEAGUE CAREER PITCHING LEADERS

### Wins

|  | Minor-League Wins | Major-League Wins |
|---|---|---|
| 1. Bill Thomas | 384 | —[1] |
| 2. Joe Martina | 349 | 6[2] |
| 3. George Payne | 348 | 1 |
| 4. Tony Freitas | 342 | 25 |
| 5. Alex McColl | 332 | 4[3] |

[1]Thomas collected 384 wins despite losing three full seasons, from 1947 through 1949, when he was declared ineligible after being implicated in an Evangeline League betting scandal.

[2]All six wins came as a 35-year-old rookie with the 1924 Washington Senators. His last major-league appearance was a perfect relief inning in the World Series that fall.

[3]Another longtime minor leaguer who got his sole major-league chance with a pennant-bound Washington team. McColl came to the Senators when he was 39—in time to pitch two perfect relief innings in the 1933 World Series.

**Most Wins in One League**
295—Frank Shellenback, Pacific Coast League. Won 10 games as a 19-year-old rookie with the 1918 White Sox, then was cut when he started poorly in 1919 and never again made it out of the high minors.

**Most Losses in One League**
235—Herman Pillette and Spider Baum, Pacific Coast League

**Most Games Pitched**
1015—Bill Thomas

# MINOR LEAGUE CAREER BATTING LEADERS
## Highest Average

|   | Minor League | Major League |
| --- | --- | --- |
| 1. Ike Boone | .370 | .319 |
| 2. Ox Eckhardt | .367 | 192[1] |
| 3. Smead Jolley | .366 | .305 |
| 4. Don Stokes | .365 | — |

## Most Home Runs

| | | |
| --- | --- | --- |
| 1. Hector Espino | 484 | — |
| 2. Nelson Barrera | 453 | — |
| 3. Andres Mora | 444 | 27 |
| 4. Buzz Arlett | 432 | 18 |
| 5. Nick Cullop | 420 | 11[2] |
| 6. Merv Connors | 400 | 8 |
| 7. Joe Hauser | 399 | 79[3] |
| 8. Bobby Prescott | 398 | 0 |
| 9. Jack Pierce | 395 | 8 |
| 10. Jack Graham | 384 | 38 |

## Most RBIs

|  | Minor League | Major League |
|---|---|---|
| 1. Nick Cullop | 1857 | 67 |
| 2. Buzz Arlett | 1786 | 72 |
| 3. Jim Poole | 1785 | 140[4] |
| 4. Spencer Harris | 1769 | 46 |
| 5. Larry Barton | 1751 | — |

## Most Hits

| | | |
|---|---|---|
| 1. Spencer Harris | 3617 | 94 |
| 2. Harry Strohm | 3486 | — |
| 3. Eddie Hock | 3474 | 1 |
| 4. George Whiteman | 3388 | 70 |
| 5. Snake Henry | 3384 | 14[5] |
| 6. Jigger Statz | 3356 | 737[6] |

## Most Stolen Bases

|  | Minor League | Major League |
|---|---|---|
| 1. George Hogriever | 947 | 48[7] |
| 2. Kid Mohler | 776 | 0 |
| 3. Count Campau | 682 | 63 |
| 4. Duke Reilley | 676 | 5 |

[1]Holds the all-time organized-baseball record for highest career batting average, even ahead of Ty Cobb's, which is lowered by his minor-league stats.

[2]One of the last American Indian players, he also showed good power in the majors but struck out too much to stick.

[3]Both preceded and followed Jim Poole as the Philadelphia A's regular first baseman. A knee injury gave the job to Poole, but Hauser later reclaimed it for a time while Jimmie Foxx was still learning the position. Small for a first sacker, only five-feet, ten-and-a-half inches—but a bomber in the high minors. In 1930 Hauser hit 63 home runs for Baltimore and had 443 total bases, an International League record. With Minneapolis in the American Association three years later, he set an all-time Triple A record when he clubbed 69 homers.

[4]Became expendable when the A's acquired Jimmie Foxx and Hauser recovered from his knee injury. His 29 seasons in organized baseball are

the most by any player who wasn't a pitcher. Among pitchers, George Brunet leads with 33 seasons, followed by Herman Pillette who, like Poole, put 29 years into the game. Brunet is an original. Apart from being the only minor-league pitching great to have a significant major-league career—324 games and 15 seasons—he's one of the small number of post-1950 players to forge a second life for himself in the minors after his major-league days ended. Still active in 1985 at age 50, Brunet had a 244–242 minor-league record in 668 games.

[5]Did poorly when the Braves gave him a crack at their first-base job in the early 1920s—but at least he got a chance in the majors, however brief. Larry Barton, who came along a few years later when the game was overstocked with good-hitting first basemen, never did.

[6]His 3356 hits all came with the Los Angeles Angels in the PCL. When his major-league total is added to them, he stands fourth on the all-time organized-baseball career hit list, behind only Pete Rose, Ty Cobb and Hank Aaron.

[7]Many of his minor-league seasons were in the 1890s before the modern rule for determining a stolen base was evolved. As a result, his true stolen base total is probably quite a bit less.

# Switch Hitters' Records

In 1950 Jim Russell of the Brooklyn Dodgers became the first switch hitter in major-league history to homer from both sides of the plate for the second time in the same game. Russell's record lasted less than six years. On May 18, 1956, Mickey Mantle of the New York Yankees had his third switch-hit homer game. By the time he was done Mantle would have 10 of them and hold most of the other all-time switch-hit slugging records as well.

### First Switch Hitter to Homer from Both Sides of the Plate in the Same Game
AL—Wally Schang, Philadelphia, September 8, 1916, at Shibe Park off Allan Russell and Slim Love of the Yankees
NL—Augie Galan, Chicago, June 15, 1937

### First Switch Hitter of Note
Bob "Death to Flying Things" Ferguson, New York Mutuals, 1871. Active in the major leagues until 1884, Ferguson was the first switch hitter to collect 1000 career hits.

### First Switch Hitter to Collect 2000 Career Hits
George Davis, Chicago White Sox, 1902. Davis collected 2655 hits altogether, the switch-hit career record until Frankie Frisch broke it in 1934.

### First Switch Hitter to Collect 3000 Career Hits
Pete Rose, Chicinnati Reds, 1978. In 1984 Rose also of course became the first switch hitter to make 4000 hits.

**First Switch Hitter to Collect 100 Hits from Each Side of the Plate in a Season**
NL—Garry Templeton, St. Louis, 1979
AL—Willie Wilson, Kansas City Royals, 1980

**First Switch Hitter to Win a Batting Title**
AA—Tommy Tucker, Baltimore Orioles, 1889
AL—Mickey Mantle, New York, 1956
NL—Pete Rose, Cincinnati, 1968

# SEASON BATTING RECORDS

| Department | National League | American League |
|---|---|---|
| Batting Average | .362, George Davis, New York, 1893 .353, Willie McGee, St. Louis, 1985* | .365, MICKEY MANTLE, New York, 1956** |
| Slugging Average | .633, Chipper Jones, Atlanta, 1999 | .705, MICKEY MANTLE, New York, 1961 |
| Home Runs | 45, Chipper Jones, Atlanta, 1999 | 54, MICKEY MANTLE, New York 1961 |
| RBIs | 136, GEORGE DAVIS, New York, 1897 130, Ken Caminiti, San Diego, 1996 | 130, Mickey Mantle, New York, 1956* |
| Hits | 230, PETE ROSE, Cincinnati, 1973 | 230, WILLIE WILSON, K.C. Royals, 1980 |
| Doubles | 55, LANCE BERKMAN, Houston, 2001 | 46, John Anderson, Milwaukee, 1901 |
| Triples | 27, GEORGE DAVIS, New York, 1893 19, Max Carey, Pittsburgh, 1923* 19, Garry Templeton, St. Louis, 1979* | 21, Willie Wilson, K. C. Royals, 1985 |
| Total Bases | 369, Ripper Collins, St. Louis, 1934 | 376, MICKEY MANTLE, New York, 1956 |
| Bases on Balls | 126, Chipper Jones, Atlanta, 1999 | 146, MICKEY MANTLE, New York, 1957 |

| Department | National League | American League |
|---|---|---|
| Runs | 140, MAX CAREY, Pittsburgh, 1922 | 133, Willie Wilson, K.C. Royals, 1980 |
| Pinch Hits | 22, Red Schoendienst, St. Louis, 1962 | 24, DAVE PHILLEY, Baltimore, 1961 |
| Stolen Bases | 110, VINCE COLEMAN, St. Louis, 1985 | 83, Willie Wilson, K.C. Royals, 1979 |
| At Bats | 695, Maury Wills, Los Angeles, 1962 | 705, WILLIE WILSON, K.C. Royals, 1980 |
| Strikeouts | 146, Todd Hundley, New York, 1996 | 160, MICKEY TETTLETON, Detroit, 1991 |
| Fewest Strikeouts (Minimum 500 ABs) | 10, FRANKIE FRISCH, St. Louis, 1927 | 21, Buck Weaver, Chicago, 1919 |

*Record since 1901
**In 1956 Mantle became the only switch hitter ever to win a Triple Crown.
Note: Tommy Tucker of the Baltimore Orioles (AA) hit .372 in 1889, the all-time highest season average by a switch hitter.

**First Switch Hitter to Hit for the Cycle**
NL—Max Carey, Pittsburgh, June 20, 1925
AL—Mickey Mantle, New York, May 23, 1957

## CAREER BATTING RECORDS

| Department | Name | Years Active | Record No. |
|---|---|---|---|
| Batting Average | Frankie Frisch | 1919–37 | .316 |
| Slugging Average | Mickey Mantle | 1951–68 | .557 |
| Home Runs | Mickey Mantle | 1951–68 | 536 |
| RBIs | Eddie Murray | 1977–97 | 1913 |
| Hits | Pete Rose | 1963–86 | 4256 |
| Doubles | Pete Rose | 1963–86 | 746 |
| Triples | George Davis | 1890–1909 | 167 |
| Total Bases | Pete Rose | 1963–86 | 5752 |
| Bases on Balls | Mickey Mantle | 1951–1968 | 1734 |
| Runs | Pete Rose | 1963–86 | 2165 |

| Department | Name | Years Active | Record No. |
|---|---|---|---|
| Pinch Hits | Jerry Hairston | 1973–89 | 94 |
| Stolen Bases | Tim Raines | 1979–2002 | 808 |
| At Bats | Pete Rose | 1963–86 | 14,053 |
| Strikeouts | Mickey Mantle | 1951–68 | 1710 |

## Most Unsung Career Record Held by a Switch Hitter

Don Buford grounded into only 33 double plays in 4553 at bats—a ratio of one to every 138 at bats, the best in history.

# Great Batting Debuts

Late in the 1951 season the St. Louis Browns brought outfielder Bob Nieman up from the Texas League. On September
14 Brownie fans watched him face pitcher Mickey McDermott
of the Red Sox and become the only player prior to the
Cards' Keith McDonald in 2000 to homer in his first two at
bats in the majors. Bert Campaneris of the Kansas City A's
is otherwise the only player in this century to hit two homers
in his initial major-league game—in his first and fourth at bats
on July 23, 1964. The first player to homer twice in his inaugural game was Princeton Charlie Reilly, who did it with Columbus in the American Association on October 9, 1889. Reilly,
a switch hitter, played in five more games and batted .478
before the curtain descended on the 1889 season. It was
mostly downhill for him after his great debut—he hit only
.250 in an eight-year career—although in 1892 he became one
of the first three players in history to get a pinch hit.

### First National League Player to Homer in His Initial at Bat
Until recently it was believed to be Phillies pitcher Bill
Duggleby, who hit a grand slam in his initial big league at
bat on April 21, 1898. Duggleby is still the only player to hit
a four-run dinger in his first at bat, but another pitcher—Billy
Gumbert of Pittsburgh on June 10, 1890—is now considered
the first NL'er to homer the initial time he stepped to the
plate.

### Second National League Player to Homer in His First at Bat
Johnny Bates, Boston Braves, April 12, 1906

### First American League Player to Homer in His First at Bat
Luke Stuart, St. Louis Browns, August 8, 1921. Stuart's feat

was buried for years because he appeared in his first major league game on July 28, 1921. His first plate appearance, however, did not come until 11 days later when he hit a two-run blast off of Walter Johnson. Stuart's landmark thrill proved to be very short-lived. He batted only twice more in the majors and was hitless in both at bats.

### First Pitcher to Homer in His First at Bat, since 1901
Clise Dudley, Brooklyn Dodgers, April 29, 1929

### First American League Pitcher to Homer in His First at Bat
Bill Lefebvre, Boston Red Sox, June 10, 1938

### First Black to Homer in His First at Bat
Dan Bankhead, Brooklyn Dodgers, August 20, 1947. It was his only hit that year and the only homer in his career.

### First American League Black Player to Homer in His First at Bat
Gates Brown, Detroit Tigers, June 19, 1963

### Only Expansion Team Player to Homer in His First at Bat in Team's Inaugural Game
Al Woods, Toronto Blue Jays, April 7, 1977, as a pinch hitter in the fifth inning.

### Only Players on Opposing Teams to Homer in Their First at Bats in the Same Game
Emmett Mueller, Philadelphia Phillies, and Ernie Koy, Brooklyn Dodgers, April 19, 1938

### Winners of the "Three Musketeers" Award
On September 20, 1981, Gary Gaetti, Tim Laudner and Kent Hrbek of the Minnesota Twins all homered in their first major league games, Gaetti's coming in his first at bat.

### Most Unlikely Player to Homer in His First at Bat (Pitchers Excluded)
Shortstop Buddy Kerr of the New York Giants hit one out the first time he stepped to the plate on September 8, 1943. Five years later Kerr became the last Giants regular to play

a full season in the Polo Grounds without hitting a single home run.

## Most Significant Homer by Player in His First at Bat
Jay Bell, Cleveland Indians, September 29, 1986, off Bert Blyleven of the Twins. Bell's clout—on the first pitch he saw in the major leagues—was the record-breaking 47th gopher ball Blyleven served up in 1986.

## Winner of the "Not Easily Intimidated" Award
Facing Warren Spahn in his initial major-league game, on May 24, 1957, Cubs outfielder Frank Ernaga homered in his first at bat and then tripled his next time up against Spahn.

## Greatest Debut by a Hall of Famer
On June 30, 1894, Louisville outfielder Fred Clarke introduced himself by clubbing five hits in his first game. The only other player to debut with a five-hit game was Cecil Travis of the Senators on May 16, 1933, in a 12-inning contest.

## Players Who Got Four Hits in Their First Games
Spud Johnson, Columbus (AA), April 18, 1889
Ray Jansen, St. Louis Browns, September 30, 1910
Casey Stengel, Brooklyn Dodgers, July 27, 1912
Art Shires, Chicago White Sox, August 20, 1928
Ed Freed, Philadelphia Phillies, September 11, 1942
Spook Jacobs, Philadelphia A's, April 13, 1954
Willie McCovey, San Francisco Giants, July 30, 1959
Mack Jones, Milwaukee Braves, July 13, 1961
Ted Cox, Boston Red Sox, September 17, 1977
Kirby Puckett, Minnesota Twins, May 8, 1984
Bill Bean, Detroit Tigers, April 25, 1987
Delino DeShields Montreal Expos, April 9, 1990
Special Mention—Pitcher Russ Van Atta debuted with the Yankees on April 25, 1933, by collecting four hits in the process of shutting out the Senators 16–0.

## The Three Greatest One-Game Wonders
First Place—The Houston Colt 45s started an all-rookie lineup on September 29, 1963, including outfielder Johnny Paciorek, who was a perfect 3-for-3, walked twice, scored four runs and drove in three. A back injury felled Paciorek in 1964, and he never worked his way back to the majors.

Second Place—Third baseman Ray Jansen of the St. Louis Browns went 4-for-5 on September 30, 1910, in his only look at major-league pitching.

Third Place—In 1933 catcher Aubrey Epps of the Pirates went 3-for-4 in his only big-league game and knocked in three runs.

# Pitchers' Records As Hitters

For a variety of reasons, almost all of the season and career records for the best offensive performance by a pitcher were established prior to expansion. Many think the most remarkable achievement of all belongs to Red Lucas. In 1936, Lucas became the first major leaguer—let alone pitcher—to collect 100 career pinch hits. He retired with 114, the ML record until 1965 and still the mark for the most pinch singles by a pitcher. However, the record holders for the highest batting average and the second-highest batting average by a pitcher who collected at least 100 career pinch-hit at bats were both prominently active during the 1942–60 era. As the chart below shows, the holder of both the all-time record for the highest season slugging average and the twentieth century season record for the most total bases by a pitcher was also prominent in that era.

## SEASON BATTING RECORDS (1893–2002)*

| Department | National League | American League |
| --- | --- | --- |
| Batting Average | .427, Jack Bentley, New York, 1923 | .433, WALTER JOHNSON, Washington, 1925 |
| Slugging Average | .632, DON NEWCOMBE, Brooklyn, 1955 | .621, Wes Ferrell, Cleveland, 1931 |
| Home Runs | 7, Don Newcombe, Brooklyn, 1955<br>7, Don Drysdale, Los Angeles, 1965 | 9, WES FERRELL, Cleveland, 1931 |

*Pitchers' hitting performances prior to 1893 when the 60'6" pitching distance was established are excluded because pitchers in the early days hurled so many games that their at-bat totals were too high to allow their feats to be compared meaningfully to post-1893 hurlers. Pitchers who played 10 or more games at other positions are likewise excluded. A minimum 80 at bats are required for batting and slugging average leaders and leaders in fewest strikeouts.

| Department | National League | American League |
|---|---|---|
| Home Runs | 7, Mike Hampton Colorado, 2001 | |
| RBIs | 42, PINK HAWLEY, Pittsburgh, 1895 | 32, Wes Ferrell Boston, 1935 |
| Since 1901: | 28, Red Lucas, Cincinnati, 1927 | |
| Hits | 57, AMOS RUSIE, New York, 1893 57, PINK HAWLEY, Pittsburgh, 1895 | 52, George Uhle, Cleveland, 1923 |
| Since 1901: | 47, Red Lucas, Cincinnati, 1927 | |
| Runs | 38, KID NICHOLS, Boston, 1894 | 31, Jack Coombs, Philadelphia, 1911 |
| Since 1901: | 25, Claude Hendrix, Pittsburgh, 1912 | |
| Doubles | 14, PINK HAWLEY Pittsburgh, 1895 | 13, Red Ruffing Boston, 1928 |
| Since 1901: | 11, Red Lucas, Cincinnati, 1932 | 13, Joe Wood, Boston 1912 |
| Triples | 8, GEORGE HEMMING, Lou-Balt, 1894 | 6, Walter Johnson, Washington, 1913 |
| Since 1901: | 6, Claude Hendrix, Pittsburgh, 1912 | 6, Jesse Tannehill, New York, 1904 |
| Total Bases | 92, PINK HAWLEY, Pittsburgh, 1895 | 70, Wes Ferrell, Cleveland, 1931 |
| Since 1901: | 74, Don Newcombe, Brooklyn, 1955 | |
| Bases on Balls | 31, TED BREITENSTEIN, St. Louis, 1894 | 23, Fred Hutchinson, Detroit, 1948 |
| Since 1901: | 20, Robin Roberts, Philadelphia, 1951 | 23, Clark Griffith, Chicago, 1901 |
| Stolen Bases | 9, Win Mercer, Washington, 1896 | 10, NIXEY CALLAHAN Chicago, 1901 |
| Since 1901: | 8, Bill Dinneen, Boston, 1901 | |
| Special Mention: | 7, Rip Sewell, Pittsburgh, 1943[1] | |
| Strikeouts: | 68, JERRY KOOSMAN, New York, 1968 | 63, DEAN CHANCE, Minnesota, 1968 |

| Fewest<br>Strikeouts | 1, JOHNNY SAIN,<br>Boston, 1947<br>(107 ABs) | 1, Fred Hutchinson,<br>Detroit, 1946<br>(89 ABs) |
| --- | --- | --- |

[1]Twentieth-century record for the most stolen bases in a season by a player who performed at no position except pitcher.

## Highest Career Batting Average as Pinch Hitter, Minimum 50 PH ABs
.390—Fred Heimach, 1920–33 (20 for 52). Jack Bentley is the only other player who was a pitcher for a significant part of his career and posted a .300+ BA as a pinch hitter (.301) in 50 or more PH at bats.

## Highest Career Batting Average as Pinch Hitter, Minimum 100 PH ABs
.284—Bob Lemon, 1941–58 (31 for 109). Second is Schoolboy Rowe at .277, and George Uhle is third at .260.

## Highest Career Batting Average as Pinch Hitter, Minimum 200 PH AB
.244—Red Ruffing, 1924–47 (58 for 238).

## Most Games, Career, Pitcher
1251—Jesse Orosco, 1979–

## Most Games, Season, Appearing as Pitcher
NL—106—Mike Marshall, Los Angeles, 1974. The previous year Marshall had appeared in 92 games to break the old record of 90 that he shared with Wayne Granger. The pre-expansion record is 76 appearances, shared by Will White (1879), Pud Galvin (1883) and Hoss Radbourn (1883). Jim Konstanty, with 74 appearances for the Phillies in 1950, the year he became the first reliever to win an MVP Award, is the 20th-century pre-expansion record holder.

Al—90—Mike Marshall, Minnesota, 1969

## Most Games, Career, Pitcher, No Relief Appearances
537—Tom Glavine, 1987–present. Dwight Gooden held the

record until he made his first relief appearance in 1989; since Glavine may yet make a relief appearance before he retires, the standard again could one day belong to Terry Larkin, the original record-holder, whose 176 pitching appearances between 1876 and 1880 all came in a starting role.

## Most Chances Accepted, Career, since 1900
1761—Christy Mathewson, 1900–16

## Most Chances Accepted, Season
AL—262—Ed Walsh, Chicago, 1907
NL—206—John Clarkson, Boston, 1889
Other—257—Will White, Cincinnati AA, 1882
NL since 1901—168—Christy Mathewson, New York, 1908

## Most Chances Accepted, Game, Nine Innings
AL—13—Nick Altrock, Chicago, August 6, 1904
         Ed Walsh, Chicago, April 19, 1907
NL—12—Rip Sewell, Pittsburgh, June 6, 1941

## Most Assists, Season
AL—227—Ed Walsh, Chicago, 1907
NL—141—Christy Mathewson, New York, 1908
Other—223—Will White, Cincinnati AA, 1882

## Most Gold Glove Awards
16—Jim Kaat, all consecutive from 1962 through 1977

# Pinch-hitting Feats

Pinch hitters really began to come into their own in the 1950s, and no player did more to elevate their status than Peanuts Lowrey when he tagged 22 pinch bingles for the Cardinals in 1953. Close on Lowrey's heels followed Ron Northey, Dave Philley, Elmer Valo, Smokey Burgess and Jerry Lynch, and by the end of the decade most teams had at least one player whose sole job was to sit patiently in the dugout and await pivotal situations, usually late in a game, when his bat was needed.

### First Pitch Hitter

Most sources say it was pitcher Mickey Welch of the New York Giants, on September 10, 1889, but Welch was almost definitely not the first pinch hitter.

### First Player to Be Used as a Pinch Hitter Twice in a Season

In 1891 the rules were changed, allowing teams to substitute for any player during a game at any time. Previously substitutes could be used only in the event of an injury or with the opposing team's permission, which was not always granted. The St. Louis Browns of the American Association used pitcher Jack Stivetts as a pinch hitter at least twice in 1891, and perhaps more than that. Preliminary evidence suggest that he may even have been the first successful pinch hitter under the new rule. In any case, Stivetts posted the highest career BA (.297) of any pitcher who worked at least 2000 innings.

### First Successful Pinch Hitter

Jack Doyle of the Cleveland Spiders is still given the honor in most record books for his pinch single against Brooklyn on June 7, 1892. However, there are several documented earlier instances when a substitute batter delivered a safe hit. The earliest came on October 2, 1873, when Jim Devlin of the

National Association Philadelphia Whites batted for a team-mate and singled.

## EVOLUTION OF THE SEASON PINCH-HIT RECORD

| Player | Team | League | Year | Pinch Hits |
|--------|------|--------|------|-----------|
| Jack Doyle | Cleveland | National | 1892 | 1[1] |
| John Sharrott | Philadelphia | National | 1893 | 2[2] |
| Doggie Miller | Louisville | National | 1896 | 6 |
| Duke Farrell | Washington | National | 1897 | 8[3] |
| Sammy Strang | New York | National | 1905 | 8 |
| Howard Wakefield | Washington | American | 1906 | 9 |
| Dode Criss | St. Louis | American | 1908 | 12[4] |
| Ted Easterly | Cleveland–Chicago | American | 1912 | 13 |
| Doc Miller | Boston | National | 1913 | 20[5] |
| Sam Leslie | New York | National | 1932 | 22[6] |
| Peanuts Lowrey | St. Louis | National | 1953 | 22[7] |
| Dave Philley | Baltimore | American | 1961 | 24 |
| Vic Davalillo | St. Louis | National | 1970 | 24 |
| Jose Morales | Montreal | National | 1975 | 25 |
| John Vander Wal | Colorado | National | 1995 | 28 |

[1]Two members of the Pittsburgh Pirates, Princeton Charlie Reilly and none other than Connie Mack, also had pinch hits in 1892.

[2]Tied by several players between 1893 and 1896.

[3]The first great pinch hitter. Until he went 1-for-11 in 1904, Farrell was averaging close to .500 in pinch-hit roles.

[4]The only player to be a league leader in pinch hits four consecutive seasons (1908–11). Criss was also the first pitcher in the American League to serve as a pinch-hitting specialist.

[5]Pinch hitters have generally followed great seasons with poor ones. Miller was one of the rare exceptions. After setting a new season pinch-hit record in 1913, he averaged .343 as a pinch hitter the following year—yet was released by the Reds.

[6]Leslie's feat was so unpublicized that when Lowrey collected 22 pinch hits in 1953 many sportswriters thought he'd set a new record and that the old one belonged to Ed Coleman of the Browns, who made 20 pinch hits in 1936.

[7]Lowrey's season is viewed as rather a fluke because he went 9-for-69 as a pinch hitter in 1954–55, but check what he did in 1952—13-for-27—one of the best years ever among pinch hitters with more than 25 at bats.

## .400 SEASONS BY PINCH HITTERS
### (Minimum 35 at bats)

| Player | Team | Year | Hits/AB's | Average |
|--------|------|------|-----------|---------|
| Ed Kranepool | New York Mets | 1974 | 17–35 | .486 |
| Frenchy Bordagaray | St. Louis Cards | 1938 | 20–43 | .465 |
| Gates Brown | Detroit Tigers | 1968 | 18–39 | .462 |
| Rick Miller | Boston Red Sox | 1983 | 16–35 | .457 |
| Jose Pagan | Pittsburgh Pirates | 1969 | 19–42 | .452 |
| Joe Cronin | Boston Red Sox | 1942 | 18–42 | .429 |
| Don Dillard | Cleveland Indians | 1961 | 15–35 | .429 |
| Candy Maldonado | San Francisco Giants | 1986 | 17–40 | .425 |
| Merritt Ranew | Chicago Cubs | 1963 | 17–41 | .415 |
| Carl Taylor | Pittsburgh Pirates | 1969 | 17–41 | .415 |
| Dave Philley | Philadelphia Phils | 1958 | 18–44 | .409 |
| Jerry Turner | San Diego Padres | 1978 | 20–49 | .408 |
| Frankie Baumholtz | Chicago Cubs | 1955 | 15–37 | .405 |
| Jerry Lynch | Cincinnati Reds | 1961 | 19–47 | .404 |
| Chet Laabs | St. Louis Browns | 1940 | 14–35 | .400 |

## Best World Series Performance by a Pinch Hitter
Dusty Rhodes of the New York Giants hit a home run and two singles and netted six RBIs as a pinch hitter in the first three games of the 1954 World Series.

## First Player to Hit a Pinch Home Run in a World Series
Yogi Berra, New York Yankees, October 2, 1947, at Ebbets Field. The first player to hit two pinch homers in a World Series was Chuck Essegian of the Los Angeles Dodgers in the second and sixth games of the 1959 Series, both coming at Comiskey Park.

## First Player to Hit Pinch Home Runs in Successive Games
Ray Caldwell, New York Yankees, June 10 and June 11, 1915. Caldwell was a pitcher.

## First Player to Hit Pinch Home Runs in Both Games of a Doubleheader
AL—Joe Cronin, Boston, June 17, 1943
NL—Hal Breeden, Montreal, July 13, 1973

**Most Pinch Home Runs, Season**
  NL—7—Dave Hansen, Los Angeles, 2000; Craig Wilson
Pittsburgh, 2001
  AL—5—Joe Cronin, Boston, 1943

**First Player to Homer as a Pinch Hitter in Three Consecutive Plate Appearances**
  Del Unser, Philadelphia Phillies, 1979. A year earlier Lee
Lacy of the Dodgers homered in three consecutive official at
bats but received a base on balls during his streak.

**First Player to Homer As a Pinch Hitter in His First Major League at Bat**
  NL—Eddie Morgan, St. Louis, April 14, 1936
  AL—Ace Parker, Philadelphia, April 30, 1937

**Most Plate Appearances, Season, by a Pinch Hitter**
  NL—88—Lenny Harris, New York, 2001
  AL—81—Elmer Valo, Washington and New York, 1960;
including an AL pinch-hit record 18 bases on balls.

**Lowest Season Batting Average by a Pinch Hitter, Minimum One Hit**
  .030—Chink Outen, Brooklyn, 1933; one hit in 33 at bats.
An outstanding hitter in the minors—he rapped .341 for Jersey City in 1932—Outen batted .248 overall for Brooklyn in
1933, his lone test against big-league pitching.

## TOP 10 IN CAREER PINCH HITS

|  | | Years Active | Pinch Hits |
|---|---|---|---|
| 1. | Lenny Harris | 1988– | 181 |
| 2. | Manny Mota | 1962–80 | 150 |
| 3. | Smokey Burgess | 1949–67 | 145[1] |
| 4. | Greg Gross | 1973–89 | 143 |
| 5. | Dave Hansen | 1990– | 128 |
| 6. | Jose Morales | 1973–85 | 123 |
|  | John Vander Wal | 1991– | 123 |
| 8. | Jerry Lynch | 1954–66 | 116 |

| | Years Active | Pinch Hits |
|---|---|---|
| 9. Red Lucas | 1923–38 | 114[2] |
| 10. Steve Braun | 1971–85 | 113 |

[1]Gets my vote as the best ever. Even as a rookie he was a rugged pinch hitter—he had 12—and if it hadn't been for a terrible final season, he would have had a career pinch-hit average of well over .300.

[2]Lucas, a pitcher, in 1935 became the first player to make 100 pinch hits, and he held the career record for most pinch hits until 1965 when Burgess broke it. Ham Hyatt, in 1917, was the first player to collect 50 career pinch hits. In 1913 Hyatt also became the first player to hit three pinch home runs in a season.

### First Player to Hit 10 Pinch Home Runs

Cy Williams. He retired in 1930 with only 41 career pinch hits, but 11 of them were homers.

### Most Career Pinch Home Runs

20—Cliff Johnson. Playing for Toronto, he broke Jerry Lynch's old mark of 18 when he hit his 19th on August 5, 1984, against Oakland.

### First Player to Hit Three Pinch Grand Slam Home Runs

Ron Northey, Chicago Cubs, September 18, 1950. Willie McCovey and Rich Reese have since tied Northey's record for the most pinch grand slams. In 1956 Northey hit .376 as a pinch hitter for the White Sox (15-for-39), remarkable in itself, but even more extraordinary is that 13 of his 15 hits came with two strikes on him.

## THE TOP 10 CAREER PINCH HITTERS

(Minimum 100 Pinch-hit at Bats; Retired Players Only)

| | Years Active | At Bats | Hits | Average |
|---|---|---|---|---|
| 1. Gordy Coleman | 1959–67 | 120 | 40 | .333 |
| 2. Ward Miller | 1909–17 | 110 | 36 | .327 |
| 3. Doc Miller | 1910–14 | 120 | 39 | .325 |

|  | Years Active | At Bats | Hits | Average |
|---|---|---|---|---|
| 4. Rod Carew | 1967–85 | 124 | 40 | .323[1] |
| 5. Al Kaline | 1953–74 | 115 | 37 | .322 |
| 6. Tommy Davis | 1959–76 | 197 | 63 | .320 |
| 7. Estel Crabtree | 1929–44 | 116 | 37 | .319 |
| 8. Earl Smith | 1919–30 | 129 | 41 | .318 |
| 9. Elmer Smith | 1914–25 | 123 | 39 | .317 |
| 10. Bib Falk | 1920–31 | 114 | 36 | .316[2] |

[1]Hall of Famers, for the most part, have been undistinguished pinch hitters. Aside from Carew and Kaline, only Bill Terry and Red Schoendienst among those with 100 or more pinch-hit at bats have career averages of over 300.

[2]The difference of only 17 points between the 1st and the 10th players on the list indicates how difficult it is to be consistently successful as a pinch hitter. Among players with 200 or more pinch-hit at bats, only Bob Fothergill, who hit exactly .300 was able to post a .300 career batting average.

## Lowest Career Batting Average as Pinch Hitter, Minimum 300 at Bats
.204—Mike Jorgensen, 1968–85; 72 hits in 353 bats

## Lowest Career Batting Average as Pinch Hitter, Minimum 200 at Bats
.176—Russ Snyder, 1959–70; 49 hits in 278 at bats

# THE 10 WORST PINCH HITTERS OF ALL TIME
(Minimum 100 Pinch-hit at Bats)

|  | Years Active | At Bats | Hits | Average |
|---|---|---|---|---|
| 1. Ivan Murrell | 1963–74 | 180 | 21 | .117 |
| 2. Ted Kubiak | 1967–76 | 123 | 15 | .122 |
| 3. Charlie Gilbert | 1940–47 | 115 | 14 | .122 |
| 4. Al Zarilla | 1943–53 | 120 | 15 | .125 |
| 5. Woody Held | 1954–69 | 147 | 19 | .129 |
| 6. Lou Klimchock | 1958–70 | 161 | 21 | .130 |
| 7. Mark Salas | 1984–91 | 114 | 15 | .132 |
| 8. Mike Mordecai | 1994– | 149 | 21 | .141 |
| 9. Roger Repoz | 1964–72 | 131 | 19 | .145 |
| 10. Dick Nen | 1963–70 | 102 | 15 | .147 |
| J. C. Martin | 1959–72 | 109 | 16 | .147 |

# Cy Young Award Winners

The Cy Young Award was originated in 1956. It was initially intended to honor only the top major-league pitcher each season, but by 1967 the feeling that the best pitcher in each league should be honored yearly had gained sway, and a second award was added.

**First Cy Young Winner**
Don Newcombe, Brooklyn Dodgers, 1956

**First Left-hander to Win a Cy Young**
Warren Spahn, Milwaukee Braves, 1957

**First American League Pitcher to Win a Cy Young**
Bob Turley, New York Yankees, 1958

**First to Win Two Cy Youngs**
Sandy Koufax, Los Angeles Dodgers, 1965. When he won again in 1966, Koufax also became the first three-time winner.

**Other Three-Time Winners**
NL—Tom Seaver, New York Mets, 1969, 1973 and 1975
AL—Jim Palmer, Baltimore, 1973, 1975 and 1976

**Four- and Five-Time Winners**
Steve Carlton, Philadelphia Phillies, 1972, 1977, 1980 and 1982. Greg Maddux, Chicago Cubs, 1992; Atlanta Braves, 1993, 1994 and 1995. Randy Johnson, Seattle, 1995; Arizona, 1999, 2000, 2001 and 2002.

**Only Six-Time Winner**
Roger Clemens, Boston Red Sox, 1986, 1987 and 1991; Toronto Blue Jays, 1997 and 1998; New York Yankees, 2001.

## First Relief Pitcher to Win a Cy Young
NL—Mike Marshall, Los Angeles, 1974
AL—Sparky Lyle, New York, 1977

## Only Rookie to Win a Cy Young
Fernando Valenzuela, Los Angles Dodgers, 1981

## Youngest Cy Young Winner
NL—Dwight Gooden, New York Mets, 1985, age 20; 15 days younger than Valenzuela the year he won
AL—Bret Saberhagen, Kansas City Royals, 1985, age 21

## Oldest Cy Young Winner
AL—Early Wynn, Chicago, 1959, age 39
NL—Steve Carlton, Philadelphia, 1982, age 37

## Most Wins by Starting Pitcher Who Won a Cy Young
AL—31—Denny McLain, Detroit, 1968
NL—27—Steve Carlton, Philadelphia, 1972

## Fewest Wins by Starting Pitcher Who Won a Cy Young (1981, 1994, 1995 Excepted)
AL—18—Pete Vuckovich, Milwaukee, 1982; Roger Clemens, Boston, 1991
NL—17—Pedro Martinez, Montreal, 1997; Randy Johnson, Arizona, 1999

## Lowest ERA by Cy Young Winner
AL—1.04—Rollie Fingers, Milwaukee, 1981
NL—1.12—Bob Gibson, St. Louis, 1968

## Highest ERA by Cy Young Winner
AL—3.66—LaMarr Hoyt, Chicago, 1983
NL—3.12—Bob Gibson, St. Louis, 1970

## Only Pitcher to Win a Cy Young after Being Traded in Midseason
Rick Sutcliffe, Chicago Cubs, 1984. Sutcliffe, who started the year with Cleveland, is also the only winner to play in both leagues in the same season.

## 25-Game Winners Who Failed to Win a Cy Young

NL—Juan Marichal, San Francisco, and on three different occasions, no less—1963, 1966 and 1968

AL—Jim Katt, Minnesota, 1966; Mickey Lolich, Detroit, 1971

## Only Pitchers to Win a Cy Young in Both Leagues

Gaylord Perry, Cleveland (AL), 1972; San Diego (NL), 1978

Pedro Martinez, Montreal (NL), 1997; Boston (AL), 1999

Randy Johnson, Seattle (AL), 1995; Arizona (NL), 1999, 2000, 2001 and 2002

# Batters' Strikeout Records

In 1956 outfielder Jim Lemon of the Washington Senators fanned 138 times, setting a new all-time record. Four years later Mickey Mantle of the Yankees collected his 1000th strikeout in only his 10th season, and another Senator, Harmon Killebrew, completed his second of a record six straight seasons in which he fanned over 100 times. Twenty years later Lemon, Mantle and Killebrew would no longer hold any major season or career strikeout records, yet they still loom today as probably the three leading harbingers of the home-run-or-bust syndrome that had already begun to permeate the game by the late 1950s.

The National League began keeping accurate batters' strikeout stats in 1910, and the American League followed suit three years later. From 1876 and 1896 the National League had counted batters strikeouts and then, for no overwhelming reason, ceased doing it for the next 14 years. The American Association kept track of the batters' strikeouts in only 2 of its 10 seasons as a major league—1889 and again in 1891. Records of batters' strikeouts are also available for the lone Players League season in 1890.

Since foul balls were not universally counted as strikes until 1903, and batters received four strikes as late as 1887, the natural assumption is that strikeouts in the game's early years were relatively infrequent. But the stats that are available to us indicate otherwise. In 1886, with the mound still only 50 feet from the plate and pitchers now allowed to throw overhand, Matt Kilroy, a rookie left-hander with the Baltimore Orioles in the American Association, fanned 513 hitters. An individual breakdown of Kilroy's victims is impossible to reconstruct a century later, but Tom Brown, rightfielder for the Pittsburgh Alleghenies, was quite likely his main one. Brown led the Players League in fanning the air in 1890, the American Association in 1891 and the National League in three of the next four seasons. Even without the strikeout totals from 6 of the 16 years he played, Brown finished in 1898 with 708 whiffs. Including his six lost years, he probably struck out around 1,100 times, making him the only player to top 1,000 until Babe Ruth came along.

## Chronology of Significant Strikeout Milestones

**1884**—Sam Wise, shortstop for the Boston Red Stockings, struck out 104 times, a record that stood until 1914.

**1887**—John Morrill of the Boston Red Stockings became the first player to strike out 500 times in his career.

**1892**—Tom Brown, playing with Louisville in the National League, became the first player to strike out 90 or more times two years in a row.

**1892**—Pud Galvin concluded his career with 630 strikeouts in only 2702 at bats; a pitcher, Galvin sometimes played the outfield between mound assignments and had a .202 batting average. despite the frequency with which he fanned.

**1930**—Babe Ruth became the first player to strike out 1000 times in his career.

**1932**—Bruce Campbell of the Chicago White Sox and St. Louis Browns struck out 104 times, the first to top 100 since 1914.

**1934**—Harlond Clift of the Browns became the first third baseman to strike out 100 or more times in a season.

**1935**—First baseman Dolph Camilli of the Phillies became the first National Leaguer since 1884 to strike out 100 times in a season.

**1937**—Frank Crosetti of the Yankees became the first shortstop to strike out 100 or more times in a season.

**1940**—Chet Ross of the Boston Braves set a new rookie strikeout record when he fanned 127 times.

**1949**—The last season in which neither league had a player who struck out 100 times.

**1958**—Harry Anderson of the Phillies topped the National League with 95 strikeouts, the last league leader to fan less than 100 times.

**1963**—John Bateman of the Houston Colt 45s became the first catcher to fan 100 or more times in a season.

**1966**—Mickey Mantle of the Yankees became the first player to fan 1500 times.

**1966**—George Scott of the Boston Red Sox set an American League rookie strikeout record by fanning 152 times.

**1978**—In his 11th season Bobby Bonds of the Texas Rangers struck out for the 1500th time, the quickest any player has ever reached 1500 K's.

**1978**—Pirates leadoff hitter Omar Moreno had only two home runs yet struck out 104 times.

**1979**—Lou Brock retired with 1730 strikeouts and only 149 home runs, further proof that it isn't only sluggers who have fallen prey to the whiff syndrome.

**1983**—Reggie Jackson of the Angels became the first player to strike out 2000 times.

**1984**—Juan Samuel of the Phillies fanned 168 times, setting an all-time rookie record.

**1986**—Pete Incaviglia of the Rangers fanned 185 times to set both a new all-time rookie and American League record, José Canseco of the A's (175) and Danny Tartabull of the Mariners (157) also topped George Scott's old AL rookie mark.

**1987**—Rob Deer of the Brewers K'd 186 times to set a new American League record.

## EVOLUTION OF BATTERS' SEASON STRIKEOUT RECORD
### (Since 1913)

|  | Team | League | Year | K's |
|---|---|---|---|---|
| Danny Moeller | Washington | American | 1913 | 103[1] |
| Gus Williams | St. Louis | American | 1914 | 120 |
| Vince DiMaggio | Boston | National | 1938 | 134 |
| Jim Lemon | Washington | American | 1956 | 138 |
| Jake Wood | Detroit | American | 1961 | 141[2] |
| Harmon Killebrew | Minnesota | American | 1962 | 142 |
| Dave Nicholson | Chicago | American | 1963 | 175[3] |
| Bobby Bonds | San Francisco | National | 1969 | 187 |
| Bobby Bonds | San Francisco | National | 1970 | 189 |

[1]The 1913 season was the first in which both leagues began keeping complete and official strikeout records. Moeller was the first documented player to fan 100 times in a season since Sam Wise in 1884.

[2]Also broke Chet Ross's rookie record in 1961; the new mark lasted only until 1966.

[3]Nicholson fanned 573 times in 1419 career at bats—a strikeout average of .404. Counting only those times his bat made contact he hit .356, making him an even more exciting player than Dave Kingman or Reggie Jackson, if they happen to be your brand of excitement. Kingman's strikeout average at retirement was .272; Jackson's was a mere .263. They rank one and two as the easiest strikeout victims among modern players with over 5000 career at bats, but in comparison to Nicholson they both seem like Joe Sewell. But before we get to Sewell and the other players at the opposite end of the spectrum from Nicholson, Kingman and Jackson, consider this: Through the 1992 season 105 players had topped 1000 career strikeouts, but only two of them—Babe Ruth and Jimmie Foxx—finished their careers prior to 1959.

## TOP 10 IN CAREER STRIKEOUTS

|  | Years Active | K's |
|---|---|---|
| 1. Reggie Jackson | 1967–87 | 2597 |
| 2. Andres Galarraga | 1985– | 2000[1] |
| 3. Jose Canseco | 1985–2001 | 1942[1] |
| 4. Sammy Sosa | 1989– | 1977[1] |
| 5. Willie Stargell | 1961–82 | 1936 |
| 6. Mike Schmidt | 1972–89 | 1883 |
| 7. Tony Perez | 1964–86 | 1867[1] |
| 8. Fred McGriff | 1986– | 1863[1] |
| 9. Dave Kingman | 1971–86 | 1816 |
| 10. Bobby Bonds | 1968–81 | 1757 |

[1]Never a league leader in K's.

## THE 10 HARDEST BATTERS TO STRIKE OUT
(Minimum 10 Seasons since 1901)

|  | Years Active | AB's | K's | AB/K Ratio |
|---|---|---|---|---|
| 1. Joe Sewell | 1920–33 | 7132 | 114 | 63 to 1 |
| 2. Lloyd Waner | 1927–45 | 7732 | 173 | 45 to 1[1] |
| 3. Nellie Fox | 1947–65 | 9232 | 216 | 43 to 1 |
| 4. Tommy Holmes | 1942–52 | 4992 | 122 | 41 to 1[2] |
| 5. Tris Speaker | 1907–28 | 7899 | 220 | 36 to 1[3] |
| 6. Stuffy McInnis | 1910–27 | 6667 | 189 | 35 to 1 |
| 7. Andy High | 1922–34 | 4400 | 130 | 34 to 1 |
| 8. Sam Rice | 1915–34 | 9269 | 275 | 34 to 1 |

| | Years Active | AB's | K's | AB/K Ratio |
|---|---|---|---|---|
| 9. Frankie Frisch | 1919–37 | 9112 | 272 | 34 to 1 |
| 10. Dale Mitchell | 1946–56 | 3984 | 119 | 34 to 1 |

[1]As a part-time outfielder and pinch hitter with the Pirates, Braves and Reds in 1941, Waner made over 230 plate appearances without striking out a single time.

[2]In 1945 Holmes led the National League in home runs with 28 and in fewest strikeouts with nine, the only such double winner in history.

[3]Speaker's and McInnis's stats prior to 1913 are excluded because their strikeout totals for their earlier seasons are unavailable.

## The Five Most Remarkable Batters' Strikeout Feats in This Century

First Place—Tommy Holmes's all-time record double win in 1945

Second Place—Ted Williams hit 521 career home runs and fanned only 709 times.

Third Place—Joe DiMaggio hit 361 career home runs and fanned only 369 times.

Fourth Place—Joe Sewell's last strikeout in the 1930 season came on May 26 when White Sox lefty Pat Caraway zapped him twice in the same game. The only other pitcher ever to fan Sewell twice in a game was the equally obscure Cy Warmoth, who did it in 1923. Warmoth had a mere 54 strikeouts in his career. In 1931 Caraway totaled only 55 strikeouts in 220 innings.

Fifth Place—Nellie Fox played 98 consecutive games in 1958 without striking out, breaking the old record of 89 games, set in 1932 by third baseman Carey Selph of the White Sox shortly before he was released.

Special Mention—In 1935 catcher Lee Head of Knoxville in the Southern Association fanned only one time in 122 games and 402 at bats.

# World Series Play:
# 1942–60

## FRANCHISE SUMMARY

| Team | League | WS Record Through 1960 | Last Year in WS |
|------|--------|------------------------|-----------------|
| Los Angeles | National | 1–0 | 1959 |
| Boston | American | 5–1 | 1946 |
| New York | American | 18–7 | 1960 |
| St. Louis | National | 6–3 | 1946 |
| Cleveland | American | 2–1 | 1954 |
| Cincinnati | National | 2–1 | 1940 |
| Pittsburgh | National | 3–2 | 1960 |
| Chicago | American | 2–2 | 1959 |
| Milwaukee | National | 1–1 | 1958 |
| Washington | American | 1–2 | 1933 |
| Detroit | American | 2–5 | 1945 |
| Chicago | National | 2–8 | 1945 |
| Philadelphia | National | 0–2 | 1950 |

### Became Defunct between 1942 and 1960

| Team | League | | |
|------|--------|------|------|
| Philadelphia | American | 5–3 | 1931 |
| Boston | National | 1–1 | 1948 |
| New York | National | 5–9 | 1954 |
| Brooklyn | National | 1–8 | 1956 |
| St. Louis | American | 0–1 | 1944 |

**Yearly Highlights**

1942—St. Louis (NL) defeated New York (AL) 4 games to 1

After dropping the Series opener, the Cards got two complete-game wins from rookie Johnny Beazley, plus a shutout from Ernie White, and took the next four games to hand the Yankees their first Series loss since 1926.

**1943—New York (AL) defeated St. Louis (NL) 4 games to 1**

The Yankees' retaliation for the 1942 wipeout featured two superbly pitched games by Spud Chandler, the AL's MVP in 1943.

**1944—St. Louis (NL) defeated St. Louis (AL) 4 games to 2**

The last series to be played entirely in one stadium—antiquated Sportsman's Park—was also the Browns' one and only fall appearance. Their pitchers allowed only 16 runs in the six games, but Cardinals pitchers gave up just 12.

**1945—Detroit (AL) defeated Chicago (NL) 4 games to 3**

Hal Newhouser of the Tigers had a Series ERA of 6.10 but won two games, including the clincher. Hank Borowy of the Cubs became the first pitcher since Jack Coombs in 1916 to win a Series game in both leagues.

**1946—St. Louis (NL) defeated Boston (AL) 4 games to 3**

Considered one of the great Series, but only the first and last games were tight. Moreover, the two stars, Ted Williams and Stan Musial, hit .200 and .222 respectively. But Harry Brecheen of the Cardinals won three games, and Enos Slaughter tallied the run that won the Series in the eighth inning of Game Seven by scoring all the way from first base on Harry Walker's single when Red Sox shortstop Johnny Pesky hesitated a fraction of a second before relaying Leon Culberson's throw to the plate.

**1947—New York (AL) defeated Brooklyn (NL) 4 games to 3**

The first Series to be televised. The opener drew a record 73,365 to Yankee Stadium as Guy Lombardo and his orchestra entertained and Met Opera soprano Helen Jepson sang the national anthem. Although sloppily played for the most part, this Series ranks among the most exciting because of two events: Bill Bevens's near no-hitter in Game Five and Al Gionfriddo's catch of Joe DiMaggio's 415-foot drive the following day with two Yankees aboard.

1948—Cleveland (AL) defeated Boston (NL) 4 games to 2

The last Series until 1967 that did not include either a New York team or a former New York team. The Braves won the opener 1–0 on a single by Tommy Holmes, which drove home Phil Masi from second base after Masi had seemingly been picked off in a carefully timed play between Indians pitcher Bob Feller and shortstop Lou Boudreau. It was the closest Feller would ever come to a Series victory. The fifth game, in Cleveland, drew a pre–1959 Series record crowd of 86,288.

1949—New York (AL) defeated Brooklyn (NL) 4 games to 1

The 1949 Series also began with a 1–0 game, won by the Yankees on Tommy Henrich's homer leading off the bottom of the ninth inning. It was the closest Don Newcombe of the Dodgers would ever come to a Series victory. Brooklyn's lone bright spot came in Game Two when Preacher Roe turned the tables on the Yankees and blanked them 1–0.

1950—New York (AL) defeated Philadelphia (NL) 4 games to 0

Phillies manager Eddie Sawyer pulled the biggest Series surprise since Connie Mack started Howard Ehmke in the 1929 opener when he named reliever Jim Konstanty to start the lid-lifter. But for the third straight year the Series began with a 1–0 game, won this time by the Yankees behind Vic Raschi. Although swept, the Phils were in every game except the last one until the final out.

1951—New York (AL) defeated New York (NL) 4 games to 2

The Giants, sparked by Eddie Stanky, won two of the first three games and then fell prey to Joe DiMaggio, playing in his last Series, and a 13–run assault in Game Five.

1952—New York (AL) defeated Brooklyn (NL) 4 games to 3

The Dodgers went up three games to two, but superlative relief pitching by Allie Reynolds helped the Yankees snatch the last two contests. Reynolds also pitched a 2–0 shutout in Game Four.

**1953—New York (AL) defeated Brooklyn (NL) 4 games to 2**

Billy Martin became the first player to make 12 hits in a 6-game Series and drove in the winning run in the ninth inning of the last game. The Dodgers became the first team to hit .300 in a Series and lose.

**1954—New York (NL) defeated Cleveland (AL) 4 games to 0**

Dusty Rhodes of the Giants delivered three game-winning hits, two of them as a pinch hitter, and Willie Mays broke hearts all over Cleveland when he robbed Vic Wertz of a probable game-winning two-run triple with a back-to-the-plate catch in the eighth inning of the opener.

**1955—Brooklyn (NL) defeated New York (AL) 4 games to 3**

In their eighth try the Dodgers finally managed to win their first and only Series while in Brooklyn. The hero was Johnny Podres with two complete-game victories, including a 2–0 shutout in the finale.

**1956—New York (AL) defeated Brooklyn (NL) 4 games to 3**

Don Larsen's perfect game gave the Yankees a 3–2 lead in the Series, but Clem Labine pitched a brilliant 10-inning 1–0 win for the Dodgers the following day, setting up what promised to be a highly dramatic final game. It disappointed—the Yankees won 9–0 behind Johnny Kucks—which is why this Series, aside from Larsen's perfect game, is seldom mentioned among the great ones even though it was Brooklyn's last fall appearance.

**1957—Milwaukee (NL) defeated New York (AL) 4 games to 3**

Lew Burdette of the Braves pitched three complete-game victories, the last two of them shutouts, and Hank Aaron had 11 hits and seven RBIs.

**1958—New York (AL) defeated Milwaukee (NL) 4 games to 3**

Down three games to one, the Yankees beat Burdette twice and Warren Spahn once to become the first team since the Pirates in 1925 to come back from so large a Series deficit.

Bob Turley pitched a 7–0 shutout in Game Five, saved Game Six and then won the final game with a six-and-two-thirds-inning relief stint.

**1959—Los Angeles (NL) defeated Chicago (AL) 4 games to 2**

The first Series involving a West Coast team and the last one involving a Chicago team. Ted Kluszewski provided most of the White Sox offense with three homers and 10 RBIs but could do little with Dodgers relief ace Larry Sherry, who won two games and saved the other two L.A. victories. Charlie Neal of the Dodgers knocked in six runs and led all batters with 10 hits.

**1960—Pittsburgh (NL) defeated New York (AL) 4 games to 3**

For the first time a seven-game Series ended with a home run when Bill Mazeroski of the Pirates led off the bottom of the ninth inning by depositing a Ralph Terry pitch over the Forbes Field left-field wall. In his last World Series as a manager, Casey Stengel saw his Yankees hit .338, set a Series record for runs and total bases, and still contrive to lose. Pittsburgh pitchers had a collective 7.11 ERA, the poorest ever by a Series winner.

# SECTION 5

# Famous Firsts:
# 1961–76

**1961**—For the first time in 60 years two cities are given new major-league franchises. One of them, the Washington Senators, replacing the old Washington Senators, who have moved to Minnesota, plays the first game involving an expansion team on April 10 at Griffith Stadium, a 4–3 loss to the Chicago White Sox, the team that, perhaps fittingly, played the very first American League game back in 1901.

**1962**—The National League reluctantly follows the American League's lead and swells to 10 teams by granting franchises to groups representing Houston and New York. Houston plays the first game involving an NL expansion team on April 10 and, perhaps fittingly, triumphs over the Chicago Cubs, the lone participant in the very first major-league season back in 1876 that has survived until 1962 without any interruptions or franchise transfers.

**1962**—Borrowing a page from the old Baltimore Orioles' scrapbook, the San Francisco Giants win the NL pennant after groundskeeper Matty Schwab drenches the infield at Candlestick Park, supposedly to keep the dust from billowing in the stiff winds there—but the Dodgers scream that it was done to slow down their leading base thief, Maury Wills, the first player in modern history to swipe more than 100 sacks in a season. Significantly, perhaps, Schwab is voted a full World Series share by Giants players.

**1965**—An amateur rookie draft is at long last instituted, major-league teams selecting free-agent players in the reverse order of their finish. The Yankees, the leading opponents of the draft, immediately topple to sixth place, their first second-division finish in 40 years.

**1965**—As a signal that the complete game is soon to become an endangered species, the Dodgers use three pitchers to shut out the Astros on September 3 and then need four pitchers to shut them out again the following day.

**1966**—Red Barber, possibly the finest baseball broadcaster ever, is fired after 34 years in the booth when he appalls the Yankees brass by asking his TV cameraman to pan the stands in Yankee Stadium on an afternoon when only 413 fans turn out to watch the Yankees first cellar finisher since 1912.

**1968**—Dick McAuliffe of the Tigers sets a record when he becomes the first American League player to play more than 150 games in a season without grounding into a double play.

**1969**—Both major leagues expand to twelve teams and divide into two divisions, the champs in each division meeting in a best-three-of-five League Championship Series at the end of the regular season to determine the pennant winner and World Series representative.

**1969**—The "Bleacher Bums" make their official debut at Wrigley field and root the Cubs to their highest finish since 1945. They are too far from the action, however, to follow the movements of the Cubs catcher Randy Hundley's flip-over mitt, the first of its kind, or to see the hands of Expos outfielder Rusty Staub, the first to popularize batting gloves.

**1969**—John Hollison dies in Chicago. His obituary neglects to mention that he was the last surviving major-league pitcher to hurl from a rectangular box only 50 feet from home plate.

**1970**—The average player's salary reaches a new high of $25,000 per year.

**1970**—Tommy Agee of the Mets becomes the first outfielder to win a Gold Glove in each league.

**1970**—Traded by the Cardinals to the Phillies, outfielder Curt Flood refuses to report to his new team and elects to test the reserve clause instead. Flood sets off a chain of events that within six years will merit him a few moments of silent thanks each evening around the dinner table of every major-league player.

**1970**—Major-league umpires refuse to work the League Championship Series games and force a settlement that increases their salaries and benefits. During the coming decade the umpires will repeatedly display their willingness to strike until their demands are met.

**1971**—The Pirates begin wearing form-fitting double-knit uniforms. Later in the decade the White Sox will experiment with short pants. In 1990 the White Sox will turn back the sartorial clock when they wear 1917-style uniforms for a home game to commemorate their last world championship.

**1971**—Ron Hunt of the Expos sets a modern record when he's hit by 50 pitches. In 1974 Hunt will retire with a 20th-century record of 243 HBP's.

**1972**—The players stage a 13-day strike, the first general strike in major-league history, and delay the opening of the season for 10 days. Commissioner Bowie Kuhn rules that games lost due to the strike will not be made up. As a result, the Tigers win the AL Eastern Division by dint of playing and winning one more game than the Red Sox. The Tigers half-game margin of victory is the smallest in either major league since 1908 when a similar ruling against playing makeup games gave the Tigers the flag by half a game over Cleveland.

**1972**—Milt Pappas of the Cubs becomes the first pitcher in history to post 200 career wins without ever winning 20 games in a season.

**1973**—The American League, after voting unanimously in favor of the designated hitter rule, uses designated hitters for pitchers for the first time in major-league history. The National League disdains the notion of a designated hitter and refuses to go along with the rule. Research into the history of the designated hitter idea reveals that it was first suggested in 1928 by National League president John Heydler, and that NL owners were all for it but couldn't get the support of the AL, which roundly vetoed it.

**1974**—Fergie Jenkins of the Texas Rangers becomes the last AL starting pitcher, prior to Cleveland's Charles Nagy in 1999, to appear in the batting order. In the game against the Twins, he singles in the sixth inning to break up a no-hitter and then goes on to triumph 2–1 for his 25th win.

**1975**—Catfish Hunter, the first star player to get himself declared a free agent, starts his first season with the Yankees, the team that won the bidding war for his services.

**1975**—Pitchers Andy Messersmith and Dave McNally, having played all season without signing contracts, demand free agency and are granted it by arbitrator Peter Seitz, the same man who declared Hunter a free agent. Seitz's decision results in a modification of the reserve clause and a shift in the balance of power from the owners to the players.

**1976**—Dan Driessen of the Reds becomes the first player to serve as a dh in a World Series game.

# Expansion Team Firsts

On April 11, 1961, the Los Angeles Angels became the first major-league expansion team to register a victory when they bested Baltimore 7–2 in their very first game. The following year the Houston Colt 45s became the first National League expansion team to win a game when they blasted the Cubs 11–2 in their inaugural contest. In contrast, the New York Mets debuted by losing their first nine games and went on to set a new 20th-century record for the most losses in a season. But in 1969 the Mets rewarded their followers and flabbergasted their critics by becoming the first expansion team to win a division title, a pennant and a World Championship.

## First American League Expansion Team to Win a Division Title
Kansas City Royals, 1976

## First American League Expansion Team to Win a Pennant
Kansas City Royals, 1980

## First American League Expansion Team to Win a World Championship
Kansas City Royals, 1985

## First Expansion Team to Occupy Sole Possession of First Place
AL—The Los Angeles Angels swept a twin bill from the Senators on July 4, 1962, and moved briefly into first place. They ultimately finished third, making them the first expansion club to achieve a first-division finish.

NL—The Mets surged past the Cubs into the NL Eastern Division lead for the first time on September 10, 1969, after taking a doubleheader from the Expos.

**First Second-Wave Expansion Team to Win a Division Title**
AL—Kansas City Royals, 1976
NL—Montreal, 1981

**First Second-Wave Expansion Team to Win a Pennant**
AL—Kansas City Royals, 1980
NL—San Diego, 1984

**First Second-Wave Team to Win a World Championship**
AL—Kansas City Royals, 1985
NL—None

**First Third-Wave Expansion Team to Win a Division Title**
AL—Toronto, 1985

**First Season Two Expansion Team Opposed Each Other in a League Championship Series**
AL—1982—California versus Milwaukee
NL—1986—New York Mets versus Houston

## FIRST EXPANSION TEAM PLAYERS TO BE LEAGUE LEADERS
### Batting

| Department | National League | American League |
|---|---|---|
| Batting Average | Al Oliver, Montreal, 1982 | ALEX JOHNSON, California, 1970 |
| Slugging Average | Darryl Strawberry, New York, 1988 | FRANK HOWARD, Washington, 1968 |
| Home Runs | Dave Kingman, New York, 1982 | FRANK HOWARD, Washington, 1968 |
| RBIs | Dave Winfield, San Diego, 1979 | FRANK HOWARD, Washington, 1970 |
| Hits | Al Oliver, Montreal, 1982 | GEORGE BRETT, Kansas City, 1975 |
| Runs | Tim Raines, Montreal, 1983 | ALBIE PEARSON, Los Angeles, 1962* |
| Doubles | RUSTY STAUB, Houston, 1967 | Amos Otis, Kansas City, 1970 |

| Department | National League | American League |
| --- | --- | --- |
| Triples | Roger Metzger, Houston, 1971 | BOBBY KNOOP, California, 1966 |
| | Joe Morgan, Houston, 1971 | |
| Total Bases | Dave Winfield, San Diego, 1979 | FRANK HOWARD, Washington, 1968 |
| Stolen Bases | Ron Le Flore, Montreal, 1980 | TOMMY HARPER, Seattle Pilots, 1969 |
| Bases on Balls | JOE MORGAN, Houston, 1965** | FRANK HOWARD, Washington, 1970 |
| Strikeouts | JIM WYNN, Houston, 1967 | FRANK HOWARD, Washington, 1967 |

*First AL major offensive department leader from an expansion team.
**First NL major offensive department leader from an expansion team.

## Pitching

| | National League | American League |
| --- | --- | --- |
| Wins | Tom Seaver, New York, 1969 | DEAN CHANCE, Los Angeles, 1964 |
| Losses | ROGER CRAIG, New York, 1962 | George Brunet, California, 1967 |
| Winning Pct. | TOM SEAVER, New York, 1969 | Paul Splittorff, Kansas City, 1979 |
| Starts | JERRY REUSS, Houston, 1973 | Dennis Leonard, Kansas City, 1978 |
| Complete Games | Tom Seaver, New York, 1973 | DEAN CHANCE, Los Angeles, 1964 |
| Innings | Randy Jones, San Diego, 1976 | DEAN CHANCE, Los Angeles, 1964 |
| Shutouts | John Matlack, New York, 1974 | DEAN CHANCE, Los Angeles, 1964 |
| ERA | Tom Seaver, New York, 1970 | DICK DONOVAN, Washington, 1961* |
| Strikeouts | TOM SEAVER, New York, 1970 | Nolan Ryan, California, 1972 |
| Bases on Balls | Bill Stoneman, Montreal, 1969 | BO BELINSKY, Los Angeles, 1962 |
| Games Pitched | RON HERBEL, N.Y.-S.D., 1970 | Ken Sanders, Milwaukee, 1971 |

| Department | National League | American League |
| --- | --- | --- |
| Saves | HAL WOODESHICK, Houston, 1964** | Minnie Rojas, California, 1967 |

## Awards

| | | |
| --- | --- | --- |
| Cy Young | Tom Seaver, New York, 1969 | DEAN CHANCE Los Angeles, 1964 |
| MVP | Jeff Bagwell, Houston, 1994 | JEFF BURROUGHS, Texas, 1974 |
| Rookie of the Year | TOM SEAVER, New York, 1967 | Lou Piniella, Kansas City, 1969 |

*First AL leader from an expansion team.
**First NL leader from an expansion team in a department other than losses.

# Home Run Feats

In 1961, to the dismay of many who regarded Babe Ruth's slugging records as inviolate, Roger Maris of the Yankees clubbed 61 home runs, breaking Ruth's season record of 60, set in 1927. Thirteen years later Hank Aaron of the Braves shattered Ruth's career record of 714 circuit clouts. Many of Ruth's home run marks still stand, however, and among them are two that will surely never be broken. In 1927 Ruth hit more home runs all by himself than every team in the American League except his own Yankees. Eight years later, upon joining the Boston Braves for what would be his final major-league season, he became the first player to hit three home runs in a game in both leagues when he thrice found the seats on May 25, 1935, at Forbes Field. Another of Ruth's records that once seemed likely to last forever was his season mark for most homers on the road—32—also set in 1927; however, Mark McGwire tied it in 1998 when he raised the homer bar to 70, and in 2001 Barry Bonds buried Ruth even deeper by clubbing 38 dingers on the road alone.

**Most Home Runs at Home, Season**
AL—39—Hank Greenberg, Detroit, 1938; he had 58 altogether
NL—38—Mark McGwire, St. Louis, 1998

**Most Seasons League Leader in Home Runs**
AL—12—Babe Ruth, last in 1931
NL—8—Mike Schmidt, 1974–76, 1980–81, 1983–84 and 1986.

**Most Home Runs, Season, 1901 through 1919**
NL—24—Gavvy Cravath, Philadelphia, 1915
AL—29—Babe Ruth, Boston, 1919; breaking Socks Seybold's league record of 16, set in 1902 with Philadelphia

## Most Home Runs, Season, 1920 through 1941
AL—60—Babe Ruth, New York, 1927
NL—56—Hack Wilson, Chicago, 1930

## Most Home Runs, Season, 1942 through 1960
NL—54—Ralph Kiner, Pittsburgh, 1949
AL—52—Mickey Mantle, New York, 1956

## Most Home Runs, Season, 1961 through 1976
AL—61—Roger Maris, New York, 1961, the AL record
NL—52—Willie Mays, San Francisco, 1965

## Most Home Runs, Season, 1977 through 1993
NL—52—George Foster, Cincinnati, 1977
AL—51—Cecil Fielder, Detroit, 1990

## Most Home Runs, Season, since 1994
NL—73—Barry Bonds, San Francisco, 2001
AL—57—Alex Rodriguez, Texas, 2002

## First Player to Homer in Every Park in Use During His Career
Harry Heilmann. He homered in Braves Field, Forbes Field, Ebbets Field, Wrigley Field, Crosley Field and the Baker Bowl for the first time in 1930, the season he came to Cincinnati from the Tigers. Previously he had homered in all nine American League stadiums in which he'd played—Shibe Park, Comiskey Park, Sportsman's Park (used also by the Cardinals), Cleveland's League Park, Navin Field, Fenway Park, Yankee Stadium, the Polo Grounds (used by both the Yankees and the Giants until 1923) and Griffith Stadium.

## First to Hit 30 Home Runs in a Season in Both Leagues
Dick Stuart, Pittsburgh, (NL) 1961, Boston (AL) 1963

## First to Hit 40 Home Runs in a Season in Both Leagues
Darrell Evans, Atlanta (NL) 1973, Detroit (AL) 1985

## Most Times Hitting Three or More Home Runs in a Game
6—Johnny Mize. First done on July 13, 1938; last done on September 15, 1950; Sammy Sosa.

## Players Who Hit Four Home Runs in a Game

AL—Lou Gehrig, New York, June 3, 1932. The first player to hit four in a game in the 20th century, he picked the day John McGraw quit as manager of the Giants to do it and so got second billing in the sports pages.

Pat Seerey, Chicago, July 18, 1948, in an 11-inning game. He hit only .231 that season with 19 homers and was cut early the following year.

Rocky Colavito, Cleveland, June 10, 1959. He did it in Baltimore's Memorial Stadium, at the time a very tough park to homer in.

NL—Bobby Lowe, Boston, May 30, 1894. In Boston's 20–11 win over Cincinnati, Lowe also singled, giving him 17 total bases.

Ed Delahanty, Philadelphia, July 13, 1896. At Chicago, in a 9–8 loss to the Colts.

Chuck Klein, Philadelphia, July 10, 1936. In a 10-inning game at Forbes Field.

Gil Hodges, Brooklyn, August 31, 1950. He did it at Ebbets Field, making him the lone player in this century prior to Bob Horner—Lowe is the only other one—to hit four homers in a game in his home park.

Joe Adcock, Milwaukee, July 31, 1954.

Willie Mays, San Francisco, April 30, 1961.

Mike Schmidt, Philadelphia, April 17, 1976. At Wrigley Field in a 10-inning game won 18–16 by the Phillies.

Bob Horner, Atlanta, July 6, 1986. At Atlanta, in an 11–8 loss to Montreal, making him the first player since Delahanty to hit four homers in a losing cause.

Mark Whiten, St. Louis, September 7, 1993. At Cincinnati, in a 15–2 Cardinals win in which he also had 12 RBIs.

Mike Cameron, Seattle, May 2, 2002. At Chicago.

Shawn Green, Los Angeles, May 23, 2002. At Milwaukee, Green, in addition, had a double and a single, giving him 19 total bases and breaking Joe Adcock's old mark of 18.

Carlos Delgado, Toronto, September 25, 2003. At Toronto.

## The "Lucky Spectator" Award

Pitcher Billy Loes was either a teammate or an opponent of four players who hit four homers in a nine-inning game—Hodges, Adcock, Colavito and Mays—and so was on hand when each of them did it.

## Only Pitchers to Hit Three Home Runs in a Game

Guy Hecker, Louisville (AA), August 16, 1886

Jim Tobin, Boston (NL), May 13, 1942. A good hitter, Tobin hammered six homers in 1942, more than anyone else on the club except Max West and Ernie Lombardi.

## Only Player to Hit Two Grand Slam Homers in Same Inning

Fernando Tatis, St. Louis (NL), April 23, 1999

## First Player to Hit Three Grand Slam Homers in a One-Week Span

Lou Gehrig, New York Yankees, August 29, August 31 and September 1, 1931. Jim Northrup of the Tigers and Larry Parrish of the Rangers have also hit three four-run homers in a week's time.

## First Team to Hit Two Grand Slam Homers in the Same Inning

Minnesota, July 18, 1962, Harmon Killebrew and Bob Allison doing the damage

## Most Grand Slam Home Runs in a Season

6—Don Mattingly, New York Yankees, 1987, breaking Ernie Banks' record of five, set in 1955

## Only Pitcher to Hit Two Grand Slam Home Runs in a Game

Tony Cloninger, Atlanta Braves, July 3, 1966. Moreover Cloninger is the only National League player ever to do it.

## Most Consecutive Games Hitting at Least One Home Run, Pitcher

4—Ken Brett, Philadelphia Phillies, June 9, 13, 18 and 23, 1973. His only home runs that season.

## Last American League Pitcher to Homer in a Regular-Season Game, Batting as Pitcher vs. AL Opponent

Roric Harrison, Baltimore, October 3, 1972

## Most Home Runs, Season, as Team's Leadoff Batter in Game

AL—12—Brady Anderson, Baltimore, 1996

NL—11—Bobby Bonds, San Francisco, 1973.

**Most Home Runs, Season, Against One Team**
   14—Lou Gehrig, New York Yankees, 1936; against Cleveland

**Most Home Runs, Season, through April 30**
   13—Ken Griffey Jr., Seattle Mariners, 1997; Luis Gonzalez, Arizona Diamondbacks, 2001

**Most Home Runs, Season, through May 31**
   28—Barry Bonds, San Francisco Giants, 2001

**Most Home Runs, Season, through June 30**
   39—Barry Bonds, San Francisco Giants, 2001

**Most Home Runs, Season, through July 31**
   45—Mark McGwire, St. Louis Cardinals, 1998; Barry Bonds, San Francisco Giants, 2001

**Most Home Runs, Season, through August 31**
   57—Barry Bonds, San Francisco Giants, 2001

**Most Home Runs, Season, through September 30**
   70—Mark McGwire, St. Louis Cardinals, 1998

**Only Team with Two Players Who Hit 50 Home Runs**
   1961 Yankees. Roger Maris, 61, Mickey Mantle, 54.

**Teams with Three Players Who Hit 40 Home Runs**
   1973 Atlanta Braves. Davey Johnson, 43, Darrell Evans, 41, and Hank Aaron, 40.
   1996 Colorado Rockies. Andres Galarraga, 47, Ellis Burks, 42, and Vinnie Castilla, 40.
   1997 Colorado Rockies. Larry Walker, 49, Andres Galarraga, 41, and Vinnie Castilla, 40.

Prior to the resumption of play after the 1994–95 strike only 17 players in all of major-league history clubbed as many as 50 home runs in a season. The total is now 36. That is correct. Since 1995 more players have amassed 50 homers in a season than achieved that formerly magic pinnacle in the previous 124 years of major-league play. Moreover, before 1998 the 60-homer mark was reached just twice; since 1998 it's already been done six times, including on three occasions by Sammy Sosa who failed to win his league's homer crown in **any** of those three seasons. As a result, the list of 50-homer men, once a hallowed repository for only the game's greatest sluggers, now houses just about every decent power hitter in recent history. Consequently the list, in this corner anyway, now begins at 55 for the sake of brevity if nothing else. Who knows? In another few years it may need to begin at 60. Or even 70.

## PLAYERS WITH 55 OR MORE HOMERS IN A SEASON

| | Team | League | Year | HRs |
|---|---|---|---|---|
| Barry Bonds | San Francisco | National | 2001 | 73 |
| Mark McGwire | St. Louis | National | 1998 | 70 |
| Sammy Sosa | Chicago | National | 1998 | 66 |
| Mark McGwire | St. Louis | National | 1999 | 65 |
| Sammy Sosa | Chicago | National | 2001 | 64 |
| Sammy Sosa | Chicago | National | 1999 | 63 |
| Roger Maris | New York | American | 1961 | 61 |
| Babe Ruth | New York | American | 1927 | 60 |
| Babe Ruth | New York | American | 1921 | 59 |
| Hank Greenberg | Detroit | American | 1938 | 58 |
| Jimmie Foxx | Philadelphia | American | 1932 | 58 |
| Mark McGwire | Oakland (AL)/St. Louis (NL) | | 1997 | 58 |
| Luis Gonzalez | Arizona | National | 2001 | 57 |
| Alex Rodriquez | Texas | American | 2002 | 57 |
| Ken Griffey, Jr. | Seattle | American | 1998 | 56 |
| Ken Griffey, Jr. | Seattle | American | 1997 | 56 |
| Hack Wilson | Chicago | National | 1930 | 56 |

## Most Controversial Home Run Ever

AL—George Brett's two-run "pine tar" blast for the Royals on July 24, 1983, which beat the Yankees 5–4 and had the odd effect, after all the disputes were settled, of causing *both* clubs to go into a tailspin and fall out of contention.

NL—The famous homer that should have been but wasn't. Dave Augustine's seeming game-winning blast for the Pirates in the 13th inning on September 20, 1973, against the Mets was ruled to have bounced off the top of the wall, allowing Cleon Jones to retrieve the ball and the Mets to throw the potential winning run out at the plate. The Mets ultimately won the game and the NL Eastern Division title. The Pirates will always feel they were robbed, and Augustine never hit another home run in the majors.

## Last Team to Go a Full Season without Finding the Seats in Its Home Park

The 1945 Washington Senators. Their only homer at Griffith Stadium was an inside-the-park four-bagger by first baseman Joe Kuhel. Griffith Stadium was so cavernous that Sam Rice played a record 19 seasons with the Senators without ever hitting a fair ball into the seats in his home park.

## Last Player to Hit Two Inside-the-Park Home Runs in a Game

Greg Gagne, Minnesota, October 4, 1986; against the White Sox. Gagne was the first player to accomplish this feat since Dick Allen of the White Sox on July 31, 1972, who did it, oddly enough, against Minnesota.

## First Player to Hit One over the Green Monster

Hugh Bradley of the Red Sox tagged the first homer over the left-field wall in Fenway shortly after the park first opened its doors in 1912. It was his only homer all season. In 1914, playing for the Pittsburgh Rebels in the Federal League, Bradley had no homers in 427 at bats.

## First Player to Clear the Left-Field Wall in Braves Field

Frank Snyder, New York Giants, 1926, more than 11 years after Braves Field hosted its first game. The place was so mammoth that between 1915 and 1928, when the fences were moved in, only seven balls were hit out of the park.

## Fewest Home Runs, Season, Since 1901, by League Leader in Home Runs

NL—6—Tommy Leach, Pittsburgh, 1902. Leach hiked his total to seven in 1903, but all of them were inside-the-park—as were most of his four-baggers in 1902.

AL—7—Sam Crawford, Detroit, 1908
        Braggo Ruth, Cleveland, 1915

**Home Run Leaders Who Never Hit Another Four-Bagger in the Majors, since 1901**
  Fred Odwell, Cincinnati Reds, 1905; Dave Brain, Boston Braves, 1907

**Most At Bats, Season, without Hitting a Home Run**
  NL—672—Rabbit Maranville, Pittsburgh, 1922
  AL—658—Doc Cramer, Boston, 1938

## PLAYERS WITH 500 OR MORE CAREER HOME RUNS

|  | Years Active | Home Runs |
|---|---|---|
| Hank Aaron | 1954–76 | 755 |
| Babe Ruth | 1914–35 | 714 |
| Willie Mays | 1951–73 | 660 |
| Barry Bonds | 1986– | 658 |
| Frank Robinson | 1956–76 | 586 |
| Mark McGwire | 1986–01 | 583 |
| Harmon Killebrew | 1954–75 | 573 |
| Reggie Jackson | 1967–87 | 563 |
| Mike Schmidt | 1972–89 | 548 |
| Sammy Sosa | 1989– | 539 |
| Mickey Mantle | 1951–68 | 536 |
| Jimmie Foxx | 1925–45 | 534 |
| Rafael Palmeiro | 1986– | 528 |
| Ted Williams | 1939–60 | 521 |
| Willie McCovey | 1959–80 | 521 |
| Eddie Mathews | 1952–68 | 512 |
| Ernie Banks | 1953–71 | 512 |
| Mel Ott | 1926–47 | 511 |
| Eddie Murray | 1977–97 | 504 |

**Most Home Runs, Career, by a Pitcher**
  38—Wes Ferrell, 1927–41. Right behind Ferrell are Bob Lemon with 37, Red Ruffing with 36 and Warren Spahn and Earl Wilson with 35.

## Most Grand Slam Home Runs, Career
23—Lou Gehrig, 1923–39

## Most Inside-the-Park Home Runs, Career
51—Sam Crawford, 1899–1917

## Most Home Runs, Career, All of Them Inside-the-Park
12—Harry Niles, 1906–10

## Most Home Runs, Career, without Ever Being a League Leader in Home Runs
475—Stan Musial, 1941–63

## Most Seasons Homering in All Parks Played In
11—Babe Ruth, last in 1931. Even granting that in Ruth's day there were only 8 parks, as opposed to 14 now in each league, it's still an extraordinary record. Hank Aaron, the NL record holder, did it nine times, last in 1966 when there were 10 different parks to conquer.

# Not with a Whimper

In 1966 an arthritic condition in his left elbow forced Sandy Koufax to retire after he'd enjoyed one of the finest seasons ever by a pitcher. Koufax easily broke Henry Schmidt's 63-year-old record for most wins by a pitcher in his final major-league season and went out with the biggest bang of any pitcher in history.

## RECORD HIGHS BY PLAYERS IN THEIR FINAL SEASON*
### Pitching

| Department | Name | Team | League | Year | Record No. |
|---|---|---|---|---|---|
| Wins | Sandy Koufax | Los Angeles | National | 1966 | 27 |
| ERA | Ned Garvin | Brooklyn-N.Y. | Nat-Am. | 1904 | 1.72 |
| Winning Pct. | Larry French | Brooklyn | National | 1942 | .789 |
| Losses | Pete Dowling | Mil.-Cleve. | American | 1901 | 26 |
| Innings | Sandy Koufax | Los Angeles | National | 1966 | 323 |
| Starts | Sandy Koufax | Los Angeles | National | 1966 | 41 |
| Complete Games | Jack Cronin | Brooklyn | National | 1904 | 33[1] |
| Shutouts | Henry Schmidt | Brooklyn | National | 1903 | 5[2] |
|  | Buttons Briggs | Chicago | National | 1905 | 5 |
|  | Joe McGinnity | New York | National | 1908 | 5 |
|  | George Kaiserling | Newark | Federal | 1915 | 5 |
|  | Sandy Koufax | Los Angeles | National | 1966 | 5 |
| Strikeouts | Sandy Koufax | Los Angeles | National | 1966 | 317 |
| Bases on Balls | Henry Schmidt | Brooklyn | National | 1903 | 120 |

| Depart-ment | Name | Team | League | Year | Record No. |
|---|---|---|---|---|---|
| Games | Mark Dewey | San Francisco | National | 1996 | 78 |
| Saves | Tom Henke | St. Louis | National | 1995 | 36 |

*Excluding players who retired before 1901 or were declared ineligible.
[1]Quit at age 30 rather than suffer through another season with Brooklyn like 1904 when he had a 2.70 ERA but lost 23 games.
[2]Even though Schmidt won 22 games in 1903, Brooklyn didn't retain him. Another of the many outstanding pitchers the club let slip through its fingers in the early part of the century, he played only that one season in the majors.

# Batting

| Depart-ment | Name | Team | League | Year | Record No. |
|---|---|---|---|---|---|
| Batting Avg. | Sam Dungan | Washington | American | 1901 | .320[1] |
| | Bill Keister | Philadelphia | National | 1903 | .320[2] |
| Slugging Avg. | Will Clark | Baltimore | American | 2000 | .546[3] |
| | | St. Louis | National | | |
| Home Runs | Dave Kingman | Oakland | American | 1986 | 35 |
| RBIs | Albert Belle | Baltimore | American | 2000 | 103 |
| Hits | Irv Waldron | Mil.-Wash. | American | 1901 | 186[4] |
| Runs | Joey Cora | Sea.-Cleve. | American | 1998 | 111 |
| Doubles | Kirby Puckett | Minnesota | American | 1995 | 39 |
| Triples | Ernie Gilmore | Kansas City | Federal | 1915 | 15[5] |
| Total Bases | Kirby Puckett | Minesota | American | 1995 | 277 |
| Games | Chick Stahl | Boston | American | 1906 | 155 |
| | Al Scheer | Newark | Federal | 1915 | 155 |
| | Joey Cora | Sea.-Cleve. | American | 1998 | 155 |
| Stolen Bases | Dave Fultz | New York | American | 1905 | 44 |
| Bases on Balls | Roy Cullenbine | Detroit | American | 1947 | 137[6] |
| Strikeouts | Howie Goss | Houston | National | 1963 | 128 |
| Fewest Strikeouts | Joe Sewell | New York | American | 1933 | 4 |
| At Bats | Tony Lupien | Chicago | American | 1948 | 617[7] |

[1]In 1900, the American League's last year as a minor league, Dungan was its leading hitter.
[2]Probably the most enigmatic figure of all time, Keister hit at least .300 in every one of his five seasons as a regular and showed good power, yet

never found a team or a position he could call home. The Phillies dropped him after 1903 even though he led the club in RBIs and was second in batting.

[3]In 1960, Ted Williams had a .645 slugging average in his final season but batted only 310 times. Similarly, Chicken Hawkes of the Phillies hit .322 in 1925 but had only 320 at bats. The all-time record for the highest batting average by a player in his final season belongs to Dave Orr, who hit .373 for the Brooklyn Players League entry in 1890 before he suffered a stroke and had to quit. Orr also holds the all-time record for most triples, RBIs and total bases.

[4]Almost as mysterious as Keister, Waldron hit .311 in 141 games and led the American League in at bats in its inaugural season. Like Arlett, he got only that one taste of major-league life; and also like Arlett, he played for years productively in the minors.

[5]For those of you who are unwilling to acknowledge the Federal League was a major circuit, the alternate record holder is: Tommy Long, 14 triples with the 1917 Cardinals.

[6]Granted, Cullenbine hit only .234 in 1947. But he led the American League in walks, ranked fourth in home runs and was second on the Tigers in RBIs. Like Lupien, he was cut; and like Lupien's replacement, George Vico, his replacement in 1948, was gone by the end of the following year.

[7]Another first baseman who got short-changed in the late 1940s. An excellent fielder and a deft base thief, Lupien wasn't considered a strong enough hitter for a first sacker—he had just six homers in 1948—and lost his job to Charlie Kress, who had all of one homer in 1949.

# Outfielders' Records

Outstanding outfielders were probably more plentiful during the 1960s and 1970s than at any other time in history. Six of the top 10 in career games played in the outfield—Willie Mays, Hank Aaron, Lou Brock, Al Kaline, Roberto Clemente and Vada Pinson—were active throughout most of the period; Curt Flood set the all-time record for the best season fielding average and several other glove marks; Aaron broke Babe Ruth's career record for home runs; Roger Maris broke Ruth's season home run record; and Brock established many new season and career stolen base standards.

## SEASON BATTING RECORDS

| Department | National League | American League |
|---|---|---|
| Batting Average | .440, HUGH DUFFY, 1894<br>.398, Lefty O'Doul, Philadelphia, 1929* | .420, Ty Cobb, Detroit, 1911 |
| Slugging Average | .863, BARRY BONDS, San Francisco, 2001 | .847, Babe Ruth, New York, 1920 |
| Home Runs | 73, BARRY BONDS, San Francisco, 2001 | 61, Roger Maris, New York, 1961 |
| RBIs | 191, HACK WILSON, Chicago, 1930 | 171, Babe Ruth, New York, 1921 |
| Hits | 254, LEFTY O'DOUL, Philadelphia, 1929 | 253, Al Simmons, Philadelphia, 1925 |
| Runs | 196, BILLY HAMILTON, Philadelphia, 1894<br>158, Chuck Klein, Philadelphia, 1930* | 177, Babe Ruth, New York, 1921 |
| Doubles | 64, Joe Medwick, St. Louis, 1936 | 67, EARL WEBB, Boston, 1931 |
| Triples | 36, OWEN WILSON, Pittsburgh, 1912 | 26, Joe Jackson, Cleveland, 1912 |

| Department | National League | American League |
|---|---|---|
| | | 26, Sam Crawford, Detroit, 1914 |
| Total Bases | 445, Chuck Klein, Philadelphia, 1930 | 457, BABE RUTH, New York, 1921 |
| Bases on Balls | 198 BARRY BONDS, San Francisco, 2002 | 170, Babe Ruth, New York, 1923 |
| Stolen Bases | 118, Lou Brock St. Louis, 1974 | 130, RICKEY HENDERSON, Oakland, 1982 |
| Strikeouts | 189, BOBBY BONDS, San Francisco, 1970 | 186, Rob Deer, Milwaukee, 1987 |
| Fewest Strikeouts (Minimum 500 ABs) | 8, LLOYD WANER, Pittsburgh, 1933 | 8, TRIS SPEAKER, Washington, 1927 |

*Record since 1901

## Most Games, Career, in the Outfield
2935—Ty Cobb, 1905–1928

## Most Consecutive Games in the Outfield
897—Billy Williams, Chicago Cubs, September 11, 1963, through June 13, 1969

## Best Career Fielding Average
.994—Darren Lewis, 1990–2002

## Most Seasons League Leader in Fielding Average
AL—6—Amos Strunk, last in 1920
NL—5—Mike Griffin, last in 1898

## Most Consecutive Errorless Games
392—Darren Lewis, Oakland A's and San Francisco Giants, August 21, 1990, through June 29, 1994. Almost immediately after making the first error of his career, Lewis made his second miscue but still only had two career errors through 1994.

## Most Consecutive Errorless Chances
938—Darren Lewis, Oakland A's and San Francisco Giants, August 21, 1990, through June 29, 1994.

# EVOLUTION OF SEASON RECORD FOR BEST FIELDING AVERAGE

|  | Team | League | Year | Average |
|---|---|---|---|---|
| Paul Hines | Chicago | National | 1876 | .923 |
| John Glenn | Chicago | National | 1877 | .948 |
| Joe Hornung | Boston | National | 1881 | .948 |
| Curt Welch | St. Louis | Amer.Assoc | 1886 | .952 |
| Pop Corkhill | Cincinnati | Amer.Assoc | 1887 | .952 |
| Pop Corkhill | Cinci-Brook | Amer.Assoc | 1888 | .961 |
| Jim Fogarty | Philadelphia | National | 1889 | .961 |
| Jim Fogarty | Philadelphia | Players | 1890 | .963 |
| Mike Griffin | Brooklyn | National | 1892 | .986 |
| Harry Bay | Cleveland | American | 1904 | .987 |
| Sam Crawford | Detroit | American | 1905 | .988 |
| Fielder Jones | Chicago | American | 1906 | .988 |
| Ed Hahn | Chicago | American | 1907 | .990 |
| Wildfire Schulte | Chicago | National | 1908 | .994 |
| Babe Ruth | Boston | American | 1919 | .996 |
| Sammy West | Washington | American | 1928 | .996[1] |
| Dick Porter | Cleveland | American | 1933 | .996 |
| Harry Craft | Cincinnati | National | 1940 | .997 |
| Danny Litwhiler | Philadelphia | National | 1942 | 1.000 |
| Rocky Colavito | Cleveland | American | 1965 | 1.000 |
| Curt Flood | St. Louis | National | 1966 | 1.000[2] |

[1]The best fielder in his time. His arm went dead in 1930 but came back as strong as ever—he led the AL in double plays in 1932.

[2]Several outfielders have had perfect fielding averages since 1966, but none had as many chances as Flood with 396.

## Most Chances Accepted, Career
7461—Tris Speaker, 1907–28

## Most Chances Accepted, Season
566—Taylor Douthit, St. Louis Cardinals, 1928. It was the only year Douthit handled anywhere near that number of chances. Second to Douthit is Richie Ashburn, who had 560 chances in 1951. Ashburn is the only outfielder to handle over 520 chances in a season more than once—he did it four times, last in 1957.

## Most Chances Accepted, Game, Nine Innings

13—Earl Clark, Boston Braves, May 10, 1929. Clark was only 21 at the time and seemed ready to take over the Braves' regular centerfield slot, but he never made it.

## Most Assists, Season, Since 1901

44—Chuck Klein, Philadelphia Phillies, 1930. Klein played shallow in his home park, the Baker Bowl, which had a short right field, and threw out several batters at first base on what ought to have been singles.

## Most Runners Thrown Out at Plate, Game

3—Jack McCarthy, Chicago Cubs, April 26, 1905. The Pirates provided the opposition that day and repeatedly challenged McCarthy's 36-year-old arm on short fly balls. Notwithstanding his having risen to the test, McCarthy lost his job to Wildfire Schulte.

## Most Gold Glove Awards

12—Roberto Clemente, 1961–72 consecutive
Willie Mays, 1957–68 consecutive

# Triple Crown Winners

In 1967 Carl Yastrzemski won the Triple Crown when he led the American League in batting and RBIs and tied Harmon Killebrew of the Twins for the top spot in home runs. Only a year earlier Frank Robinson had won the Triple Crown after the Orioles acquired him from the Reds. After a ten-year hiatus since Mickey Mantle's Triple Crown season in 1956, Robinson's and Yastrzemski's triumphs seemed to signal that hitters like Chuck Klein, Jimmie Foxx, Lou Gehrig and Ted Williams, who were capable of winning a Triple Crown and who had been relatively abundant in the 1930s and 40s, were once again going to emerge. Instead, however, 35 seasons have passed since 1967, and Yastrzemski still remains the last Triple Crown winner.

### Closest Since 1967 to Winning a Triple Crown

AL—Dick Allen, Chicago, led in homers and RBIs and tied for third in batting in 1972. Jim Rice, Boston, also led in homers and RBIs and was third in batting in 1978.

NL—Mike Schmidt, Philadelphia, led in homers and RBIs and was fourth in batting in 1981

## TRIPLE CROWN WINNERS

|  | Team | League | Year | HRs | RBIs | BA |
|---|---|---|---|---|---|---|
| Paul Hines | Providence | National | 1878 | 4 | 58 | .358[1] |
| Tip O'Neill | St. Louis | Association | 1887 | 14 | 123 | .435[2] |
| Nap Lajoie | Philadelphia | American | 1901 | 14 | 125 | .422 |
| Ty Cobb | Detroit | American | 1909 | 9 | 115 | .377[3] |
| Heinie Zimmerman | Chicago | National | 1912 | 14 | 103 | .372 |

| | Team | League | Year | HRs | RBIs | BA |
|---|---|---|---|---|---|---|
| Rogers Hornsby | St. Louis | National | 1922 | 42 | 152 | .401[4] |
| Rogers Hornsby | St. Louis | National | 1925 | 39 | 143 | .403 |
| Chuck Klein | Philadelphia | National | 1933 | 28 | 120 | .368[5] |
| Jimmie Foxx | Philadelphia | American | 1933 | 48 | 163 | .356 |
| Lou Gehrig | New York | American | 1934 | 49 | 165 | .363 |
| Joe Medwick | St. Louis | National | 1937 | 31 | 154 | .374[6] |
| Ted Williams | Boston | American | 1942 | 36 | 137 | .356[7] |
| Ted Williams | Boston | American | 1947 | 32 | 114 | .343 |
| Mickey Mantle | New York | American | 1956 | 52 | 130 | .353[8] |
| Frank Robinson | Baltimore | American | 1966 | 49 | 122 | .316 |
| Carl Yastrzemski | Boston | American | 1967 | 44 | 121 | .326 |

[1]Disputed. Some sources give the batting title in 1878 to Abner Dalrymple.
[2]Led the American Association in every major hitting department in 1887—runs, hits, total bases, slugging average, doubles and triples as well as the three TC departments.
[3]The only TC winner also to lead his league in stolen bases.
[4]The case against Hornsby being the all-time greatest second baseman always starts with the fact that everybody hit a ton during his peak years. Really? Who else between 1920 and 1940 won two Triple Crowns, let alone hit .400 three times?
[5]Despite winning the Triple Crown, he wasn't selected the MVP.
[6]Last National League player to win a Triple Crown.
[7]Lost out in the MVP voting to Joe Gordon of the Yankees.
[8]The only TC winner who also hit 50 homers in the same season.

## NUMBER OF TIMES LED THE THREE TC DEPARTMENTS*

| | BA | HRs | RBIs | Total Wins |
|---|---|---|---|---|
| Babe Ruth | 1 | 12 | 6 | 19 |
| Ty Cobb | 12 | 1 | 4 | 17 |
| Ted Williams | 6 | 6 | 4 | 16 |
| Rogers Hornsby | 7 | 2 | 4 | 13 |
| Honus Wagner | 8 | 0 | 4 | 12 |
| Hank Aaron | 2 | 4 | 4 | 10 |
| Cap Anson | 2 | 0 | 8 | 10 |
| Dan Brouthers | 5 | 2 | 2 | 9 |
| Stan Musial | 7 | 0 | 2 | 9 |
| Lou Gehrig | 1 | 3 | 5 | 9 |

*Includes only players who won at least one batting title and one of the other two TC departments.

|  | BA | HRs | RBIs | Total Wins |
|---|---|---|---|---|
| Jimmie Foxx | 2 | 4 | 3 | 9 |
| Johnny Mize | 1 | 4 | 3 | 8 |
| Nap Lajoie | 3 | 1 | 3 | 7 |
| Chuck Klein | 1 | 4 | 2 | 7 |
| Ed Delahanty | 2 | 1 | 3 | 6 |
| Mickey Mantle | 1 | 4 | 1 | 6 |
| Joe DiMaggio | 2 | 2 | 2 | 6 |
| Sam Thompson | 1 | 2 | 2 | 5 |
| Carl Yastrzemski | 3 | 1 | 1 | 5 |
| Willie Mays | 1 | 4 | 0 | 5 |
| Joe Medwick | 1 | 1 | 3 | 5 |

## Active Players

|  | BA | HRs | RBIs | Total Wins |
|---|---|---|---|---|
| Andres Galarraga | 1 | 1 | 2 | 4 |
| Larry Walker | 3 | 1 | 0 | 4 |
| Barry Bonds | 1 | 2 | 1 | 4 |
| Manny Ramirez | 1 | 0 | 1 | 2 |

## Close, But No Cigar, Awards

First Prize—Cy Seymour of the Reds led the National League in every major hitting department except home runs in 1905. He lost the TC by the margin of one home run; the NL leader in homers that year was a teammate of Seymour's, Fred Odwell, who never hit another home run in the majors.

Second Prize—Ted Williams led the AL in homers and RBIs in 1949 but missed taking his third Triple Crown when he lost the batting title to George Kell by .00016 of a point.

Third Prize—Stan Musial missed a Triple Crown in 1948 by a single home run; that season he led the National League in every other major hitting department.

Fourth Prize—Al Rosen of the Indians led the American League in homers and RBIs in 1953 but lost the batting title to Mickey Vernon by a single point when he failed by an eyelash to beat out an infield hit in his last at bat of the season.

Fifth Prize—By today's rules Jimmie Foxx would have won a Triple Crown in 1932 as well as in 1933. He led in homers and RBIs but lost the AL batting title by three points to Dale

Alexander, who had only 392 at bats. Foxx came close again in 1938 when he led in batting and RBIs and clubbed 50 homers but lost the home run crown to Hank Greenberg, who had 58.

Sixth Prize—Ty Cobb led the AL in batting and RBIs in 1911 but fell one home run short of winning his second TC. In 1907 Cobb also missed a TC when he finished tied for second in homers.

Seventh prize—Rogers Hornsby came nearly as close as Ted Williams to winning three TCs. In 1921 he led the NL in batting and RBIs but trailed home run leader George Kelly by two circuit clouts.

Eighth Prize—Gavvy Cravath of the Phillies led the NL in homers and RBIs in 1913 but lost the batting crown to Jake Daubert of the Dodgers by nine points.

## Closest Babe Ruth Came to Winning a Triple Crown

In 1924 Ruth led the AL in homers and batting average but finished second in RBIs, eight behind Goose Goslin of the Senators. Two years later Ruth won the homer and RBI crowns but trailed batting leader Heinie Manush of the Tigers by six points.

## Closest Hank Aaron Came to Winning a Triple Crown

In 1963 Aaron led the NL in homers and RBIs but finished third in batting seven points behind the winner, Tommy Davis.

# Great Shutout Feats

More shutouts were pitched in 1968 than in any other season since the end of the deadball era as pitchers savored their last months before mound heights were shaved and the strike zone was reduced to edge the balance of power once again toward the batters' side of the scale. That year Don Drysdale established a new all-time record for consecutive shutout innings, Bob Gibson fashioned the most shutouts by any pitcher since the end of the deadball era, and the Mets' Jim McAndrew also set a shutout record, albeit one he would rather not own.

**Most Shutout Games, Season, since 1901**
  NL—16—Pete Alexander, Philadelphia, 1916
  AL—13—Jack Coombs, Philadelphia, 1910

**Most Shutout Games, Season, since 1920**
  NL—13—Bob Gibson, St. Louis, 1968
  AL—11—Dean Chance, Los Angeles, 1964

**Most Shutout Games, Season, 1920 through 1941**
  NL—10—Carl Hubbell, New York Giants, 1933
  AL—6—Done by nine pitchers, last by Bob Feller, Cleveland, 1941

**Most Shutout Games, Season, 1942 through 1960**
  NL—10—Mort Cooper, St. Louis, 1942
  AL—9—Bob Feller, Cleveland, 1946
          Bob Lemon, Cleveland, 1948

**Most Shutout Games by Left-hander, Season, since 1901**
  NL—11—Sandy Koufax, Los Angeles, 1963. Second only to Ed Morris of the Pittsburgh Alleghenies in the American Association, who had 12 in 1886.

AL—9—Ron Guidry, New York, 1978
   Babe Ruth, Boston, 1916

## Most Seasons League Leader in Shutouts
NL—7—Pete Alexander, last in 1921
AL—7—Walter Johnson, last in 1924

## Most Consecutive Shutouts Pitched
NL—6—Don Drysdale, Los Angeles, 1968
AL—5—Doc White, Chicago, 1904

## Most Consecutive Shutout Innings Pitched
NL—59—Orel Hershiser, Los Angeles, 1988. Hershiser's streak was maintained at one point by a questionable interference call, but Don Drysdale of the Dodgers, the previous record-holder with 58 consecutive innings, was the beneficiary of an even more controversial ruling. In 1968, after pitching four shutouts in succession, he led the Giants 3–0 in the ninth inning on May 31 at Dodger Stadium and then filled the bases with none out. With a 2–2 count, Drysdale's next pitch hit Giants catcher Dick Dietz, apparently forcing home a run and ending the shutout skein. But plate umpire Harry Wendelstadt ruled that Dietz hadn't tried to dodge the pitch. With the count now, 3–2, Dietz popped out to short left field, and Drysdale then got the next two batters, preserving his streak. The Dodgers claimed that Wendelstadt's call was both correct and courageous; Giants vice president Chub Feeney said it would have been courageous if he'd made it in San Francisco.

AL—55⅔—Walter Johnson, Washington, 1913; including two relief appearances

## Most Consecutive Shutout Innings Pitched by Left-hander
45⅓—Carl Hubbell, New York Giants, 1933

## Most Consecutive Shutout Innings Pitched, Beginning of Career
NL—25—George McQuillan, Philadelphia, 1908
AL—22—Boo Ferriss, Boston, 1945. Ferriss is one of eight pitchers who threw shutouts in their first two major-league games. McQuillan, whose shutout string included relief appearances, is not among them.

**Most Spectacular Pitching Job, First Two Major-League Games**
Jim Hughes of the Baltimore Orioles threw a two-hit shutout in his major-league debut on April 18, 1898, then no-hit the Boston Beaneaters four days later in his second start. Hughes won 23 games as a rookie and 28 in his sophomore year, then got married and spent the 1900 season pitching in a California outlaw league after his new bride refused to go East.

**Most Innings Needed to Win Shutout in First Start**
13—In his first (and only) career start, the Giants' Don Fisher earned a complete-game 13-inning 1–0 win against the Braves in the first game of a season-closing doubleheader on September 30, 1945. Despite his dazzling debut start, Fisher never threw another pitch in the majors.

**Most Unusual League Leader in Shutouts**
In 1935, Freddie Fitzsimmons of the New York Giants hurled just 94 innings and had an uninspiring 4–8 record. He nevertheless tied for the NL lead in shutouts when all four of his wins were whitewashes.

**Most Hits Surrendered While Pitching a Shutout**
NL—14—Larry Cheney, Chicago, versus the New York Giants on September 14, 1913
AL—14—Milt Gaston, Washington, versus Cleveland on July 10, 1928

**The Team That Never Learned How to Pick Them II**
The only time a St. Louis Browns pitcher led the American League in whitewashes was in 1929 when three Brownies—Sam Gray, George Blaeholder and Al Crowder—all tied for the top spot with four shutouts.

**Most Shutout Games Lost, Season**
NL—11—Bugs Raymond, St. Louis, 1908
AL—10—Walter Johnson, Washington, 1909; five of them to the White Sox.

**Most Consecutive Shutout Games Lost, Start of Career**
4—Jim McAndrew, New York Mets, 1968

### Pitcher with Whom McAndrew Could Most Sympathize

In 1908, Bugs Raymond posted a 2.06 ERA for the Cardinals but nevertheless topped the NL with 25 losses when he dropped a post-1900 record 11 games by shutout.

### Most Consecutive Shutout Wins, Team

NL—6—Pittsburgh, June 2 through June 6, 1903, amid an all-time record 56 straight shutout innings from June 1 to June 9

AL—5—Baltimore, September 2 through September 6, 1974

### Most Shutout Games Won in a Season, Team

NL—32—Chicago, 1907 and 1909

AL—30—Chicago, 1906

### Most Shutout Games Lost in a Season, Team

NL—33—St. Louis, 1908; 11 of them behind Bugs Raymond

AL—29—Washington, 1909; 10 of them behind Walter Johnson

### Most Consecutive Games Without Being Shut Out, Team

AL—308—New York, August 3, 1931, through August 2, 1933. The streak was ended by Lefty Grove of the A's, who blanked the Yankees 7–0.

NL—182—Philadelphia, August 17, 1893, through May 10, 1895

## TOP 10 IN CAREER SHUTOUTS

|  | | Years Active | Shutouts |
|---|---|---|---|
| 1. | Walter Johnson | 1907–27 | 110 |
| 2. | Pete Alexander | 1911–30 | 90 |
| 3. | Christy Mathewson | 1900–1916 | 78 |
| 4. | Cy Young | 1890–1911 | 76 |
| 5. | Eddie Plank | 1901–17 | 69[1] |
| 6. | Warren Spahn | 1942–65 | 63 |
| 7. | Tom Seaver | 1967–86 | 61 |
|  | Nolan Ryan | 1966–93 | 61 |
| 9. | Bert Blyleven | 1970–92 | 60 |
| 10. | Don Sutton | 1966–88 | 58 |

[1]Southpaw record.

## Most Consecutive Innings Without Scoring, Team

AL—48—Philadelphia, September 22 to September 26, 1906

NL—48—Chicago, June 15 to June 21, 1968. During their scoreless skeins both the A's and the Cubs lost four consecutive shutout games, tying a record held by several teams but most notably the Astros, who had it happen to them in 1963 and again only three years later.

## Most 1–0 Games Won, Career

38—Walter Johnson, Johnson also lost an all-time record 26 1–0 games and 65 shutout games altogether, also an all-time record.

## Only Pitcher to Complete 100 or More Games without Ever Pitching a Shutout

Jim Hughey, 1891–1900, registered exactly 100 complete games but no shutouts. His career record was 29–80, giving him a .266 winning percentage, the all-time poorest among pitchers in over 100 decisions. In Hughey's defense he pitched for the 1898 St. Louis Browns and the 1899 Cleveland Spiders, two of the worst teams in the last century.

## Most Complete Games since 1901 without Pitching a Shutout

45—Roy Mahaffey, 1927–36

## Only Pitcher since 1901 to Throw a No-hitter But Never a Shutout

Ed Lafitte of the Brooklyn Tip Tops in the Federal League held the Kansas City Packers hitless on September 19, 1914, while beating them 6–2. Lafitte, whose family tree included the pirate Jean Lafitte, won 35 games in the majors between 1909 and 1915, but none was a shutout. Bumpus Jones, who no-hit Pittsburgh 7–1 on October 15, 1892, in his first major-league game, also never pitched a shutout. The following year the mound was moved 10½ feet farther from the plate, and Jones, unable to adjust to the added distance, was cut by Cincinnati after being battered to the tune of a 10.32 ERA in his first seven games.

# The Three Most Interesting Teams Between 1961 and 1976

## 1967 CHICAGO WHITE SOX
### W-89 L-73
### Manager: Eddie Stanky

**Regular Lineup**—1B, Tom McGraw; 2B, Wayne Causey; 3B, Don Buford; SS, Ron Hansen; RF, Ken Berry; CF, Tommy Agee; LF, Pete Ward; C, J. C. Martin; P, Gary Peters; P, Joel Horlen; P, Tommy John; P, Bob Locker; P, Hoyt Wilhelm; P, Wilbur Wood.

Nobody ever thought much of Stanky as a manager, but he kept this club in the tight 1967 American League race until the last week of the season when a doubleheader loss to Kansas City left the battle to the Red Sox, Twins and Tigers. The White Sox best hitters in 1967, Buford and Berry, batted .241; Ward led in RBIs with 62; Agee in runs with 73 and total bases with 196; and the club scored almost 200 runs less than pennant-winning Boston. But Stanky's pitching tandem of Peters and Horlen, coupled with a superlative bullpen crew of Wilhelm, Locker and Wood, made for a lot of close low-scoring games. The Sox team batting average of .225 and slugging average of .320 are both record lows for a first-division team since the end of deadball era. Horlen, Peters and John ranked first, second and fourth in the AL in ERA, but John's 2.47 figure was a shade too high for a team that averaged just over three runs a game, and he finished with a 10–13 record.

# 1972 CINCINNATI REDS
## W-95 L-59
## Manager: Sparky Anderson

**Regular Lineup**—1B, Tony Perez; 2B, Joe Morgan; 3B, Dennis Menke; SS, Dave Concepcion; RF, Cesar Geronimo; CF, Bobby Tolan; LF, Pete Rose; C, Johnny Bench; P, Jack Billingham; P, Ross Grimsley; P, Gary Nolan; P, Clay Carroll, P, Tom Hall; P, Pedro Borbon; P, Don Gullett; P, Wayne Simpson; P, Jim McGlothlin.

The Reds easily won the NL Western Division by 10½ games over the Astros, beat the favored Pirates in the LCS when Bob Moose wild-pitched home the pennant-winning run in the bottom of the ninth inning of Game Five, then took the A's to seven games in the World Series before losing the finale 3–2. Unlike Cincy teams later in the decade, this club had only one .300 hitter, Rose at .307, and only Bench with 100 RBIs. The Reds trailed the Astros uncharacteristically in batting, runs and even home runs and got a league-low 25 complete games from their starters. But what Anderson lacked in mound quality he made up for in depth. Much like the 1939 Yankees, who lacked a real staff leader but had nine heavy contributors, the Reds had eight pitchers who worked in more than 120 innings and a ninth, Carroll, who saved 37 games. The staff workhorse was Billingham with only 218 innings, and fragile Nolan, the top winner, had just 15 victories. The team won the division with timely hitting and a strong bullpen, but in the postseason the hitters did little, and it was the starting pitchers who, unexpectedly, came through. In the Series the Reds got only one poor starting effort—from McGlothlin in Game Five. Likewise, only Gullett in the first game of the LCS put on a bad show. The 1972 season was Joe Morgan's first as a Red—and the first time the public really became aware of his tremendous versatility, as he led the NL in runs, bases on balls, steals and fielding while hitting .292.

# 1974 OAKLAND ATHLETICS
## W-90 L-72
## Manager: Al Dark

**Regular Lineup**—1B Gene Tenace; 2B, Dick Green; 3B, Sal Bando; SS, Bert Campaneris; RF, Reggie Jackson; CF, Bill North; LF, Joe Rudi; C, Ray Fosse; P, Catfish Hunter; P, Vida Blue; P, Ken Holtzman; P, Rollie Fingers.

The A's won their division with the second-lowest team batting average in the AL, no reliable dh's, no .300 hitters and only Catfish Hunter of the starters having a good season—Holtzman was 19–17, Blue was 17–15—but the staff had the league's top ERA, and Fingers posted 17 saves. In the LCS The A's beat Baltimore in four games, losing only the first one, and then almost swept the Dodgers in the Series dropping only Game Two. Dark got solid years from Rudi and Jackson and 103 RBIs from Bando on a .243 average, but the A's hit only .183 as a team in the LCS and .211 in the Series, creating the impression, in retrospect, that they won their third straight world title on habit as much as anything else.

# Relievers' Records

In 1970 Hoyt Wilhelm became the first pitcher to appear in 1000 games, Mike Marshall gave up trying to be a starter and moved permanently to the bullpen, and Rollie Fingers, after registering only one complete game in 19 starts, began thinking that he might be wise to do the same. Fifteen years later the three of them held almost every major season and career relief record and were all strong candidates for the title of best relief pitcher ever.

Asked to name the first great reliever, most historians cite Firpo Marberry, but I'd split the honor between Three Finger Brown and Ed Walsh, with Christy Mathewson and Chief Bender only a notch beyond. When those four pitched, a "save" was still some 50 years away from being added to the game's vocabulary, but managers were already well aware that certain pitchers were especially adept at protecting a late-inning lead and were not at all hesitant to yank their starters when the game was on the line and to bring on the staff ace. Brown, for example, averaged over 10 relief appearances a season, and after it was decided what constituted a save and today's standards were applied to yesterday's box scores, he was credited with leading the National League in saves four consecutive years and being the first pitcher to chalk up more than 10 saves in a season. Walsh was only slightly less prized for his relief work. Four of his 40 wins in 1908 came as a reliever, and in addition he collected seven saves.

Just as effective as Brown and Walsh, a generation later, was Lefty Grove. During his peak years he was probably the best southpaw bullpen stopper in the game. After he was traded to the Red Sox, Grove was used almost exclusively as a starter, but between 1925 and 1933 he won 28 games in relief and saved 51 others.

## Greatest Season by a Relief Pitcher Prior to 1893

First Prize—Jack Manning, Boston Red Caps, 1876. Manning, a rightfielder, doubled as a change pitcher and won four games and saved five others in relief of starters.

Second Prize—Bill Hutchison, Chicago White Stockings, 1891. The last pitcher to win 40 games two years in a row, Hutchinson numbered 7 relief victories and a save among his 43 wins in 1891.

## Greatest Season by a Relief Pitcher Between 1893 and 1920

First Prize—Tom Hughes, Boston Braves, 1915. He had a 16–14 record overall but was a perfect 6–0 as a reliever and led the NL in saves with nine.

Second Prize—Nig Cuppy, Cleveland Spiders, 1894. He was 8–0 in relief, the first great season by a bullpenner after the mound was moved to its present location.

## First Relief Pitcher to Collect 100 Saves

Firpo Marberry, in 1934, pitching for the Tigers. He retired with 101 saves and also won 94 games as a starter.

## First Relief Pitcher to Collect 200 Saves

Hoyt Wilhelm, in 1969, pitching for the Angels. He finished with 227 saves.

## First Relief Pitcher to Collect 300 Saves

Rollie Fingers, in 1982, pitching for the Brewers. He retired at the end of the 1985 season with 347 saves, the career record until 1992.

## First Relief Pitcher Selected for an All-Star Game

Jack Russell, Washington Senators, 1934. The first reliever to pitch in an All-Star Game was Mace Brown of the Pirates, in 1938.

## First Relief Pitcher to Appear in 60 or More Games Two Consecutive Seasons

Ace Adams, New York Giants, 1942–43. He went on to appear in 60-plus games four straight seasons during World War II.

## First Relief Pitcher to Appear in Half His Team's Games
John Wyatt, Kansas City A's, 1964. He had a 9–8 record in 81 games.

## First Relief Pitcher to Appear in 90 Games in a Season
Wayne Granger, Cincinatti Reds, 1969. Posted 27 saves in 90 games.

## First Relief Pitcher to Appear in 100 Games in a Season
Mike Marshall, Los Angeles Dodgers, 1974. He made 106 appearances, the all-time record and also set the current American League record in 1979 when he appeared in 90 games for the Twins.

## Most Relief Appearances, Season, by a Left-hander
NL—89—Steve Kline, St. Louis, 2001
AL—88—Sean Runyan, Detroit, 1998; Mike Myers, Detroit, 1997

## Most Relief Innings, Season
NL—208—Mike Marshall, Los Angeles, 1974, shattering the old all-time record of 167 innings, set in 1945 by Andy Karl of the Phillies.
AL—168⅓—Bob Stanley, Boston, 1982

## Season Tandem Record for Relief Appearances
NL—178—Kent Tekulve (94) and Enrique Romo (84), Pittsburgh, 1979
AL—160—Wilbur Wood (88) and Hoyt Wilhelm (72), Chicago, 1968
—160—Paul Quantrill (82) and Dan Plesac (78), Toronto, 1998

## Relief Pitcher with the Most Underappreciated Career
Lindy McDaniel. He pitched in 987 games and 2140 innings between 1955 and 1975. Never on a pennant winner, he had 172 saves and also won 22 games as a starter.

## Best Career by a Starter Turned Reliever, Prior to Dennis Eckersley
Phil Regan. Dropped in 1965 by the Tigers after successive seasons in which he went 4–10 and 1–5 as a starter, Regan was used exclusively in relief by the Dodgers in 1966 and responded with a 14–1 record and 21 saves, the best all-

around season ever by a National League reliever. He finished in 1972 with 92 career saves and 58 relief wins.

### Best Career by a Starter Who Began as a Reliever

Phil Niekro, hands down. The runner-up is just as clear-cut. Wilbur Wood, after eight years in the bullpen, was made a starter by the White Sox in 1971 and won 20 games the next four years in a row.

### Best Final Season by a Reliever

Prior to his tragic death in the spring of 1993, Cleveland's Steve Olin notched eight wins and 29 saves in 1992 with a 2.34 ERA in 72 appearances. Previously the best final season had belonged to another Cleveland hurler, Russ Christopher, who had 17 saves and a 2.90 ERA as the Indians bullpen ace in 1948 before a weak heart forced him to retire prematurely.

### Greatest One-Game Relief Performance

Ernie Shore. On June 23, 1917, in the first game of a doubleheader at Fenway Park, Shore relieved Babe Ruth after Ruth was booted by homeplate umpire Brick Owens for arguing a ball-four call to Washington leadoff hitter Ray Morgan. Red Sox catcher Pinch Thomas was also ejected for joining Ruth's protest. The new catcher, Sam Agnew, cut down Morgan trying to steal second, and Shore then retired the next 26 batters in a row and was once credited with having pitched a perfect game despite not pitching a complete game.

### Relief Pitcher Who Did the Most to Aid His Own Cause

NL—Emil Yde, Pittsburgh, June 15, 1924. Trailing the Cubs in the ninth inning, Yde doubled home the tying run and then tripled home the winning run in the 14th inning.

AL—Babe Birrer, Detroit, July 19, 1955. After entering the game in relief, he hit two three-run homers.

### Relief Pitcher Who Did the Least to Aid His Own Cause

Ed Rommel, Philadelphia A's, July 10, 1932. In the process of working an American League-record 17 innings in relief, he gave up 29 hits and 14 runs to Cleveland batters, yet emerged the winning pitcher when the A's pushed across their 18th run in the top of the 18th inning. It was Rommel's 171st and last major-league victory, and he had the additional distinction of helping Johnny Burnett of the Indians make nine hits, an all-time one-game record. The A's stuck with Rommel because they brought only two able-bodied pitchers to Cleveland that day and had no one left after Connie Mack lifted starter Lew Krausse.

## Least Productive Season by a Reliever

In 1991, Jeff Innis of the New York Mets came out of the pen 69 times without recording a single win or save. The distinction for having the least productive season by an AL reliever belongs to Arnie Earley, who worked 57 games for the Red Sox in 1965 without notching either a win or a save .

## Most Career Mound Appearances by a Reliever Who Never Started a Game

1050—Kent Tekulve, 1974–89

## Winners of the "You-Had-to-Be-Paying-Attention-to-See-Them-in-Action" Award

In major league history a total of six pitchers have appeared in 500 or more games while logging fewer innings than mound appearances. Interestingly, none saw action in the majors prior to 1989.

First Prize—Mike Stanton (1989– ), 885 games but only 869 innings.

Second Prize—Buddy Groom (1992– ), 679 games but only 641 innings.

Third Prize—Mike Myers (1995– ), 609 games but, amazingly, only 376.2 innings.

Fourth Prize—Graeme Lloyd (1993– ), 568 games but only 533 innings.

Fifth Prize—Scott Radinsky (1990–2001), 557 games but only 481.1 innings.

Sixth Prize—Steve Kline (1997– ), 522 games but only 473.1 innings.

## Proof That It Doesn't Pay for a Reliever to Start Off Too Meteorically

Butch Metzger began his career in the mid-1970s with 12 straight wins in relief, breaking the rookie record of 10 straight relief wins set in 1952 by Eddie Yuhas of the Cardinals. Before Yuhas, the record belonged to Joe Pate, who was 9–0, all in relief, for the 1926 Athletics. Now you probably know that Metzger won only 18 games before his arm went, but Yuhas and Pate fared even worse. Neither ever won another game after his rookie season.

## Best Season Ever by a Reliever

True, Roy Face was 18–1 in 1959, Phil Regan went 14–1 in 1966, Jim Konstanty and Willie Hernandez both were selected MVPs, and Hernandez, Rollie Fingers and Sparky Lyle all won Cy Young Awards, but John Hiller still gets my vote. In 1973 he had a 10–5 record in relief, a 1.44 ERA, 124 strikeouts in 125 innings—but the clincher was his 38 saves, a southpaw record until 1986 when Dave Righetti of the Yankees netted 46 saves.

## EVOLUTION OF THE SEASON SAVE RECORD SINCE 1901

| | Team | League | Year | Saves |
|---|---|---|---|---|
| Joe McGinnity | New York | National | 1904 | 5[1] |
| Claude Elliott | New York | National | 1905 | 6[2] |
| George Ferguson | New York | National | 1906 | 7 |
| Ed Walsh | Chicago | American | 1908 | 7 |
| Frank Arellanes | Boston | American | 1909 | 8[3] |
| Three Finger Brown | Chicago | National | 1911 | 13 |
| Firpo Marberry | Washington | American | 1924 | 15 |
| Firpo Marberry | Washington | American | 1925 | 15 |
| Firpo Marberry | Washington | American | 1926 | 26[4] |
| Joe Page | New York | American | 1949 | 27 |
| Ellis Kinder | Boston | American | 1953 | 27 |
| Luis Arroyo | New York | American | 1961 | 29 |
| Ted Abernathy | Chicago | National | 1965 | 31[5] |
| Jack Aker | Kansas City | American | 1966 | 32 |
| Wayne Granger | Cincinnati | National | 1970 | 35 |
| Clay Carroll | Cincinnati | National | 1972 | 37 |
| John Hiller | Detroit | American | 1973 | 38 |
| Dan Quisenberry | Kansas City | American | 1983 | 45 |
| Bruce Sutter | St. Louis | National | 1984 | 45 |

[1]Before 1904 the 20th-century record was three, held by many, McGinnity tied Jack Manning's all-time record, set in 1876.

[2]Never pitched again in the majors after 1905.

[3]The only saves of his career.

[4]By 1926 Marberry, you'd think, would have spawned an onslaught of bullpen records, but over the next 30 years Johnny Murphy was the only other relief pitcher to collect 100 saves, and as late as 1946 Ken Raffensberger, mainly a starter, led the National League in saves with just six.

[5]Had 148 career saves, all of them after he passed his 30th birthday.

| | Team | League | Year | Saves |
|---|---|---|---|---|
| Dave Righetti | New York | American | 1986 | 46 |
| Bobby Thigpen | Chicago | American | 1990 | 57[6] |

[6]The current NL record is 55, set by John Smoltz of Atlanta in 2002.

# EVOLUTION OF SEASON RECORD FOR RELIEF WINS, SINCE 1893

| | Team | League | Year | Relief Wins |
|---|---|---|---|---|
| Frank Killen | Pittsburgh | National | 1893 | 5 |
| Nig Cuppy | Cleveland | National | 1894 | 8[1] |
| Tom Hughes | Boston | National | 1916 | 9 |
| Rosy Ryan | New York | National | 1923 | 9 |
| Allan Russell | Washingtron | American | 1923 | 9 |
| Ken Holloway | Detroit | American | 1924 | 9 |
| Elam Vangilder | St. Louis | American | 1925 | 11 |
| George Dauss | Detroit | American | 1926 | 11[2] |
| Wilcy Moore | New York | American | 1927 | 13[3] |
| Mace Brown | Pittsburgh | National | 1938 | 15 |
| Jim Konstanty | Philadelphia | National | 1950 | 16[4] |
| Roy Face | Pittsburgh | National | 1958 | 18[5] |

[1]Four other pitchers also had 8 prior to 1916.
[2]The final 11 wins of a career in which he won 221, all for the Tigers.
[3]Won 19 games altogether and also had 13 saves.
[4]Probably the finest season by a reliever prior to Hiller's 1973 season—he also had 22 saves and appeared in 74 games, the most ever by a pitcher in a 154-game season.
[5]The American League record belongs to John Hiller, who won 17 for the Tigers in 1974.

# TOP 10 IN CAREER SAVES

| | Years Active | Saves |
|---|---|---|
| 1. Lee Smith | 1980–98 | 478 |
| 2. John Franco | 1984– | 424 |
| 3. Dennis Eckersley | 1975–98 | 390 |
| 4. Jeff Reardon | 1979–94 | 367 |
| 5. Trevor Hoffman | 1993– | 352 |

|  | Years Active | Saves |
|---|---|---|
| 6. Randy Myers | 1985–2000 | 347 |
| 7. Rollie Fingers | 1968–85 | 341 |
| 8. John Wetteland | 1989–2000 | 330 |
| 9. Roberto Hernandez | 1991– | 320 |
| 10. Rick Aguilera | 1985–2000 | 318 |

## TOP 10 IN CAREER RELIEF WINS

|  | Years Active | Relief Wins |
|---|---|---|
| 1. Hoyt Wilhelm | 1952–72 | 124 |
| 2. Lindy McDaniel | 1955–75 | 119 |
| 3. Goose Gossage | 1972–94 | 115 |
| 4. Rollie Fingers | 1968–85 | 107 |
| 5. Sparky Lyle | 1967–82 | 99 |
| 6. Roy Face | 1953–69 | 96 |
| 7. Kent Tekulve | 1974–89 | 94 |
| Gene Garber | 1969–88 | 94 |
| 9. Mike Marshall | 1965–81 | 92 |
| 10. Don McMahon | 1957–74 | 90 |

# Workhorse Records

In 1971 Mickey Lolich of the Tigers pitched 376 innings, the most by any hurler since 1917. The following year Wilbur Wood topped Lolich's post-deadball record when he logged 377 innings for the White Sox. Wood's total was the most by a left-hander since Irv Young pitched 378 innings for the Boston Braves in 1905.

Before 1893, when the mound distance was increased by 10½ feet, pitchers routinely worked 500 or more innings in a season, led by Will White of Cincinnati, who pitched 683 innings in 1879 while the mound was still only 45 feet from the plate. Until the early 1920s pitchers were still expected to finish almost every game they started and paced themselves accordingly. After that, inning totals dipped so sharply that in 1925, for the first time in major-league history, a league leader in innings pitched worked fewer than 300 innings.

**Most Innings Pitched, Season, since 1901**
AL—464—Ed Walsh, Chicago, 1908
NL—434—Joe McGinnity, New York Giants, 1903

**Most Innings Pitched, Season, 1920 through 1941**
NL—363—Pete Alexander, Chicago, 1920
AL—358—George Uhle, Cleveland, 1923

**Most Innings Pitched, Season, 1942 through 1960**
AL—371—Bob Feller, Cleveland, 1946; the post-deadball record for a 154-game season
NL—347—Robin Roberts, Philadelphia, 1953

**Most Innings Pitched, Season, 1961 through 1976**
AL—377—Wilbur Wood, Chicago, 1972
NL—346—Steve Carlton, Philadelphia, 1972

## Most Innings, Pitched, Season, since 1977
NL—342—Phil Niekro, Atlanta, 1979
AL—319—Jim Palmer, Baltimore, 1977

## Most Seasons League Leader in Innings Pitched
NL—7—Pete Alexander, last in 1920
AL—5—Bob Feller, last in 1947; Walter Johnson, last in 1916

## Fewest Innings Pitched by League Leader in Innings Pitched, 1981, 1994 and 1995 Excluded
AL—231.2—David Wells, Toronto, 1999
NL—250—Frank Viola, New York, 1990

## First Season League Leader in Innings Pitched Had Fewer than 300 Innings
AL—1925—Herb Pennock, New York, led with 277 IPs
NL—1926—Pete Donohue, Cincinnati, led with 286 IPs

## Most Seasons 400 or More Innings Pitched, since 1901
2—Ed Walsh, Chicago White Sox, 1907 and 1908; Joe McGinnity, New York Giants, 1903 and 1904

## Most Seasons 300 or More Innings Pitched, since 1901
11—Christy Mathewson, last in 1914

## Most Consecutive Seasons 300 or More Innings Pitched, since 1901
9—Walter Johnson, 1910–18

## Most Consecutive Seasons 300 or More Innings Pitched, since 1920
NL—6—Robin Roberts, Philadelphia,. 1950–55
AL—4—Wilbur Wood, Chicago, 1971–74; Mickey Lolich, Detroit, 1971–74; Gaylord Perry, Cleveland, 1972–75

## Most Innings Pitched, Game
NL—26—Leon Cadore, Brooklyn, and Joe Oeschger, Boston, May 1, 1920
AL—24—Jack Coombs, Philadelphia, and Joe Harris, Boston, September 1, 1906

## Second-Most Innings Pitched, Game
NL—22—Bob Smith, Boston, May 17, 1927. Smith lost 4–3

to the Cubs in 22 innings, the longest complete-game decision in National League history.

AL—21—Ted Lyons, Chicago, May 24, 1929, lost 6–5 to Detroit in 21 innings.

**Most Relief Innings Pitched, Game**

NL—18⅓—Zip Zabel, Chicago, June 17, 1915, winning 4–3 in 19 innings over Jeff Pfeffer to the Dodgers, who went all the way

AL—17—Ed Rommel, Philadelphia, July 10, 1932, winning 18–17 in 18 innings over Cleveland.

**Most Relief Innings Pitched, Career**

1870—Hoyt Wilhelm, 1952–72

## TOP 10 IN CAREER INNINGS PITCHED

|  | | Years Active | Innings |
|---|---|---|---|
| 1. | Cy Young | 1890–1911 | 7356 |
| 2. | Pud Galvin | 1879–92 | 5941.1 |
| 3. | Walter Johnson | 1907–27 | 5914.1 |
| 4. | Phil Niekro | 1964–87 | 5404.1 |
| 5. | Nolan Ryan | 1966–93 | 5386 |
| 6. | Gaylord Perry | 1962–83 | 5350.1 |
| 7. | Don Sutton | 1966–88 | 5282.1 |
| 8. | Warren Spahn | 1942–65 | 5243.2 |
| 9. | Steve Carlton | 1965–88 | 5217.1 |
| 10. | Pete Alexander | 1911–30 | 5190 |

# Great Feats of Precocity

Robin Yount became the youngest regular in American League history when he won the Brewers shortstop job in 1974 shortly after celebrating his 18th birthday. The youngest National League regular, also only 18 at the time, was Johnny Lush, who alternated between first base and the outfield for the 1904 Phillies. Unlike Yount who went on to become a long-time star, Lush was gone from the majors by the age of 24 after leading a hapless Cardinals team in wins and ERA. Trapped on weak clubs, embroiled in frequent holdouts and disputes with managers, he took his talented arm to the Pacific Coast League where he pitched with equal distinction—and bad luck—for several more seasons. With Portland in 1914 for example, he tossed a no-hitter against Venice that he lost 1–0 on a teammate's two-base error followed by a passed ball. Lush was the first player in this century to leave his mark on the game before the age of twenty, but he and Yount were far from being the only players who carved their first niches in the record book while they were still teenagers.

**Youngest Player to Hit a Home Run since 1901**
   Tommy Brown, who in 1944 played 46 games at shortstop for the Dodgers as a 16-year-old high school student, banged a circuit clout off Preacher Roe of the Pirates on August 20, 1945, when he was just 17 years, 4 months and 14 days old.

**Youngest Player to Get a Pinch Hit since 1901**
   AL—Mel Acosta, Washington, 1913, at age 17
   NL—Mel Ott, New York Giants, 1926, at age 17; he was 9-for-24 that season as a pinch hitter.

**Youngest to Pitch in a Game since 1901**
   NL—Joe Nuxhall, still a month and a half shy of his 16th

birthday, pitched two-thirds of an inning for Cincinnati on June 10, 1944, in the Reds' 18–0 loss to the Cardinals.

AL—Carl Scheib, Philadelphia, September 6, 1943, when he was 16 years, 8 months and 5 days old

## Youngest Pitcher to Start a Game since 1901

Bonus baby Jim Derrington was still a couple of months shy of his 17th birthday when the White Sox gave him a starting assignment in 1956. He lost it, was 0–1 in 20 games in 1957 and as gone from the majors before he turned eighteen.

## Youngest 20-Game Winner

No pitcher has been a 20-game winner before his 20th birthday since the mound was moved to its present distance from the plate. But before that happened there were several teenage 20-game winners. The youngest was Willie McGill, who won 20 in the American Association in 1891 at age 17; as a 16-year-old McGill had become the youngest ever to pitch a complete-game victory when he beat Buffalo on May 20, 1890, while toiling for Cleveland in the Players League. By 1896 McGill, one of the more prodigious imbibers of his day, was finished.

## Youngest 25-Game Winner

Jumbo McGinnis, St. Louis Browns (AA), 1882, at age 18 won 25 games; the following year he won 28, giving him 53 wins before his 20th birthday.

## First Teenage 20-Game Winner

Among those who consider the National Association a major league, Tommy Bond is regarded as the first teenage 20-game winner—he had a 22–32 record at age 18 with the 1874 Brooklyn Atlantics. In any case, Bond became the youngest 30-game winner in 1876 when he racked up 31 victories for Hartford while still just 20 years old, as well as being the youngest 40-game winner the following season with Boston.

## Most Luckless Teenage Pitcher

Larry McKeon set an American Association record for most losses in a season when he was beaten 41 times in 1884 as an 18-year-old rookie with Indianapolis.

**Best Debut by a Teenager Pitcher**

Von McDaniel of the Cardinals threw a two-hit 2–0 shutout against the Dodgers at age 18 on June 21, 1957.

**All-Time Youngest Player**

Fred Chapman, Philadelphia, American Association, pitched a game in 1887 when he was just 14.

# BEST SEASONS BY TEENAGERS*

## Batting

| Department | National League | American League |
|---|---|---|
| Batting Average | .322, MEL OTT, New York, 1928 | .290, Tony Conigliaro, Boston, 1964 |
| Slugging Average | .524, Mel Ott, New York, 1928 | .530, TONY CONIGLIARO, Boston, 1964 |
| Home Runs | 18, MEL OTT, New York, 1928 | 24, TONY CONIGLIARO, Boston, 1964 |
| RBIs | 82, PHIL CAVARRETTA, Chicago, 1935 | 65, Mickey Mantle, New York, 1951 |
| Hits | 162, PHIL CAVARRETTA, Chicago, 1935 | 139, Al Kaline, Detroit, 1954 |
| Runs | 85, PHIL CAVARRETTA, Chicago, 1935 | 69, Tony Conigliaro, Boston, 1964 |
| Doubles | 28, PHIL CAVARRETTA, Chicago, 1935 | 23, Ken Griffey Jr., Seattle, 1989 |
| Triples | 12, PHIL CAVARRETTA, Chicago, 1935 12, FRED LINDSTROM, New York, 1925 | 5, done by four players |
| Total Bases | 238, PHIL CAVARRETTA, Chicago, 1935 | 214, Tony Conigliaro, Boston, 1964 |
| Stolen Bases | 17, Cesar Cedeno, Houston, 1970 | 23, TY COBB, Detroit, 1906 |
| Bases on Balls | 59, RUSTY STAUB, Houston, 1963 | 35, Tony Conigliaro, Boston, 1964 |
| Strikeouts | 73, Les Mann, Boston, 1913 | 83, KEN GRIFFEY JR., Seattle, 1989 |
| Wins | 17, Dwight Gooden, New York, 1984 | 19, WALLY BUNKER, Baltimore, 1964 |

# Pitching

| Department | National League | American League |
|---|---|---|
| Losses | 13, Pete Schneider, Cincinnati, 1914 | 14, CHIEF BENDER, Philadelphia, 1903 |
| Starts | 32, Gary Nolan, Cincinnati, 1967 | 36, BOB FELLER, Cleveland, 1938 |
| Complete Games | 11, Pete Schneider, Cincinnati, 1914 | 29, CHIEF BENDER, Philadephia, 1903 |
| Innings | 227, Gary Nolan, Cincinnati, 1967 | 278, BOB FELLER, Cleveland, 1938 |
| Games | 44, Don Gullett, Cincinnati, 1970 | 45, TERRY FORSTER, Chicago, 1971 |
| Shutouts | 5, GARY NOLAN, Cincinnati, 1967 | 4, Joe Wood, Boston, 1909 |
| Bases on Balls | 108, Curt Simmons, Philadelphia, 1948 | 208, BOB FELLER, Cleveland, 1938 |
| Strikeouts | 276, DWIGHT GOODEN, New York, 1984 | 240, Bob Feller, 1938 |
| ERA | 2.58, Gary Nolan, Cincinnati, 1967 | 2.18, JOE WOOD, Boston, 1909 |

*Includes players since 1901 who ended the season still short of their 20th birthday—batters in at least 100 games, pitchers in at least 154 innings.

# Great Milestone Achievements

On April 8, 1974, Hank Aaron of the Braves surpassed what had once seemed an unattainable milestone when he hit his 715th home run off Al Downing of the Dodgers. The only comparable achievement occurred on September 11, 1985, at Riverfront Stadium when Pete Rose singled off Eric Show of San Diego to collect his 4192d career hit 57 years to the day after Ty Cobb played his last game and retired with a record that for the next half-century was believed to be even more unassailable than Ruth's. Here is a partial chronology of other great milestone achievements.

**1897**—On July 18 Cap Anson became the first player in history to make 3000 hits.

**1910**—Pitching for Cleveland, Cy Young won his 500th game on July 19, beating Washington 5–4 in 11 innings.

**1914**—On June 9 Honus Wagner of the Pirates became the first player in this century and only the second in history to make 3000 career hits.

**1915**—Eddie Plank of the Federal League St. Louis Terriers became the first southpaw to win 300 games.

**1916**—Sam Crawford of Detroit collected his 311th and final triple.

**1921**—Still in the early stages of his career, Babe Ruth of the Yankees hit his 137th home run, breaking Roger Connor's career record of 136.

**1923**—On May 25 Ty Cobb scored his 1741st run, moving him ahead of Wagner. Cobb retired with 2244 runs, an all-time record that has since been challenged only by Pete Rose and Hank Aaron.

**1923**—Cobb went 4-for-4 on September 20 against the Red Sox at Fenway Park, breaking Wagner's record for career hits.

**1927**—On July 19, now with the Athletics, Cobb wreaked

revenge on Detroit for letting him go by garnering his 4000th career hit, a double, off Sam Gibson of the Tigers. Remarkably, Cobb himself didn't realize what he'd achieved in that less record-concerned time until he read about it in the paper that evening.

**1927**—On September 30 Babe Ruth shattered his own record of 59 when he hammered his 60th homer of the season off Tom Zachary of Washington.

**1928**—Tris Speaker of the A's collected his 793rd and last career double.

**1929**—Pete Alexander of the Cardinals netted his 373d career victory, staggering to a 19–16 decision over the Phillies. Released shortly thereafter by the Cards, Alexander left convinced that his last victory had put him one ahead of Christy Mathewson and given him the National League record for career wins, but 15 years later a review of Mathewson's stats revealed he'd been deprived of a win in 1902 that ought to have been credited to him, bringing his total also up to 373 and tying him with Alexander.

**1935**—Babe Ruth, wearing a Boston Braves uniform, collected his 2062nd and last walk.

**1936**—Outfielder Woody Jensen of the Pirates totaled 696 at bats, the all-time record for a 154-game season. The quintessential contact hitter, Jensen struck out only 19 times that year and picked up just 16 walks.

**1937**—Rogers Hornsby hit .321 in 20 games for the St. Louis Browns and then retired at 41 with a .358 career average, the all-time highest by a right-handed hitter.

**1939**—On May 2 the Yankees beat Detroit 22–2 at Briggs Stadium without Lou Gehrig's name appearing in the box score for the first time in 2131 games played by the Yankees.

**1941**—Lefty Grove of the Red Sox, after a long struggle, became the second left-hander to win 300 games.

**1942**—Paul Waner of the Braves made his 3000th career hit, the last player to do so until 1958.

**1960**—On July 19 Juan Marichal of the Giants experienced the best mound debut ever by a future Hall of Famer when he pitched a 2–0 one-hitter against the Phillies.

**1961**—Roger Maris of the Yankees broke Ruth's season home run record when he hit his 61st round-tripper on October 1 off Tracy Stallard of the Red Sox.

**1963**—Warren Spahn's first win of the season gave him 328 career victories, breaking Eddie Plank's southpaw record.

**1963**—Early Wynn became the first American League hurler since 1941 to win 300 games when he beat Kansas City.

**1970**—Willie Mays became the first black player to make 3000 hits.

**1972**—Roberto Clemente made his 3000th and final career hit, a double off John Matlack of the Mets in the Pirates' last night home game of the season.

**1974**—Al Kaline of the Tigers became the first American Leaguer since Tris Speaker in 1925 to collect 3000 hits when he doubled on September 24 against Dave McNally of Baltimore.

**1975**—Bob Watson of Houston scored the 1,000,000th major-league run on May 4 in a game against the Giants.

**1979**—On September 23, against the Mets, Lou Brock of the Cardinals stole his 938th and final base.

**1981**—On June 10, just before the players went out on strike, Pete Rose of the Phillies made his 3630th hit to tie Stan Musial's National League record.

**1981**—Steve Carlton of the Phillies broke Bob Gibson's National League record when he recorded his 3118th career strikeout on September 21 in a 17-inning 1–0 loss to Montreal.

**1983**—Cal Ripken of the Orioles set a new all-time record when he played every inning of every regular-season, League Championship Series and World Series game played by his team.

**1984**—Pete Rose played in his 3309th game, breaking Carl Yastrzemski's all-time record for the most games played.

**1984**—Pete Rose collected his 4000th hit, a double off Jerry Koosman of the Phils, exactly 21 years after making his first hit.

**1958**—On July 11 Nolan Ryan of the Astros became the first pitcher in history to notch 4000 strikeouts when he fanned Danny Heep of the Mets.

**1985**—Rod Carew of the Angels collected his 3000th hit on August 4 off Frank Viola of the Twins, making him the first infielder since Eddie Collins to attain the 3000-hit circle. That same day Tom Seaver of the White Sox beat the Yankees 4–1 at Yankee Stadium for his 300th win. It was the first time in history that two players had achieved such important milestone figures on the same date.

**1985**—Cal Ripken of the Orioles played his 5342d consecutive inning, breaking the all-time record of 5341 consecutive innings, set by Buck Freeman of the Red Sox on June 5, 1905.

**1985**—Phil Niekro of the Yankees nailed his 300th win on October 6, the last day of the season, by beating Toronto 8–0. It was the first time since 1890 that two pitchers picked up their 300th wins in the same year.

**1986**—Steve Carlton of the Giants on August 5 became the first southpaw to collect 4000 strikeouts.

**1987**—Lou Whitaker and Alan Trammell of the Tigers became the first keystone combo to play regularly for the same team for ten years.

**1988**—Jose Canseco of the A's became the first player in history to hit 40 home runs and steal 40 bases in the same season.

**1989**—Nolan Ryan of the Rangers notched his 5000th strikeout en route to becoming the first pitcher ever to collect 300 K's in a season after age 40.

**1990**—George Brett of the Royals became the first AL player to win a batting title in three different decades (1976, 1980 and 1990).

**1991**—Cal Ripken Jr. of the Orioles became the first shortstop in AL history to collect 30 or more home runs, 100 or more RBIs and hit .300.

**1993**—Sparky Anderson of Detroit became the first pilot since Connie Mack retired in 1950 to manage 24 consecutive seasons in the majors.

**1993**—Carlos Baerga of Cleveland became the first second baseman in major league history to collect 20 or more home runs, 200 or more hits, 100 or more RBIs and hit .300 two years in a row.

**1994**—San Diego's Tony Gwynn hit .394, the highest batting average since Ted Williams topped .400 in 1941.

**1995**—Lou Whitaker and Alan Trammell of the Tigers played in their 1915th game together on September 13 against Milwaukee to set a new AL record for most games as teammates; the NL record is 2015, held by Billy Williams and Ron Santo of the Cubs.

**1996**—Paul Molitor became the first member of the 3000-hit club whose career batting average was below .300 at age 30 and above .300 at age 40.

**1998**—Barry Bonds became the first player to amass 400 career home runs and 400 career stolen bases.

**1999**—Mark McGwire became the first slugger to reach major home run milestones in consecutive seasons when he hit his 500th homer in 1999 after hitting his 400th in 1998.

# World Series Play: 1961–76

## FRANCHISE SUMMARY

| Team | League | WS Record Thru 1976 | Last WS | LCS Record Thru 1976 | Last LCS |
|------|--------|---------------------|---------|----------------------|----------|
| Oakland | American | 3–0 | 1974 | 3–2 | 1975 |
| New York | American | 20–10 | 1976 | 1–0 | 1976 |
| St. Louis | National | 8–4 | 1968 | — | — |
| Pittsburgh | National | 4–2 | 1971 | 1–4 | 1975 |
| Cleveland | American | 2–1 | 1954 | — | — |
| Boston | American | 5–3 | 1975 | 1–0 | 1975 |
| Los Angeles | National | 3–2 | 1974 | 1–0 | 1974 |
| Cincinnati | National | 4–4 | 1976 | 4–1 | 1976 |
| Chicago | American | 2–2 | 1959 | — | — |
| Baltimore | American | 2–2 | 1971 | 3–2 | 1974 |
| New York | National | 1–1 | 1973 | 2–0 | 1973 |
| Detroit | American | 3–5 | 1968 | 0–1 | 1972 |
| Chicago | National | 2–8 | 1945 | — | — |
| Minnesota | American | 0–1 | 1965 | 0–2 | 1970 |
| San Francisco | National | 0–1 | 1962 | 0–1 | 1971 |
| Philadelphia | National | 0–2 | 1950 | 0–1 | 1976 |
| Atlanta | National | | | 0–1 | 1969 |

## Became Defunct between 1961 and 1976

| | | | |
|---|---|---|---|
| Milwaukee | National | 1–1 | 1958 |

### Yearly Highlights
1961—New York (AL) defeated Cincinnati (NL) 4 games to 1

Whitey Ford broke Babe Ruth's World Series record for consecutive scoreless innings as the Yankees won easily under their new manager, Ralph Houk.

1962—New York (AL) defeated San Francisco (NL) 4 games to 3

Ralph Terry nearly became the first pitcher to lose the seventh game in two World Series on the final pitch of the game. Instead he became the first pitcher to win a seventh game 1–0 as Yankees second baseman Bobby Richardson speared Willie McCovey's line drive in the bottom of the ninth inning with two out and runners on second and third.

1963—Los Angeles (NL) defeated New York (AL) 4 games to 0

The first renewal of the Yankees-Dodgers rivalry since the Brooklyn franchise had fled to the West coast, and the first time the Yankees had been swept in a Series since the Giants did it to them in 1922.

1964—St. Louis (NL) defeated New York (AL) 4 games to 3

Also for the first time since 1922, the Yankees lost back-to-back Series—despite Bobby Richardson's all-time record 13 hits—when a weary Bob Gibson of the Cardinals staggered to a 7–5 win in the deciding game.

1965—Los Angeles (NL) defeated Minnesota (AL) 4 games to 3

The Dodgers dropped the first two games in Minnesota but then got three shutouts, two of them by Sandy Koufax, to win a Series that had only one close game, the finale.

1966—Baltimore (AL) defeated Los Angeles (NL) 4 games to 0

The Dodgers were held scoreless the last 33⅔ innings of the Series by Orioles reliever Moe Drabowsky, who fanned a record-tying six in a row in the opener, followed by three Orioles starting pitchers—Jim Palmer, Wally Bunker and Dave McNally—who had notched only one shutout among them during the regular season.

1967—St. Louis (NL) defeated Boston (AL) 4 games to 3

The seventh game found both Bob Gibson of the Cardinals and Jim Lonborg of the Red Sox shooting for their third wins, the first time that so dramatic a matchup had ever occurred in a Series. Gibson emerged with the victory but shared laurels with teammate Lou Brock, who hit .414 and stole a record seven bases.

## 1968—Detroit (AL) defeated St. Louis (NL) 4 games to 3

Once again Brock hit over .400 and swiped seven bases, and Gibson and his mound rival both started the seventh game in search of their third Series victories. But this time Gibson's opponent, Mickey Lolich, prevailed as Curt Flood of the Cardinals misplayed a long fly ball into a two-run triple. An inning earlier Lolich had extinguished a St. Louis rally by picking both Flood and Brock off first base. The Series MVP, Lolich brought the Tigers back after they trailed three games to one and aided his own cause in his first Series win by hitting the only home run of his long major-league career. Gibson achieved a measure of solace when he set an all-time Series record by fanning 17 Tigers in the opener.

## 1969—New York (NL) defeated Baltimore (AL) 4 games to 1

The most improbable world champs ever, the Mets fulfilled their fans' wildest fantasy by capturing four straight after dropping the opener. Prior to the 1969 season each league had expanded to 12 teams and split into two divisions, necessitating a best-three-of-five league Championships Series to determine the pennant winner. The Mets won the first National League LCS, besting the Atlanta Braves three games to none. The Orioles likewise won the first American League LCS three games to none over Minnesota.

## 1970—Baltimore (AL) defeated Cincinnati (NL) 4 games to 1

The Reds won the fourth game to avert a sweep. Both LCS runners-up, Minnesota and Pittsburgh, once again fell in three straight.

## 1971—Pittsburgh (NL) defeated Baltimore (AL) 4 games to 3

Led by Roberto Clemente's bat, Nelson Briles's shutout in Game Four and Steve Blass's two complete-game wins, including the series finale, the Pirates rallied after being down two games to none. Game Three, in Pittsburgh, was the first Series contest to be played at night. In LCS play, the Orioles swept Oakland and Pittsburgh bested San Francisco three games to one.

1972—Oakland (AL) defeated Cincinnati (NL) 4 games to 3

The A's Series hero, Gene Tenace, hit .348 and collected four homers and nine RBIs after hitting .225 in the regular season. For the first time in Series history no pitcher on either team registered a complete game. Also for the first time, both LCSes were competitive, the A's needing five games to dispose of Detroit and Pittsburgh taking the Reds to the full five games before losing on a ninth-inning wild pitch.

1973—Oakland (AL) defeated New York (NL) 4 games to 3

Well-pitched games from starters Jerry Koosman and John Matlack, abetted by Tug McGraw's superb relief work, nearly brought the Mets their second World Championship in five years, but the A's got even better relief pitching from Rollie Fingers, who had two saves, and Darold Knowles, who also had two saves and became the first pitcher to appear in every game of a seven-game Series. Again, both LCSes went down to the wire, the Mets beating the Reds in five behind Tom Seaver while Catfish Hunter shut down the Orioles in the fifth game without a single Baltimore runner getting as far as third base.

1974—Oakland (AL) defeated Los Angles (NL) 4 games to 1

The A's got complete games from Vida Blue and Ken Holtzman to beat the Orioles 3–1 in the LCS, and Don Sutton blanked the Pirates in the opener of the National League LCS, which the Dodgers also won three games to one. But in the World Series, for the third year in a row, no pitcher tossed a complete game. Reliever Rollie Fingers, with a win and two saves, was the Series MVP. The A's, in becoming the first team other than the Yankees to win three straight World Championships, also may have become, in the opinion of many, the last team besides the Yankees ever to do it.

1975—Cincinnati (NL) defeated Boston (AL) 4 games to 3

In LCS play, the Reds took out the Pirates in three straight, and the Red Sox did the same to Oakland, setting up what promised to be one of the better Series of the decade. It turned out to be possibly the best Series ever. Boston's Luis Tiant broke what was becoming a disturbing pattern by pitching two complete-game victories, and the Red Sox came from three runs back in the eighth inning of Game Six to tie the Reds in regulation length and then even the Series on a 12th-inning homer by Carlton Fisk. But in Game Seven, the Reds rallied from a 3–0 deficit to win their first World Championship in 35 years on Joe Morgan's two-out single in the ninth inning. The Reds scored 29 runs in the Series, the Red Sox scored 30, and both pitching staffs had near identical ERAs. The most even matchup in history, both statistically and on the field, was probably resolved by the Reds having a deeper bullpen. At the wire, Red Sox manager Darrell Johnson found himself with no one to bring in but rookie lefty Jim Burton. Burton's loss in the seventh game was the last decision he recorded in the majors.

## 1976—Cincinnati (NL) defeated New York (AL) 4 games to 0

The most one-sided Series since 1963—the Yankees were competitive only in the second game—followed the Reds' three-zip blowout of the Phillies in the National League LCS. The Yankees, on the other hand, needed five games in the LCS to shake the Kansas City Royals, the first American League expansion team to qualify for postseason play. The fifth game seemed headed for extra innings until Chris Chambliss of the Yankees snapped a 6–6 deadlock by leading off the bottom of the ninth inning with a homer off Royals reliever Mark Littell. Mobbed by Yankees fans, Chambliss was unable to complete his home run trot around the bases. Hours later he crept out of the clubhouse, accompanied by two policemen, and touched home plate to make his pennant-winning run official.

# SECTION 6

# Famous Firsts:
# 1977–93

**1977**—The American League bloats to 14 teams after granting new franchises to Toronto and Seattle. There are now 26 clubs in the major leagues, the most since the frantically unstable 1884 season when the uninvited Union Association joined the American Association in its war with the National League.

**1977**—Paddy Livingston dies in Cleveland. His obituary notes that he played for the Indians but neglects to mention that he was the last surviving member of the American League's class of 1901, its first year as a major circuit.

**1978**—The Yankees beat the Red Sox 5–4 at Fenway Park to cop the first division playoff game in history.

**1979**—Willie Stargell of the Pirates and Keith Hernandez of the Cardinals become the first players to be selected co-MVPs.

**1981**—On June 12 the players go on strike for the second time in history and shut down the season for 50 days.

**1982**—Joel Youngblood becomes the first player to get hits for two different teams in two different cities on the same day when he's traded by the Mets to the Expos following an afternoon game on August 4 and scurries to Philadelphia in time to play in the game that night for Montreal.

**1982**—Relief pitcher Greg Minton of the Giants set a new major-league record when he twirls 269⅓ innings over four seasons without surrendering a home run.

**1982**—In the wake of dire forecasts that the 1981 strike will disenchant fans with the game, the Dodgers demolish the season attendance record by drawing 3,608,881 fans.

**1983**—First baseman Pete Rose of the Phillies becomes the first player since the end of the deadball era to play a full season at the position for a pennant winner without hitting a home run.

**1984**—Jim Rice of the Red Sox sets a new major-league record when he grounds into 36 double plays.

**1985**—Don Sutton, never a strikeout leader, becomes the first pitcher ever to fan 100 or more hitters in 20 consecutive seasons. By September he is on the same team with Reggie Jackson, the first hitter to fan 100 or more times in 17 consecutive seasons (1981 excepted).

**1985**—The two League Championship Series are expanded to a best 4-of-7 format, and the Kansas City Royals promptly establish the record for being the first team to rally from a 3–1 deficit to win an LCS.

**1986**—Don Sutton of the Angels beats the Texas Rangers 5–1 on June 18 for his 300th career victory, making him the first 300-game winner in history who needed more than 20 full seasons to do it and only once was a 20-game winner.

**1986**—Don Baylor of the Red Sox breaks the American League record that he previously shared with Kid Elberfeld when he is hit by 35 pitches. His career total of 227 leaves him only 16 short of Ron Hunt's modern record.

**1986**—Bert Blyleven of the Twins surrenders 50 home runs, shattering Robin Roberts's former all-time record of 46 by a comfortable margin.

**1986**—On September 29, for the first time in history, two brothers face each other as rookie starting pitchers when Greg Maddux of the Cubs beats older brother Mike of the Phillies, 8–3.

**1987**—Benito Santiago of the Padres sets a new rookie record when he hits safely in 34 straight games.

**1988**—Jerry Ruess of the White Sox becomes the first southpaw to collect 200 career victories without ever winning 20 games in a season.

**1990**—Willie McGee becomes the first absentee batting titlist in history when he is traded from the National League to the American League shortly after he collected enough plate appearances to qualify for the NL crown.

**1991**—The Braves become the first NL or AL team to leap from worst to first when they win the NL pennant after posting the poorest record in the majors in 1990.

**1992**—Tim Wakefield of Pittsburgh becomes the first rookie to hurl two complete game wins in an LCS.

**1993**—The Oakland A's become the first defending division champions to finish in the league cellar the following season.

# The Most Difficult Pitchers to Beat

His 24–4 record and .857 winning percentage in 1986 not only brought Boston's Roger Clemens the Cy Young and MVP awards but narrowly missed equalizing Ron Guidry's incredible performance eight years earlier for the Yankees. In 1978 Guidry had the greatest season ever by a left-hander, a 25-game winner and, for that matter, a 20-game winner when he posted a 25–3 record and an .893 winning percentage. Guidry's mark shattered the old record for the highest winning percentage by a 20-game winner—.880—set by Preacher Roe of the Brooklyn Dodgers in 1951 when he won 22 games and lost only 3. But Roe still holds the National League record.

**Highest Winning Percentage, Season, Minimum 15 Wins**
    NL—.947—Roy Face, Pittsburgh, 1959 (18–1). At one point in the season Face had a 17–0 record.
    AL—.938—Johnny Allen, Cleveland, 1937 (15–1). Allen was 15–0 until he lost his last start of the season.

**Most Wins in a Season without a Loss**
    AL—12—Tom Zachary, New York, 1928. The runner-up is Dennis Lamp, who had a perfect 11–0 record for Toronto in 1985.
    NL—10—Howie Krist, St. Louis, 1941. One runner-up, Ken Holtzman of the Cubs, began the 1967 season by winning his first nine games, then was called away to do military service.

**Highest Winning Percentage by a Rookie 20-Game WInner**
    NL—.838—Bill Hoffer, Baltimore, 1895 (31–6)
    AL—.813—Russ Ford, New York, 1910 (26–6)

**Highest Winning Percentage by a Rookie since 1893, Minimum 10 Decisions**
 NL—1.000—Howie Krist, St. Louis, 1941 (10–0)
 AL—.923—Jim Nash, Kansas City A's, 1966 (12–1)

**Most Wins without a Loss, Only Season in Majors**
 3—Luke Nelson, New York Yankees, 1919
  Danny Osborn, Chicago White Sox, 1975

**Most Seasons League Leader in Winning Percentage**
 AL—5—Lefty Grove, last in 1939
 NL—3—Ed Reulbach, 1906–08 consecutive

**Only Pitchers to Lead Both the NL and the AL in Winning Percentage**
 Jack Chesbro, Pittsburgh (NL), 1901 and 1902; New York (AL), 1904; Randy Johnson, Seattle (AL) 1995 and 1997; Arizona (NL) 2001 and 2002

**Most Seasons League Leader in Winning Percentage before 1901**
 3—Bob Caruthers, St. Louis (AA), 1885 and 1887; Brooklyn (AA), 1889

**Only Two-Time League Leader in Winning Percentage with a Career WP below .500**
 Larry Benton of the New York Giants led the National League in winning percentage in 1927 and again in 1928 but finished with a 127–128 record.

**Highest Career Winning Percentage, Minimum 150 Decisions**
 .717—Spud Chandler, 1937–47 (109–43). Chandler didn't win his first game until he was nearly 30. He lost almost two full seasons to military service during World War II and parts of several other seasons to arm ailments. Against that he played for the Yankees, who won seven pennants while he was with them. Prior to joining the Yankees, Chandler posted a mediocre 47–41 record in six minor-league seasons.

**Highest Career Winning Percentage, Pitcher Never on a Pennant Winner, Minimum 150 Wins**
 .626—Addie Joss, Cleveland, 1902–10 (159–95)

# TOP 10 IN CAREER WINNING PERCENTAGE*
## (Minimum 200 Decisions, Retired Pitchers Only)

|  | | Years Active | Wins | Losses | Pct. |
|---|---|---|---|---|---|
| 1. | Whitey Ford | 1950–67 | 236 | 106 | .690[1] |
|  | Dave Foutz | 1884–94 | 147 | 66 | .690 |
| 3. | Bob Caruthers | 1884–92 | 218 | 99 | .688[2] |
| 4. | Lefty Grove | 1925–41 | 300 | 141 | .680[3] |
| 5. | Christy Mathewson | 1900–16 | 373 | 186 | .665 |
|  | Larry Corcoran | 1880–87 | 177 | 89 | .665 |
| 7. | Sam Leever | 1898–1910 | 195 | 100 | .661[4] |
| 8. | Roger Clemens | 1984–2003 | 310 | 160 | .660 |
| 9. | Sandy Koufax | 1955–66 | 165 | 87 | .655 |
| 10. | Johnny Allen | 1932–44 | 142 | 75 | .654 |

[1]Had a .720 winning percentage through 1964, then lost 22 games and won only 20 in his last three seasons.

[2]Had a .708 winning percentage before posting a 2–10 record for the 1892 St. Louis Browns in his final season as a pitcher.

[3]The top winning percentage among 300-game winners.

[4]Had a 37–36 career record after his first three seasons but then fashioned an incredible .712 winning percentage from 1901 through 1910.

## Highest Career Winning Percentage since 1961 (Retired Pitchers Only)
.686—Don Gullett, 1970–78 (109–50). In his last four seasons he won 44 games, lost only 13 and had a .772 winning percentage.

## Highest Career Winning Percentage, Minimum 40 Decisions
.771—Howie Krist, 1937–46 (37–11). After his first four seasons he had an unbelievable 26–4 career record.

## Highest Career Winning Percentage, Minimum 20 Decisions
.871—Luis Aloma, 1950–53 (18–3). In between bouts of arm trouble he also netted 15 saves and pitched a shutout in his only starting assignment.

## Most Career Wins Without a Loss
4—Ben Shields, 1924–31. Although pounded in almost every game he pitched—he had an 8.27 career ERA—he was somehow never beaten.

**Highest Career Winning Percentage as a Relief Pitcher, Minimum 50 Decisions**
    .718—Hugh Casey, 1935–49 (51–20).

**Only Pitcher with a .600 Career Slugging Average and Winning Percentage**
    Babe Ruth, 1914–35; had a .671 winning percentage (94–46) and a .690 slugging average.

# The All-time Worst Fielders

When third baseman Butch Hobson of the Red Sox fielded
.899 in 133 games in 1978, he became the first regular player
in 62 years to post a fielding average that was below .900.
Rather incredibly, however, since 1978 two other regular players have posted sub-.900 fielding averages.

**Last Regular Prior to Hobson to Field below .900**
Charlie Pick, Philadelphia A's, 1916. Primarily a third baseman, Pick fielded .899 in 116 games.

**Most Recent Regular to Field Below .900**
Third sacker Gary Sheffield, while splitting the 1993 season
between San Diego and Florida, clocked an .899 FA when he
committed 34 errors in 338 chances. Nine years earlier, in
1984, Joel Youngblood fielded just .887 in 117 games at third
base for the San Francisco Giants.

**Last Regular Outfielder to Field Below .900**
Guy Zinn, New York Yankees, 1912; fielded .893 in 106
games. Also in 1912, Jay Kirke of the Boston Braves fashioned a meager .862 FA when he was guilty of 23 boots in
just 167 outfield chances. Kirke played only 71 games in the
pasture that year, however.

**Lowest Fielding Average by a Regular Player since 1901**
If we drop back a year to 1900, we find Piano Legs Hickman at third base for the New York Giants fielding a grand
.842 and making 86 errors. But the record since 1901, when
the majors became a two-league operation, belongs to Bill
Keister, who fielded .851 and made 97 errors while playing
shortstop for the 1901 Baltimore Orioles.

## Most Errors, Season, by a Player since 1901

Johnny Gochnauer, Cleveland shortstop, 1903; made 98 errors and fielded .869.

## Most Errors, Season, by First Baseman since 1901

Once again, by dropping back a year to 1900, we find Jack Doyle, who made 43 errors with the Giants, most of them, we might imagine, while trying to handle Piano Legs Hickman's throws. The record since 1901 is held by Jerry Freeman, who racked up 41 miscues with Washington in 1908.

## Most Errors, Season, by a Catcher since 1901

41—Oscar Stanage, Detroit Tigers, 1911. Rather bizarrely, Stanage also holds the American League record for most assists in a season.

## Most Errors, Season, All-time Record

122—Herman Long, Kansas City, AA, 1889
—Billy Shindle, Philadelphia, PL, 1890

## Last Players to Make 100 Errors in a Season

Joe Sullivan, 102 errors, Washington, 1893.
Herman Long, 100 errors, Boston, 1893.

## Last Player to Make 90 or More Errors in a Season

Johnny Gochnauer, Cleveland, 1903; along with his 98 errors he batted .185.

## Last Player to Make 80 or More Errors in a Season

Neal Ball, shortstop New York Yankees, 1908; a year before he became the first player to perform an unassisted triple play.

## Last Player to Make 70 Errors in Consecutive Seasons

Buck Weaver, shortstop Chicago White Sox, made exactly 70 errors in 1913. The year before he had 71 boots. Despite his high number of miscues, Weaver had relatively decent fielding averages for that time, and one suspects that he accumulated so many errors mostly because he got to more balls than the average shortstop. Switched to third base in 1916, he became one of the outstanding hot corner glove men of his era.

**Last Player to Make 60 or More Errors in a Season**

Al Brancato, shortstop Philadelphia A's. 1941; 61 errors and a .915 fielding average.

**Last Player to Make 50 or More Errors in a Season**

Roy Smalley, shortstop Chicago Cubs, 1951; 51 errors and a .945 fielding average. No apologies here. Cubs fans in the early fifties, harkening back to Tinker to Evers to Chance, cynically coined the chant "Miksis to Smalley to Addison Street." When Cubs managers Frankie Frisch and Phil Cavarretta wanted to rest Smalley's scatter-arm, they were stuck with Tommy "Buckshot" Brown at shortstop. In 1951 Brown fielded .911 and was second on the team in errors to Smalley, although he played in just 61 games.

# Base-stealing Feats

What player was the most proficient base thief ever? The most prolific? We're watching both of them perform right now. Indeed the majority of season and career base-stealing records have been set in the past 15 years.

**Most Stolen Bases, Season**

AL—130—Rickey Henderson, Oakland, 1982; also swiped 108 bases in 1983 and 100 in 1980.

NL—118—Lou Brock, St. Louis, 1974. The only other players who stole 100 or more bases in a season were Maury Wills, who grabbed 104 with the 1962 Dodgers, and Vince Coleman, 110, as a rookie with the 1985 Cardinals and 107 in 1986, his sophomore season.

**Most Stolen Bases, Season, 1901 through 1919**

AL—96—Ty Cobb, Detroit, 1915
NL—81—Bob Bescher, Cincinnati, 1911

**Most Stolen Bases, Season, 1920 through 1941**

AL—63—Sam Rice, Washington, 1920
NL—52—Max Carey, Pittsburgh, 1920

**Most Stolen Bases, Season, 1942 through 1960**

AL—61—George Case, Washington, 1943
NL—50—Maury Wills, Los Angeles, 1960

**Most Stolen Bases without Being Caught, Season**

NL—21—Kevin McReynolds, New York, 1988
AL—20—Paul Molitor, Toronto, 1994

**Most Consecutive Stolen Bases without Being Caught**

NL—50—Vince Coleman, St. Louis, 1988–89; streak ended

on July 28, 1989, when he was nailed by Nelson Santovenia of the Expos.

AL—32—Willie Wilson, Kansas City Royals, 1980; Todd Cruz, Chicago, 1980–81. Prior to Wilson and Cruz, the AL record was 26, set in 1977 by Mitchell Page of Oakland.

## Most Successful Thefts of Home, Season
AL—7—Rod Carew, Minnesota, 1969
NL—7—Pete Reiser, Brooklyn, 1946

## First Player to Steal Home Twice in a Game
Joe Tinker, Chicago Cubs, June 28, 1910

## Last Pitcher to Steal Home
NL—Darren Dreifort, Los Angeles, June 12, 2001
AL—Harry Dorish, St. Louis Browns, June 21, 1951

## Most Stolen Bases, Game
6—Eddie Collins, Philadelphia A's September 11 and September 22, 1912. Collins's dual feats, occurring only 11 days apart, were the only times in modern history that a player stole more than five bases in a game.

## Most Seasons League Leader in Stolen Bases
NL—10—Max Carey, last in 1925
AL—10—Rickey Henderson, last in 1998

## Most Seasons 50 or More Stolen Bases
AL—13—Rickey Henderson, last in 1998
NL—12—Lou Brock, last in 1976

## Most Players with 50 or More Stolen Bases in a Season, Team
AL—3—Oakland, 1976; Bill North (75), Bert Campaneris (54), Don Baylor (52)
NL—3—San Diego, 1980: Gene Richards (61), Ozzie Smith (57), Jerry Mumphrey (52).

## Most Stolen Bases, Season, Team
NL—347—New York Giants, 1911
AL—341—Oakland, 1976

**Best Stolen Base Percentage, Season, Minimum 35 Attempts**
   NL—.962—Max Carey, Pittsburgh, 1922; 51 steals in 53 tries
   AL—.943—Amos Otis, Kansas City Royals, 1970; 33 steals
in 35 tries

**Lowest Stolen Base Percentage, Season, Minimum 20 Attempts**
   .133—Lary Gardner, Cleveland Indians, 1920; three steals
in 23 tries

**Most Times Caught Stealing, Season**
   AL—42—Rickey Henderson, Oakland, 1982; 130 steals in
172 tries.
   NL—36—Miller Huggins, St. Louis, 1914; 32 steals in 68
tries. Huggins's stolen base percentage that season—well
below .500—was not atypical of the deadball era.

**Most times Caught Stealing, Season, Team**
   NL—149—Chicago, 1924; 137 steals in 286 tries
   AL—123—Oakland, 1976; 341 steals in 464 tries

**Fewest Stolen Bases, Season, by League Leader in Stolen Bases**
   AL—15—Dom DiMaggio, Boston, 1950
   NL—18—Stan Hack, Chicago, 1938

**Fewest Stolen Bases, Season, by Team**
   AL—13—Washington, 1957; club leader was Julio Becquer
with 3
   NL—17—St. Louis, 1949; club leader was Red Schoendienst
with 8

**Highest Batting Average, Season, since 1901, by League Leader in Steals**
   AL—.420—Ty Cobb, Detroit, 1911
   NL—.354—Honus Wagner, Pittsburgh, 1908

**Lowest Batting Average, Season, since 1901, by League Leader in Steals**
   NL—.219—Danny Murtaugh, Philadelphia, 1941
   AL—.225—George Case, Cleveland, 1946

### Winner of the "Making Them Count" Award

In 1958 Vic Power stole only three bases all year, but two of them were thefts of home—and in the same game, no less.

### Winner of the "Right Man for the Job" Award

Inserted as a pinch runner on September 1, 1909, rookie Bill O'Hara of the New York Giants promptly stole both second and third base; called on again to pinch run the following day, he did the same thing.

### Winner of the "Stemming the Tide" Award

On May 11, 1897, catcher Duke Farrell of Washington threw out a record eight would-be base thieves.

### Most Combined Home Runs and Stolen Bases, Season, Minimum 30 Home Runs

88—Alex Rodriguez, Seattle, 1998, 42 homers and 46 steals.

## OTHER CURRENT TOP 20 MEMBERS OF THE 30/30 CLUB

| | Team | Year | Homers | Steals | Total |
|---|---|---|---|---|---|
| 2. Eric Davis | Cincinnati Reds | 1987 | 37 | 50 | 87 |
| 3. Ken Williams | St. Louis Browns | 1922 | 39 | 47 | 86 |
| Barry Bonds | Pittsburgh | 1990 | 33 | 53 | 86 |
| 5. Alfonso Soriano | New York Yankees | 2002 | 39 | 45 | 84 |
| 6. Bobby Bonds | San Francisco | 1973 | 39 | 43 | 82 |
| Jose Canseco | Oakland | 1988 | 42 | 40 | 82 |
| Barry Bonds | San Francisco | 1996 | 42 | 40 | 82 |
| Larry Walker | Colorado Rockies | 1997 | 49 | 33 | 82 |
| 10. Vladimir Guerrero | Montreal Expos | 2002 | 39 | 41 | 80 |
| 11. Bobby Bonds | California Angels | 1977 | 37 | 41 | 78 |
| 12. Bobby Bonds | San Francisco | 1969 | 32 | 45 | 77 |
| Howard Johnson | New York Mets | 1989 | 36 | 41 | 77 |
| Barry Bonds | San Francisco | 1997 | 40 | 37 | 77 |
| 15. Willie Mays | New York Giants | 1956 | 36 | 40 | 76 |
| 16. Hank Aaron | Milwaukee Braves | 1963 | 44 | 31 | 75 |
| Darryl Strawberry | New York Mets | 1987 | 39 | 36 | 75 |
| 18. Bobby Bonds | White Sox-Texas | 1978 | 31 | 43 | 74 |
| 19. Willie Mays | New York Giants | 1957 | 35 | 38 | 73 |
| Barry Bonds | Pittsburgh | 1992 | 34 | 39 | 73 |

**Most Consecutive games without Being Caught Stealing**
    1,206—Gus Triandos, 1953—65. Triandos played his entire career without ever being caught stealing. He tried only once to swipe a base, and that was while playing for Baltimore in 1958 in a game the Orioles were losing so badly to the Yankees that the Yankees didn't bother to make a play on him.

**Fewest Stolen Bases, Career, 2,400 or More Games Played**
    19—Harmon Killebrew, 1954–75 (2,435 games). Nearly half of Killebrew's thefts—8—came in 1969. Killebrew also has the fewest triples (24) of any player in over 2400 games.

## LEADERS IN CAREER STOLEN BASES

|  | *Years Active* | *Stolen Bases* |
|---|---|---|
| 1. Rickey Henderson | 1979– | 1406[1] |
| 2. Lou Brock | 1961–79 | 938 |
| 3. Ty Cobb | 1905–28 | 892 |
| 4. Tim Raines | 1979–2002 | 808 |
| 5. Vince Coleman | 1985–97 | 752 |
| 6. Eddie Collins | 1906–30 | 743 |
| 7. Max Carey | 1910–29 | 738 |
| 8. Honus Wagner | 1897–1917 | 703[2] |
| 9. Joe Morgan | 1963–84 | 689 |
| 10. Willie Wilson | 1976–94 | 668 |
| 11. Bert Campaneris | 1964–83 | 649[3] |

[1]The most prolific base thief in history, he has averaged 56.2 stolen bases a season.

[2]In 1897, Wagner's rookie year, a stolen base was still often awarded whenever a runner advanced an extra base on a hit or an out. As a result, all stolen base records set before 1898, when the modern scoring rule was established, are impossible to compare to records set afterward and have been omitted from this section.

[3]In 1969 he stole 62 bases in 70 tries, the highest success rate of any American League player with more than 60 attempts in a season. Tim Raines of the Expos, who swiped 70 sacks in 79 attempts for an .886 percentage in 1985, holds the all-time record; in 1986 Raines posted identical stolen base stats to tie his own mark.

**Most Career Thefts of Home**
    35—Ty Cobb, 1905–28. George Burns, 1911–25, is second with 27.

**Most Times Caught Stealing, Career**
  335—Rickey Henderson, 1979–

**Highest Stolen Base Percentage, Career, Minimum 400 Attempts**
  .847—Tim Raines. Upon retiring after the 2002 season Raines had 808 thefts in 954 attempts; his success rate is easily the best ever among players with a minimum of 500 career steal attempts.

# Loyalty Records

In 1983 Carl Yastrzemski completed his 23d season in a Boston Red Sox uniform, tying Brooks Robinson's all-time record for playing the most seasons with the same team. Yastrzemski's retirement left Bill Russell heir to the loyalty record among active players. In 1986 Russell played his 18th consecutive season with the Dodgers. Since free agency was made part of the game in 1975, only nine other players who began their careers before then—Mike Schmidt, Robin Yount, Dave Concepcion, Dennis Leonard, Dwight Evans, Bob Forsch, Jim Rice, Charlie Moore and George Brett—were still playing with their original teams during the 1986 season.

**Record for Most Seasons with One Team Before Brooks Robinson Broke It**
22—Al Kaline, Detroit Tigers, 1953–74
Mel Ott, New York Giants, 1926–47
Stan Musial, St. Louis Cardinals, 1941–63
Cap Anson, Chicago White Stockings, 1876–97. Anson's share of the record is open to dispute since he played with the Rockford Forest Citys and Philadelphia Athletics in the National Association for five seasons prior to 1876.

**Team That for Some Perverse Reason Inspired the Most Loyalty**
The Chicago White Sox from 1914 through 1950. Beginning in 1914, Red Faber pitched 20 years for them without ever playing with another team. Ted Lyons pitched 21 years for the Pale Hose from 1923 through 1946. And shortstop Luke Appling gave the Sox his entire 20-year career from 1930 through 1950. Faber came to the club in time to play on two

pennant winners, but Lyons and Appling were not so fortunate. Lyons holds the record for playing the most pennantless seasons with the same team, and Appling is second to him.

## ENTIRE CAREER WITH ONE TEAM
## RECORD HOLDERS
### Batting

| Department | Name | Years Active | Team | Record |
|---|---|---|---|---|
| Games | Carl Yastrzemski | 1961–83 | Boston Red Sox | 3308 |
| At Bats | Carl Yastrzemski | 1961–83 | Boston Red Sox | 11,988 |
| Hits | Stan Musial | 1941–63 | St. Louis Cardinals | 3630 |
| Home Runs | Mike Schmidt | 1972–89 | Philadelphia Phillies | 548 |
| RBIs | Lou Gehrig | 1923–39 | New York Yankees | 1991 |
| Runs | Stan Musial | 1941–63 | St. Louis Cardinals | 1949 |
| Doubles | Stan Musial | 1941–63 | St. Louis Cardinals | 725 |
| Triples | Bid McPhee | 1882–99 | Cincinnati Reds | 189 |
| Total Bases | Stan Musial | 1941–63 | St. Louis Cardinals | 6134 |
| Stolen Bases | Clyde Milan | 1907–22 | Washington Senators | 495 |
| Bases on Balls | Ted Williams | 1939–60 | Boston Red Sox | 2019 |
| Strikeouts | Mickey Mantle | 1951–68 | New York Yankees | 1710 |
| Batting Average | Ted Williams | 1939–60 | Boston Red Sox | .344 |
| Slugging Average | Ted Williams | 1939–60 | Boston Red Sox | .634 |

### Pitching

| | | | | |
|---|---|---|---|---|
| Wins | Walter Johnson | 1907–27 | Washington Senators | 416 |
| Losses | Walter Johnson | 1907–27 | Washington Senators | 279 |
| Winning Pct. | Whitey Ford | 1950–67 | New York Yankees | .690 |

| Department | Name | Years Active | Team | Record |
|---|---|---|---|---|
| Games | Walter Johnson | 1907–27 | Washington Senators | 802 |
| Innings Pitched | Walter Johnson | 1907–27 | Washington Senators | 5924 |
| Starts | Walter Johnson | 1907–27 | Washington Senators | 666 |
| Complete Games | Walter Johnson | 1907–27 | Washington Senators | 532 |
| ERA | Addie Joss | 1902–10 | Cleveland Indians | 1.88 |
| Strikeouts | Walter Johnson | 1907–27 | Washington Senators | 3508 |
| Bases on Balls | Bob Feller | 1936–56 | Cleveland Indians | 1764 |

## The All-time Loyalty All-Star Team*

| Position | Name | Team | Years Played | Total |
|---|---|---|---|---|
| First Base | Cap Anson | Chicago White Stockings | 1879–97 | 19 |
| Second Base | Bid McPhee | Cincinnati Reds | 1882–99 | 18 |
| Third Base | Brooks Robinson | Baltimore Orioles | 1958–75 | 18 |
| Shortstop | Dave Concepcion | Cincinnati Reds | 1970–86 | 17 |
| Outfield | Al Kaline | Detroit Tigers | 1954–72 | 19 |
| Outfield | Roberto Clemente | Pittsburgh Pirates | 1955–72 | 18 |
| Outfield | Clyde Milan | Washington Senators | 1908–21 | 14 |
| Catcher | Bill Dickey | New York Yankees | 1929–43 | 15 |

*Limited to players who became institutions both because they spent their entire careers with the same team and because they were regulars at the same positions without any interruptions during the years cited. The lone exceptions are Lyons, who lost years to the military service, Kaline, who was a utility outfielder during the regular season in 1968 but played every game in the World Series, and Concepcion, the Reds regular shortstop in 1986 until injured in mid-season.

| Position | Name | Team | Years Played | Total |
|----------|------|------|--------------|-------|
| Pitcher | Walter Johnson | Washington Senators | 1907–27 | 21 |
| Pitcher | Ted Lyons | Chicago White Sox | 1923–46 | 21 |
| Picher | Red Faber | Chicago White Sox | 1914–33 | 20 |
| Pitcher | Mel Harder | Cleveland Indians | 1928–47 | 20 |

## Mobility Records

Carl Yastrzemski and Alex Johnson dovetailed in 1970 when they fought it out all season for the American League batting crown, which Johnson won by a fraction of a point, but from then on their careers diverged probably as much as those of any two players in modern history. By the time Johnson left in 1976 he had played at least one full season with eight different teams, at the time a post–1900 record.

## Most Teams Played for between 1901 and 1960

Since 1961, when expansion increased the number of teams in the major leagues, pitcher Mike Morgan has worn an all-time record 12 different uniforms, but prior to expansion the record was held by Dick Littlefield, who pitched for nine different teams between 1950 and 1958. He appeared with the Red Sox, the White Sox, the Tigers, the Browns, the Pirates, the Cardinals, the Giants, the Cubs and the Milwaukee Braves—and, in addition, pitched three games in a Baltimore uniform after the Browns franchise was transferred there in 1954.

## One of a Kind

Mike Torrez. Between 1974 and 1978 he pitched for the Expos, the Orioles, the A's, the Yankees and the Red Sox, winning at least 14 games with each club. No other player in history has done so much for so many teams in such a short space of time.

## Proof That the More Things Change the More They Stay the Same

Due to the expansion and free agency, player mobility seems to be at an all-time apex in the 1990s, but that isn't really the case. Exactly a century ago things were equally in a state of flux, as can be seen by the career of Jersey Bakely. In 1884 Bakely embarked on an odyssey that took him not only to four different teams in his next four seasons in the majors but also to four different leagues. Bakely actually pitched for six different clubs during that span. He spent the 1884 season with Philadelphia, Wilmington and Kansas City in the Union Association, then was out of the majors until 1888, when he pitched for Cleveland in the American Association. The following year he found himself still with Cleveland but in the National League, and in 1890 he jumped to the Cleveland entry in the Players League. In each of the four seasons he pitched at least 300 innings, giving him an additional record for being the only pitcher ever to figure in a minimum of 30 decisions in four different major leagues.

## Proof That the More Things Change the More They Stay the Same, II

Don Mincher broke in with the Washington Senators in 1960, then went to Minnesota when the franchise transferred there the following year. In 1971 he found himself with the expansion Washington Senators and must have felt that he'd come full circle upon learning that the franchise would be transferring to Texas in 1972 and he'd be going with it.

## Players in 1000 or More Games at Two Different Positions

Ernie Banks (1953–71); 1259 games at first base, 1125 games at shortstop

Stan Musial (1941–1963); 1896 games in the outfield, 1016 games at first base

Ron Fairly (1958–1978); 1218 games at first base; 1037 games in the outfield.

Rod Carew (1967–85); 1128 games at second base, 1065 games at first base

Robin Yount (1974–93); 1479 games at shortstop, 1104 games in the outfield

## Only Players Who Were Regulars at Four Different Positions

Dennis Menke (1962–74); shortstop, third base, second base, first base.

Pete Rose (1963–86); second base, third base, outfield, first base.

Gregg Jefferies (1987–2000); third base, second base, first base, outfield.

## Players Who Were Regulars at Three Different Positions
(since 1893)

Wid Conroy, (1901–11); shortstop, third base, outfield
Frankie Gustine, (1939–50); second base, third base, shortstop
Nixey Callahan, (1894–1913); pitcher, outfield, third base
Eric McNair, (1929–42); shortstop, second base, third base
Billy Goodman, (1947–62); second base, first base, third base
Ray Boone, (1948–60); shortstop, third base, first base
Gil McDougald, (1951–60); third base, shortstop, second base
Harmon Killebrew, (1954–75); third base, first base, outfield
Joe Torre, (1960–77); catcher, third base, first base
Pete Runnels, (1951–64); shortstop, second base, first base
Dick Allen, (1963–77); third base, outfield, first base
Jimmy Brown, (1937–46); second base, shortstop, third base
Don Buford, (1963–72); second base, third base, outfield
Buddy Myer, (1925–41); second base, shortstop, third base
Dan Meyer, (1974–85); outfield, first base, third base
Don Money, (1968–83); third base, second base, shortstop
Deron Johnson, (1960–76); first base, third base, outfield
Bill Keister, (1896–1903); second base, shortstop, outfield
Barry McCormick, (1895–1904); second base, shortstop, third base
Hubie Brooks, (1980–94); outfield, third base, shortstop
Toby Harrah, (1969–86); shortstop, third base, second base
Buck Herzog, (1908–20); second base, third base, shortstop
Frank O'Rourke, (1912–31); shortstop, second base, third base
Jim Delahanty, (1901–15); second base, third base, outfield
Tony Phillips, (1982–99); shortstop, third base, outfield
Tony Fernandez, (1983–2001); shortstop, second base, third base
B. J. Surhoff (1987–); catcher, third base, outfield
Todd Zeile (1989–); catcher, third base, first base
Tony Womack (1997–); second base, outfield, shortstop
Craig Biggio (1988–), catcher, second base, outfield

## Players since 1893 Who Pitched in 100 Games and Had 1000 Hits

Babe Ruth (1914–1935); 163 games pitched, 2873 hits
Cy Seymour (1896–1913); 140 games pitched, 1723 hits

## Only Player since 1901 to Play 15 or More Games at Every Position

Art Hoelskoetter, (1905–08). The all-time jack-of-all-trades, in his four seasons with the St. Louis Cardinals, he was tried at every job, including that of pinch hitter, in at least 15 games.

# The Hitless Wonders

Duane Kuiper and Johnnie LeMaster both finished their careers in 1985 with performances that cemented their rankings among the leading Hitless Wonders of all time. Kuiper, by failing to hit a home run, kept intact his record for the fewest home runs of any player in history with 3000 or more career at bats, and LeMaster's .119 season vaulted his career batting average into 11th place on the list of the all-time weakest hitters.

## THE 20 WORST HITTERS*

| | Years Active | At Bats | Batting Ave. | Slugging Ave. |
|---|---|---|---|---|
| 1. Jerry Kindall | 1956–65 | 2057 | .213 | .327 |
| 2. Bobby Wine | 1960–72 | 3172 | .215 | .286 |
| 3. Dal Maxvill | 1962–75 | 3443 | .217 | .259[1] |
| 4. Joe Quest | 1871–76 | 2295 | .217 | .267 |
| 5. Darrell Chaney | 1969–79 | 2113 | .217 | .288 |
| 6. George McBride | 1901–20 | 5526 | .218 | .264[2] |
| 7. Skeeter Webb | 1932–48 | 2274 | .219 | .268 |
| 8. Lee Tannehill | 1903–12 | 3778 | .220 | .273 |
| 9. Rob Deer | 1984–96 | 3881 | .220 | .445 |
| 10. Rafael Belliard | 1982–98 | 2301 | .221 | .259 |
| 11. Johnnie LeMaster | 1978–87 | 3191 | .222 | .289 |
| 12. Pop Smith | 1880–91 | 4238 | .222 | .313 |
| 13. Art Whitney | 1880–91 | 3681 | .223 | .285 |
| 14. Jimmy Canavan | 1891–97 | 2072 | .224 | .345 |
| 15. Ed Brinkman | 1961–75 | 6045 | .224 | .300 |
| 16. George Strickland | 1950–60 | 2824 | .224 | .311 |

|  | Years Active | At Bats | Batting Ave. | Slugging Ave. |
|---|---|---|---|---|
| 17. Enzo Hernandez | 1971–78 | 2327 | .224 | .266[3] |
| 18. Roger Repoz | 1964–72 | 2145 | .224 | .390[4] |
| 19. John Kennedy | 1962–74 | 2110 | .225 | .323[5] |
| 20. Gorman Thomas | 1973–86 | 4677 | .225 | .448[6] |

*Minimum 2000 career at bats. Pitchers and catchers excluded.

[1]Has the lowest slugging average of any player since 1901 who batted over 3000 times.

[2]A model of consistency. As Washington's regular shortstop from 1908 through 1916, he never hit more than .235 or less than .203.

[3]No fewer than seven of the top 15 on this list were shortstops active since expansion. Hernandez was the prototype—low average, low on base percentage, little run production.

[4]If you remember Repoz at all, you remember him as one of a host of slugging outfielders in the 1960s who connected now and then but mostly just struck out a lot. More than that, he had the lowest career average ever among outfielders with 2000 or more at bats until Rob Deer recently surpassed him. In 1992, however, Deer hiked his career BA four points, putting Repoz once again in jeopardy of being the negative record-holder.

[5]The list, as you've already spotted, is constituted almost entirely of players active before 1920 and after 1960. The weakest hitter between 1920 and World War II, and also the only member of the top 25, was Rabbit Warstler, a shortstop and second baseman, who hit .229 between 1930 and 1940.

[6]Despite his low average, Thomas was a steady, and sometimes spectacular, run producer. In contrast, Rick Miller, also an outfielder from the same period, had a .269 career average on 3887 at bats but only 369 RBIs and 552 runs.

# LOWEST SEASON BATTING AVERAGE
## BY POSITION
### (Minimum 300 at Bats)

| Position | Name | Team | Year | At Bats | BA | SA |
|---|---|---|---|---|---|---|
| First Base | George Scott | Boston Red Sox | 1968 | 350 | .171 | .237 |
| Second Base | Mickey Doolan | Brooklyn Dodgers | 1918 | 308 | .179 | .218 |
| Third Base | Dave Roberts | San Diego Padres | 1974 | 318 | .167 | .252 |
| Shortstop | George McBride | St. Louis Cards | 1906 | 313 | .169 | .208 |
| Outfield | George Wright | Texas Rangers | 1985 | 363 | .190 | .242 |
| Catcher | Bill Bergen | Brooklyn Dodgers | 1909 | 346 | .139 | .156 |

(Minimum 400 at Bats)

| | | | | | | |
|---|---|---|---|---|---|---|
| First Base | Mark McGwire | Oakland A's | 1991 | 483 | .201 | .383 |

| Position | Name | Team | Year | At Bats | BA | SA |
|----------|------|------|------|---------|-----|-----|
| Second Base | Billy Hallman | Cleveland-Phillies | 1902 | 464 | .185 | .235[1] |
| Third Base | Eddie Zimmerman | Brooklyn Dodgers | 1911 | 417 | .185 | .264 |
| Shortstop | Ed Brinkman | Washington Senators | 1965 | 444 | .185 | .257[2] |
| Outfield | Rob Deer | Detroit Tigers | 1991 | 448 | .178 | .386 |
| Catcher | Billy Sullivan | Chicago White Sox | 1908 | 430 | .191 | .228 |

(Minimum 500 at Bats)

| Position | Name | Team | Year | At Bats | BA | SA |
|----------|------|------|------|---------|-----|-----|
| First Base | Dave Kingman | New York Mets | 1982 | 535 | .204 | .432 |
| Second Base | Bobby Lowe | Detroit Tigers | 1904 | 507 | .207 | .258 |
| Third Base | Charles Moran | Wash.-St. Lou. | 1904 | 405 | .196 | .225 |
| Shortstop | Monte Cross | Philadelphia A's | 1904 | 503 | .189 | .256 |
| Outfield | Charlie Jones | Washington Senators | 1905 | 544 | .208 | .267 |
| Catcher | Randy Hundley | Chicago Cubs | 1968 | 553 | .226 | .311[3] |

(Prior to 1901*)

| Position | Name | Team | Year | At Bats | BA | SA |
|----------|------|------|------|---------|-----|-----|
| First Base | Milt Scott | Baltimore (AA) | 1886 | 482 | .190 | .242 |
| Second Base | Joe Gerhardt | New York (NL) | 1885 | 399 | .155 | .195[4] |
| Third Base | Art Whitney | Kansas City (AA) | 1891 | 358 | .193 | .240 |
| Shortstop | Charlie Bastian | Philadelphia (NL) | 1885 | 389 | .167 | 252[5] |
| Outfield | Jim Lillie | Kansas City (NL) | 1886 | 416 | .175 | .197 |
| Catcher | Henry Sage | Toledo (AA) | 1890 | 275 | .149 | .229[6] |

*Minimum 350 at bats; for catchers, participation in at least half of team's games.

[1] In 1902 the Phillies replaced Hallman with Pete Childs, who hit .194 and had a .206 slugging average, the lowest in this century among players with over 400 at bats.

[2] Cleveland shortstop Johnny Gochnauer hit .185 both in 1902 and 1903, but each year his average was a few thousandths of a point higher than Brinkman's.

[3] Hundley's not-all-that-terrible batting average in 1968 ranks as the worst mostly because catchers who aren't hitting much seldom got 500 at bats in a season.

[4] Called "Move Up Joe," Gerhardt did anything but that with men on base. A decent hitter early in his career, he tailed off dramatically after pitchers began throwing overhand.

[5] Bastian, Tom McLaughlin and Henry Easterday were the three most inept of the many weak-hitting shortstops in the 1880s, suggesting that the philosophy then with regard to shortstops may have been very like that in our own time.

[6] Because there were three major leagues in 1890, the supply of good catchers was short. Another AA receiver, Herman Pitz of Brooklyn and Syracuse, hit .165 in 90 games and collected just 47 hits in 284 at bats, all of them singles, making him the only player in history without an extra base hit in over 200 at bats.

**Most Consecutive at Bats without Hitting a Home Run**
    3278—Eddie Foster, 1910–23. Foster collected six career home runs in 5652 at bats, but all came early in his career. He connected for the last time near the beginning of the 1916 season.

**Most Career at Bats without Hitting a Home Run, since 1901**
    1931—Tom Oliver, 1930–33. Second to Oliver is Irv Hall, an infielder with the Philadelphia A's during World War II who went homerless in 1904 at bats.

## THE 17 LOWEST CAREER HOME RUN PERCENTAGES*

| | Years Active | At Bats | Home Runs | HR Pct. |
|---|---|---|---|---|
| 1. Bill Holbert | 1876–88 | 2335 | 0 | .00000[1] |
| 2. Davy Force | 1871–86 | 4256 | 1 | .00023 |
| 3. Bob Ferguson | 1871–84 | 3470 | 1 | .00028 |
| 4. Duane Kuiper | 1975–85 | 3379 | 1 | .00029 |
| 5. Emil Verban | 1944–50 | 2911 | 1 | .00034[2] |
| 6. Jimmy Slagle | 1899–1908 | 4994 | 2 | .00040 |
| 7. Johnny Bassler | 1913–27 | 2319 | 1 | .00043[3] |
| 8. Joe Quest | 1871–86 | 2295 | 1 | .00044 |
| 9. Floyd Baker | 1938–49 | 2280 | 1 | .00044 |
| 10. Woody Woodward | 1963–71 | 2187 | 1 | .00047 |
| 11. Freddie Maguire | 1922–31 | 2120 | 1 | .00047 |
| 12. Joe Gedeon | 1913–20 | 2109 | 1 | .00047 |
| 13. Al Newman | 1985–92 | 2107 | 1 | .00047 |
| 14. Al Bridwell | 1905–15 | 4169 | 2 | .00048 |
| 15. Tommy Thevenow | 1924–38 | 4164 | 2 | .00048 |
| 16. Ed Hahn | 1905–10 | 2045 | 1 | .00049 |
| 17. Frank Taveras | 1971–82 | 4043 | 2 | .00049 |

*Players who had home run percentages below .00050 in 2000 or more career at bats.

[1]Holds the all-time record for the most career at bats without hitting a home run.

[2]Got his chance during the war when he was 29. Did little his rookie year, but then hit .412 in the 1944 World Series and went on to a productive career. In 1949 he struck out only twice in 343 at bats.

[3]Shared the Detroit catching job during the 1920s with Larry Woodall, who hit only one home run in 1317 career at bats. The only .300 career hitter on the "Powerless" list, Bassler was still catching in the Pacific Coast League when he was in his middle forties.

**Lowest Career Batting Average, Minimum 1,000 at Bats**

.175—Ray Oyler, 1965–70. Detroit won the pennant in 1968 with Oyler playing shortstop and hitting .135 in 111 games. The only other player in the 20th century who posted a sub-.200 career batting average in 1000 or more at bats—catchers again excepted—was Rich Morales, 1967–74, who finished at .195.

**Lowest Career Batting Average, Minimum 500 at Bats**

.161—John Vukovich, 1970–81. In 1971, while sharing the Phillies' third-base job with Don Money, Vukovich hit .166 in 74 games and had a .189 slugging average.

**Most Career at Bats without Ever Getting a Hit, Pitchers Included**

41—Randy Tate, New York Mets, 1975; went 0-for-41 in his only season. Excluding pitchers, the lowest career average among players who got at least one hit belongs to Skeeter Shelton, an outfielder who was given a 10-game trial by the Yankees in 1915 and went 1-for-40, giving him an .025 career mark.

**Most Career at Bats without Ever Getting a Hit, Pitchers Excluded**

23—Mike Potter, St. Louis Cardinals, 1976–77
    Larry Littleton, Cleveland Indians, 1981

**Most Career at Bats Exclusively as a Pinch Hitter, .000 Career Batting Average**

13—Paul Dicken, Cleveland Indians, 1964, 1966

## LOWEST CAREER BATTING AVERAGE
## BY POSITION
### (Minimum 3,000 at Bats)

| Position | Name | Years Active | At Bats | BA |
|----------|------|--------------|---------|-----|
| First Base | Steve Balboni | 1981–93 | 3120 | .229[1] |
| Second Base | Bobby Knoop | 1964–72 | 3622 | .236 |
| Shortstop | Bobby Wine | 1960–72 | 3172 | .215 |

| Position | Name | Years Active | At Bats | BA |
|----------|------|--------------|---------|-----|
| Third Base | Lee Tannehill | 1903–12 | 3778 | .220[2] |
| Outfield | Rob Deer | 1984–96 | 3881 | .220[1] |
| Catcher | Bill Bergen | 1901–11 | 3028 | .170[3] |
| Pitcher | Ron Herbel | 1963–71 | 206 | .029[4] |
| (Minimum 200 ABs) | | | | |

[1] Also played as a designated hitter.

[2] Also played some at shortstop and second base; the only Hitless Wonder who was actually a member of the original Hitless Wonders—the 1906 Chicago White Sox.

[3] Had only a .201 career slugging average. Reportedly a great defensive catcher, but I'm more inclined to believe he stuck around so long because he spent his last eight seasons with Brooklyn. The Dodgers in those years seemed to have entered into some sort of Faustian compact to make their pitchers survive on as little hitting support as possible.

[4] Went 0-for-47 in 1964, his worst season, but the record belongs to Bob Buhl, who went 0-for-70 in 1962 for the Braves and Cubs. The AL Season record for futility is held by Bill Wight of the White Sox, who went 0-for-61 in 1950.

# The Three Most Interesting Teams Between 1977 and 1993

## 1977 KANSAS CITY ROYALS
### W-102 L-60
### Manager: Whitey Herzog

**Regular Lineup**—1B, John Mayberry; 2B, Frank White; 3B, George Brett; SS, Freddie Patek; RF, Al Cowens; CF, Amos Otis; LF, Tom Poquette; C. Darrell Porter; P, Dennis Leonard; P, Jim Colborn; P, Paul Splittorff; P, Andy Hassler; P, Marty Pattin; P, Doug Bird; P, Larry Gura.

After posting the best regular-season record prior to 2001 by an AL expansion club, the Royals were only three outs away from winning the American League pennant. Before they got them the Yankees scored three runs and beat them in the ninth inning of the fifth and final LCS game for the second year in a row. Probably the finest Royals team ever, much stronger than either the 1980 or 1985 clubs, they not only had a solid lineup but a good bench and the deepest pitching staff in the league. With just a very slight reordering of events, Herzog could have taken them to four pennants in five years—and they didn't miss by all that much in 1979, either. The Yankees, Reds and A's are remembered as the dominant teams of the 1970s, but the Royals were on a par with them and may even have been the best of them all.

# 1980 HOUSTON ASTROS
## W-93 L-70
## Manager: Bill Virdon

**Regular Lineup**—1B, Art Howe; 2B, Joe Morgan; 3B, Enos Cabell; SS, Craig Reynolds; RF, Terry Puhl; CF, Cesar Cedeno; LF, Jose Cruz; C, Alan Ashby; P, Joe Niekro; P, Nolan Ryan; P, Ken Forsch; P, Vern Ruhle; P, J. R. Richard; P, Joe Sambito; P, Dave Smith; P, Frank LaCorte.

The Astros came to Dodger Stadium on the last weekend of the season needing to win only one game of a three-game set to clinch their first division title. They lost all three but won the one-game playoff for the right to meet the Phillies in the LCS. After splitting the first two games in Philadelphia, Virdon got a super 11-inning 1–0 shutout from Niekro and Dave Smith in Game Three. Playing at home and only one step away from taking the pennant, the Astros then dropped two straight 10-inning games. In Game Five, they led 5–2 in the top of the eighth with Ryan pitching, but Ryan couldn't hold off the Phillies, nor could relief ace Sambito. The Astros, in 1980, had two .300 hitters, Cedeno and Cruz, plus a pitching staff that could have been unstoppable if Richard hadn't suffered a midseason stroke. An ill-fated club, tenacious to the end, but one break short of winning it all. The same could be said for the 1981 team, which lost the division playoff by a hair to the Dodgers, who went on to win the World Series, and, of course, the 1986 team.

# 1983 PHILADELPHIA PHILLIES
## W-90 L-72
## Manager: Pat Corrales and Paul Owens

**Regular Lineup**—1B, Pete Rose; 2B, Joe Morgan; 3B, Mike Schmidt; SS, Ivan DeJesus; RF, Von Hayes; CF, Gary Maddox; LF, Gary Matthews; C, Bo Diaz; P, Steve Carlton; P, John Denny; P, Ron Reed; P, Charlie Hudson; P, Al Holland, P, Marty Bystrom.

Maddox, their top-hitting regular, hit only .275; they had only one regular younger than 30, no 20-game winners, got only a 15–16 season from staff ace Carlton, eight wins from their number three starter Hudson, and a 6–9 record from Bystrom, their fourth starter. Yet they won their division by six games, romped over the Dodgers in the LCS and won the World Series opener before the Orioles burst their bubble and took four straight. The three big reasons for their unexpected win were Denny's 19 victories, Holland's 25 saves and Schmidt's 40 homers and 109 RBIs. But other contenders got equally good seasons from their top players, and none had a first baseman who hit .245 and had just 45 RBIs. The real catalyst on this club was 39-year-old Morgan, who hit only .230 but scored 72 runs and collected 89 walks in just 404 at bats. Many believe this team, and not the 1973 Mets, was the weakest pennant winner since the 1944 St. Louis Browns—but it may also have been the most savvy team ever. Whether they would have come together if Corrales had remained at the helm may be the only real grist for argument here.

# Third Baseman's Records

The proliferation of great third basemen in the past 20 years has yet to be studied and understood. As a point of comparison, only one third baseman active before 1908—Jimmy Collins—is in the Hall of Fame. No one can predict for sure how many third basemen active in recent years will make it, but three seems an extremely conservative guess, and it may be as many as six or seven. From whence did they suddenly all appear?

## SEASON BATTING RECORDS

| Department | National League | American League |
|---|---|---|
| Batting Averages | .391, JOHN MCGRAW, Baltimore, 1899<br>.379, Fred Lindstrom, New York, 1930* | .390, George Brett, K.C. Royals, 1980 |
| Slugging Average | .644, Mike Schmidt, Philadelphia, 1981 | .664, GEORGE BRETT, K.C. Royals, 1980 |
| Home Runs | 48, MIKE SCHMIDT, Philadelphia, 1980 | 47, Troy Glaus, Anaheim, 2000 |
| RBIs | 144, Vinny Castilla, Colorado, 1998 | 145, AL ROSEN, Cleveland, 1953 |
| Runs | 143, John McGraw, Baltimore, 1898<br>130, Pete Rose, Cincinnati, 1976* | 145, HARLOND CLIFT, St. Louis, 1936 |
| Hits | 231, Fred Lindstrom, New York, 1928, 1930 | 240, WADE BOGGS, Boston, 1985 |
| Doubles | 53, Jeff Cirillo, Colorado, 2000 | 56, GEORGE KELL, Detroit, 1950 |

| Department | National League | American League |
|---|---|---|
| Triples | 28, JIMMY WILLIAMS, Pittsburgh, 1899 | 22, Bill Bradley, Cleveland, 1903 |
| | 22, Tommy Leach, Pittsburgh, 1902* | |
| Total Bases | 380, VINNY CASTILLA, Colorado, 1998 | 367, Al Rosen, Cleveland, 1953 |
| Bases on Balls | 131, Bob Elliott, Boston, 1948 | 151, EDDIE YOST, Washington, 1956 |
| Stolen Bases | 59, Art Devlin, New York, 1905 | 74, FRITZ MAISEL, New York, 1914 |
| Strikeouts | 180, MIKE SCHMIDT, Philadelphia, 1975 | 172, Jim Presley, Seattle, 1986 |
| Fewest Strikeouts (Minimum 500 ABs) | 7, Pie Traynor, Pittsburgh, 1929 | 3, JOE SEWELL, New York, 1932 |

*Record since 1901.

Note: Harmon Killebrew of the Twins hit 49 homers in 1969 but played almost half the season at first base. Woody English of the Cubs scored 152 runs in 1930 while playing 83 games at third base and 78 games at shortstop; since his total is higher than the record at both positions, he can conceivably be regarded as the all-time record holder at either.

## Most Games, Career, at Third Base
2,870—Brooks Robinson, 1955–77

## Most Consecutive Games at Third Base
576—Eddie Yost, Washington, July 3, 1951, through May 11, 1955

## Best Career Fielding Average
.971—Brooks Robinson, 1955–77

## Most Seasons League Leader in Fielding Average
AL—11—Brooks Robinson, last in 1975
NL—6—Heinie Groh, last in 1924
　　　Ken Reitz, last in 1981

# EVOLUTION OF SEASON RECORD FOR BEST FIELDING AVERAGE

| | Team | League | Year | Average |
|---|---|---|---|---|
| Joe Battin | St. Lous | National | 1876 | .867[1] |
| Bill Hague | Providence | National | 1878 | .925[2] |
| Chippy McGarr | Boston | National | 1890 | .933 |
| George Pinkney | Brooklyn | Amer.Assoc | 1890 | .933 |
| Billy Nash | Boston | National | 1894 | .933[3] |
| Lave Cross | Philadelphia | National | 1895 | .940 |
| Billy Clingman | Louisville | National | 1897 | .947 |
| Lave Cross | Cleve-StL | National | 1899 | .959[4] |
| Harry Steinfeldt | Chicago | National | 1907 | .967 |
| Terry Turner | Cleveland | American | 1911 | .970[5] |
| Hans Lobert | Philadelphia | National | 1913 | .974 |
| Larry Gardner | Cleveland | American | 1920 | .976 |
| Heinie Groh | New York | National | 1924 | .983[6] |
| Willie Kamm | Cleveland | American | 1933 | .984[7] |
| Hank Majeski | Philadelphia | American | 1947 | .988 |
| Don Money | Milwaukee | American | 1974 | .989 |

[1]A victim of the fair-foul rule change. Slumped to .199 in 1877 after hitting .300 the previous year.

[2]A fluke season—Hague never again came within 80 points of his record. Art Whitney's .924 FA with Pittsburgh in 1887 is probably a truer figure for the period.

[3]Rated by many the best fielding third baseman prior to 1900.

[4]Never received anywhere near the press that Hall of Famer Jimmy Collins did, but had better career stats in almost every major department.

[5]Also played shortstop and second base in 1910 but was in enough games at third base to be the recognized fielding leader. Led AL third basemen in FA again in 1912.

[6]Still the NL season record; broke his own former record of .975, set in 1923.

[7]Those who saw both Kamm and Brooks Robinson play rank them about equal and, in any case, the two best glovemen ever at third base.

## Most Consecutive Errorless Games

99—John Wehner, Pittsburgh and Florida, August 2, 1992, through September 29, 2000. Never more than an obscure utilityman in his lengthy career, Wehner made errors at other positions while handling 202 chances at third base over an eight-year span without making a miscue.

## Most Consecutive Errorless Chances
261—Don Money, Milwaukee Brewers, September 28, 1973, through July 16, 1974. Money's season FA record was largely the result of his long errorless streak.

## Most Chances Accepted, Career
8,902—Brooks Robinson, 1955–77

## Most Chances Accepted, Season
603—Harlond Clift, St. Louis Browns, 1937

## Most Chances Accepted, Game, Nine Innings
13—Done by several third basemen; last by Roy Hughes, Chicago Cubs, August 29, 1944

## Most Assists, Season
412—Graig Nettles, Cleveland Indians, 1971

## Most Seasons League Leader in Assists
AL—8—Brooks Robinson, last in 1974
NL—7—Ron Santo, 1962–68 consecutive

## Greatest Left-handed Third Baseman
Hick Carpenter, 1879–92, played 1,059 games at third base and a scattering of games at shortstop and second base. Carpenter was probably not only the best southpaw third baseman but the best southpaw infielder, period. The last lefty infielder of note was Kid Mohler, a second baseman with the San Francisco Seals in the Pacific Coast League as late as the early teens. Mohler played three games in the majors at age 19 in 1894 before commencing his long minor-league career. The last southpaw infielder to play regularly in the majors was Billy Huhlen, a shortstop with the 1896 Phillies. Don Mattingly of the Yankees, who played several games at third base in 1986, is the most recent southpaw infielder.

## Most Gold Glove Awards
16—Brooks Robinson, 1960–75 consecutive. Only pitcher Jim Kaat has won as many Gold Gloves.

# Red-hot Rookies

Fernando Valenzuela and Dwight Gooden, the most exciting rookie pitchers since Herb Score, exploded onto the scene in the 1980s only four years apart, and in 1986 Todd Worrell of the Cardinals shattered the yearling record for saves by a wide margin in the process of copping the NL Rookie of the Year Award. None of the three managed to win 20 games, something only one first-year pitcher—Tom Browning of the Reds—has done in recent years, but Valenzuela and Gooden also each set a post–1901 rookie record. Gooden's is well known, but you may need to check the list below before you remember Valenzuela's.

## ROOKIE RECORD HOLDERS*
### Batting

| Department | National League | American League |
|---|---|---|
| Batting Average | .373, George Watkins, St. Louis, 1930 | .408, JOE JACKSON, Cleveland, 1911 |
| Slugging Average | .621, GEORGE WATKINS, St. Louis, 1930 | .609, Ted Williams, Boston, 1939 |
| Home Runs | 38, Wally Berger, Boston, 1930<br>38, Frank Robinson, Cincinnati, 1956 | 49, MARK MCGWIRE, Oakland, 1987 |
| RBIs | 130, Albert Pujols, St. Louis, 2001 | 145, TED WILLIAMS, Boston, 1939 |
| Hits | 223, Lloyd Waner, Pittsburgh, 1927 | 242, ICHIRO SUZUKI, Seattle, 2001 |

*Qualifications for rookie status are the same as those employed by the Official Major League Scoring Committee as of 1971.

| Department | National League | American League |
|---|---|---|
| Runs | 135, ROY THOMAS, Philadelphia, 1899<br>133, Lloyd Waner, Pittsburgh, 1927** | 132, Joe DiMaggio, New York, 1936 |
| Doubles | 52, JOHNNY FREDERICK, Brooklyn, 1929 | 47, Fred Lynn, Boston, 1975 |
| Triples | 27, JIMMY WILLIAMS, Pittsburgh, 1899<br>25, Tommy Long, St. Louis, 1915** | 19, Home Run Baker, Philadelphia, 1909<br>19, Joe Cassidy, Washington, 1904 |
| Total Bases | 360, Albert Pujols, St. Louis, 2001 | 374, HAL TROSKY, Cleveland, 1934<br>374, TONY OLIVA, Minnesota, 1964 |
| Stolen Bases | 110, VINCE COLEMAN, St. Louis, 1985 | 66, Kenny Lofton, Cleveland, 1992 |
| Bases on Balls | 115, ROY THOMAS, Philadelphia, 1899<br>100, Jim Gilliam, Brooklyn, 1953** | 107, Ted Williams, Boston, 1939 |
| Pinch Hits | 20, JOE FRAZIER, St. Louis, 1954 | 17, Sammy Hale, Detroit, 1920 |
| Strikeouts | 168, Juan Samuel, Philadelphia, 1984 | 185, PETE INCAVIGLIA, Texas, 1986 |
| Fewest Strikeouts (Minimum 500 ABs) | 17, BUDDY HASSETT, Brooklyn, 1936 | 25, Tom Oliver, Boston, 1930 |

## Pitching

| Department | National League | American League |
|---|---|---|
| Wins | 31, BILL HOFFER, Baltimore, 1895<br>28, Pete Alexander, Philadelphia, 1911** | 26, Russ Ford, New York, 1910 |
| Losses | 48, JOHN COLEMAN, Philadelphia, 1883 | 26, Bob Groom, Washington, 1901 |

**Record since 1901.

| Department | National League | American League |
|---|---|---|
| | 25, Harry McIntyre, Brooklyn, 1905** | |
| Games | 78, Tim Burke, Montreal, 1985 | 88, SEAN RUNYAN, Detroit, 1998 |
| Starts | 41, IRV YOUNG, Boston, 1905 | 36, Roscoe Miller, Detroit, 1901 |
| Complete Games | 41, IRV YOUNG, Boston, 1905 | 35, Roscoe Miller, Detroit, 1901 |
| Innings Pitched | 378, IRV YOUNG, Boston, 1905 | 332, Roscoe Miller, Detroit, 1901 |
| Winning Pct. | .838 BILL HOFFER, Baltimore, 1895 | .813, Russ Ford, New York, 1910 |
| | .833, King Cole, Chicago, 1910** | |
| Strikeouts | 276, DWIGHT GOODEN New York, 1984 | 245, Herb Score, Cleveland, 1955 |
| Bases on Balls | 185, SAM JONES, Chicago, 1955 | 168, Elmer Myers, Philadelphia, 1916 |
| Shutouts | 9, GEORGE DERBY, Detroit, 1881 | 8, Russ Ford, New York, 1910 |
| | 8, Fernando Valenzuela, L.A., 1980** | 8, Red Russell, Chicago, 1913 |
| Saves | 36, Todd Worrell, St. Louis, 1986 | 37, KAZUHIRO SASAKI, Seattle, 2000 |
| ERA | 1.11, BABE ADAMS, Pittsburgh, 1909 | 1.39, Harry Krause, Philadelphia, 1909 |

## Only Rookies to Win a Batting Title
Pete Browning, Louisville (AA), 1882 (.378)
Tony Oliva, Minnesota Twins, 1964 (.323)
Ichiro Suzuki, Seattle Mariners, 2001 (.350)
Dave Orr, New York (AA), 1884 (.354)

## Only Rookies to Be League Leaders in Home Runs
Harry Lumley, Brooklyn, 1904 (9); Tim Jordan, Brooklyn, 1906 (6); Braggo Roth, Chicago–Cleveland, 1915 (7), Al Rosen, Cleveland Indians, 1950 (37); Mark McGwire, Oakland A's, 1987 (49), Ralph Kiner, Pittsburgh, 1946 (23).

## Only Rookie Pitcher to Win 20 Games While Pitching Less Than 200 Innings
Bob Grim, New York Yankees, 1954 (20–6; 199 innings

pitched). Prior to Pedro Martinez in 2002, Grim was the only pitcher in history to win 20 games in less than 200 innings.

## Most Recent Rookie 20-Game Winners
NL—Tom Browning, Cincinnati, 1985 (21–9)
AL—Bob Grim, New York, 1954 (20–6)

## Best Season by Rookie Batter Who Failed to Win Rookie of the Year Award
Minnie Minoso, Chicago White Sox, 1951, hit .326, led the AL in triples and stolen bases and was fifth in slugging, but lost out to the Yankees Gil McDougald.

## Best Season by Rookie Pitcher Who Failed to Win Rookie of the Year Award
Gene Bearden, Cleveland Indians, 1948, had a 20–7 record and led the AL with a 2.43 ERA, but lost the award to Al Dark of the Boston Braves in the last season only one rookie honor was given.

## Only Team in Existence since 1947 That Has Never Had a Rookie of the Year Winner
Pittsburgh. Ironically, in 1946, the last season no official rookie award was given, Ralph Kiner of the Pirates was generally regarded to be the top rookie in the majors, although Del Ennis of the Phillies copped the *Sporting News* yearling award.

# The Leading Losers

Hugh Mulcahy is the only major leaguer who has ever been saddled with the unwelcome nickname of "Losing Pitcher," but rather surprisingly he owns none of the major records for pitching losses. Three of them have been set since 1981—by Jose DeLeon, Terry Felton and George Frazier. Do you know what they are?

**Lowest Winning Percentage, Season, Minimum 20 Decisions**
    AL—.048—Jack Nabors, Philadelphia, 1916 (1–20)
    NL—.095—Jose DeLeon, Pittsburgh, 1985 (2–19)

**Most Losses, Season, without a Win**
    AL—13—Terry Felton, Minnesota, 1982
    NL—12—Russ Miller, Philadelphia, 1929

**Most Consecutive Losses, Season**
    AL—19—Bob Groom, Washington, 1909
            Jack Nabors, Philadelphia, 1916
    NL—18—Roger Craig, New York Mets, 1963
            Cliff Curtis, Boston, 1910. Curtis also lost his first
            five decisions in 1911, giving him 23 consecutive
            losses, a record that lasted until 1993 when An-
            thony Young of the New York Mets dropped 27
            straight decisions before beating Florida in relief,
            5–4, on July 28.

**Most Seasons League Leader in Losses**
    NL—4—Phil Niekro, Atlanta, 1977–80 consecutive
    AL—4—Bobo Newsom, last in 1945; done with four differ-
            ent teams
            Pedro Ramos, 1958–61, consecutive

## Most Consecutive Losses, Start of Career

16—Terry Felton, Minnesota, April 18, 1980, through September 12, 1982; breaking Guy Morton's record of 13, set with Cleveland in 1914.

## Last 25-Game Loser

Ben Cantwell, Boston Braves, 1935. His 4–25 record is the worst since 1901 by a 25-game loser. Just two years earlier, in 1933, Cantwell had rung up a 20–10 record with the Braves to lead all National League pitchers in *winning* percentage.

## Most Losses, Season, 162-Game Schedule

24—Roger Craig, New York Mets, 1962
    Jack Fisher, New York Mets, 1964

## Most Losses, Season, by Relief Pitcher

NL—16—Gene Garber, Atlanta, 1979 (6–16)
AL—14—Darold Knowles, Washington, 1970 (2–14 but had 27 saves)
        John Hiller, Detroit, 1974 (17–14)
        Mike Marshall, Minnesota, 1979 (10–14)

## Most Losses, Season

48—John Coleman, Philadelphia Phillies, 1883 (12–48). Despite his monstrous number of losses, Coleman was the Phillies' ace—the rest of their mound staff had an aggregate 5–33 record.

## Most Losses, Season, since 1893

35—Red Donahue, St. Louis Browns, 1897. But Donahue was not the last 30-game loser. That distinction belongs to Jim Hughey of Cleveland, who had a 4–30 record in 1899.

## Most Losses, Season, since 1901

29—Vic Willis, Boston Braves, 1905. He also dropped 25 decisions in 1904, making him the last pitcher to lose 24 or more games two years in a row.

## Most Losses, Season, since 1920

27—Paul Derringer, St. Louis Cardinals—Cincinnati Reds, 1933

## Most Losses, Only Major-League Season

37—George Cobb, Baltimore Orioles, 1892 (10–37). In 1876, his one and only season, Dory Dean had a 4–26 record with Cincinnati, which played just 65 games. Cobb's record, in contrast, came in the first season that the National League experimented with a 154-game schedule. Another one-year hurler, Florence Sullivan of the AA Pittsburgh Alleghenies, lost 35 of his team's 108 decisions in 1884.

## Most Losses, Only Major-League Season, since 1901

NL—18—Ham Iburg, Philadelphia, 1902
AL—13—Orie Arntzen, Philadelphia, 1945
    Troy Herriage, Kansas City A's, 1956
    Jeff Byrd, Toronto, 1977
FL—20—Hank Keupper, St. Louis, 1914

## Only 30-Game Winner Since 1920, Later a 20-Game Loser

Denny McLain, Washington, 1971 (10–22); Detroit, 1968 (31–6)

## Only Pitcher since 1901 to Lose 20 Games for a Pennant-winning Team

George Mullin, Detroit, 1907 (20–20)

## Lowest Winning Percentage by Pitcher on a Pennant-Winner, Minimum 20 Decisions

NL—.345—Larry French, Chicago, 1938 (10–19)
AL—.350—Bill Bevens, New York, 1947 (7–13). In 1986 Tom Seaver of the pennant winning Red Sox also had a 7–13 record, but six of his losses came with the second-division White Sox.

## Most Losses, Season, in a World Series (Best 4-of-7)

3—George Frazier, New York Yankees, 1981; all of them in relief

## Most Fantastic Turnaround from One Season to the Next

Earl Hamilton was cut by the St. Louis Browns after he had a 0–9 record in 1917. Brought back to the majors by Pittsburgh in 1918, Hamilton posted a perfect 6–0 record and an 0.83 ERA in six starts.

# TOP 10 IN CAREER LOSSES

|  | Years Active | Losses |
|---|---|---|
| 1. Cy Young | 1890–1911 | 316 |
| 2. Pud Galvin | 1879–92 | 308 |
| 3. Nolan Ryan | 1966–93 | 292 |
| 4. Walter Johnson | 1907–27 | 279 |
| 5. Phil Niekro | 1964–87 | 274 |
| 6. Gaylord Perry | 1962–83 | 265 |
| 7. Jack Powell | 1897–1912 | 257[1] |
| 8. Don Sutton | 1966–88 | 256 |
| 9. Eppa Rixey | 1912–33 | 251 |
| 10. Robin Roberts | 1948–66 | 245 |
| Warren Spahn | 1942–65 | 245 |

[1]Has a .488 career winning percentage, one of only two 200-game winners who finished below .500. The other is Bobo Newsom with a .487 winning percentage.

## MOST LOSSES, CAREER, WITH .000 WINNING PERCENTAGE

|  | Years Active | Career Record |
|---|---|---|
| Terry Felton | 1979–82 | 0–16 |
| Steve Gerkin | 1945 | 0–12 |
| Bill Stecher | 1890 | 0–10 |
| Ed O'Neil | 1890 | 0–8 |
| Ed Albosta | 1941, 1946 | 0–8 |
| Archie Reynolds | 1968–72 | 0–8 |
| Paul Brown | 1961–63, 1968 | 0–8 |
| Scott Ruffcorn | 1993–97 | 0–8 |
| Tommy McCarthy | 1884–94 | 0–7[1] |
| Walter Craddock | 1955–58 | 0–7 |
| Roy Bruner | 1939–41 | 0–7 |
| Walter Moser | 1906, 1911 | 0–7 |
| Charlie Barnabe | 1927–28 | 0–7 |
| Joe Fontenot | 1997–98 | 0–7 |
| Brian Reith | 2001 | 0–7 |

[1]Made the Hall of Fame as an outfielder, but his first season, as a 19-year-old pitcher-outfielder with the 1884 Boston Union Association team, is best forgotten. He was 0–7 on the mound and hit only .215.

## Lowest Career Winning Percentage since 1901, Minimum 200 Decisions

.372—Milt Gaston, 1924–34 (97–164). Gaston, who never pitched in the minor leagues, had a 5–3 record as a 28-year-old rookie with the 1924 Yankees and was 15–14 with the Browns in 1925 after being traded to them but finished below .500 every other season.

## Lowest Career Winning Percentage since 1901, Minimum 150 Decisions

.331—Buster Brown, 1905–13 (51–103); died before the 1914 season began.

## Lowest Career Winning Percentage since 1901, Minimum 100 Decisions

.299—Happy Townsend, 1901–06 (35–82). Townsend spent the bulk of his career with dismal Washington teams, and it's impossible now to gauge whether he was unlucky or simply a poor pitcher carried by a club that could find no one better.

## Lowest Career Winning Percentage since 1901, Minimum 50 Decisions

.206—Ike Pearson, 1939–48 (13–50); including a 7–40 record as a starter. Signed by the pitcher-hungry Phillies after graduating from the University of Mississippi, Pearson was thrown into the breech without a minor-league apprenticeship and suffered for it his whole career.

## Lowest Career Winning Percentage, Cy Young Award Winner

.378—Mark Davis (1980–97) 51–84

## Lowest Career Winning Percentage, Pitcher with ERA below 3.00 in over 100 Decisions

.352—George Bell, 1907–11 (43–79). Seventeen of Bell's 43 wins were shutouts, and he had a fine 2.85 ERA. One of the most luckless pitchers ever, his misfortune was twofold: He was bound by the reserve clause to Brooklyn, at the time a rotten team, and he didn't get to the majors until he was 32 years old.

## All-time Winner of the Hugh Mulcahy Award

Ike Butler had a 1–10 record with the 1902 Baltimore Orioles in his only year in the majors. Discouraged, he signed with Portland, where he set a Pacific Coast League record in 1903 when he lost 31 games and then tied his own mark the following year when he dropped 31 more.

# Father-and-Son Firsts

In 1989, Ken Griffey of the Reds not only had the ultimate thrill a baseball-playing parent can receive when his son Ken, Jr., cracked the Mariners' starting lineup, he became the elder half of the first father-son duo to be active in the majors in the same season.

### First Son to Play for a Team Managed by His Father

Earle Mack, Philadelphia A's, 1910; son of Connie Mack. When Dale Berra played with the Yankees for a short while under his father's tutelage in 1985, it was only the second time in major-league history a son had been managed by his father. In 1987 Cal Ripken became the first son to play as a regular for his father.

### First Father and Son to Play in the Majors

Herman and Jack Doscher. A third baseman with Troy, beginning in 1879, Herman wasn't much of a player, nor was his son, who pitched briefly for the Cubs and Dodgers in the early 1900s. The second father-and-son combo to make the majors, the Meinkes—Frank and son Bob—had even less impact.

### First Father and Son Who Both Had Lengthy Careers

The Sullivans, Billy, Sr., and Billy, Jr. The elder Sullivan played for the White Sox in the first part of the century and was a fine catcher but a weak hitter. His son, also a catcher, was the antithesis. Billy, Jr., hit .351 for Cleveland in 1935, but his defensive skills were such that he caught more than half his team's games only once and was moved behind the plate after failing to cut it as both a third baseman and a first baseman. The Sullivans were also the first father and son to play in a World Series—Billy I in 1906 with the White Sox, and Billy II in 1940 with the Tigers.

## Some Other Fathers and Sons Who Had Lengthy Careers

Earl Averill, Sr., and Jr. George and Dick Sisler. Ray and Bob Boone. Marty and Matt Keough. Ernie and Don Johnson. Mike and Tommy Tresh. Pinky and Milt May. Joe Schultz, Sr., and Jr. Mel Queen and son Mel. Dick Schofield and son Dick. Yogi and Dale Berra. Bob and Terry Kennedy. Maury and Bump Wills. Joe Coleman and son Joe. Dizzy and Steve Trout. Jim Bagby, Sr., and Jr. Vern and Vance Law. Jim and Mike Hegan. Max and Hal Lanier. Dolf and Doug Camilli. Gus and Buddy Bell. Roy Smalley, II and III. Oscar Ray Grimes, Sr., and Jr. Thornton and Don Lee.

## First Father and Son to Play for the Same Team in the Same Decade

Earle Brucker, Sr., and Jr., both caught for the A's in the 1940s. Although he didn't make the majors until he was 36 years old, the elder Brucker, a long-time A's coach under Connie Mack, posted a .290 average over a five-year career. The Griffeys in 1990 of course became the first father and son to play for the same team in the same *season*.

## First Father and Son Both to Pitch in the Majors

Willie Mills, New York Giants, 1901; Art Mills, Boston Braves, 1927. Neither ever won a game.

## Only Father and Son Each to Win a Game before His 20th Birthday

Lew Krausse, Sr., Philadelphia A's, 1931; Lew Krausse, Jr., Kansas City A's, 1961.

## Only Father and Son Each to Be a League Leader in Innings Pitched

Jim Bagby, Sr., Cleveland, 1920, led the AL with 340 innings pitched; Jim Bagby, Jr., Cleveland, 1943, equaled his father's feat by pitching in 273 innings.

## Only Father and Son Each to Be a League Leader in Losses

Herman Pillette, Detroit, 1923, led the AL with 19 losses; Duane Pillette, St. Louis, 1951, tied for the AL lead with 14 losses.

**Only Father and Son Each to Be a League Leader in Pinch Hits**

Joe Schultz, Sr., St. Louis Cardinals, 1919, led the NL with eight pinch hits; Joe Schultz, Jr., St. Louis Browns, led the AL in pinch hits in both 1945 and 1946.

**First Black Father and Son to Play in the Majors**

Sam Hairston, Chicago White Sox, 1951, saw two of his sons make the majors—John in 1969 with the Cubs, and later Jerry, who broke in with the 1973 White Sox. Maury Wills became the second black father to have a son make it when Bump won the Rangers' second base job in 1977.

**Longest Span between First Games Played in Majors by a Father and Son, Since 1901**

36 years—Jack Lively, Detroit Tigers, 1911; Bud Lively, Cincinnati Reds, 1947. Both were pitchers; Jack was 62 years old when his son reached the majors.

**All-time Longest Span between First Games Played in Majors by a Father and Son**

43 years—Charlie Ganzel, St. Paul (UA), 1884; Babe Ganzel, Washington Senators, 1927. The elder Ganzel, among the game's leading catchers in the 1890s, had been dead 13 years by the time Babe made the majors, but his younger brother John, a first baseman with several teams in the early part of the century, was still alive to see it.

**Only Father to Have Two Sons Who Won Batting Titles**

Ewart Walker, who pitched for Washington between 1909 and 1912, fathered both Dixie and Harry Walker. Dixie won the NL batting title in 1944; Harry won it in 1947. Moreover, Ewart's brother Ernie played in the majors for the Browns in the mid-teens, giving the Walkers a second record for being the only family who had two generations of brothers to make it to the top.

**First Three-Generation Family in Majors**

When Bret Boone joined Seattle in 1992, following on the heels of his grandfather Ray and his father Bob, the Boones became the first father-son-grandson trio in big league history.

# LEADERS IN COMBINED CAREER HITS*

| | |
|---|---|
| 1. Ray, Bob, Bret and Aaron Boone | 5344 |
| 2. Gus, Buddy, David, and Mike Bell | 5143 |
| 3. Bobby and Barry Bonds | 4481 |
| 4. Pete Rose, Sr. and Jr. | 4258 |
| 5. Ken Griffey, Sr. and Jr. | 4223 |
| 6. Felipe and Moises Alou | 3689 |
| 7. George, Dick and Dave Sisler | 3557 |
| 8. Hal and Brian McRae | 3427 |
| 9. Eddie Collins, Sr. and Jr. | 3377 |
| 10. Tony and Eduardo Perez | 3050 |

# LEADERS IN COMBINED CAREER WINS*

| | |
|---|---|
| 1. Mel and Todd Stottlemyre | 302 |
| 2. Dizzy and Steve Trout | 258 |
| 3. Jim Bagby, Sr. and Jr. | 224 |
| 4. Ed Walsh and son Ed | 206 |
| 5. Joe Coleman and son Joe | 194 |

*Batters contributing at least one hit and pitchers at least one win to the family total.

# The Most Prolific Hitters

In 1985 Pete Rose established a new all-time record for career base hits and Wade Boggs became the first American League player since 1928 to make 240 hits in a season.

## PLAYERS WHO MADE 240 HITS IN A SEASON

|  | Team | League | Year | Hits |
|---|---|---|---|---|
| George Sisler | St. Louis | American | 1920 | 257 |
| Lefty O'Doul | Philadelphia | National | 1929 | 254 |
| Bill Terry | New York | National | 1930 | 254 |
| Al Simmons | Philadelphia | American | 1925 | 253 |
| Rogers Hornsby | St. Louis | National | 1922 | 250 |
| Chuck Klein | Philadelphia | National | 1930 | 250 |
| Ty Cobb | Detroit | American | 1911 | 248 |
| George Sisler | St. Louis | American | 1922 | 246 |
| Ichiro Suzuki | Seattle | American | 2001 | 242 |
| Babe Herman | Brooklyn | National | 1930 | 241 |
| Heinie Manush | Detroit | American | 1928 | 241 |
| Jesse Burkett | Cleveland | National | 1896 | 240 |
| Wade Boggs | Boston | American | 1985 | 240 |
| Darin Erstad | Anaheim | American | 2000 | 240 |

**Most Seasons League Leader in Hits**
AL—8—Ty Cobb, last in 1919
NL—7—Pete Rose, last in 1981
Tony Gwynn, last in 1997

**Most Seasons 200 or More Hits**
NL—10—Pete Rose, last in 1979
AL—9—Ty Cobb, last in 1924

**Most Consecutive Seasons 200 or More Hits**
NL—8—Willie Keeler, 1894 through 1901

NL since 1901—5—Chuck Klein, 1929 through 1933
AL—7—Wade Boggs, 1983 through 1989

## Most Consecutive Seasons 200 or More Hits, Start of Career
3—Johnny Pesky, Boston Red Sox, 1942, 1946 and 1947; he missed the 1943 through 1945 seasons while in military service.

## First Players to Make 200 or More Hits in a Season
NL—Sam Thompson, Detroit, 1887 (203 hits)
AA—Tip O'Neill, St. Louis, 1887 (225 hits)
    Pete Browning, Louisville, 1887, (220 hits)
    Denny Lyons, Philadelphia, 1887 (209 hits)
AL—Nap Lajoie, Philadelphia, 1901 (232 hits)

## All-Time Organized-Baseball Record for Most Hits in a Season
325—Paul Strand, Salt Lake City, Pacific Coast League, 1923. Strand, who had earlier flopped as a teenage pitcher with the Boston Braves, returned to the majors at age 30 in 1924, but finished his career in the minors after hitting .228 in 47 games for the Philadelphia A's.

## Fewest Hits, Season, Minimum 150 Games
NL—80—Dal Maxvill, St. Louis, 1970; batted 399 times in 152 games.
AL—82—Ed Brinkman, Washington, 1965; batted 444 times in 154 games.

## Most Hits in a Nine-Inning Game
NL—7—Wilbert Robinson, Baltimore, June 10, 1892; went 7-for-7. Rennie Stennett, Pittsburgh, September 16, 1975; went 7-for-7 and twice had two hits in an inning as the Pirates blasted the Cubs 22–0, the worst shutout shellacking in this century.
AL—6—Held by many players. Only one AL player, Cesar Gutierrez of Detroit, has ever gone 7-for-7, and that was in a 12-inning game on June 21, 1970. For the season Gutierrez netted only 101 hits and hit .243; after 1970 he made just seven more hits in the majors.

## All-Time Major-League Record for Most Hits in a Game
9—Johnny Burnett, Cleveland, July 10, 1932; went 9-for-11 in an 18-inning game against Philadelphia.

**First Player to Go 6-For-6 in a Nine-Inning Game**
Davy Force, Philadelphia, June 27, 1876.

**First Teammates Each to Get Six Hits in the Same Nine-Inning Game**
Hick Carpenter and Long John Reilly of the American Association Cincinnati Red Stockings on September 12, 1883.

## PLAYERS WHO MADE 3,000 OR MORE CAREER HITS (1876–2003)[1]

| | Years Active | Hits |
|---|---|---|
| Pete Rose | 1963–86 | 4256 |
| Ty Cobb | 1905–28 | 4191[2] |
| Hank Aaron | 1954–76 | 3771 |
| Stan Musial | 1941–63 | 3630 |
| Tris Speaker | 1907–28 | 3515 |
| Honus Wagner | 1897–1917 | 3430 |
| Carl Yastrzemski | 1961–83 | 3419 |
| Paul Molitor | 1978–98 | 3319 |
| Eddie Collins | 1906–30 | 3313 |
| Willie Mays | 1951–73 | 3283 |
| Eddie Murray | 1977–97 | 3255 |
| Nap Lajoie | 1896–1916 | 3251 |
| Cal Ripken | 1981–2001 | 3184 |
| George Brett | 1973–93 | 3154 |
| Paul Waner | 1926–45 | 3152 |
| Robin Yount | 1974–93 | 3142 |
| Tony Gwynn | 1982–2001 | 3141 |
| Dave Winfield | 1973–95 | 3110 |
| Rickey Henderson | 1979– | 3055 |
| Rod Carew | 1967–85 | 3053 |
| Lou Brock | 1961–79 | 3023 |
| Wade Boggs | 1982–99 | 3010 |
| Al Kaline | 1953–74 | 3007 |
| Roberto Clemente | 1955–72 | 3000 |

[1]Cap Anson made 3415 career hits, but 420 of them came pre-1876 in the National Association, not recognized as a major league.

[2]Disputed figure. Many historians believe that Cobb was credited with an extra hit in 1910 and his correct total should be 4190.

# World Series Play: 1977–93

## FRANCHISE SUMMARY

| Team | League | WS Record through 1993 | Last WS | LCS Record through 1993 | Last LCS |
|------|--------|------------------------|---------|-------------------------|----------|
| Toronto | American | 2–0 | 1993 | 2–3 | 1993 |
| Pittsburgh | National | 5–2 | 1979 | 2–7 | 1992 |
| New York | American | 22–11 | 1981 | 4–1 | 1981 |
| Oakland | American | 4–2 | 1990 | 6–4 | 1992 |
| Cleveland | American | 2–1 | 1994 | — | — |
| New York | National | 2–1 | 1986 | 3–1 | 1988 |
| Minnesota | American | 2–1 | 1991 | 2–2 | 1991 |
| St. Louis | National | 9–6 | 1987 | 3–0 | 1987 |
| Cincinnati | National | 5–4 | 1990 | 5–2 | 1990 |
| Los Angeles | National | 5–4 | 1988 | 5–2 | 1988 |
| Boston | American | 5–4 | 1986 | 2–2 | 1990 |
| Baltimore | American | 3–3 | 1983 | 5–2 | 1983 |
| Chicago | American | 2–2 | 1959 | 0–2 | 1993 |
| Kansas City | American | 1–1 | 1985 | 2–4 | 1985 |
| Detroit | American | 4–5 | 1984 | 1–2 | 1987 |
| Philadelphia | National | 1–4 | 1993 | 3–3 | 1993 |
| Chicago | National | 2–8 | 1945 | 0–2 | 1989 |
| San Francisco | National | 0–2 | 1989 | 1–2 | 1989 |
| Atlanta | National | 0–2 | 1992 | 2–3 | 1992 |
| Milwaukee | American | 0–1 | 1982 | 1–0 | 1982 |
| San Diego | National | 0–1 | 1984 | 1–0 | 1984 |
| California | American | — | — | 0–3 | 1986 |
| Houston | National | — | — | 0–2 | 1986 |
| Montreal | National | — | — | 0–1 | 1981 |

## Yearly Highlights

**1977—New York (AL) defeated Los Angeles (NL) 4 games to 2**

The Royals for the second year in a row took the Yankees to five games in the LCS before succumbing in the ninth inning of the finale. The Dodgers beat the Phillies 3–1 in the LCS but fell prey in the Series to Mike Torrez's two complete-game wins and Reggie Jackson's three-homer barrage in Game Six. Jackson had five homers and 8 RBIs in the Series.

**1978—New York (AL) defeated Los Angeles (NL) 4 games to 2**

For the first time all four divisions had repeat winners. Both the Yankees and the Dodgers won their LCSes three games to one, and the Yankees then completed the reprise of the 1977 season by winning the Series in six after losing the opening two games in Los Angeles. Bucky Dent, whose three-run homer sparked the Yankees in their division playoff win over th Red Sox, had 10 hits in the Series, and his Dodgers counterpart at shortstop, Bill Russell, led all players with 11.

**1979—Pittsburgh (NL) defeated Baltimore (AL) 4 games to 3**

The Orioles held a 3–1 lead in games and had their three mound aces, Mike Flanagan, Jim Palmer and Scott McGregor, ready to apply the clincher. But all three lost, giving the Pirates their second seven-game Series win over Baltimore in the decade. The Orioles beat California 3–1 in the LCS while the Pirates swept Cincinnati.

**1980—Philadelphia (NL) defeated Kansas City (AL) 4 games to 2**

To win their first world title in their 98-year history, the Phillies beat not only a hot Kansas City team that had knocked off the Yankees three straight in the LCS, but the Astros with a pair of come-from-behind 10th-inning victories in the final two games of the National League LCS. After a disappointing LCS, Mike Schmidt had two homers and seven RBIs in the Series and was outdone only by Amos Otis of the Royals, who led both clubs with 11 hits and a .438 average.

**1981—Los Angeles (NL) defeated New York (AL) 4 games to 2**

The Dodgers came back from a 2–1 deficit in the LCS to defeat the Expos, then lost the first two Series games. Returning to Los Angeles, they took three straight from the Yankees and then journeyed back to Yankee Stadium and won the closer 9–2 in a fashion that made Yankees owner George Steinbrenner apoplectic and spoiled for him the taste of the Yankees' LCS sweep of Oakland, managed by Billy Martin.

**1982—St. Louis (NL) defeated Milwaukee (AL) 4 games to 3**

The Brewers became the first team to win an LCS after trailing two games to zip when they took three straight from the Angels at Milwaukee. But in the Series the Brewers had to play the last two games on the road, and the Cardinals won both, led by Keith Hernandez's eight RBIs and Joaquin Andujar's two wins. Mike Caldwell of the Brewers also had two wins and was only one out away, in Game Five, from being the first pitcher since 1977 to complete two games in a Series. To earn the right to meet the Brewers, the Cardinals pasted Atlanta three straight times in the National League LCS.

**1983—Baltimore (AL) defeated Philadelphia (NL) 4 games to 1**

The Phillies rode Steve Carlton's two wins to a victory over the Dodgers in the LCS, then took the Series opener before the Orioles got untracked. For the Orioles, Cal Ripken hit only .167 in the Series and Gary Roenicke went 0-for-7 after both had murdered White Sox pitchers in the American League LCS.

**1984—Detroit (AL) defeated San Diego (NL) 4 games to 1**

The Tigers swept the Royals in the LCS and had little trouble in the Series with the Padres as Jack Morris posted two complete-game wins and Alan Trammell hit .450 and knocked in six runs. All the postseason drama occurred in the National League LCS when the Padres took three straight from Chicago after the Cubs were poised to win their first pennant since 1945.

1985—Kansas City (AL) defeated St. Louis (NL) 4 games to 3

The majors changed to a best-four-of-seven format in the LCSes, giving the Royals an opportunity to snatch the AL pennant from the Blue Jays after trailing three games to one. In the Series they likewise fell behind the Cardinals 3–1 but then won three straight to become the first AL expansion team to win a world title. The Cardinals cited umpire Don Denkinger's questionable safe call in Game Six as the reason for their defeat, but their .185 team batting average was a much larger factor. In the LCS, the Cardinals beat the Dodgers 4 games to 2, homers by Jack Clark and switch hitter Ozzie Smith—his first ever left-handed—hanging consecutive defeats on Dodgers reliever Tom Neidenfuer in the final two contests.

1986—New York (NL) defeated Boston (AL) 4 games to 3

After an uneventful regular season in which all four division races were resolved by Labor Day, the Mets beat the Astros four games to two in a National League LCS that was arguably the best-played and most dramatic fall series ever. It culminated in a see-saw 16-inning game—the longest post-season contest in history—which the Mets won 7–6 behind Jesse Orosco, the first relief pitcher to win three games in a championship series. Orosco saved two more contests in the World Series, including the deciding seventh game, but was only one of many Mets heroes in the most remarkable comeback in Series history. Trailing 5–3 with two out in the bottom of the 10th inning of Game 6 and only one strike away from elimination, the Mets rallied for three runs and thereby became the first team on the brink of extinction to overcome so large a deficit in its last turn at bat and then go on to win the Series. The Mets' triumph deprived Boston pitcher Bruce Hurst of the MVP Award—he had already been voted the trophy on the basis of his two Series wins before New York launched its last-ditch comeback—but the Red Sox, although frustrated once again in a bid to claim their first World Championship since 1918, had the satisfaction of staging an equally incredible come-from-behind win in the AL LCS. Down three games to one, Boston trailed the Angels 5–4 in the top of the ninth inning of Game 5 when Red Sox centerfielder Dave Henderson uncorked a two-out, two-strike, two-run homer. The Angels fought back to tie the game in the bottom of the ninth, but lost 7–6 in 11 innings and then were blown out in the final two contests in Boston. Houston starter Mike Scott and Boston second baseman Marty Barrett were the individual pitching and hitting standouts in post-season play, but in the end the Mets superior bullpen, one of the deepest in recent history, was the deciding factor.

1987—Minnesota (AL) defeated St. Louis (NL) 4 games to 3

The Twins posted the poorest road record of any flag winner in history and then won only one away game in post-season play, that against the Tigers in the AL LCS. But that win was enough to bring Minnesota its first world championship when neither Detroit nor the Cardinals, the NL champs, could manage a win in the Metrodome, the first indoor park to host a World Series game. Minus their top slugger, Jack Clark, who was idled by an ankle injury, the Cards needed seven games to defeat the Giants, the NL West winners. The crucial contest—and probably the 1987 post-season highlight—was the third NL LCS game at Candlestick Park when St. Louis rallied from a 4–0 deficit to triumph 6–5. Frank Viola of the Twins, who sandwiched wins in the Series opener and finale around a shellacking in Game 4, copped the Series MVP Award, and Minnesota outfielder Dan Gladden was the top offensive performer in fall play, knocking five runs in the LCS and seven more in the Series.

1988—Los Angeles (NL) defeated Oakland (AL) 4 games to 1

In perhaps the most stunning Series upset since the Mets beat the vaunted Orioles in 1969, Dodgers pitchers held Oakland hitters to a .177 batting average and just 11 runs. Led by Orel Hershiser's two complete-game wins and Kurt Gibson's two-strike, two-out, two-run homer in the bottom of the ninth inning in Game 1, Los Angeles lost only the third Series game—on a dramatic solo homer in the last of the ninth by the A's Mark McGwire. That four-bagger was McGwire's lone Series hit. Jose Canseco, the other half of the A's heralded slugging duo, also was held hitless save for a grand slam homer in the opening game. In contrast, Mickey Hatcher of the Dodgers, a sub during the regular season, hit .368 and clubbed two key homers. Hatcher typified the outstanding efforts Los Angeles received from unlikely sources. Gibson's homer, for example, came in his lone Series appearance after he injured his knee. To add insult, his victim was Dennis Eckersley, who set an LCS record when he saved all four of the A's wins in their AL LCS sweep of the Red Sox. Gibson's long-ball heroics and Hershiser's four-star pitching likewise thwarted the heavily favored Mets in the NL LCS. Hershiser deservedly was an easy winner of both the LCS and the Series MVP Awards.

## 1989—Oakland (AL) defeated San Francisco (NL) 4 games to 0

The long-awaited first Bay Area World Series—and the Giant's first fall appearance in 27 years—was on course to being the most one-sided championship match since 1976 before a massive earthquake interrupted play for ten days with the A's ahead 2 games to 0. When action resumed Oakland completed its sweep of San Francisco. The A's were so thoroughly dominant that for the first time in Series history the losing team not only never had the lead in any of the four games but never once had the tying run at the plate in its final turn at bat. Dave Stewart was voted the MVP, but the award could as easily have gone to any one of several A's. The Giant's Will Clark, who had destroyed the Cubs in the NL LCS, was held in check by A's pitchers throughout the Series, and none of the other San Francisco hitters was able to take up the slack. Indeed, the Blue Jays, who fell to the A's in five games in the AL LCS, may well have been the second-best team in post-season action—albeit a very distant second best. In any case, the A's ended the 1980s as probably the strongest team since the 1975–76 Reds.

## 1990—Cincinnati (NL) defeated Oakland (AL) 4 games to 0

In their first year under manager Lou Piniella, the Reds became one of the few teams in history to lead their league from wire to wire and then capped their remarkable season by defeating the Pirates in the National League LCS and sweeping the heavily favored defending-champion A's in the World Series. Billy Hatcher of the Reds set a new Series BA record and Cincinnati third sacker Chris Sabo had nine hits and five RBIs in the four-game fray. The MVP award was copped by Reds hurler Jose Rijo, who bested A's ace Dave Stewart twice after Stewart had beaten the Red Sox a pair of games in the American League LCS. Boston fireballer Roger Clemens exemplified the Sox frustration in their second one-sided loss to the A's in three years when he was heaved out early in the final ALCS game for moaning too graphically about ball and strike calls.

## 1991—Minnesota (AL) defeated Atlanta (NL) 4 games to 3

The Twins continued to be winless on the road in fall classics since moving to Minnesota, but nevertheless snatched their second World Championship in five years when ex-Tiger ace Jack Morris won a gutty 1–0 ten-inning verdict in Game 7. The best Series since 1975 featured two of the poorest teams in the majors in 1990, both of which had been revitalized by free-agent signings and an influx of young talent. Atlanta took seven games to edge Pittsburgh in the NLCS, while the Twins needed only five ALCS contests to polish off Toronto. The 1991 Series was the first seven-game affair since 1962 with a 1–0 finale, and the first fall fray since 1924 to go the ultimate limit—an extra-inning contest won by the home team in its final at bat.

## 1992—Toronto (AL) defeated Atlanta (NL) 4 games to 2

An electrifying extra-inning triumph in Game 6 rendered the Blue Jays the first team outside the USA to cop a World Championship and put Jack Morris on his third different title team in a nine-year period. Morris failed in his bid to become the first hurler to bag Series wins with three different clubs, but Juan Guzman and the other Jays pitchers more than took up the slack. After becoming the oldest to homer in a Series earlier in the affair, 41-year-old Dave Winfield garnered the Series-winning hit. Toronto catcher Pat Borders meanwhile grabbed the Series MVP prize, mainly on the strength of his timely hitting. The Jays needed only six games to dispose of Oakland in the ALCS, but Pittsburgh took the Braves to the absolute limit before falling 3–2 in Game 7 of the NLCS to a two-out two-run single by seldom used sub Francisco Cabrera.

## 1993—Toronto (AL) defeated Philadelphia (NL) 4 games to 2

Joe Carter's three-run homer in the bottom of the ninth inning of Game 6 gave the Blue Jays a come-from-behind 8–6 win against Phils reliever, Mitch Williams, and made them the first team since the 1977–78 Yankees to bag consecutive world titles. Williams was also the loser in Game 4, a 15–14 slugfest that broke the record for the most runs in a post-season fray (25), last done by the St. Louis Browns and New York Giants in the finale of the 1888 World Series. Paul Molitor was the Series MVP as he continued to excel in post-season action, but the award could well have gone to Phils centerfielder Len Dykstra in a losing cause. Molitor's bat also sparked the Jays in their six-game triumph over the White Sox in the ALCS. Led by Dykstra and pitcher Curt Schilling, the Phils likewise put away the favored Braves in six rounds in the NLCS to earn their third Series appearance in the past 14 seasons after making just two stabs at the world title in the previous 97 years.

# SECTION 7

# Famous Firsts:
# 1994–2003

**1994**—Greg Maddux of Atlanta is the first pitcher ever to post an ERA a full two runs below the top team ERA in his circuit when he compiles a 1.56 ERA to the Montreal Expos' NL-leading 3.56 ERA.

**1994**—A season-ending strike on August 12 leaves the game without a major-league champion for the first time since professional baseball began in 1871.

**1995**—In the course of becoming the first player ever to average better than a dozen home runs per 100 at bats (12.3), Mark McGwire of the Oakland A's shatters the record for the most home runs in a season in under 350 ABs (39).

**1995**—Playing at a torrid pace in a strike-shortened season, Cleveland becomes the first team in American League history to win 100 games on a schedule that calls for fewer than 154 games.

**1996**—En route to a total of 52 home runs, Oakland's Mark McGwire becomes the first slugger ever to collect 50 homers in a season before he compiles 400 at bats.

**1996**—The first major league game ever to be played outside the United States or Canada takes place on August 16 at Monterrey Stadium in Monterrey, Mexico, with San Diego topping the New York Mets, 15–10.

**1996**—On September 15, Mike Piazza of Los Angeles becomes the first catcher in major league history to be leading his league in batting with as many as 500 at bats when he ends the day with 501 at bats and an NL pace-setting .347 batting average.

**1996**—Alex Rodriguez of the Seattle Mariners is the first shortstop in 52 years to cop an American League batting title.

**1996**—For the first time in franchise history, the Cleveland Indians showcase the best record in the major leagues two years in a row.

**1996**—The Baltimore Orioles become the first team since 1894 to qualify for postseason play with a staff ERA above 5.00 when they nab the American League wild-card slot despite surrendering an average of 5.14 earned runs per game.

**1997**—Mark McGwire is the first player to lead the majors in homers without being a league leader when he raps 34 dingers for Oakland (AL) and 24 for St. Louis (NL), giving him a total of 58.

**1998**—Alex Rodriguez of the Seattle Mariners is the first infielder to achieve 40 home runs and 40 stolen bases in the same season.

**1999**—Mark McGwire of the St. Louis Cardinals is the first to hammer 50 or more home runs four years in a row.

**1999**—The Cleveland Indians are the first team to score 1000 runs (1009) on a 162-game schedule.

**2000**—The New York Mets and Chicago Cubs open the 2000 season by playing the first major-league game outside the North American continent when the Cubs win 5–3 in front of 55,000 at the Tokyodome in Tokyo, Japan.

**2000**—For the first time in major-league history no team finishes above .600 or below .400.

**2000**—The Cincinnati Reds become the first team to go through an entire season without being shut out since the schedule was expanded to 162 games.

**2001**—Jason Jennings of Colorado becomes the first pitcher since 1901 to throw a shutout and also hit a home run in his first major-league game.

**2001**—Roger Clemens of the Yankees becomes the first pitcher in major-league history to reach 20 wins with only one loss.

**2001**—Sammy Sosa of the Cubs is the first slugger to achieve 60 home runs in a season three times.

**2002**—Pedro Martinez of the Red Sox becomes the first man in major-league history to win 20 games as a starting pitcher (20–4) in less than 200 innings (199.1).

# Life-Begins-At-40 Records

In 1996, Paul Molitor of the Twins celebrated turning 40 by not only compiling his 3000th hit but by demolishing no fewer than *four* "Life-Begins-at-40" records.

### Oldest Player to Throw a Shutout
When 46-year-old Phil Niekro bagged his 300th win by blanking Toronto on the last day of the 1986 season, he surpassed Satchel Paige who was a few months younger when he whitewashed Detroit 1–0 in 12 innings on August 6, 1952.

### Oldest Player to Hit a Home Run
AL—46—Jack Quinn, Philadelphia, 1930. Quinn, a pitcher, is also the oldest player to make more than one hit in a season—he collected four in 1932 when he was 48.

NL—46—Cap Anson, Chicago, 1897

### Oldest Player to Hit a Grand Slam Home Run Since 1901
43—Carlton Fisk, Chicago White Sox, on October 3, 1991

### Oldest Player to Participate in a Major-League Game
Satchel Paige pitched three shutout innings for the Kansas City A's at age 59 (or maybe older) on September 25, 1965, against the Boston Red Sox.

### Oldest Player to Hit Safely in a Major-League Game
Minnie Minoso went 1-for-8 at age 53 as a dh for the White Sox in 1976; his lone hit, a single, came on September 12. Nick Altrock was a slightly younger 53-year-old when he played right field for the White Sox on October 6, 1929, and got a hit in his only trip to the plate.

## First 40-Year-Old to Play in a Major-League Game

Dickey Pearce, a standout shortstop in the 1850s, hung on long enough to play 25 games with St. Louis in 1876, the National League's inaugural year. But if you're among those who credit the National Association with being a major league, the honor goes to Nate Berkenstock, who played a single game in the outfield for the 1871 Philadelphia Athletics after he turned 40..

## First Player Who Was Still a Regular at Age 40

Joe Start, Providence Grays, 1883. Start, a first baseman, remained a regular player until he was nearly 44 years old.

## Oldest Rookie

NL—43—Diomedes Olivo, Pittsburgh, 1962, had a 5–1 record and seven saves in 62 games.

AL—42—Satchel Paige, Cleveland, 1948, had a 6–1 record in 27 games.

## Oldest Rookie to Play in Over Half His Team's Games

Chuck Hostetler hit .298 in 90 games as a 41-year-old rookie outfielder with the 1944 Detroit Tigers.

## Oldest Rookie to Play Enough to Qualify for a Batting Title

Earle Brucker played 102 games for the 1937 Philadelphia A's at age 36—the rules then required a player to participate in two-thirds of his team's games to qualify for a batting title. In 1938 Brucker actually did lead all American League batters when he hit .374—but in only 53 games.

## Oldest Rookie to Go on to a 20-Year Career

Hoyt Wilhelm, 29 when he came to the New York Giants in 1952, retired in 1972 after playing 21 years in the majors.

## Most Games Caught after Age 40 Prior to 1980s

220—Deacon McGuire, 1884–1912. Some historians, myself among them, consider this to be the most impressive of all the "Life-Begins-at-40" accomplishments.

## Oldest 20-Game Winner

NL—42—Warren Spahn, Milwaukee, 1963 (23–7)

AL—41—Cy Young, Boston, 1908 (21–11)

**Oldest League Leader in a Major Pitching Department**

NL—48—Jack Quinn, Brooklyn, 1932; led in saves with 8. Also the NL save leader in 1931 with 15.

AL—42—Jim Turner, New York, 1945, led in saves with 10.

**Oldest League Leader in a Major Batting Department**

AL—40—Ted Williams, Boston, 1958, hit .328 to win the batting title.

NL—40—Cap Anson, Chicago, 1891, led in RBIs with 120.

## LIFE BEGINS-AT-40 SEASON BATTING RECORDS

| Department | National League | American League |
|---|---|---|
| Batting Average | .335, Cap Anson, Chicago, 1895 .325, Pete Rose, Philadelphia, 1981* | .357, TY COBB, Philadelphia, 1927 |
| Slugging Average | .508, STAN MUSIAL, St. Louis, 1962 | .501, Darrell Evans, Detroit, 1987 |
| Home Runs | 20, Hank Aaron, Atlanta, 1974 | 34, DARRELL EVANS, Detroit, 1987 |
| RBIs | 120, CAP ANSON, Chicago, 1891 82, Stan Musial, St. Louis, 1962* | 113, Paul Molitor, Minnesota, 1996 |
| Hits | 172, Pete Rose, Philadelphia, 1982 | 225, PAUL MOLITOR, Minnesota, 1996 |
| Runs | 89, Rickey Henderson, New York, 1999 | 121, SAM RICE, Washington, 1930 |
| Doubles | 34, Gary Gaetti, StL-Chi, 1998 | 41, PAUL MOLITOR, Minnesota, 1996 |
| Triples | 17, HONUS WAGNER, Pittsburgh, 1915 | 13, Sam Rice, Washington, 1930 |

*Record since 1901.

Note: Record holders are players who were at least 40 years old before the end of the season in which they set the mark. Batting and slugging average record holders must have had enough plate appearances to qualify for the batting title.

| Department | National League | American League |
|---|---|---|
| Total Bases | 239, Honus Wagner, Pittsburgh, 1915 | 309, PAUL MOLITOR, Minnesota, 1996 |
| Stolen Bases | 47, DAVEY LOPES, Chicago, 1985 | 22, Ty Cobb, Philadelphia, 1927 |
| Bases on Balls | 112, Willie Mays, San Francisco, 1971 | 121, LUKE APPLING, Chicago, 1949 |
| Strikeouts | 123, WILLIE MAYS, San Francisco, 1971 | 115, Reggie Jackson, California, 1986 |
| Fewest Strikeouts (Minimum 500ABs) | 28, Rabbit Maranville, Boston, 1932 | 14, SAM RICE, Washington, 1930 |

# Team Records since 1901

## Most Consecutive Wins Since 1876

On September 7, 1916, the New York Giants embarked on a 26-game winning streak, the longest victory skein since the National League was formed in 1876, by beating the Dodgers 4–1 at the Polo Grounds. All 26 victories came in their home park, giving them a second record for the most consecutive wins at home. In the course of the streak the Giants beat every National League rival at least once. The only blemish on their record was a 1–1 tie with the Pirates on September 18 in the second of three straight doubleheaders that postponements forced the two clubs to play.

Earlier in the 1916 season the Giants had rattled off 17 straight victories away from the Polo Grounds, the last coming on May 29 when Christy Mathewson beat the Braves 3–0 and registered the final shutout of his career. On the strength of Mathewson's arm, the Giants broke the previous record for most consecutive road wins—16, set by the Washington Senators between May 30 and June 15, 1912. Despite two long streaks the Giants finished with an 86–66 mark, good only for fourth place.

### Most Consecutive Wins without a Tie

NL—21—Chicago, 1935. The 1881 Chicago White Stockings also won 21 in a row, but tied a game with Providence.

AL—20—Oakland, 2002, surpassing the former record of 19 set by New York in 1947.

### Most Consecutive Wins Prior to 1876

The National Association Boston Red Caps won 26 straight in 1875. If you recognize the NA as a major league—and many do—then the 1875 Red Caps share the all-time major-league record with the 1916 Giants. The record for the most consecutive wins by a professional team was set by the

1869–70 Cincinnati Red Stockings, who won 130 straight games with one tie before losing 8–7 to the Brooklyn Atlantics on June 14, 1870, in 11 innings. After scoring two runs in the top of the 11th to go ahead 7–5, the Red Stockings let the game slip away when second baseman Charlie Sweasy threw the ball away while trying for a double play on a ground ball with runners on first and second. Bob Ferguson, the lead runner, scored the winning run on the error. Ironically, at the end of the nine innings the Red Stockings had refused the Atlantics' offer of a tie and insisted on playing to a decision.

## Most Consecutive Doubleheaders Won

5—New York Yankees, 1906; the last one on September 4 when they beat the Red Sox 7–0 and 1–0

## Most Consecutive Wins, Start of Season

NL—13—Atlanta, April 6 to April 21, 1982
AL—13—Milwaukee, April 6 to April 20, 1987

## Most Consecutive Wins, Start of Season, before 1901

20—St. Louis Maroons, Union Association, April 20 to May 22, 1884. The runaway UA pennant winners didn't suffer their first loss untl May 24, when they were beaten 8–1 by Boston's Tommy Bond.

## Most Consecutive Losses

NL—23—Philadelphia, 1961; the streak ended on August 20 when the Phils beat the Braves in the second game of a doubleheader
AL—21—Baltimore, 1988

## Most Consecutive Losses Prior to 1901

26—Louisville Eclipse, American Association, May 22 to June 22, 1889. Louisville finished in the cellar with a 27–111 record. In 1890 the club won 61 more games, the largest improvement in major-league history, and became the first major-league team to vault from last place to a pennant the following season.

## Most Consecutive Losses, Expansion Team

NL—20—Montreal, 1969
AL—15—Texas, 1972

## Most Consecutive Losses on the Road

NL—22—New York Mets, June 16 through July 28, 1963. The Mets played some home games, which they won, in the midst of their road losing streak, but the Pittsburgh Innocents, co-holders of the all-time record, in 1890 dropped 22 straight, all on the road.

AL—19—Philadelphia, July 25 through August 8, 1916; in the process the A's also set an all-time record for the most losses—19—in a two-week span.

## Most Consecutive Losses at Home

AL—20—St. Louis, June 3 through July 7, 1953
NL—15—New York, August 1 through 1st game, September 1, 2002

## Most Consecutive Doubleheaders Lost

In 1929 weather postponements forced the Boston Braves to play a record nine doubleheaders in a row from September 4 through September 15; at one point in their travails they lost five consecutive twin bills, one at Philadelphia and four straight to the Giants in Boston.

## Most Consecutive Losses, Start of the Season

AL—21—Baltimore, 1988
NL—14—Chicago, 1997

## Special Mention

In 1899 the Cleveland Spiders, playing their final season in the National League, had losing streaks of 24 games, 16 games and 14 games.

## Highest Batting Average, Season

NL—.319—New York Giants, 1930
AL—.316—Detroit, 1921

## Lowest Batting Average, Season

AL—.212—Chicago, 1910
NL—.213—Brooklyn, 1908

## Highest Slugging Average, Season

AL—.489—New York, 1927
NL—.483—Colorado, 2001

## Lowest Slugging Average, Season

AL—.261—Chicago, 1910. Patsy Dougherty led the club with a .300 slugging average, 85 points below Ty Cobb's *batting* average that season.

NL—.274—Boston, 1909

## Most Runs, Season

AL—1067—New York, 1931

NL—1004—St. Louis, 1930

## Fewest Runs, Season

NL—372—St. Louis, 1908; only three fewer than Brooklyn scored that year

AL—380—Washington, 1909

## Most Home Runs, Season

AL—264—Seattle, 1997

NL—239—Colorado, 1997

## Fewest Home Runs, Season

AL—3—Chicago, 1908; pitcher Ed Walsh tied for the club lead with one homer.

NL—7—Pittsburgh, 1917

## Most Pennants

AL—39—New York, last in 2003

NL—18—Brooklyn-Los Angeles, last in 1988

## Fewest Pennants

AL—0—Seattle; Washington-Texas; Tampa Bay

NL—0—Houston; Montreal; Colorado

## Most Consecutive Pennants

AL—5—New York, 1949–53; 1960–64

NL—4—New York Giants; 1921–24

## Most Consecutive Seasons without Winning a Pennant

NL—58—Chicago, 1946–2003

AL—42—St. Louis, 1902–43

## Most Seasons Finishing in Last Place

AL—26—Philadelphia-Kansas City-Oakland, last in 1997

NL—26—Philadelphia, last in 2000

## Most Consecutive Seasons Finishing in Last Place
    AL—7—Philadelphia, 1915–21
    NL—5—Philadelphia, 1938–42

## Most Consecutive Seasons Avoiding a Last-Place Finish
    NL—86—Brooklyn-Los Angeles, 1906–91
    AL—71—Boston, 1933–2003. No, the Sox, unlike L.A., didn't finish last in 1992, just last in the AL East.

## Highest Winning Percentage, Season
    NL—.763, Chicago, 1906 (116–36)
    AL—.721, Cleveland, 1954 (111–43)

## Highest Winning Percentage, Season, 162 Games
    AL—.716—Seattle, 2001 (116–46)
    NL—.667—Cincinnati, 1975 (108–54)
              New York Mets, 1986 (108–54)

## Lowest Winning Percentage, Season
    AL—.235—Philadelphia, 1916 (36–117)
    NL—.248—Boston, 1935 (38–115)

## Lowest Winning Percentage, Season, 162 Games
    NL—.250—New York Mets, 1962 (40–120)
    AL—.265—Detroit, 2003 (43–119)

## Lowest Winning Percentage, Pennant Winner
    NL—.509—New York Mets, 1973 (82–79)
    AL—.525—Minnesota, 1987 (85–77)

## Highest Winning Percentage, Non-Postseason Qualifier
    NL—.680—Chicago, 1909 (104–49)
    AL—.669—New York, 1954 (103–51)

## Fewest Games Needed to Clinch Pennant, 154-Game Schedule
    AL—136—New York, 1941
    NL—137—New York, 1904

## Fewest Games Needed to Clinch Pennant or Division, 162-Game Schedule, Two-Division League
    NL—142—Cincinnati, 1975
    AL—146—Baltimore, 1969

**Largest Margin of Victory by Pennant Winner**
 NL—27½ games—Pittsburgh, 1902
 AL—22 games—New York, 1998. (In 1995 Cleveland won the Central Division by 30 games but finished just 14 games ahead of Boston, which had the AL's second-best record.)

**Most Games Finishing behind Pennant Winner**
 NL—66½—Boston, 1906
 AL—64½—St. Louis, 1939

**Fewest Games Finishing behind Pennant Winner, Last Place Team, Prior to 1969**
 NL—21—New York Giants, 1915
 AL—25—Washington, 1944

**Largest Improvement by Pennant Winner over Previous Season's Record**
 AL—33 games—Boston, 1946
 NL—29 games—Atlanta Braves, 1991

**Most Consecutive Years Finishing in First Division**
 39—New York Yankees, 1926–64

**Most Consecutive Years Finishing in Second Division**
 20—Chicago Cubs, 1947–66

**Best Home Record, Season**
 AL—.805—New York, 1932 (62–15)
 NL—.789—Pittsburgh, 1902 (56–15)

**Worst Home Record, Season**
 AL—.234—St. Louis, 1939 (18–59)
 NL—.260—Boston, 1911 (19–54)

**Best Road Record, Season**
 NL—.800—Chicago, 1906 (60–15)
 AL—.730—New York, 1939 (54–20)

**Worst Road Record, Season**
 NL—.167—Boston, 1935 (13–65)
 AL—.169—Philadelphia, 1916 (13–64)

## Most Consecutive Games Won from One Club

AL—23—Baltimore from Kansas City Royals, May 10, 1969, through August 12, 1970

NL—20—Pittsburgh from Cincinnati, last 17 in 1937, first 3 in 1938

## Most Games Won from One Club, Season

AL—21—New York from St. Louis, 1927

NL—21—Chicago from Cincinnati, 1945; Chicago from Boston, 1909. In 1909 the Braves also lost 20 of 21 games to Pittsburgh, giving them a 2–41 record against the NL's top two teams that year.

# One-Year Wonders

Baseball historians divide one-year wonders into two categories: men who literally played only one season in the majors and those who, for one reason or another, had just one exceptional season in an otherwise mediocre career that in many cases never again saw them even play regularly for a full campaign. Arguably, the greatest one-year wonders in the first category were Henry Schmidt among pitchers and Buzz Arlett among hitters. Of the men in the second category, Phil Plantier currently must stand high just about everyone's list. In 1993, Plantier not only shattered the all-time record for the fewest hits (111) by a player with 100 or more RBIs, but he also set new NL one-year regular records for homers and RBIs. Here are the all-time record holders in the second category. Active players are excluded except in the case of Plantier, who at the moment seems a darkhorse ever again to have a season in the majors in which he collects 400 or more at bats.

## BATTING RECORDS

### Highest Batting Average, Only Season as Regular, 400 or More At Bats
AL—.370—Al Wingo, Detroit, 1925
NL—.353—Wilbert Robinson, Baltimore, 1894
NL since 1901—.329—Dick Cox, Brooklyn, 1925

### Highest Slugging Average, Only Season, 400 or More At Bats
NL—.540—Cliff Lee, Philadelphia, 1922
AL—.527—Al Wingo, Detroit, 1925

## Highest On-Base Percentage, Only Season, 400 or More At Bats

AL—.456—Al Wingo, Detroit, 1925
NL—.421—Tommy Glaviano, St. Louis, 1950

## Most Home Runs, Only Season, 400 or More At Bats

NL—34—Phil Plantier, San Diego, 1993. The former record-holder was Stan Lopata, who hammered 32 dingers for the Phillies in 1956, his lone year with 400 or more ABs.
AL—27—Gary Alexander, Oakland-Cleveland, 1978
—27—Norm Zauchin, Boston, 1955

## Most Triples, Only Season, 400 or More At Bats

All-time—22—Joe Visner, Pittsburgh, Players League, 1890
20th century—17—Jim Kelly, Pittsburgh, Federal League, 1915
AL—16—Hank Edwards, Cleveland, 1946
NL since 1901—14—Chet Ross, Boston, 1940
—14—Lou Klein, St. Louis, 1945

## Most Doubles, Only Season, 400 or More At Bats

AL—42—Carl Lind, Cleveland, 1928
Other—40—Duke Kenworthy, Kansas City, Federal League, 1914
NL—39—Jim Gleeson, Chicago, 1940

## Most RBIs, Only Season, 400 or More At Bats

AL—114—Bob Fothergill, Detroit, 1927
Other—106—Jocko Milligan, Philadelphia, American Association, 1891
NL—100—Phil Plantier, San Diego, 1993 (Stan Lopata, with 95 RBIs for the Phils in 1956, was the former NL record-holder.)

## Most Hits, Only Season, 400 or More At Bats

NL—200—Chick Fullis, Philadelphia, 1933
AL—200—Dick Wakefield, Detroit, 1943

## Most Runs, Only Season, 400 or More At Bats

All-time—140—Tom Poorman, Philadelphia, American Association, 1887
AL—105—Ike Davis, Chicago, 1925
NL—98—Lefty Davis, Brooklyn-Pittsburgh, 1901

## Most At Bats, Only Season, 400 or More At Bats
AL—663—Jake Wood, Detroit, 1961
NL—653—Marvell Wynne, Pittsburgh, 1984

## Most Total Bases, Only Season, 400 or More At Bats
Other—286—Duke Kenworthy, Kansas City, Federal League, 1914
NL—286—Stan Lopata, Philadelphia, 1956
AL—275—Dick Wakefield, Detroit, 1943

## Most Stolen Bases, Only Season, 400 or More At Bats
All-time—88—Tom Poorman, Philadelphia, American Association, 1887
NL—64—Eric Yelding, Houston, 1990
AL—61—Miguel Dilone, Cleveland, 1980

## Most Walks, Only Season, 400 or More At Bats
AL—106—Les Fleming, Cleveland, 1942
NL—95—Billy Grabarkewitz, Los Angeles, 1970

## Most Strikeouts, Only Season, 400 or More At Bats
AL—175—Dave Nicholson, Chicago, 1963
NL—149—Billy Grabarkewitz, Los Angeles, 1970

# PITCHING RECORDS

## Most Wins, Season, Only Season ERA Qualifier (average of 1 inning pitched for each game team played)
NL—26—Bill James, Boston, 1914
Other—23—Bill Wise, Washington, Union Association, 1884
AL—20—Buck O'Brien, Boston, 1912
        Bob Grim, New York, 1954

## Most Losses, Season, Only Season ERA Qualifier
NL—37—George Cobb, Baltimore, 1892
Other—35—Fleury Sullivan, Pittsburgh, American Association, 1884
NL since 1901—25—Stoney McGlynn, St. Louis, 1908
AL—20—Brian Kingman, Oakland, 1980
        Roy Wilkinson, Chicago, 1921

20—Jack Nabors, Philadelphia, 1916
Other since 1901—20—Henry Keupper, St. Louis Federal League, 1914

## Lowest ERA, Only Season ERA Qualifier
NL—1.90—Bill James, Boston, 1914
AL—1.95—Fred Olmstead, Chicago, 1910

## Most Strikeouts, Only Season ERA Qualifier
Other—268—Bill Wise, Washington, Union Association, 1884
NL—239—Bill Stemmeyer, Boston, 1886
NL since 1901—202—Floyd Youmans, Montreal, 1986
AL—189—Ed Correa, Texas, 1986

## Most Walks, Only Season ERA Qualifier
AL—157—Grover Lowdermilk, StL-Det, 1915
Other—148—John Keefe, Syracuse, American Association, 1890
NL—139—Johnny Lindell, Pitt-Phila, 1953

## Most Shutouts, Only Season, ERA Qualifier
AL—6—Rube Vickers, Philadelphia, 1908
NL—5—Lee Grissom, Cincinnati, 1937. Sharing the record with Grissom is Larry Jaster, who tossed five shutouts for St. Louis in 1966 in just 151.2 innings; remarkably, Jaster never got enough work in *any* season to be an ERA qualifier.
Other—5—Clint Rogge, Pittsburgh, Federal League, 1915

## Most Innings, Only Season ERA Qualifier
Other—441—Fleury Sullivan, Pittsburgh, American Association, 1884
NL—394.1—George Cobb, Baltimore 1892
NL since 1901—352.1—Stoney McGlynn, St. Louis, 1908
AL—317—Rube Vickers, Philadelphia, 1908

## Highest Winning Percentage, Only Season ERA Qualifier, Minimum 20 Wins
NL—.793—Jocko Flynn, Chicago, 1886 (23–6)
NL since 1900—.788—Bill James, Boston, 1914 (26–7)
AL—.769—Bob Grim, New York, 1954 (20–6)

Among the men who literally played only one season in the majors, here are your current all-time record holders.

# SEASON BATTING RECORDS*

| Department | | National League | American League |
|---|---|---|---|
| Batting Average | | .313, Buzz Arlett, Philadelphia, 1931 | .311, Irv Waldron, Mil-Wash, 1901 |
| | Other: | .336, HARRY MOORE, Washington UA, 1884 | |
| Slugging Average | | .538, BUZZ ARLETT, Philadelphia, 1931 | .397, Buddy Blair, Philadelphia, 1942 |
| Home Runs | | 18, BUZZ ARLETT, Philadelphia, 1931 | 15, Jim Baxes, Cleveland, 1959[1] |
| RBIs | | 72, Buzz Arlett, Philadelphia, 1931 | 66, Buddy Blair, Philadelphia, 1942 |
| | Pre-1900: | 76, Ace Stewart, Chicago, 1895 | |
| | Other: | 77, CHARLIE HAMBURG, Louisville AA, 1890 | |
| Hits | | 131, Buzz Arlett, Philadelphia 1931 | 186, IRV WALDRON, Mil-Wash, 1901 |
| | Other: | 132, Charlie Hamburg, Louisville AA, 1890 | |
| Runs | | 73, Goat Anderson, Pittsburgh, 1907 | 102, IRV WALDRON, |
| | Other: | 93, Charlie Hamburg, Louisville AA, 1890 | |
| Doubles | | 26, BUZZ ARLETT, Philadelphia, 1931 | 26, BUDDY BLAIR, Philadelphia, 1942 |
| | Other: | 26, AL BOUCHER, St. Louis FL, 1914 | |
| Triples | | 7, Buzz Arlett, Philadelphia, 1931 | 9, Irv Waldron, Mil-Wash, 1901 |
| | Pre-1901: | 10, ACE STEWART, Chicago, 1895 | 9, Joe Martin, Was-STL, 1903 |
| Total Bases | | 225, BUZZ ARLETT, Philadelphia, 1931 | 224, Irv Waldron, Mil-Wash, 1901 |
| Bases on Balls | | 80, GOAT ANDERSON, Pittsburgh, 1907 | 47, Hector Rodriguez, Chicago, 1952 |
| | Other: | 69, Charlie Hamburg, Louisville AA, 1890 | |
| Stolen Bases | | 27, Goat Anderson, Pittsburgh, 1907 | 20, Irv Waldron, Mil-Wash, 1901 |
| | Other: | 46, CHARLIE HAMBURG, Louisville AA, 1890 | |

*Includes only men who played one season in the majors with the lone exception of Jocko Flynn, who played a couple of innings as an outfield defensive replacement the year following his only season as a pitcher.

[1] Also hit two home runs for Los Angeles NL in 1959 for a total of 17

# SEASON PITCHING RECORDS*

| Department | | National League | American League |
|---|---|---|---|
| Wins | | 22, Henry Schmidt, Brooklyn, 1903 | 8, Ed Smith, St. Louis, 1906 |
| | Pre-1901: | 23, JOCKO FLYNN, Chicago, 1886,[2] | Other: 12, Erv Lange, Chicago, FL, 1914 |
| Losses | | 18, Ham Iburg, Philadelphia, 1902 | 13, Orie Arntzen, Philadelphia, 1943 |
| | Other since 1901: | 20, Henry Keupper, St. Louis, FL, 1914 | 13, Troy Herriage, Kansas City, 1956 |
| | Pre-1900: | 37, GEORGE COBB, Baltimore, 1892 | 13, Jeff Byrd, Toronto, 1977 |
| Winning Pct. | | 618, Henry Schmidt, Brooklyn, 1903 | .421, Ed Smith, St. Louis, 1906 |
| | Pre-1900: | .793, JOCKO FLYNN, Chicago, 1886 | |
| Starts | | 36, Henry Schmidt, Brooklyn, 1903 | 20, Orie Arntzen, Philadelphia, 1943 |
| | Pre-1901: | 47, George Cobb, Baltimore, 1892 | |
| | Other: | 51, FLEURY SULLIVAN, Pittsburgh AA, 1884 | |
| Complete Games | | 29, Henry Schmidt, Brooklyn, 1903 | 13, Ed Smith, St. Louis, 1906 |
| | Pre-1901: | 42, George Cobb, Baltimore, 1892 | |
| | Other: | 51, FLEURY SULLIVAN, Pittsburgh AA, 1884 | |
| Innings | | 301, Henry Schmidt, Brooklyn, 1903 | 164.1, Orie Arntzen, Philadelphia, 1943 |
| | Pre-1901: | 394.1, George Cobb, Baltimore, 1892 | |
| | Other: | 441, FLEURY SULLIVAN, Pittsburgh AA, 1884 | |
| Shutouts | | 5, HENRY SCHMIDT, Brooklyn, 1903 | 3, Tex Neuer, New York, 1907 |
| ERA | | 3.83, Henry Schmidt, Brooklyn, 1903 | 3.72, Ed Smith, St. Louis, 1906 |
| | Pre-1900: | 2.36, WILL SAWYER, Cleveland, 1883 | Other: 2.23, Erv Lange, Chicago, FL, 1914 |
| Strikeouts | | 106, Ham Iburg, Philadelphia, 1902 | 75, Bill Mooneyham, Oakland, 1986 |
| | Pre-1901 | 159, GEORGE COBB, Baltimore, 1892 | |
| | Other: | 147, Park Swartzel, Kansas City AA, 1889 | |

*Includes only men who played one season in the majors with the lone exception of Jocko Flynn, who played a couple of innings as an outfield defensive replacement the year following his only season as a pitcher.

[2]Disputed total—some authorities credit Flynn with 24 wins in 1886.

| Department | | National League | American League |
|---|---|---|---|
| Bases on Balls | | 120, Henry Schmidt, Brooklyn, 1903 | 69, Orie Arntzen, Philadelphia, 1943 |
| | Pre-1901: | 140, George Cobb, Baltimore, 1892 | |
| | Other: | 148, JOHN KEEFE, Syracuse AA, 1890 | |
| Games Pitched | | 62, BILL WAKEFIELD New York, 1964 | 45, Bill Mooneyham, Oakland, 1986 |
| Saves | | 7, LLOYD MERRITT, St. Louis, 1957 | 5, Pete Gebrian, Chicago, 1947 |

# RBI Records

The official tabulation of RBIs was not adopted by both major leagues until 1920 when all slugging statistics suddenly took on an increased importance with Babe Ruth's emergence as the game's greatest home run hitter and the accompanying surge in attendance. Prior to 1920 RBI statistics were kept unofficially, and there were many seasons, especially in the 1880s, when some team scorers noted how runs were brought home and others didn't. As a result it is now impossible to determine with absolute certainty who led the American Association in RBIs in 1882, for example, or how many career RBIs Pete Browning, Dave Orr, Harry Stovey and many other early-day stars had.

## EVOLUTION OF THE SEASON RBI RECORD

|                  | Year | Team     | League   | RBIs    |
|------------------|------|----------|----------|---------|
| 1. Sam Thompson  | 1887 | Detroit  | National | 166[1]  |
| 2. Babe Ruth     | 1921 | New York | American | 171     |
| 3. Lou Gehrig    | 1927 | New York | American | 175[2]  |
| 4. Hack Wilson   | 1930 | Chicago  | National | 191[3]  |

[1]Some purists prefer to start with the 1888 season when both the National League and the American Association began keeping reasonably accurate RBI data. Even if you align yourself with their thinking, Thompson remains the pre-Ruth record holder, with 165 RBIs for the 1895 Philadelphia Phillies. In addition, Thompson was the most prolific player ever at knocking in runs—.921 per game. Lou Gehrig ranks second with .919 per game; Hank Greenberg is third with .915 per game.

[2]In 1931 Gehrig set an American League record, which still stands, when he had 184 RBIs; six years later Hank Greenberg of Detroit had 183.

[3]In 1930 Gehrig led the AL with 174 RBIs, and Chuck Klein of the Phillies had 170 RBIs; the season was so skewed that Bill Terry's RBI total of 129, good for only fifth place in 1930, would have led the NL the following year.

**Most RBIs, Season, 1901 through 1919**
    AL—130—Home Run Baker, Philadelphia, 1912, although some sources still credit Ty Cobb with 144 RBIs in 1911
    NL—128—Gavvy Cravath, Philadelphia, 1913

**Most RBIs, Season, 1941 through 1960**
    AL—159—Vern Stephens and Ted Williams, Boston, 1949
    NL—143—Ernie Banks, Chicago, 1959

**Most RBIs, Season, 1961 through 1977**
    NL—153—Tommy Davis, Los Angeles, 1962
    AL—142—Roger Maris, New York, 1961

**Most RBIs, Season, 1977 through 1993**
    NL—149—George Foster, Cincinnati, 1977
    AL—145—Don Mattingly, New York, 1985

**Most RBIs, Season, since 1994**
    AL—165—Manny Ramirez, Cleveland, 1999
    NL—160—Sammy Sosa, Chicago, 2001

**Most Seasons League Leader in RBIs**
    AL—6—Babe Ruth, last in 1928 when he tied with Gehrig
    NL—5—Honus Wagner, last in 1912

**Fewest RBIs, Season, League Leader in RBIs, since 1920**
    AL—105—Al Rosen, Cleveland, 1952
    NL—105—Gary Carter, Montreal, and Mike Schmidt, Philadelphia, 1984

**Fewest RBIs, Season, League Leader in RBIs, Prior to 1920**
    NL—80—Bill Dahlen, New York Giants, 1904
    AL—83—Harry Davis, Philadelphia, 1905

**Most RBIs, Game**
    NL—12—Jim Bottomley, St. Louis, September 16, 1924
    —12—Mark Whiten, St. Louis, September 7, 1993
    AL—11—Tony Lazzeri, New York, May 24, 1936

**Most RBIs, Doubleheader**
    NL—13—Nate Colbert, San Diego, August 1, 1972
    —13—Mark Whiten, St. Louis, September 7, 1993

AL—No American League player has ever collected more than 11, the number Lazzeri amassed in a single game.

**Fewest RBIs, Season, Outfielder, Minimum 400 at Bats**
11—Charlie Jamieson, Philadelphia A's, 1918, 416 at bats

**Fewest RBIs, Season, First Baseman, Minimum 400 at Bats**
20—Ivy Griffin, Philadelphia A's, 1920, 467 at bats, and Joe Agler, Buffalo Buffeds (FL), 1914, 463 at bats

**Fewest RBIs, Season, Third Baseman, Minimum 400 at Bats**
14—Bobby Byrne, St. Louis Cardinals, 1908, 439 at bats, and Eddie Yost, Washington, 1947, 428 at bats

**Fewest RBIs, Season, Minimum 500 at Bats**
12—Enzo Hernandez, San Diego Padres, 1971, 549 at bats

**Fewest RBIs, Season, Minimum 150 Games**
19—Morrie Rath, Chicago White Sox, 1912, 157 games

**Greatest Margin, Season, Between Runs and RBIs, since 1901**
106—Lloyd Waner, Pittsburgh Pirates, 1927, scored 133 runs and had only 27 RBIs. The all-time record for the greatest margin between runs and RBIs is held by John McGraw, with 140 runs and 33 RBIs for the 1899 Baltimore Orioles, a difference of 107.

## PLAYERS WITH 40 HOMERS AND FEWER THAN 100 RBIS IN A SEASON (1994 EXCLUDED)

|  | Year | Team | League | Homers | RBIs |
|---|---|---|---|---|---|
| Duke Snider | 1957 | Brooklyn | National | 40 | 92 |
| Mickey Mantle | 1958 | New York | American | 42 | 97 |
| Mickey Mantle | 1960 | New York | American | 40 | 94 |
| Harmon Killebrew | 1963 | Minnesota | American | 45 | 96 |
| Hank Aaron | 1969 | Atlanta | National | 44 | 97 |
| Rico Petrocelli | 1969 | Boston | American | 40 | 97 |
| Hank Aaron | 1973 | Atlanta | National | 40 | 96 |
| Davy Johnson | 1973 | Atlanta | National | 43 | 99 |
| Darrell Evans | 1985 | Detroit | American | 40 | 94 |
| Ken Griffey, Jr. | 1994 | Seattle | American | 40 | 90 |
| Matt Williams | 1994 | San Fran. | National | 43 | 96 |

## Most RBIs, Season, Since 1901, Fewer Than 10 Home Runs
NL—131—Paul Waner, Pittsburgh, 1927, 9 home runs
AL—127—Ty Cobb, Detroit, 1911, 8 home runs

## Most Seasons with 100 or More RBIs and Fewer Than 10 Home Runs
7—Honus Wagner, last in 1912.

## Last Player to Collect 100 or More RBIs and Fewer Than 10 Home Runs
Paul Molitor, Minnesota, 1996; 9 home runs and 113 RBIs. Molitor and Tommy Herr (1985) are the only two players to do it since George Kell in 1950.

## Most RBIs, Season, With No Home Runs
121—Hughie Jennings, Baltimore Orioles, 1896

## Last Player to Lead League in RBIs with Fewer Than 10 Home Runs
Dixie Walker, Brooklyn, led the National League in 1945 with 124 RBIs despite hitting only eight homers.

## Special Mention
In 1979 Jim Rice of the Boston Red Sox became the first player ever to string together three successive seasons in which he had, at minimum, 110 RBIs, 35 home runs and 200 hits.

## Most Seasons 150 or More RBIs
7—Lou Gehrig, last in 1937.

## Most Consecutive Seasons 100 or More RBIs
13—Lou Gehrig, 1926–38; Jimmie Foxx, 1929–41

## Most RBIs Per Each Home Run, Career
1.77—Lou Gehrig, 873 RBIs on 493 home runs.

## First Player to Lead Majors in RBIs Three Years In a Row, since 1920
Cecil Fielder, 1990–92. Prior to 1920, when RBIs became an official stat, Babe Ruth started a three-year skein that ran from 1919 through 1921.

# TOP TEN IN CAREER RBIS

|  | Years Active | RBIs |
|---|---|---|
| 1. Hank Aaron | 1954–76 | 2297[4] |
| 2. Babe Ruth | 1914–35 | 2209[3] |
| 3. Lou Gehrig | 1923–39 | 1990 |
| 4. Stan Musial | 1941–63 | 1951 |
| 5. Ty Cobb | 1905–28 | 1933[2] |
| 6. Jimmie Foxx | 1925–45 | 1922 |
| 7. Eddie Murray | 1977–97 | 1907 |
| 8. Willie Mays | 1951–73 | 1902[5] |
| 9. Cap Anson | 1876–97 | 1879[1] |
| 10. Mel Ott | 1926–47 | 1860 |

[1]The first player to accumulate 1,000 RBIs.
[2]Broke Anson's career RBI record in 1927.
[3]Broke Cobb's career mark in 1931.
[4]Broke Ruth's career mark in 1975 while serving as a DH for the Milwaukee Brewers.
[5]Although eighth on the all-time list, Mays never led the National League in RBIs.

# TOP 10 IN CAREER RBIS, PLAYERS ACTIVE THROUGH 2002 SEASON

|  | First Year | RBIs |
|---|---|---|
| 1. Barry Bonds | 1986 | 1742 |
| 2. Rafael Palmiero | 1986 | 1687 |
| 3. Fred McGriff | 1986 | 1543 |
| 4. Sammy Sosa | 1989 | 1450 |
| 5. Andres Galarraga | 1985 | 1423 |
| 6. Jeff Bagwell | 1991 | 1421 |
| 7. Frank Thomas | 1990 | 1390 |
| 8. Juan Gonzalez | 1989 | 1387 |
| 9. Ken Griffey, Jr. | 1989 | 1384 |
| 10. Gary Sheffield | 1988 | 1232 |

# Men for All Seasons

At the moment Deion Sanders is still the first and only athlete to play in both a World Series and a Super Bowl, but he is far from being the only—or even the most outstanding—multisport star in major league history.

## Heisman Trophy Winners to Play Major-League Baseball

In 1986, Auburn running back Bo Jackson, the number one pick in the NFL draft, spurned a reported $7 million deal with the Tampa Bay Buccaneers to sign a baseball contract with the Kansas City Royals. When Jackson was added to the Royals' roster in September, he became only the second former Heisman Trophy winner to play in a major-league game. The first was one of the last great single-wing tailbacks: Vic Janowicz, Ohio State, 1950. Janowicz won as a junior, then floundered through his final college season after the new Buckeye coach, Woody Hayes, installed a T-formation, which diluted his triple-threat talents. But the Pirates still made him a bonus baby. After two undistinguished seasons with the Pirates in the mid-1950s, Janowicz opted to pursue a pro football career with the Washington Redskins instead, but that too was ended by a near-fatal auto accident.

## Members of the Pro Football Hall of Fame Who Played Major League Baseball

There are seven: Jim Thorpe, Paddy Driscoll, Red Badgro, Ernie Nevers, George Halas, Greasy Neale and Ace Parker. None of them even remotely threatened to become a Hall of Famer in both sports, but all except Driscoll and Badgro had their moments. Parker homered in his first major-league at bat; Nevers surrendered two of Babe Ruth's 60 home runs in 1927; Thorpe drove in the winning run in the famous double no-hit game in 1917; Neale starred for the Reds in the 1919

World Series; and Halas played a few games for the 1919 Yankees in right field, a position that would be occupied the following year by Babe Ruth.

## Only Member of Both the Pro Football and Pro Baseball Hall of Fame

Cal Hubbard, a star tackle in the NFL, was enshrined in Cooperstown as well as in Canton, Ohio, after a long career as an American League umpire. Hank Soar, Charlie Moran and George Magerkurth were other umpires who played in the NFL. Soar also coached the Providence Steamrollers in the Basketball Association of American, a forerunner of the NBA.

## Only Major-League Manager Who also Served as Head Coach in the NFL

Hugo Bezdek managed the Pirates from 1917 through 1919 and later coached the Pittsburgh Steelers.

## First Athlete to Play in Both a Rose Bowl Game and a World Series

Jackie Jensen, an All-American running back at Cal, played in the 1949 Rose Bowl game against Northwestern and later played for the Yankees in the 1950 World Series. Chuck Essegian, who teamed with Gary Kerkorian and Harry Hugasian to give Stanford the nation's best-ever Armenian backfield, in 1959 became the second athlete to play in both a Rose Bowl game and a World Series.

## Other College Football Stars Who Played in the Major Leagues

The list is too long to mention everyone. Among those who had successful major-league careers were Jackie Robinson, Glenn Wright, Lou Gehrig, George Stirnweiss, Spud Chandler, Blondie Ryan, Billy Werber, Del Pratt, Luke Sewell, Ted Kluszewski, Sam Chapman, Eldon Auker, Lloyd Merriman, Frank Grube, Harvey Hendrick, Wes Schulmerich, Eddie Morgan, Rick Leach, Bill Carrigan, Red Wilson, Joe Sparma, Tom Haller, Galen Cisco, Harry Agganis, Carl Reynolds, Riggs Stephenson, Gee Walker, Kirk Gibson, Al Dark, Jake Gibbs, Bernie Allen, Ron Darling, Norm Cash and Frankie Frisch. Bud Metheny, Eric Tipton and Bob Finley were three outstanding running backs who played in the majors during World War II when rosters were thinned by the draft; Finley, the catalyst on the top-ranked SMU Mustangs in 1935, was never more than a reserve catcher even with draft-depleted Philadelphia Phillies and might have done better to consider a pro football career. Among the others who achieved stardom on college gridirons but were only marginal major leaguers were Jesse Hill, Johnny Herrnstein, Tom Gastall, Dean Look, Bill Renna, Harley Boss, Chink Outen, Larry Bettencourt, Don Lund, Steve Korcheck, Carroll Hardy, Jerry Schoonmaker, Paul Giel, David Morey, Tom Yewcic, Haywood Sullivan, George Spencer and Mike Miley.

## Athletes who Played Both Pro Football and Major-League Baseball Prior to World War II

In the 1920s and 1930s it was not at all uncommon for major-league baseball players to give pro football a whirl during the off-season. Among the many not previously mentioned who did were Chuck Dressen, Evar Swanson, Tom Whelan, Mike Wilson, Russ Young, Ab Wright, Ernie Vick, Pid Purdy, Jim Levey, Hoge Workman, Joe Vance, Al Pierotti, Ossie Orwoll, Garland Buckeye, Walt Masters, Bert Kuczynski, Red Smith, Walter French, Bob Fothergill, Charlie Berry and Walt Gilbert.

## Athletes Who Played Both Pro Football and Major-League Baseball after World War II

Beginning in the early 1940s it became increasingly difficult to combine both sports. Until Bo Jackson came along and played for both the Royals and the NFL Raiders, the last athlete to play both pro spots on a major-league level was Tom Brown, an outfielder with the 1963 Senators who later played on the first Super Bowl winner, the 1966 Green Bay Packers. Among the other two-sport pro athletes since 1941 are Jim Castiglia, Steve Filipowicz, Pete Layden, Norm Bass, Rex Johnston, Cliff Aberson and Deion Sanders.

## Only College Basketball All-American to Win a Major-League MVP Award

Dick Groat, winner of the National League MVP award in 1960, had been an All-American at Duke before he signed a bonus contract with the Pirates. Groat also played for a short time in the National Basketball Association.

## Athletes Who Played Both Pro Basketball and Major-League Baseball Prior to World War II

Before World War II a number of major leaguers regularly switched their sliding pads for short pants during the winter months. Pro basketball was a loose operation then at best with a short season and lots of franchise transfers, but the biggest reason it was relatively simple for major leaguers to play both sports was that pro basketball teams hadn't yet become repositories for seven-footers. The game still had plenty of room for a good small man, and there were many of them, including several of the following two-sporters: Harry Riconda, Ralph Miller, Ed Wineapple, Bert Lewis and Rusty Saunders. No famous baseball names here, but Saunders, a four-game outfielder with the 1927 Philadelphia A's, was well known among court followers. He played some 20 years on the pro circuit and was deep into his forties before he finally put away his sneakers.

## Athletes Who Played Both Pro Basketball and Major-League Baseball after World War II

The most recent athlete to play both is Toronto lefty Mark Hendrickson, who made his major league debut in 2002 after playing with four NBA teams from 1996 to 2000. Others who have had dual careers since World War II are Frankie Baumholtz, Howie Schultz, Chuck Connors, Del Rice, Bill McCahan, Hank Biasetti, George Crowe, Irv Noren, Steve Hamilton, Cotton Nash, Dave DeBusschere, Ron Reed, Johnny Gee, Danny Ainge, Dick Ricketts and Gene Conley. Conley was the best in both worlds; DeBusschere, the best pro basketball player also to play major-league baseball; and Reed, a teammate of DeBusschere's on the 1966–67 Detroit Pistons, the best baseball player also to play pro basketball.

## Other Athletes for All Seasons

The best major-league baseball player who later became a pro golfer was Ken Harrelson, but Sammy Byrd, known in his days with the Yankees as "Babe Ruth's Caddy" because he often served as a late-inning defensive replacement for Ruth, was the best pro golfer who had been a former major-league baseball player. The greatest track-and-field athlete who also played major-league baseball was of course Jim Thorpe. Not far behind Thorpe, who was probably the greatest all-around athlete in major-league history, was Vern Kennedy, a 21-game winner for the White Sox in 1936 and winner of the decathlon at the Penn Relays in 1927.

# Eagle-eyed Hitters

Ted Williams owned many records when he retired in 1960. Most have since been broken, but one that still stands is his career mark for the highest bases on balls average. Williams walked .208 percent of the times he stepped to the plate. Max Bishop, with a career bases on balls average of .204, is the only other retired player above .200, but Frank Thomas is currently threatening to join this very select list after topping the junior loop in walks in four of his first five full seasons. Thomas may also one day challenge Williams's record for the most consecutive seasons as a league leader in bases on balls—six, from 1941 through 1949, excepting the 1943, 1944 and 1945 seasons when he was in the armed services.

**Most Seasons League Leader in Bases on Balls**
   AL—11—Babe Ruth, last in 1933
   NL—9—Barry Bonds, last in 2003

**Most Seasons 100 or More Bases on Balls**
   AL—13—Babe Ruth, last in 1934
   NL—11—Barry Bonds, last in 2003. Only an injury-riddled season in 1999 prevented Bonds from stringing together 10 straight 100-walk seasons.

**Most Bases on Balls, Season**
   NL—198—Barry Bonds, San Francisco, 2002
   AL—170—Babe Ruth, New York, 1923

**Fewest Bases on Balls, Season, Minimum 500 at Bats**
   AL—6—George Stovall, Cleveland, 1909; 565 at bats
   NL—6—Art Fletcher, New York, 1915; 562 at bats
   Pre-1900—5—Hick Carpenter, Cincinnati AA, 1889; 551 at bats

## Fewest Bases on Balls, 154-Game Season, League Leader in Bases on Balls
NL—69—Hack Wilson, Chicago, 1926
AL—90—Willie Kamm and Johnny Mostil, Chicago, 1925

## Most Intentional Bases on Balls, Season
68—Barry Bonds, San Francisco, 2002

## Most Bases on Balls, Season, Pinch Hitter
NL—20—Matt Franco, New York, 2000
AL—18—Elmer Valo, Washington, 1960

## Most Consecutive Games Receiving at Least One Base on Balls
AL—22—Roy Cullenbine, Detroit, July 2 through July 24, 1947
NL—20—Barry Bonds, San Francisco. Streak began September 9, 2002, and ended the third game of the 2003 season.

## Most Bases on Balls, Game, Since 1893
AL—6—Jimmie Foxx, Boston, June 16, 1938
NL—5—held by many players, but Mel Ott of the New York Giants, who walked five times in a game on four separate occasions, is the only player ever to do it more than twice.

## Most Intentional Bases on Balls, Game
5—Mel Ott, New York Giants, on October 5, 1929, in the second game of the doubleheader against the Phillies and the last game of the season. Ott began the game one home run behind the Phillies Chuck Klein in the NL home run derby; to ensure Klein of the crown, Phillies pitchers purposely passed Ott every time he came to bat.

## First Player to be Given an Intentional Pass with the Bases Loaded
Nap Lajoie, Philadelphia Athletics, May 23, 1901.

## Most Bases on Balls, Season, Team
AL—835—Boston, 1949
NL—732—Brooklyn, 1947

**Fewest Bases on Balls, Career, Minimum 5000 at Bats**
   172—George Stovall, 1904–15; 5222 at bats

**Fewest Bases on Balls, Career, Minimum 4000 at Bats**
   138—Jesus Alou, 1963–79; 4345 at bats. Alou also seldom struck out, so fielders, knowing that contact was imminent, were unusually alert when he came to bat.

**Fewest Bases on Balls, Career, Minimum 1500 at Bats**
   25—Rob Picciolo, 1977–85; 1628 at bats. In 1979 Picciolo, probably the most impatient hitter in history, walked only three times in 348 at bats.

## MOST BASES ON BALLS, CAREER, TOP 10

|   | | Years Active | Bases on Balls |
|---|---|---|---|
| 1. | Rickey Henderson | 1979– | 2190 |
| 2. | Barry Bonds | 1986– | 2070 |
| 3. | Babe Ruth | 1914–35 | 2062[1] |
| 4. | Ted Williams | 1939–60 | 2021 |
| 5. | Joe Morgan | 1963–84 | 1865 |
| 6. | Carl Yastrzemski | 1961–83 | 1845 |
| 7. | Mickey Mantle | 1951–68 | 1733 |
| 8. | Mel Ott | 1926–47 | 1708 |
| 9. | Eddie Yost | 1944–62 | 1614[2] |
| 10. | Darrell Evans | 1969–89 | 1605[3] |

Frank Thomas also currently has the highest career on-base percentage of any player active since Ted Willams retired. Not far behind Thomas are Edgar Martinez and Barry Bonds. All three look like safe bets to crack the "On-Base Percentage Career Top 10" before they retire.

[1]The only player on the top 10 list who was active before 1920.
[2]The only player on the list with fewer than 2000 career hits.
[3]With so many modern players on the list, you should rightfully wonder where the eagle-eyed hitters of the game's early days rank. Ty Cobb, for one, is only 32nd in career bases on balls. Willie Keeler, five feet, four-and-a-half inches and reputedly the most deft bat handler ever, is nowhere to be found—he had just 524 walks in 8594 at bats.

# EVOLUTION OF THE SEASON ON-BASE
# PERCENTAGE RECORD, SINCE 1889*

|  | Year | Team | League | OBP |
|---|---|---|---|---|
| Fred Carroll | 1889 | Pittsburgh | National | .486 |
| Billy Hamilton | 1893 | Philadelphia | National | .490 |
| Billy Hamilton | 1894 | Philadelphia | National | .523 |
| John McGraw | 1899 | Baltimore | National | .547[1] |
| Ted Williams | 1941 | Boston | American | .551 |
| Barry Bonds | 2002 | San Francisco | National | .582 |

[1]Post-1889 National League record
*The 1889 season was the first time only four balls were needed to receive a walk. The pre-1889 record-holder is Tip O'Neill with a .490 OBP in 1887.

## Highest OBP, Season, 1901 through 1919
AL—.486—Ty Cobb, Detroit, 1915
ML—.453—Roy Thomas, Philadelphia, 1903

## Highest OBP, Season, 1920 through 1941
AL—.551—Ted Williams, Boston, 1941
NL—.507—Rogers Hornsby, St. Louis, 1924 (the 20th-century National League record)

## Highest OBP, Season, 1942 through 1960
AL—.528—Ted Williams, Boston, 1957
NL—.460—Eddie Stanky, New York, 1950

## Highest OBP, Season, 1961 through 1977
AL—.488—Norm Cash, Detroit, 1961
—.488—Mickey Mantle, New York, 1962
NL—.471—Joe Morgan, Cincinnati, 1975

## Highest OBP, Season, 1978 through 1993
AL—.480—Wade Boggs, Boston, 1988
NL—.463—Barry Bonds, San Francisco, 1993

## Highest OBP, Season, 1994 to Present
NL—.582—Barry Bonds, San Francisco, 2002
AL—.494—Frank Thomas, Chicago, 1994

## Most Seasons League Leader in OBP
AL—12—Ted Williams, last in 1958
NL—8—Rogers Hornsby, last in 1928

## Lowest OBP, Season, Major League Leader in OBP, since 1889
.399—Willie Mays, San Francisco NL, 1965. The 1965 season was the only one since 1889 when no major league batting title qualifiers compiled an OBP of at least .400, as Carl Yastrzemski topped the AL with a .398 mark.

## Lowest OBP, Season, League Leader in OBP, since 1889
NL—.379—Gavvy Cravath, Philadelphia, 1916
AL—.394—Doc Gessler, Boston, 1908

## Lowest Batting Average, Season, by OBP League Leader
.231—Yank Robinson, St. Louis AA, 1888. The 1888 season was the last in which a batter had to look at five bad pitches before he received a walk. Bases on balls, accordingly, were hard to obtain. Nevertheless, Robinson collected 116 walks to establish a new major league record. Even more remarkably, he totaled 11 more walks than he did hits (105). Three times during his relatively short career Robinson collected 100 or more walks and totaled more walks than he did hits. Only one other 19th-century player—Jack Crooks—ever accomplished that feat even once.

## Lowest Batting Average, Season, .400 or Above OBP
.213—Jack Crooks, St. Louis NL, 1892. In 1892, while collecting just 95 hits, Crooks somehow coaxed 136 walks to set a major league record that stood until 1911. The 20th-century record for the lowest batting average by a player with a .400 OBP and enough plate appearances under current rules to qualify for the batting title belongs to Wes Westrum. In 1951, Westrum racked up 104 walks and a .400 OBP while hitting just .219. His modern record has been threatened twice in recent years. Jim Wynn batted just .207 for Atlanta in 1976, but managed to post a .386 OBP when he collected 127 walks. The following year Gene Tenace had a .417 OBP for San Diego despite batting a meager .233.

**Lowest OBP Season, Batting Crown Winner, since 1889**

NL—.357, Bill Buckner, Chicago, 1980 (.324 BA); breaking Larry Doyle's old mark of .358, set in 1915.

AL—.361, Tony Oliva, Minnesota, 1964 (.323 BA). Oliva also holds the record for the lowest career OBP (.356) by a multiple batting crown winner.

**Lowest Career OBP, Career Batting Average above .340, Minimum 3000 ABs**

.379—George Sisler, 1915–30, (.340 BA). Sisler was the most impatient great hitter in history. It is undoubtedly significant that the only two seasons he managed to collect more than 40 walks he batted .400.

**Lowest Career OBP, Career Batting Average above .300, Minimum 3000 ABs**

.333—Emmet Heidrick, 1898–1908 (.300 BA). He had just 146 walks in 3047 ABs.

# HIGHEST ON-BASE PERCENTAGE, CAREER, TOP TEN RETIRED PLAYERS

(Minimum 1000 games)

| | | Years Active | One Base Pct. |
|---|---|---|---|
| 1. | Ted Williams | 1939–1960 | .483 |
| 2. | Babe Ruth | 1914–35 | .474 |
| 3. | John McGraw | 1891–1906 | .460[1] |
| 4. | Billy Hamilton | 1888–1901 | .455 |
| 5. | Lou Gehrig | 1923–39 | .447 |
| 6. | Rogers Hornsby | 1915–37 | .434 |
| 7. | Ty Cobb | 1905–28 | .432 |
| 8. | Jimmie Foxx | 1925–45 | .428 |
| 9. | Tris Speaker | 1907–28 | .427 |
| 10. | Ferris Fain | 1947–55 | .425[2] |

[1]McGraw and Hamilton were two of the best players in the 1890s at coaxing walks. Even so, the generally inflated batting averages of the period resulted in their being higher on the list than they probably deserve to be.

[2]The one real surprise on the list. Eddie Yost, Ted Williams, Eddie Joost and Eddie Stanky were the recognized masters at drawing walks in the late 1940s and early 1950s, but Fain was just as good. One illustration of how difficult it is to achieve a career on-base percentage of .400 or better: Except for the recently retired Wade Boggs, Mike Hargrove is the only player to retire in the past 20 years with a .400 career on-base percentage. However, several current players are a virtual lock to top that figure.

# Doubles Records

Earl Webb of the Boston Red Sox socked an all-time major-league record 67 doubles in 1931. The 1931 season was the only one in which Webb collected more than 30 doubles. In contrast, Joe Medwick, who set the National League record when he rapped 64 doubles in 1936, had 40 or more doubles seven years in a row. Webb's and Medwick's loop marks—both of which looked safe forever just a few years ago—are now suddenly under assault as an all-time record 21 performers in 1996 collected 40 or more two-baggers.

**Most Doubles, Season, 1901 through 1919**
 AL—53—Tris Speaker, Boston, 1912
 NL—44—Honus Wagner, Pittsburgh, 1904

**Most Doubles, Season, 1942 through 1960**
 AL—56—George Kell, Detroit, 1950
 NL—53—Stan Musial, St. Louis, 1953

**Most Doubles, Season, 1961 through 1976**
 NL—51—Frank Robinson, Cincinnati, 1962
 AL—47—Fred Lynn, Boston, 1975

**Most Doubles, Season, 1977 through 1993**
 AL—54—Hal McRae, Kansas City Royals, 1978
   —54—John Olerud, Toronto, 1993
 NL—51—Pete Rose, Cincinnati, 1978

**Most Doubles, Season, since 1994**
 NL—59—Todd Helton, Colorado, 2000
 AL—57—Carlos Delgado, Toronto, 2000

**Most Seasons League Leader in Doubles, since 1901**
AL—8—Tris Speaker, last in 1923
NL—8—Stan Musial, last in 1954

**Most Seasons 50 or More Doubles**
AL—5—Tris Speaker, last in 1926
NL—3—Paul Waner, last in 1936; Stan Musial, last in 1953.

**Most Doubles, Season, All-time Organized Baseball Record**
100—Lyman Lamb, Tulsa (Western League), 1924.

**Most Doubles, Season, Team**
373—St. Louis Cardinals, 1930; eight players had 32 or more doubles.

**Most Doubles, Season, Team, since 1942**
310—Boston Red Sox, 1979

**Fewest Doubles, Season, League Leader in Doubles**
AL—32—Sal Bando, Oakland, and Pedro Garcia, Milwaukee, 1973
NL—32—Sam Mertes, New York Giants, Harry Steinfeldt, Cincinnati, and Fred Clarke, Pittsburgh, 1902

**Fewest Doubles, Season, since 1901, Minimum 500 at Bats**
NL—4—Roy Thomas, Philadelphia, 1902; 531 at bats
AL—5—Donie Bush, Detroit, 1915, 542 at bats

## TOP 10 IN CAREER DOUBLES

|  |  | Years Active | Doubles |
|---|---|---|---|
| 1. | Tris Speaker | 1907–28 | 793 |
| 2. | Pete Rose | 1963–86 | 746 |
| 3. | Stan Musial | 1941–63 | 725 |
| 4. | Ty Cobb | 1905–28 | 724 |
| 5. | George Brett | 1973–93 | 665 |
| 6. | Honus Wagner | 1897–1917 | 651 |
| 7. | Nap Lajoie | 1896–1916 | 648 |
| 8. | Carl Yastrzemski | 1961–83 | 646 |
| 9. | Hank Aaron | 1954–76 | 624 |
| 10. | Paul Molitor | 1978–98 | 605 |

# The Three Most Interesting Teams since 1994

## 1994 CHICAGO WHITE SOX
### W-67 L-46
### Manager: Gene Lamont

**Regular Lineup**—1B, Frank Thomas; 2B, Joey Cora; 3B, Robin Ventura; SS, Ozzie Guillen; RF, Darrin Jackson; CF, Lance Johnson; LF, Tim Raines; C, Ron Karkovice; DH, Julio Franco; P, Jack McDowell; P, Alex Fernandez; P, Wilson Alvarez; P, Jason Bere; P, Roberto Hernandez.

Would they have brought the city of Chicago its first world champion since 1917? Thanks to the game's first season-ending strike, we will never know. At the time the strike rang down the curtain on the 1994 season, the Sox were in a furious three-way battle for first place in the AL Central Division with the resurrected Cleveland Indians and a stubborn Kansas City team. But Chicago's superior pitching—Lamont's crew had the best ERA in the AL by a comfortable margin and sat nearly a full run below the loop average—seemed certain to hold off all challengers. When the strike dragged on for so long that the 1995 season was jeopardized, Franco and Jackson defected to play in Japan. Cora and McDowell also abandoned the Sox when the Mariners and the Yankees, respectively, waved more money in front of them, leaving Lamont with too many holes to fill by the time action, finally, was resumed. Manager of the year in 1993—and a good bet to become the first pilot ever to cop the award two seasons in a row if the Sox had won the flag in 1994—Lamont was fired just 31 games into the 1995 campaign when his charges started 11–20.

# 1995 COLORADO ROCKIES
## W-77 L-67
### Manager: Don Baylor

**Regular Lineup**—1B, Andres Galarraga; 2B, Jason Bates; 3B, Vinny Castilla; SS, Walt Weiss; RF, Larry Walker; CF, Mike Kingery; LF, Dante Bichette; C, Joe Girardi; P, Kevin Ritz; P, Bill Swift; P, Curtis Leskanic; P, Marvin Freeman; P, Armando Reynoso.

Bichette, Galarraga, Walker and Castilla made the Rockies only the second team in history to feature a lineup studded with four 30-homer men. A shell-shocked pitching staff that produced just one complete game (by rookie Brian Rekar) gave the Rockies a 4.97 ERA, at that point the second highest in history (the 1894 Baltimore Orioles went to the Temple Cup series with a 5.00 ERA) by a postseason qualifier. Baylor's bombers somehow managed to play .611 ball in their new home park, Coors Field, despite being outscored by their opponents 490 to 485. On the road the Rockies tallied seven more runs than their opposition—300 to 293—but were .458, with 39 losses and just 33 wins. All of these paradoxical achievements went virtually unnoted when Colorado edged Houston by one game to become the first wildcard qualifier in NL history and the youngest expansion team to achieve a postseason berth. For their first-round opponents, the Rockies drew heavily favored Atlanta and threw a scare into the Braves in every game before succumbing in three of the four matches. Baylor bagged NL managerial honors and Bichette nearly got the MVP for leading the loop in homers and RBIs, but the team's most important contributor may have been Weiss, who led all shortstops in double plays and was second only to Barry Bonds in walks.

# 1996 MONTREAL EXPOS
## W-88 L-74
### Manager: Felipe Alou

**Regular Lineup**—1B, David Segui; 2B, Mike Lansing; 3B, Shane Andrews; SS, Mark Grudzielanek; RF, Moises Alou; CF, Rondell White; LF, Henry Rodriguez; C, Darrin Fletcher;

Util F. P. Santangelo; P, Jeff Fassero; P, Pedro Martinez; P, Mark Leiter; P, Rheal Cormier; P, Ugie Urbina; P, Mel Rojas.

Grudzielanek started the season as if he, and not Alex Rodriguez, would shatter the shortstops' record for most hits, and Henry Rodriguez looked for a long while as if he might become one of the most improbable home-run kings ever. Both cooled markedly after the All-Star break, taking the rest of the team down with them. A late-season spiral prevented the Expos from claiming the NL wildcard spot with just about the lowest payroll in the game. Montreal's valiant effort to remain competitive on the cheap had seemed destined to pay dividends in 1994 too, before the strike kept us from finding out whether Alou and son could have held off the richer and much more talented Atlanta Braves for a full season. The Expos are truly a modern Gas House Gang: 25 guys who fight hard every day, most of them products of the shrewdest farm system in the majors, and all of them knowing they'll be shopped elsewhere when their tastes become too expensive. In 1997 no Montreal regulars were as old as 30 when season began and it's likely to continue to be that way in Canada's largest city for some time to come.

# Catchers' Records

Until very recently the 1942–60 era was the most fertile for outstanding catchers. In 1996 alone, however, Ivan Rodriguez, Todd Hundley and Terry Steinbach not only set several new all-time batting records for backstoppers, but Rodriguez fell only two runs short of shattering Mickey Cochrane's mark for the most tallies by a catcher and Mike Piazza very nearly became the first catcher ever to lead his league in hitting while collecting as many as 500 at bats.

## SEASON BATTING RECORDS

| Department | National League | American League |
|---|---|---|
| Batting Average | .394, JACK CLEMENTS, Philadelphia, 1895 .367, Babe Phelps, Brooklyn, 1936* | .362, Bill Dickey, New York, 1936 |
| Slugging Average | .630, GABBY HARTNETT, Chicago, 1930 | .617, Bill Dickey, New York, 1936 |
| Home Runs | 42, JAVY LOPEZ, Atlanta, 2003 | 35, Terry Steinbach, Oakland, 1996 35, Ivan Rodriguez, Texas, 1999 |
| RBIs | 142, ROY CAMPANELLA, Brooklyn, 1953 | 133, Bill Dickey, New York, 1937 |
| Runs | 112, Jason Kendall, Pittsburgh, 2000 | 118, MICKEY COCHRANE, Philadelphia, 1932 |
| Hits | 201, MIKE PIAZZA, Los Angeles, 1997 | 199, Ivan Rodriguez, Texas, 1999 |
| Doubles | 42, Terry Kennedy, San Diego, 1982 | 47, IVAN RODRIGUEZ, Texas, 1996 |

| Department | National League | American League |
|---|---|---|
| Triples | 13, TIM McCARVER. St. Louis, 1966 13, JOHNNY KLING, Chicago, 1903 | 12, Mickey Cochrane, Philadelphia, 1928 |
| Total Bases | 355, MIKE PIAZZA, Los Angeles, 1997 | 335, Ivan Rodriguez, Texas, 1999 |
| Bases on Balls | 125, GENE TENACE, San Diego, 1977 | 121, Darrell Porter, K.C. Royals, 1979 |
| Stolen Bases | 26, Jason Kendall, Pittsburgh, 1998 | 36, JOHN WATHAN, K.C. Royals, 1982 |
| Strikeouts | 146, Todd Hundley, New York, 1996 | 151, JORGE POSADA, New York, 2000 |
| Fewest Strikeouts | 14, Ernie Lombardi, Cincinnati, 1938 | 7, MICKEY COCHRANE, Philadelphia, 1927 |

*Record since 1901

Note: All catchers' seasons that contained more than 15 games at other positions are excluded, and where ties exist the record holder is considered to be the catcher who played the fewest games elsewhere. The lone exception is Tenace who played more than 15 games at other positions but collected so many more bases on balls than the runner up to his league record that excluding him would result in recognizing a much lesser achievement.

## Most Games, Career, at Catcher

2226—Carlton Fisk, 1969–93. Fisk lasted just long enough to break Bob Boone's old record of 2223 games.

## Most Consecutive Games at Catcher

312—Frankie Hayes, Philadelphia A's and Cleveland Indians, October 3, 1943, through April 21, 1946

# EVOLUTION OF SEASON RECORD FOR BEST FIELDING AVERAGE

| | Team | League | Year | Average |
|---|---|---|---|---|
| Doug Allison | Hartford | National | 1876 | .881[1] |
| Pop Snyder | Lousville | National | 1877 | .910[2] |
| Pop Snyder | Boston | National | 1878 | .912 |
| Pop Snyder | Boston | National | 1879 | .925 |

| | Team | League | Year | Average |
|---|---|---|---|---|
| Silver Flint | Chicago | National | 1880 | .934 |
| Charlie Bennett | Detroit | National | 1881 | .962[3] |
| Chief Zimmer | Cleveland | National | 1896 | .972 |
| Chief Zimmer | Cleve-Louis | National | 1899 | .978 |
| Malachi Kittredge | Boston | National | 1901 | .984 |
| O. Schrecongost | Philadelphia | American | 1905 | .984 |
| Johnny Kling | Chicago | National | 1907 | .987 |
| Bill Bergen | Brooklyn | National | 1908 | .989 |
| George Gibson | Pittsburgh | National | 1912 | .990[4] |
| Hank Severeid | St. Louis | American | 1923 | .993 |
| Mickey Cochrane | Philadelphia | American | 1930 | .993 |
| Shanty Hogan | New York | National | 1931 | .996 |
| Bill Dickey | New York | American | 1931 | .996 |
| Earl Grace | Pittsburgh | National | 1932 | .998 |
| Buddy Rosar | Philadelphia | American | 1946 | 1.000[5] |
| Charles Johnson | Florida | National | 1997 | 1.000 |

[1]The catcher for the 1869–70 Cincinnati Red Stockings, Allison was 30 years old by the time the National League was formed, and 1876 was his last season as a regular.

[2]May have been the best catcher in his era, but he jumped to the American Association in 1882, thereby sacrificing the disproportionate recognition that National League players have received from historians.

[3]Bennett had a .966 fielding average in 1888 but in only 74 games, fewer than the 60 percent of his team's games required to qualify as a fielding leader. Another catcher, Farmer Vaughn, fielded .969 in 1893, but included in his average were some 40 games he played at other positions.

[4]In only 94 games, just barely qualifying as the new record holder.

[5]Rosar and Johnson are the only two backstoppers to catch 100 games in a season without making an error.

## Best Career Fielding Average
.993—Bill Freehan, 1961–76

## Most Seasons League Leader in Fielding Average
AL—8—Ray Schalk, last in 1922
NL—7—Gabby Hartnett, last in 1937

## Most Consecutive Errorless Games
171—Charles Johnson, Florida Marlins, June 23, 1996, through the close of the 1997 season. Johnson broke both Yogi Berra's record of 950 consecutive errorless chances and Rick Cerone's mark of 159 straight errorless games before committing a bobble on Opening Day in 1998.

**Most Chances Accepted, Career**
12,988—Gary Carter, 1974–92

**Most Chances Accepted, Season**
1221—Johnny Edwards, Houston Astros, 1969. That year the Astros' pitchers set a new all-time season record for most strikeouts. All the one-game records for most chances accepted are similarly held by the batterymates of strikeout record-setters.

**Most Assists, Season**
NL—214—Pat Moran, Boston 1903
AL—212—Oscar Stanage, Detroit, 1911

**Most Seasons League Leader in Assists**
AL—6—Jim Sundberg, last in 1981
NL—6—Gabby Hartnett, last in 1935
Del Crandall, last in 1960

**Most No-hitters Caught, Career**
4—Ray Schalk; the last one was Charlie Robertson's perfect game on April 30, 1922

**Only Catchers since Ernie Lombardi to Hit .300 Five Times or More**
Thurman Munson, last in 1977; Mike Piazza, 1993–2001; Ivan Rodriguez, 1995–99

**Most Recent Left-hander to Catch in a Major-League Game**
Benny Distefano, Pittsburgh, last in 1989

**Most Games Caught by Left-hander, Since 1901**
43—Jiggs Donahue, Pittsburgh Pirates, 1901 (1); Milwaukee Brewers, 1901 (19); St. Louis Browns, 1902 (23).

**Greatest Left-handed Catcher**
Jack Clements, 1884–1900; .286 career batting average in 1157 games

**Most Gold Glove Awards**
10—Johnny Bench, 1969–78 consecutive
—Ivan Rodriguez, 1992–2001 consecutive

# The Strikeout Kings

On September 18, 1996, Roger Clemens of the Red Sox tied his own single-game mark of 20 strikeouts when he blanked Detroit, 4–0. Clemens became the first pitcher to fan as many as 20 batters in a nine-inning game against Seattle on April 30, 1986. Less than a month later, on May 28, 1986, Joe Cowley of the White Sox set a modern record when he started off his game against the Rangers by striking out the first seven hitters who faced him. Cowley's record lasted only until September 23, 1986, when Jim Deshaies of the Astros fanned the first eight Dodgers he faced. Clemens, Cowley and Deshaies are just three of the multitude of pitchers in recent years who have toppled almost all the existing season and career strikeout records.

**Most Consecutive Strikeouts, Game**
10—Tom Seaver, New York Mets, April 22, 1970. Seaver fanned 19 San Diego Padres in the game, tying the former nine-inning record, and broke Mickey Welch's old mark of nine consecutive strikeouts, set against Philadelphia on August 28, 1884, when Welch, pitching for the New York Gothams (soon to become the Giants), opened the game by fanning the first nine Phillies he faced—the all-time record Deshaies was shooting for until he faltered after striking out Jose Gonzalez.

**Most Consecutive Strikeouts by a Rookie in His First Game**
7—Sammy Stewart, Baltimore Orioles, September 1, 1978, against Cleveland. A starting pitcher at the time, Stewart failed to finish the game despite his strikeout skein and was also knocked out early in his next start. The following season Earl Weaver made him a reliever.

## Most Strikeouts by a Rookie in His First Start
NL—15—Karl Spooner, Brooklyn, September 22, 1954
J. R. Richard, Houston, September 5, 1971
AL—12—Elmer Myers, Philadelphia, October 6, 1915.
Steve Woodard, Milwaukee, July 28, 1997

## First Pitcher to Strike Out 19 Batters in a Game
Charlie Sweeney, Providence Grays, June 7, 1884. Exactly one month later Hugh Daily of Chicago fanned 19 hitters in a Union Associaton game. Daily, as you no doubt know, had only one arm, but Sweeney apparently had a less overt but ultimately more insidious handicap. He jumped to the Union Association in the midst of the 1884 season, paving the way for Hoss Radbourn to set all sorts of iron-man records while bringing Providence the pennant. By 1887 Sweeney, possibly the most gifted pitcher of his time, had drifted from the majors altogether although just 24 years old, and shortly thereafter he wound up in San Quentin, convicted of manslaughter.

## First Pitcher to Strike Out 18 Batters in a game, Mound 60 Feet 6 Inches From The Plate
AL—Bob Feller, Cleveland, October 2, 1938, against Detroit
NL—Sandy Koufax, Los Angeles, August 31, 1959, against San Francisco. Koufax also fanned 18 Cubs on April 24, 1962, making him the only NL pitcher who twice struck out 18 or more batters in a game.

## First Pitcher to Strike Out 19 Batters in a Game, Mound 60 Feet 6 Inches From The Plate
NL—Steve Carlton, St. Louis, September 15, 1969, against the pennant-winning Mets. The following year Tom Seaver of the Mets, while breaking Welch's consecutive strikeout mark, became the second pitcher to do it.
AL—Nolan Ryan, California, August 12, 1974. In 1976 Ryan also had an 18-K effort and became the first AL hurler who twice fanned 18 or more batters in a game.

## Most Strikeouts, Game, by a Rookie
20—Kerry Wood, Chicago Cubs, May 6, 1998

## Most Strikeouts, Game, Extra Innings Included

21—Tom Cheney, Washington Senators, September 12, 1962, against Baltimore, in 16 innings

## Most Strikeouts, Season

AL—383—Nolan Ryan, California, 1973. His record-breaking strikeout was Rich Reese of the Twins—on his last pitch of the season.

NL—382—Sandy Koufax, Los Angeles, 1965

## Most Strikeouts, Season, 1901 Through 1919

AL—349—Rube Waddell, Philadelphia, 1904. Waddell's total is now universally accepted, but after Bob Feller notched 348 K's in 1946 it was hotly contested for some while by many authorities, who felt that Waddell had been credited with more strikeouts in 1904 than he'd earned and Feller was now the true modern record holder.

NL—267—Christy Mathewson, New York Giants, 1903

## Most Strikeouts, Season, 1920 through 1941

NL—262—Dazzy Vance, Brooklyn 1924

AL—261—Bob Feller, Cleveland, 1940

## Most Strikeouts, Season, 1942–60

AL—348—Bob Feller, Cleveland, 1946

NL—246—Don Drysdale, Los Angeles, 1960

## Most Strikeouts, Season, since 1977

NL—372—Randy Johnson, Arizona, 2001

AL—341—Nolan Ryan, California, 1977

## Most Seasons League Leader in Strikeouts

AL—12—Walter Johnson, last in 1924

NL—7—Dazzy Vance, 1922–28 consecutive

## Most Seasons 300 or More Strikeouts

6—Nolan Ryan, last in 1989; Randy Johnson, last in 2002

## Most Consecutive Seasons, 300 or More Strikeouts

5—Randy Johnson, 1998–2002

## Most Consecutive Seasons 200 or More Strikeouts
9—Tom Seaver, 1968–76

## Most Significant Milestone Strikeout
My vote goes to Ryan's whiff of the Expos' Brad Mills on April 27, 1983, giving him his 3508th career strikeout and tying him with Walter Johnson.

## Most Strikeouts, Season, Team
NL—1404—Chicago, 2003; led by Kerry Wood with 266
AL—1266—New York, 2001; led by Mike Mussina with 214

## First Team to Top 1000 Strikeouts in a Season
Los Angeles Dodgers, 1959, notched 1077; led by Don Drysdale with 242

## Fewest Strikeouts, Season, Since 1901, by League Leader in Strikeouts
AL—113—Bobo Newsom, Washington, and Tex Hughson, Boston, 1942
NL—134—Dazzy Vance, Brooklyn, 1922

## Most Recent League Leader to Have Fewer Than 200 Strikeouts (1981 and 1994 Excluded)
AL—187—Len Barker, Cleveland, 1980
NL—188—Jack Sanford, Philadelphia, 1957

## Most Consecutive Years, League, without a Pitcher Who Had 200 or More Strikeouts
NL—16—1942 through 1957, from Johnny Vander Meer, who had 202 K's in 1941, to Sam Jones with 205 K's in 1958
AL—13—1917 through 1929, from Walter Johnson with 228 K's in 1916 to Lefty Grove, 209 K's in 1920

## Most Consecutive Years, Individual, without Registering 100 Strikeouts in a Season
21—Ted Lyons, 1923–46. Lyons, a 260-game winner, never once in his long career came even close to notching 100 strikeouts in a season; his high was 74 in 1933.

# TOP 10 IN CAREER STRIKEOUTS

|  | Years Active | Strikeouts |
|---|---|---|
| 1. Nolan Ryan | 1966–93 | 5714 |
| 2. Steve Carlton | 1965–88 | 4136[1] |
| 3. Roger Clemens | 1984–2003 | 4099 |
| 4. Randy Johnson | 1988– | 3871 |
| 5. Bert Blyleven | 1970–92 | 3701[2] |
| 6. Tom Seaver | 1967–86 | 3640 |
| 7. Don Sutton | 1966–88 | 3574[3] |
| 8. Gaylord Perry | 1962–83 | 3534 |
| 9. Walter Johnson | 1907–27 | 3509[4] |
| 10. Phil Niekro | 1964–87 | 3342[5] |

[1]Southpaw record. Mickey Lolich, the runner-up, is 12th on the all-time list.

[2]Replaced Jim Bunning on the top 10 list in 1985. Bunning's departure from it left Johnson as the lone member who collected a significant portion of his career strikeouts—let alone all of them—prior to expansion.

[3]Never a league leader in strikeouts; nor, for that matter, was Perry.

[4]The only top 10 member who was active before 1959.

[5]Niekro, Jenkins, and Blyleven all were league leaders in strikeouts just once.

# World Series Play
# 1994–2003

## Franchise Summary

| Team | League | WS Record Thru 2003 | Last WS | LCS Record Thru 2003 | Div Playoff Record Thru 2003 |
|---|---|---|---|---|---|
| Florida | National | 2–0 | 2003 | 2–0 | 2–0 |
| Toronto | American | 2–0 | 1993 | 2–3 | — |
| Arizona | National | 1–0 | 2001 | 1–0 | 1–2 |
| Anaheim | American | 1–0 | 2002 | 1–3 | 1–0 |
| Pittsburgh | National | 5–2 | 1979 | 2–7 | — |
| New York | American | 26–13 | 2003 | 10–1 | 6–3 |
| Oakland | American | 4–2 | 1990 | 6–4 | 0–4 |
| Minnesota | American | 2–1 | 1991 | 2–3 | 1–1 |
| St. Louis | National | 9–6 | 1987 | 3–3 | 3–1 |
| Cincinnati | National | 5–4 | 1990 | 5–3 | 1–0 |
| Los Angeles | National | 5–4 | 1988 | 5–2 | 0–2 |
| Boston | American | 5–4 | 1986 | 2–4 | 2–2 |
| Baltimore | American | 3–3 | 1983 | 5–4 | 2–0 |
| New York | National | 2–2 | 2000 | 4–2 | 2–0 |
| Chicago | American | 2–2 | 1959 | 0–2 | 0–1 |
| Kansas City | American | 1–1 | 1985 | 2–4 | — |
| Detroit | American | 4–5 | 1984 | 1–2 | — |
| Cleveland | American | 2–3 | 1997 | 2–1 | 3–3 |
| Atlanta | National | 1–3 | 1999 | 5–3 | 5–3 |
| Philadelphia | National | 1–4 | 1993 | 3–3 | — |
| Chicago | National | 2–8 | 1945 | 0–3 | 1–1 |
| San Francisco | National | 0–3 | 2002 | 2–2 | 1–3 |
| San Diego | National | 0–2 | 1984 | 2–0 | 1–1 |
| Milwaukee | American | 0–1 | 1982 | 1–0 | — |
| Seattle | American | — | — | 0–2 | 2–1 |
| Houston | National | — | — | 0–2 | 0–3 |
| Montreal | National | — | — | 0–1 | — |
| Texas | American | — | — | — | 0–3 |
| Colorado | American | — | — | — | 0–1 |

**1994**—On August 12 a player strike halted the season, making it the first since 1904 without a World Series and the first since professional baseball began in 1871 to lack even a pennant winner.

**1995**—Atlanta (NL) defeated Cleveland (AL) 4 games to 2.

Leading 3 games to 1 with four-time Cy Young winner Greg Maddux slated to pitch Game 5, the Braves looked certain to nail their first world title in Atlanta. But Cleveland upset Maddux 5–4, only to succumb 1–0 two nights later when David Justice's solo homer provided all the scoring as Series MVP Tom Glavine and Mark Wohlers combined to hurl the first Series one-hitter since 1967. Despite being held to a .179 BA, the Indians hung tight all the way, losing three games by one run. In the first year the playoffs were expanded to include eight teams, Cleveland blanked Boston 3–0 in the first round and then outbattled Seattle 4–2 in the ALCS. The Mariners stunned the AL wild-card Yankees in round one by winning three straight games at the Kingdome after trailing 2–0 in games. Colorado, the NL wild card, fell in four to the Braves in round one while Cincinnati humbled the Dodgers 3–0. Atlanta then ruined hopes of a first-ever all-Ohio World Series by sweeping the Reds in the NLCS with the same formula that stymied the Indians: super pitching.

**1996**—New York (AL) defeated Atlanta (NL) 4 games to 2

Trailing St. Louis 3 games to 1 in the NLCS, the Braves put together the most remarkable five-game run in postseason history. Led by Greg Maddux, John Smoltz and Tom Glavine, the strongest trio of starters in recent times, Bobby Cox's crew buried the Cardinals in the final three NLCS contests and rolled up a quick 2–0 lead on the Yankees after grabbing the first two frays in New York by a combined 16–1 score. Atlanta then fell prey to Yankees skipper Joe Torre's two season-long fortes: the best bullpen anywhere and an eerie invincibility in road games against his chief foes. Drawing upon a gutty outing by starter David Cone in Game 3 and a game-tying three-run homer by Jim Leyritz the next night that rallied the Yankees from a 6–0 deficit, Torre manipulated his relief corps so that closer John Wetteland faced a save situation three nights in a row in Atlanta. When Wetteland prevailed all three times and then got Mark Lemke on a foul pop to seal a tense 3–2 verdict in Game 6 at New York, the Yankees were champs for the first time since 1978. In the ALCS, New York erased Baltimore in five frames, helped by a 12-year-old fan's interference in Game 1, but more by a complete mastery of the Orioles in their Camden Yards home. The Yankees had evidenced a similar prowess against Texas in the first playoff round while wild-card Baltimore shocked Cleveland, owner of the best record in the majors, by long-balling the Indians into early submission. The two NL division playoffs proved humiliating for the West Division representatives when both the San Diego Padres and the wild-card Los Angeles Dodgers were swept 3–0 by the Cardinals and the Braves, respectively. Indeed, only the Yankees' startling Series turnaround saved a postseason that might otherwise have been remembered most for sloppy umpiring and the inept handling of Orioles second sacker Roberto Alomar's tawdry spitting episode on the final weekend of the season.

**1997**—Florida (NL) defeated Cleveland (AL), 4 games to 3.

At long last it was the year to be a Cleveland fan . . . almost. Two outs away from bringing the Indians their first world crown in 49 years, Tribe closer Jose Mesa surrendered a game-tying sac fly to Florida's Craig Counsell in the bottom of the ninth inning of Game 7. Two frames later Edgar Renteria's bases-loaded single plated Counsell with the overtime run that gave Florida a thrilling 3–2 win and a championship in only the franchise's fifth year in existence. Marlins rookie Livan Hernandez garnered the Series MVP for his two wins, but had Mesa closed out Game 7 successfully, Cleveland rookie Jaret Wright would also have collared two Series wins and probably the MVP prize. Wright had previously spearheaded Cleveland's improbable march to a near championship by halting the New York Yankees twice in an AL division playoff that went the limit. The down-to-the-wire five-game set with the Yanks seemed certain to drain the Indians for Baltimore in the ALCS. Instead Cleveland won four excruciatingly tense one-run games, two in overtime and all in a bizarre fashion, culminated by Tony Fernandez's 11th-inning solo homer to defeat Baltimore reliever Armando Benitez, 1–0. Benitez had earlier been part of a glittering bullpen brigade that sparked the O's to a remarkably easy division playoff win over the hard-hitting Seattle Mariners. The NL division playoffs were both three-and-out affairs, with Florida dropping the San Francisco Giants and the Atlanta Braves decimating the Houston Astros. Atlanta, owner of the best regular-season record in the majors, then was victimized in the NLCS by Hernandez's pitching, erratic umpiring, and its own uncharacteristically shaky fielding. Hernandez and popular Marlins pilot Jim Leyland were the top postseason stories, but the media darlings could as easily have been Jaret Wright, Chad Ogea (winner of two Series games for Cleveland and the "hitting star" of Game 6), and Indians skipper Mike Hargrove, who came within minutes of celebrating both his 48th birthday and a long-sought Tribe world title on the same day.

**1998**—New York (AL) defeated San Diego (NL), 4 games to 0

After the Yankees won an AL-record 114 games, pundits feared the only lingering question in the postseason was what team would prove to be second-best. They were right. The answer was the Cleveland Indians, who pushed the Bombers to six games in the ALCS after dumping the Boston Red Sox in four hard-fought division playoff contests. The Yanks meanwhile swept the Texas Rangers in their own division playoff series. San Diego was the NL upset winner, topping the Houston Astros in the division playoffs and then erasing the heavily favored Atlanta Braves in six games in the NLCS. Atlanta had dispatched the wild-card Chicago Cubs three straight in the division playoffs. The Yankees unlikely postseason heroes were third sacker Scott Brosius in the Series and rookie hurler Orlando Hernandez in the ALCS.

**1999**—New York (AL) defeated Atlanta (NL), 4 games to 0

Billed as the match that would establish the team of the '90s, the 1999 World Series proved to be a cruel letdown when the Yankees easily swept. As in 1998, the second-best team in the postseason may have been the ALCS loser, the Boston Red Sox, the only team to beat the Yankees even a single game in the postseason. In the AL first round the Sox rallied from a 2–0 deficit in games to bury Cleveland in three straight contests while New York swept Texas. Atlanta and the New York Mets needed just four games each to win their NL first-round matches with Houston and Arizona, respectively. The NLCS was the best senior-loop postseason match since 1992 as the Mets called on a raft of obscure heroes to rally from a 3–0 hole in games and nearly force a seventh game before falling in Game 6, 9–8 in 11 innings.

**2000**—New York (AL) defeated New York (NL), 4 games to 1

Except in New York, the first "Subway Series" since 1956 was a clinker, at least on the surface, in that it pitted the team with only the fifth best record in the AL against the NL wild card and lasted just five games. In the process of winning their third straight World Championship, however, Joe Torre's Yankees also won their record 12th straight World Series contest AND their record 9th straight postseason affair. Only the surprising Oakland A's posed a serious challenge to the Yankees, taking them down to the wire in their best-of-five division series. Wildcard Seattle meanwhile disposed of the White Sox, the team with the best record in the AL, in three quick frames. The NL's best regular-season team, San Francisco, was likewise slammed to the mat by the Mets in the opening round while St. Louis swept the perennially disappointing Atlanta Braves. Both St. Louis and Seattle suffered a hitting drought in their respective LCSes, allowing the Mets and Yankees to romp. The Yanks' Derek Jeter was the runaway World Series MVP, but Mets journeyman Bobby Jones provided the postseason highlight when he one-hit the Giants to wrap up the division series.

**2001**—Arizona (NL) defeated New York (AL), 4 games to 3

In the dramatic culmination to a season that was extended for a week by the tragic events of September 11, 2001, the Arizona Diamondbacks outscored the New York Yankees 37–15 and sported the dual World Series MVPs, Randy Johnson and Curt Schilling, but still were forced to rally for two runs in the bottom of the ninth in Game 7 against the Bombers' previously indomitable relief ace Mariano Rivera to bag their first championship in only their fourth year of existence. Luiz Gonzalez's bases-loaded looping single over a drawn-in infield provided the winning run in the D'backs' 3–2 triumph in a Series marked by last-ditch heroics. Twice, in Games 4 and 5, the Yankees stunned D'backs closer Byung-Hyun Kim with game-tying two-run homers with two outs in the bottom of the ninth and then went on to win in extra innings. The LCS battles, in contrast, were routine affairs. Seattle, after winning a record-tying 116 games in the regular season, won just one of five contests against the Yankees, and Atlanta likewise fell in five to Arizona. In their respective division series, however, both WS entries were severely tested. The Yankees managed to subdue the wild-card Oakland A's despite losing the first two games of the series in their home park. Arizona also needed the full five games to hold off the NL wild-card St. Louis Cardinals. In the other two opening rounds, Houston, the NL's top-seeded team, continued its disappointing postseason history by losing to Atlanta in just three games while the AL's bottom seed, Cleveland, narrowly missed knocking off heavily favored Seattle before succumbing in five games thanks to two superb starts from Mariners lefty Jamie Moyer, at age 38 the oldest first-time 20-game winner in major-league history.

**2002**—Anaheim (AL) defeated San Francisco (NL), 4 games to 3

For the first time since wildcards were added to the postseason mix in 1995, two wildcard teams vied for the ultimate prize—the World Series championship trophy. The two upstarts also represented cities that had never won a world title, guaranteeing a first-time champion. In effect the seventh and eighth seeds in an eight-team tourney, between them the Angels and the Giants either set or tied all manner of postseason records, led by San Francisco's Barry Bonds, who collected eight home runs overall and 13 walks in the World Series alone, but the Angels garnered the two records that mattered most when John Lackey became the first rookie starter in AL history to bag a decisive Game 7 World Series victory and in so doing gave the Angels a new mark for the fewest career wins (48) by the winning pitchers on a World Series champion. Two other Anaheim frosh, Brendan Donnelly and Francisco Rodriguez, combined with Lackey to enable the Angels in addition to register a new mark for the most Series innings pitched by rookies—28⅔—and Rodriguez also tied the record for the most wins in a postseason with five. Rodriguez, who had never won a game in the majors prior to the postseason, was just one of the many Angels that began the first round of the playoffs not only as heavy underdogs but for the most part as unknown names to most of the baseball public. Still, for all their heroics in ending the Yankees' four-year reign as AL champs in the division series in only four games and then swiftly scorching the hopes of Minnesota, another upset division-series winner, in the ALCS, the Angels appeared doomed to fall short of the big prize when the Giants led 3–2 in games and took a seemingly safe 5–0 lead into the bottom of the seventh inning in Game 6 at Anaheim's Edison Field. But a three-run homer by first baseman Scott Spiezio, followed by three more runs in the eighth off the Giants' two top relievers, Tim Worrell and Robb Nen, keyed an unprecedented rally by a team on the brink of

World Series elimination and a 6–5 win that knotted matters. Much as the 1985 Cardinals and 1986 Red Sox that likewise had suffered shocking zero-hour defeats in Game 6 after appearing to have a lock on Series rings, the Giants seemed listless and demoralized in Game 7 and offered only token resistance before bowing 4–1. In the preliminary rounds San Francisco, down 2 games to 1, rebounded to knock off the top seeded Braves and then in the NLCS routed a Cardinals' team that proved unable to surmount the injury loss of slugging third baseman Scott Rolen after themselves sweeping a badly crippled Arizona team in the division series. The eighth and final entry in the postseason hunt, the Oakland A's, saw their hopes of making 2002 a reprise of the 1989 Bay Bridge Series vanish in the decisive 5th game of their opening division match when closer Billy Koch, with the A's trailing just 2–1, coughed up three runs to the Twins in the top of the ninth and then had the agonizing task of watching as his team staged a last-ditch charge at Minnesota closer Eddie Guarado that fell one run short when second sacker Denny Hocking made a superb catch of a foul fly to strand the potential tying run on first base.

**2003**—Florida (NL) defeated New York (AL), 4 games to 2

Arguably, both the hero and goat of the 2003 postseason was shortstop Alex Gonzales. In the NLCS, Chicago Cubs shortstop Alex Gonzalez muffed a potential double-play grounder in the eighth inning of Game 6, opening the floodgates for the Florida Marlins to overcome a 3–0 deficit and pin a stunning loss on Cubs' co-ace Mark Prior just when Chicago denizens had begun to feel certain that their beloved Bruins were finally about to make their first World Series appearance in 58 years. The following night the Marlins rocked the Cubs' other co-ace, Kerry Wood, to complete a stunning comeback after being down 3 games to 1 and make Florida the first team to reach the World Series twice as a wildcard. In the Fall Classic the New York Yankees posted a dazzling 2.13 staff ERA, but all it earned them was the distinction of achieving the lowest ERA by a Series loser since 1944 as the Marlins, an improbable amalgam of unknown young players and 72-year-old Jack McKeon, the oldest manager in history to win a World Championship, dumped the Yankees in six games on the strength of Series MVP 23-year-old Josh Beckett's 2–0 shutout in the finale before an incredulous Yankee Stadium full house. Marlins catcher Ivan Rodriguez earned overall postseason plaudits for providing a continuous stream of key base hits and stellar defensive plays throughout the three-round tourney, but the blow that most demoralized the Yankees was a walkoff home run by Florida shortstop Alex Gonzalez in the bottom of the twelfth inning of Game 4. The two Gonzalezes made history when they became the first performers with the same name to play the same position for a pair of postseason combatants in the NLCS, but the ALCS showcased an equally monumental historical pairing as six-time Cy Young winner Roger Clemens, verging on retirement, twice opposed Pedro Martinez, the multiple Cy Young winner the Boston Red Sox corralled following the 1997 season rather than attempting to re-sign Clemens. The first Clemens-Martinez clash evolved into an ugly beanball war and near riot, won by the Yankees, but Martinez seemed headed for revenge when he took a three-run lead into the bottom of the eighth inning in Game 7 at Yankee Stadium. Instead, a chain of Yankees hits tied the game and doomed Red Sox manager Grady Little in the eyes of Boston brass for allegedly leaving his ace in too long when the Yankees subsequently won the pennant on Aaron Boone's leadoff homer in the bottom of the eleventh inning. Quickly forgotten by Little's critics was the masterful job he had done rallying the Red Sox from a 2–0 deficit against the Oakland A's in their division series, helped by two egregious base-running blunders that prevented the A's from sweeping the match in three games. The A's cross-bay neighbor, the San Francisco Giants, likewise failed to apply the hammerlock in their division series with Florida after winning the opening game and taking a seemingly prohibitive lead early in Game 2 before succumbing to Ivan Rodriguez's sensational work both at bat and behind it as well as on the bases. In the other two division series the Yankees routinely dispensed with Minnesota, the AL Central winner, in four games and the Cubs likewise needed only four contests to subdue perennial NL East champ, Atlanta. Florida, though at first glance a wildcard Series winner in much the same mold as Anaheim, the previous year's unlikely champion, was in actuality the hottest club in the majors heading into the postseason. After luring McKeon out of retirement some six weeks into the 2003 campaign to replace Jeff Torborg, the Marlins posted the best record in either league after May 23 and in the process became the only team other than the Miracle Braves in 1914 to cop a World Championship after being as many as 10 games below .500 during the season.

# 1,001 BASEBALL QUESTIONS YOUR FRIENDS CAN'T ANSWER

## Dom Forker

Baseball savants can test their knowledge against an arsenal of the toughest trivia questions covering every aspect of the game, in a collection of quizzes that shows them how to formulate their expertise in the form of a career batting average.

0-451-19132-3

Available im Paperback

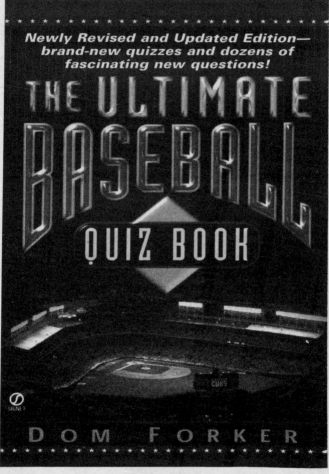

Newly Revised and Updated Edition—
brand-new quizzes and dozens of
fascinating new questions!

THE ULTIMATE BASEBALL QUIZ BOOK

DOM FORKER

Signet
0-451-20601-0